THROUGH THE LENS
OF ANTHROPOLOGY

THROUGH THE LENS OF ANTHROPOLOGY

An Introduction to Human Evolution and Culture

Robert Muckle
and
Laura Tubelle de González

UNIVERSITY OF TORONTO PRESS

Library and Archives Canada Cataloguing in Publication

Muckle, Robert James, author
 Through the lens of anthropology : an introduction to human evolution and culture / Robert J. Muckle and Laura Tubelle de González.

Includes bibliographical references and index.
Issued in print and electronic formats.
ISBN 978-1-4426-0864-1 (bound).—ISBN 978-1-4426-0863-4 (paperback).—ISBN 978-1-4426-0865-8 (pdf).
—ISBN 978-1-4426-0866-5 (html).

1. Anthropology—Textbooks. I. González, Laura Tubelle de, 1969–, author II. Title.

GN25.M82 2015 301 C2015-903721-2
C2015-903722-0

We welcome comments and suggestions regarding any aspect of our publications—please feel free to contact us at news@utphighereducation.com or visit our Internet site at www.utppublishing.com.

North America
5201 Dufferin Street
North York, Ontario, Canada, M3H 5T8

2250 Military Road
Tonawanda, New York, USA, 14150
ORDERS PHONE: 1-800-565-9523
ORDERS FAX: 1-800-221-9985
ORDERS E-MAIL: utpbooks@utpress.utoronto.ca

UK, Ireland, and continental Europe
NBN International
Estover Road, Plymouth, PL6 7PY, UK
ORDERS PHONE: 44 (0) 1752 202301
ORDERS FAX: 44 (0) 1752 202333
ORDERS E-MAIL: enquiries@nbninternational.com

Every effort has been made to contact copyright holders; in the event of an error or omission, please notify the publisher.

The University of Toronto Press acknowledges the financial support for its publishing activities of the Government of Canada through the Canada Book Fund.

Cover Image: urbancow/iStock

Printed in Canada.

Our book is dedicated to the domestication of coffee, barley, and hops. The writing of this book was fueled by coffee and will be celebrated with beer.

North Pacific Ocean

North Atlantic Ocean

South Pacific Ocean

Locations
Mentioned in
the Book

Brief Contents

Contents

Illustrations

Tables

Maps

Boxes

Acknowledgments

The authors acknowledge the contributions of many. We appreciate our families for their patience, and for not complaining too much while we were writing. Laura would like to express her love and gratitude especially for the support of her husband, Luis; and daughters, Maya and Lirén; and her two dogs, Mochi and Ginger, for accompanying her in the office while writing. She would also like to dedicate her writing to her father Larry, who inspired her to write by example. Bob expresses appreciation for the support of his wife, Victoria, and his yours-mine-and-ours children: Miriam, Esther, Jonathan, Cody, Tomas, and Anna. He does not feel he received any support from his cat, Whisky; dog, Rosie; or any of the finches, all named Darwin.

We are very appreciative of all those friends, colleagues, and former students who have contributed photos at no cost, in order to keep the cost of production low and ultimately make the book affordable to students. This includes Gillian Crowther, Emma Kimm-Jones, Nadine Ryan, Michelle Malham, Sashur Henninger, Luis A. González, Angel Piedad, Barbara Zaragoza, Daniel Chit, Carole Counihan, the Mays-Agate family, Anabel de Krogstad, and Tad McIlwraith. We are also indebted to our good friend and colleague Barry Kass, owner of imagesofanthropology.com, who has provided many photos at a deep discount.

Of course we thank the good people at the University of Toronto Press, especially executive editor Anne Brackenbury who has guided us through the process from proposal to publication. We also thank those in the production process, proofreaders, and designers, including Ashley Rayner, Megan Pickard, Beate Schwirtlich, and copyeditors Beth McAuley, Barbara Kamienski, and Chris Cameron of The Editing Company. They make us look like better writers than we really are. We also thank the good work of those in marketing, sales, and shipping. Without those folks, there is really no point in writing the book, because no one would ever see it.

About the Authors

Each author has primary responsibility for several chapters, but there was considerable discussion and contributions that overlap. Bob Muckle had primary responsibility for the introduction and the chapters on evolutionary thought, archaeology, and biological anthropology (Chapters 1–7). Laura González had primary responsibility for the chapters on cultural anthropology and sustainability, integrating linguistic anthropology throughout (Chapters 8–14).

Robert (Bob) Muckle is a professor in the anthropology department at Capilano University in North Vancouver, Canada. He has been practicing, teaching, and writing about anthropology since the 1980s. His primary teaching and research interests are in archaeology, biological anthropology, and the Indigenous peoples of North America. He also is interested in applying archaeology to help solve issues related to sustainability. He has worked on dozens of field projects in North America and Africa, including working collaboratively with Indigenous peoples of North America. Publications include *Introducing Archaeology*, Second Edition (2014), *Indigenous Peoples of North America: A Concise Anthropological Overview* (2012), and *The First Nations of British Columbia: An Anthropological Overview*, Third Edition (2014). He also edited a volume of readings for students titled *Reading Archaeology* (2008). If he could live anywhere at any time in the past, he would choose North America about 10,000 years ago. This is because he prefers low population densities, enjoys using an atlatl, and would like to taste fresh mammoth. Alternatively, he would like to be hanging out around Stonehenge about 4,000 years ago, drinking a drink we now call beer. As long as he remembers, he's had a thing for Stonehenge.

Laura Tubelle de González is a professor in the anthropology department at San Diego Miramar College in Southern California. She has taught cultural anthropology, physical anthropology, and the Cultures of Mexico courses for 15 years. She specializes in cultural anthropology, having done ethnographic fieldwork in Mexico and India. Her current research interest is in food studies with a focus on sustainable food systems, and she is involved in sustainability initiatives on campus. She is also a past president of the Society for Anthropology in Community Colleges, a section of the American Anthropological Association that focuses on teaching anthropology. Currently she administrates their Facebook page and twitter feed (@SACC_L). If Laura had limitless funds, she would travel the world with the express purpose of tasting every local cuisine, preferably with a book, a camera, and some dancing shoes. Alternatively, she would like to pilot a dirigible and be addressed as "Captain."

Preface

The ultimate objective of this book is to provide students with an appreciation of what we call the lens of anthropology, in other words, the way in which anthropology frames and views the world. *Through the Lens of Anthropology* introduces the perspective, methods, and ideas of anthropology as well as some of its theories. The book also contains highlights of some anthropological research in order to provide students with concrete examples. We hope that this book will contribute in a positive way to students learning about anthropology in its many forms and applications.

We realize that for many students, a single introductory anthropology course may be their only formal education in anthropology, and this book may be the only one they ever read that is explicitly devoted to the subject. While keeping the text readable and user-friendly, the authors strive to provide enough information so that students can appreciate the broad and detailed fields of the discipline. It's not important to us that, 20 years from now, students still recall specific details, such as the number of australopithecine species. Rather, we hope that students will at least understand and appreciate the anthropological lens and how it is applied.

Several key themes set this book apart from others. First, we have written the book with an emphasis on food and sustainability, topics in which both authors have an interest. The book has boxes inset into every chapter with each of these themes highlighted. Sustainability is explored in three contexts: environmental, social, and economic. As well, most chapters have additional examples related to aspects of food and sustainability. Finally, we have devoted an entire chapter to anthropology and sustainability (Chapter 14), to emphasize the connections between them.

Secondary themes of the book include the Indigenous peoples of North America, and how anthropology is embedded in popular culture. Finally, although the second half of the book emphasizes cultural anthropology, with one chapter focusing especially on linguistic anthropology (Chapter 9), more ways to talk about language are embedded in each of the cultural chapters. In the remaining cultural chapters, "Talking about ..." boxes focus on one aspect of language as it relates to the theme of the chapter.

About the Cover

The cover photo shows a young woman in Barsana, Rajasthan, India, as she records action from the 2014 Holi Festival on her mobile phone. The authors chose this photo for the ways it highlights the anthropological lens. First, although readers may never have thrown brightly colored pigment to celebrate Holi, they can easily identify with and understand the young woman's wish to capture the moment on video. In this way, the photo highlights both our different and same experiences, as humans participating in cultural life. We recognize ourselves in her. Second, today we live in a globally connected world. People in all societies use cultural artifacts—such as smart phones—in new and creative contexts. Culture is constantly changing, and anthropologists are interested in how and why. This book shows how anthropology seeks to understand, and help provide solutions for, human issues at a time of rapid change to cultures, economies, and the environment.

Note to Instructors

We have designed the book so that topical coverage is not restricted to the sequence of the chapters as laid out. Following the introductory chapter, the sequence leads to the primate background (Chapter 2), followed by evolutionary thought (Chapter 3), human biological evolution (Chapter 4), archaeology (Chapters 5, 6, and 7), and then cultural anthropology and linguistic anthropology (Chapters 8–14). We know that some instructors prefer to begin with cultural anthropology, for example. Similarly, some may choose to cover evolutionary thought before primates. One of the ways we have accommodated alternate coverage sequences is to bold important glossary terms multiple times in the book, for instance, the first time it appears in the archaeology section and then again the first time it appears in the cultural anthropology section. This way, the book doesn't assume the student knows the term when it appears in the latter half.

Although different parts of the book have different foci (i.e., biological anthropology, archaeology, and cultural anthropology with linguistics), we strive to integrate the four-field approach where appropriate. Our primary themes of food and sustainability, for example, are one way of showing the integration, and the incorporation of linguistics into various contexts another. In addition, when a topic is addressed multiple times in the book, we cross-reference the chapters.

Each chapter includes a list of learning objectives, a chapter summary, and questions to guide students' reading and provide a framework for thinking about the issues covered. In addition, the authors and the University of Toronto Press provide a full set of ancillaries for instructors adopting the text. These ancillaries include an instructor's manual with chapter outlines and key points, lecture suggestions, assignments and activities, answers to the review questions found in the book, lists of key terms with page references, further reading, Web links, PowerPoint slides, and a test bank. For more information about the instructor's manual, PowerPoint slides, and test bank, and to download the images, maps, figures, and tables from the book, instructors should visit www.lensofanthropology.com.

We wanted to keep the book in a concise format for two main reasons: First, the concise format brings the cost of the book down for students; the high cost of textbooks is a concern for many instructors, including us. Second, we know that you, the instructor, have your own knowledge, experience, and goals for your courses. We have provided the basic structure upon which we hope you will build, utilizing examples of your own that will make the course come to life.

Note to Students

More than 300 words in the text appear in boldface, indicating that they are in the glossary. Students are encouraged to check the glossary to see how these words are defined. Many of them have a particular meaning in anthropology that may be different from the way they are used in common conversation (words such as *theory* or *gender*, for example). Many words are boldfaced two or three times in the text. This accommodates courses that follow a different sequence of chapters than that laid out in the book. We also encourage you to use the learning objectives to guide your reading, as well as the review and discussion questions to reflect and apply what you have read to your own experience.

The term *North America* is used frequently throughout this book. We recognize that there are multiple ways of defining North America, but when we use North America in this book, we are primarily referring to the United States and Canada.

There are free online learning resources that can greatly enhance each student's engagement with the book's content. Visit www.lensofanthropology.com for self-study questions, chapter outlines, Web links, further reading, and to download the images, maps, figures, and tables contained in the book.

PLACES MENTIONED IN CHAPTER 1

1 Island of Flores, Indonesia
2 Cahokia Mounds (St. Louis, Missouri)
3 New York
4 Kalahari Desert, Botswana
5 Afghanistan
6 Germany

INTRODUCTION: VIEWING THE WORLD THROUGH THE LENS OF ANTHROPOLOGY

Anthropology is a kind of lens, bringing focus and clarity to human diversity #lensofanthropology

Learning Objectives

In this chapter students will learn:

- the nature and scope of anthropology, including its use as a lens or framework, the major branches and subfields, and the anthropological perspective.
- the nature of culture, with particular attention to its definition, components, interconnectedness, and ever-changing dynamic.
- the history of anthropology in North America, focusing on principal contributions, dominant figures, relationships with Indigenous peoples, and the diversity of anthropologists and interests today.
- how anthropology is situated within the contexts of academia, the business world, and popular culture.
- how anthropology is important in an increasingly connected world.

Introduction

How, why, and when did **humans** come to be? Why do various groups of people around the world have different physical characteristics, and why do so many people speak, think, and do things differently than those you are most familiar with?

The short answer is that **science** in general, and **anthropology** in particular, tells us that humans have been around a very long time. Habitually walking on two legs was the first important thing to occur in the human lineage, intelligence the second. Differences in languages, thoughts, and customs arise from many things, but are usually the result of humans' successful adaptation to the environment and other people around them. A longer, more thorough, answer requires some knowledge of anthropology. This text is designed to give students some of that fundamental knowledge and the anthropological thinking skills to address these questions and others like them.

To make sense of the world around us and our place in it, it's useful to have a framework. Frameworks help organize thoughts and guide our understanding of both the natural and cultural worlds. Many frameworks exist. Traditional mainstream religions offer one major kind of framework, Indigenous ideologies another. Science and academic enquiry are frameworks as well. Just as there are many different religious and Indigenous frameworks, there are also different kinds of scientific, academic, and scholarly frameworks. All frameworks are valid.

It is important to have a framework for understanding phenomena. Frameworks help people work toward explanations. Frameworks narrow down the kinds of information to consider. What constitutes a framework is a set of principles, methods, theories; and knowledge to investigate, understand, and explain phenomena.

Anthropology is one such framework, a way of understanding how humans came, and continue, to be. It isn't the only way, but it is one way. In practical terms, this means that anthropology has a particular set of characteristics that distinguish it from other ways of knowing. These characteristics are clarified later in this and subsequent chapters.

In this book we refer to the anthropological framework as the **lens of anthropology**. As with any framework, it provides a basic structure to help organize our thoughts. It provides focus and clarity. The lens is a particular set of ideas, methods, theories, ethics, views, and research results.

This book introduces the discipline of anthropology, mostly in the context of the academic world, but also from the perspective of practical applications. Mostly, it informs readers about the human world as seen through the lens of anthropology. This opening chapter outlines the nature of anthropology, the **anthropological perspective**, the history of anthropology, how anthropology is situated within the world today, and the importance of anthropology in an increasingly connected world. Subsequent chapters turn the lens toward our place in the world of **primates**, human biological evolution, cultural evolution, and the wide range of cultural diversity among the world's populations today. Where appropriate, the chapters include references to underlying anthropological methods and theories as well as research findings and insight.

Box 1.1
Anthropology and Food

It is hard to think of a more essential thing in human existence than food. People need nourishment to survive. Therefore, much of the social and cultural life that embeds humans in their daily activities results from finding, distributing, preparing, consuming, and disposing of food. For this reason, anthropologists across the four fields have addressed the questions surrounding the human relationship to food since the beginning of the discipline.

There are many ways in which food issues are similar across cultures. All humans may consume a wide variety of foods to support health. As omnivores, people choose from foods available in the environment—which may vary greatly from one ecosystem to another—and receive the nutrients the human body requires. In addition, humans prepare food by cooking it. This is grounded in an ancient legacy in which hominins' bodies and communal life were greatly affected by the cooking process. Finally, the activities around food procurement are deeply embedded in a complex system of social, economic, political, and religious norms and expectations. People's daily lives are limited, supported, and enriched by eating as a cultural and symbolic act.

Anthropologists interested in food issues may identify themselves simply as biological, cultural, archaeological, or linguistic anthropologists with an emphasis on foodways. They may also choose a more specialized subfield, such as nutritional anthropology (which takes a biocultural approach), ethnoecology (which examines traditional foodways), gastronomy (which combines cooking, food science, and cultural meanings, especially of fine foods), or food studies (which tends to focus on issues of culture, history, and identity).

Studying peoples' foodways has become more important than ever in light of the impacts of climate change and globalization. Due to unpredictable weather patterns, farmers may lose entire harvests during a severe storm or heat wave. Inuit ice fishermen can no longer reliably read the sky to know if they should undertake a fishing expedition. Because of a globalized economy that opens up access to land and water, companies and nations claim ownership of resources that are outside of their boundaries. Water, privatized by a bottling company, vanishes in underground aquifers, leaving less for farmers seeking to irrigate crops. The World Bank funds massive food aid programs, while African farmers' harvests rot in granaries, owing to lack of demand.

Food issues are sustainability issues, and also anthropological issues. What is more central to people's lives than food?

Besides offering an overview of the basic framework of anthropology, this book highlights two themes of contemporary interest in anthropology: food and sustainability.

Food is an area of considerable interest in anthropology, including such topics as the emergence of meat eating, the origins of cooking, processes involved in food production, cooking and gender, patterns of eating across cultures, food security, and food taboos. Explicit references to food are made in most of the chapters, in both the main part of the writing and the box features.

Anthropology and Sustainability

It has been clear to scientists for some time that life on our planet is becoming unsustainable. Louder and more urgent calls to action emerge every few years. In 1992, the scientific community published the "World Scientists' Warning to Humanity." In 2000, the United Nations Millennium goals were published; they included specific targets to aim for by 2015 in social, environmental, and economic realms to mitigate some of the most detrimental effects. Seeing that we hadn't yet reached these targets, in 2014, the Intergovernmental Panel on Climate Change (IPCC) published their synthesis report, which states bluntly that if we don't act now to cut carbon pollution, there will be severely damaging and "irreversible impacts" that will hamper our ability to survive as a species.

Clearly, the sustainability of people and life on earth is an issue that we cannot ignore. Why include anthropology in a discussion about sustainability? Anthropology, across its fields, is uniquely positioned as a field of study to provide the kinds of broad and deep understandings about people in their environments— understandings that can lead to solutions. Since the beginning of the discipline, anthropologists have sought to learn about the long-term interactions of people in their environments.

From the time of hominin evolution, through more recent prehistory, to the rise and fall of civilizations, anthropologists have sought to understand the reasons for successes and failures in all of the ecosystems on earth.

Today, anthropologists study some of the most marginalized people living on the planet, including Indigenous people living in small-scale, traditional societies. As the world becomes more connected through globalization and industry, these groups are often the most oppressed. At the same time, these groups hold vast amounts of traditional knowledge about the ecosystems in which they live. This knowledge appears to be more important than ever to save the biodiversity of the planet. As these small-scale cultures disappear, so do their knowledge, languages, understanding and use of flora and fauna, and pre-industrialized ways of making a living.

It is here among the people who are on the edges of the modern Western world that anthropologists discover the kinds of connections with the natural world that modernization has largely discarded in the quest for status and power that characterizes the contemporary world. Therefore, anthropology can not only provide holistic and long-term views of why cultures succeed or fail in their ecosystems but also illuminate the kinds of human connections to one another and to the natural world that characterize our species.

Sustainability is another area of considerable interest in anthropology, including such topics as nonhuman primates' contributions to sustainable environments, the identification of sustainability (or lack thereof) in the human past, and maintaining environmental sustainability in contemporary times. This book understands sustainability as having three main aspects: environmental, social, and economic. As with food, explicit references are made to sustainability in most chapters, in both the main writing and some of the box features. Sustainability is also the entire focus of Chapter 14.

Defining Anthropology, Defining Human, and Defining Culture

Three of the most important words a student of anthropology should become familiar with, at least in regard to how they are used in anthropology, are *anthropology*, *human*, and *culture*. There is a good chance most students already have some idea of the meaning of these words, but they may not be aware of specific meanings and how they may vary depending on context. There is little consensus, even among anthropologists, about what these words mean, but this is not necessarily a bad thing. There are some general understandings of what each word means in anthropology, but it isn't necessary that everyone use the same definition in every context.

There are many definitions of anthropology. The one constant in all valid definitions is that anthropology involves the study of humans. Beyond this, however, how one defines the discipline depends on context. Outside of North America, anthropology is often considered to focus on peoples and cultures of contemporary times (or the very recent past). In North America, however, anthropology is usually considered to include studies of human cultures and human biology, past and present.

In many instances, such as when general distinctions between various fields of study are being made, a simple definition such as "anthropology is the study of humans" may be sufficient. There are many disciplines that focus on humans, however, so it is often desirable to distinguish between the particular kinds of things about humans that anthropologists are interested in, such as human culture and human biology, or methods or perspectives. The inclusion of the "evolutionary, comparative, and holistic perspectives," for example, distinguishes anthropology. Other uniquely anthropological perspectives are included later in this chapter.

Human has a distinct meaning in anthropology and may be used in ways that are unfamiliar. For many people, human equates with *Homo sapiens*, the genus and species to which we all belong. For anthropologists interested in the human past, however, *Homo sapiens* is insufficient. As will be clarified and expanded upon in subsequent chapters, many anthropologists equate human with a certain kind of primate whose normal means of moving around is walking on two legs (**bipedalism**) and who emerged several million years ago. Those who accept that bipedalism is the distinguishing characteristic of humans therefore equate

> ## Defining Anthropology
> Anthropology is ...
> - The study of humans
> - The study of human culture
> - The study of humans, in all places and at all times
> - The study of human culture and biology
> - The study of humans, focusing on the description and explanation of human cultures and human biology, and including the scholarly collection, analysis, and interpretation of data related to humans, past and present
> - The scholarly study of humans through evolutionary, comparative, and holistic perspectives

human with the biological family **Homininae**, which includes the genus *Homo* as well as other genera (plural of genus) existing between seven million and one million years ago. Some anthropologists, especially those focusing on the past cultures, equate human with the genus *Homo*, for the simple reason that it is with the emergence of the genus *Homo* more than two million years ago that we have first undeniable physical evidence of human culture. In sum, some anthropologists equate human with *Homo sapiens*, some equate human with the genus *Homo* (which includes *sapiens* as well as other now extinct species), and some equate human with the biological family *Homininae*.

Culture, too, has a distinct meaning in anthropology, which may not correspond to its usage in other contexts. Culture is a core concept in anthropology and is covered more fully in Chapter 8. As with the definitions of anthropology and human, there are many different ways to define culture, even within the discipline of anthropology. Some definitions focus on the mental templates that govern peoples' behavior; others focus on customs. The authors of this textbook consider culture to include aspects of **ideology** and behavior, as well as the products of those thoughts and behaviors (i.e., material culture). Thus, we define culture as the learned and shared things that people think, do, and have as members of a society. "Things that people think" refers to ideology, which includes belief systems and values. "Things that people do" includes behaviors that are commonly referred to as customs. "Things that people have" is commonly referred to as material culture.

There are many components of culture including those relating to subsistence, diet, technology, communication, economies, social and political systems, ideology, arts, and health. All cultures have these components, and each is discussed more fully in later chapters. When anthropologists speak of **subsistence**, food procurement, or foodways, they are usually referring to the methods by which people get their food, such as **foraging** (also known as hunting and gathering), **pastoralism**, **horticulture**, **agriculture**, or industrialism. Diet refers to the specific kinds of food eaten. Technology refers to the way people have made or used things, including such things as making and using tools, cooking, harvesting, and building. Communication refers to all ways people have of communicating, including speech, sounds, gestures, art, and writing. Settlement patterns refer to the movements of people within their territories, and the ways in which they create their living spaces. Economic systems focus on the way people obtain and distribute resources. Social systems include the methods by which order is maintained within a community or group, and political systems involve the processes in which order is maintained with other groups. Ideology includes shared beliefs and values. Art includes both visual and performing

Components of Culture

- Subsistence/ food-getting/food procurement
- Diet
- Technology
- Language and communication
- Settlement patterns
- Economic systems
- Social systems
- Political systems
- Belief systems and ideology
- Arts
- Health and healing

arts, and health and healing refers to both physical and mental health, illnesses, and methods of treatment.

It is important to understand that culture is dynamic, fluid, and ever-changing. All components of culture do not change at the same rate, and the components do not change in the same order, but they all do eventually change.

It is possible to be part of multiple cultures and subcultures at the same time. Based on language alone, there are several thousand distinct cultures in the world today. This is based on the notion that where languages are distinct, other aspects of ideology, customs, and material culture are typically distinct as well. Most elements of any one culture are shared with other cultures as well. It is the suite of characteristics that distinguish distinct cultures and subcultures. Consider, for example, that readers of this text may identify with North American culture, which has some distinct values, behaviors, and other things unique to North Americans but not shared widely with people outside of North America. Beyond that, people may also identify with other cultures associated with their heritage, country, or geography. Although they share many aspects of North American culture, for example, there are distinct differences between American and Canadian cultures, east coast or west coast subcultures, southern and northern subcultures; Indigenous and non-Indigenous, or corporate and non-corporate subcultures. Readers of this text are also likely to share the same particular set of values, customs, and items as those attending colleges and universities anywhere in North America, as part of college and university subculture.

Many people are also often able to operate within multiple cultures. It is common, for example, for some Indigenous peoples in North America to move between their Indigenous culture, especially as it is on their reserves or reservation, and the typically more dominant non-Indigenous cultures in urban areas.

Figure 1.1
The Branches of Anthropology
This illustration represents the four main branches of anthropology. Each branch also includes an "applied" component.

The Four Fields and Applied Anthropology

Anthropology in North America is usually considered to have four academic fields, sometimes referred to as branches or subfields: **cultural anthropology**, **archaeology**, **biological anthropology**, and **linguistic anthropology**. As illustrated in Figure 1.1, anthropologists often also apply their skills outside academia in a branch called **applied anthropology**, which utilizes skills and methods of each of the other branches.

Cultural anthropology, also known as social anthropology or socio-cultural anthropology, focuses on cultures of the present and

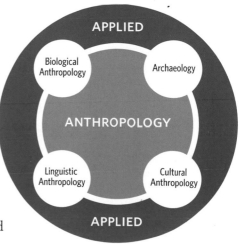

Figure 1.2

Indigenous Men in the Kalahari

Cultural anthropologists study peoples and cultures all over the globe. Pictured here are two Indigenous men in the Kalahari Desert region of Botswana, Africa. Anthropological studies of Indigenous peoples of this area, sometimes known as the San, typify anthropological interests in the foreign and unfamiliar to North Americans. It would be incorrect to think, however, that it is only the foreign and unfamiliar that anthropologists study.

Credit: © Afripics.com/Alamy

Figure 1.3

Times Square

In addition to the strange, unfamiliar, and exotic, anthropologists also study North American culture. What may seem normal to North Americans is strange and unfamiliar to others.

Credit: © Barry D. Kass/Images of Anthropology

recent past. Training in this branch often involves immersing oneself within a culture for several months or more and then producing an **ethnography**, which is a written description of that culture. Immersion in a culture is often called **ethnographic research**, and the method itself, whereby one both observes and participates in a culture, is known as **participant observation**. Thousands of ethnographies have been written by cultural anthropologists over the past 150 years, and they provide much of the raw data of anthropology. Beyond simply describing peoples' lifeways, cultural anthropologists also seek to interpret and explain larger patterns of culture. Cultural anthropologists often work in the academic world; however, there are many who find themselves working in the world of business, governments, and the not-for-profit sectors. Insight into the world of contemporary cultures through cultural anthropology is the focus of Chapters 8 through 14.

Archaeology (also spelled archeology) may be defined as the study of humans through their material remains, which essentially means the physical evidence of their activities. Most archaeology is focused on **prehistory** and the historic period, but some archaeologists focus on the contemporary world. The primary raw data of archaeology includes **archaeological sites** and **artifacts**, which are usually found during fieldwork. The primary objectives of archaeologists are to describe and explain the human past and to document the rapidly disappearing physical record of the human past. About 90 per cent of archaeologists working in North America are involved in a kind of archaeology known as **cultural resource management**, or **commercial archaeology**, which essentially involves looking for and recording archaeological sites in advance of development projects. The results of archaeological research, especially in regard to outlining the development of human culture over the past two million years, are the focus of Chapters 5, 6, and 7.

Biological anthropology, also known as **physical anthropology**, focuses on human biology, past and present. This includes the study of human biological evolution as well as the study of contemporary biological variability. Biological

anthropologists study skeletal material (e.g., bones and teeth) as well as DNA and other molecular substances.

Primatology, which is the study of nonhuman primates within a framework of anthropology, is usually considered a subfield of biological anthropology. Biological anthropologists are interested in the study of other primates to help us better understand our place in the animal world from a biological perspective and also to provide us with models of how early humans may have behaved. Primate taxonomy, evolution, and behaviour are covered in Chapter 2.

Palaeoanthropology, which involves the study of early human biology and culture, is often considered to be part of biological anthropology, although it tends to involve the recovery, analysis, and interpretation of both early human biological and cultural evidence. The study of human biological evolution, mostly based on studies by palaeoanthropologists, is the focus of Chapter 4. The study of early human cultural evolution is the focus of Chapter 5.

Most biological anthropologists work in the academic world, but some also are employed elsewhere, in such fields as **ergonomics** or forensics. Forensic anthropologists use their expertise in biological anthropology mostly to identify victims; they typically ascertain an individual's sex, age at death, and cause of death, but their duties may also include such things as identifying the ancestral population of the individual and his or her medical and nutritional history.

Linguistic anthropology is the study of human languages within the framework of anthropology. This includes classifying languages (such as putting them into taxonomic categories); determining past migrations and interactions by examining languages; and studying language change, the influence of language on other elements of culture and their influences on it, and language usage. Most linguistic anthropologists work in academic institutions, but there are also career opportunities elsewhere, such as with **Indigenous** groups and not-for-profits seeking to document the rapidly disappearing languages of the world.

Figure 1.4
Doing Archaeology
Archaeologists at work. Most anthropologists prefer to collect their own data. In archaeology, this usually involves excavation. Archaeologists here are excavating an early twentieth-century Japanese camp in Canada.
Credit: Nadine Ryan

Figure 1.5
A Macaque Eating
Macaque eating jackfruit. Primatology is often considered a subfield of biological anthropology. Anthropologists are interested in nonhuman primates, both to learn about these species and to better understand humans.
Credit: Nadine Ryan

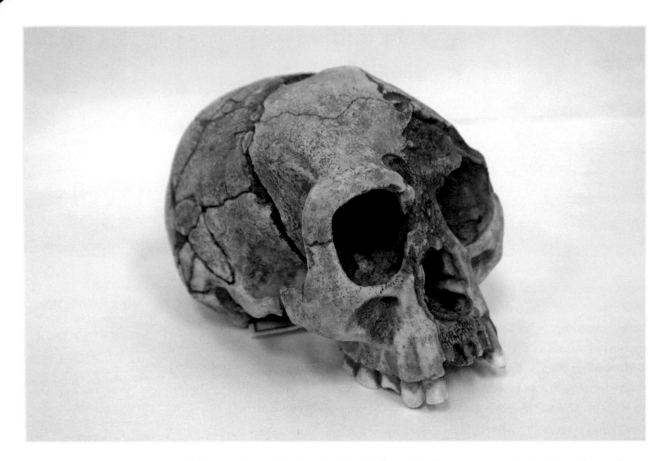

Figure 1.6 **Homo floresiensis Skull**

Skull of *Homo floresiensis*. *Homo floresiensis* was a very small human species, often described as hobbits, that lived as recently as 12,000 years ago on the island of Flores in Southeast Asia.

Credit: Nadine Ryan

Most anthropologists in North America have some training in at least three, and often four, of the major branches of anthropology. It is common, for example, for one who primarily identifies as an archaeologist to also have training in and a good understanding of cultural anthropology and biological anthropology. A cultural anthropologist usually has some training in and understanding of linguistic anthropology and archaeology.

While each branch has an applied anthropology component, it is clearly in the field of archaeology that the largest percentage of anthropologists practice the discipline outside of the purely academic arena. Many cultural anthropologists are employed by Indigenous groups, helping them document their cultures, especially in the areas of **Traditional Use Studies (TUS)** and **Traditional Ecological Knowledge (TEK)**. Corporations employ cultural anthropologists to help them with their own internal organizations as well as to learn how to better deal with consumers or people in other countries. Some cultural anthropologists have even found employment working for the US military in conflict zones, on the assumption that the expertise a cultural anthropologist has is likely to lead to better-informed decisions by military personnel. A recent program by the US military in this regard is known as the **Human Terrain System**, the ethics of which are highly controversial and debated widely among professionals (see Box 8.4).

The Anthropological Perspective

It is primarily the anthropological perspective that constitutes the lens of anthropology. This perspective has several elements, including being holistic, evolutionary, comparative, qualitative, focused on linkages, focused on change, and based on fieldwork. Taking a **holistic** perspective means that anthropologists view all aspects of human biology and culture as being interrelated. That is, for a thorough understanding of any one component of human biology or culture, anthropologists recognize that a full understanding involves studying the links. In the study of early human evolution, for example, anthropologists understand that intelligence is correlated with brain size, making tools is linked with dexterity, meat eating correlated with digestive enzymes, and so on. They also recognize that all components of culture are intricately interrelated, so that an anthropologist primarily interested in art recognizes that art may influence or be influenced by politics, social systems, ideology, technology, and more. Anthropologists also understand that a change in one component of a culture invariably causes changes in other components.

Taking an evolutionary perspective means that a good understanding of biological and cultural traits is best considered in regard to long-term evolutionary changes. Anthropologists use a database that extends millions of years into the past. They understand that changes rarely occur in a vacuum, and while some changes can occur quickly across time and space, it is at least worth considering the record of the past.

Taking a comparative perspective means that anthropologists often compare things in their research. For biological anthropologists this may mean that when they find an ancient bone that looks as if it may be human, they compare it to known human bone matter to determine what species it may best be classified as. When archaeologists find an ancient tool of unknown function they may compare it to similar-looking things in use today to make inferences about its use. Linguistic anthropologists often compare the vocabularies of languages to draw inferences about interactions in the past. Cultural anthropologists compare various components of multiple cultures in studies, to reveal how people may adapt to similar circumstances.

Taking the **qualitative** perspective means that anthropologists tend to focus on descriptive research rather than **quantitative** data. Anthropologists do use statistics, but it is rarely the primary method of research. Rather than have people complete surveys and then quantify the results, for example, anthropologists tend to seek deeper meaning and insight by focusing on fewer individuals for longer periods.

Focusing on linkages relates to the holistic perspective. Much more so than other disciplines, anthropology tends to focus on the linkages between human biology

> ## Key Elements of the Anthropological Perspective
> - Holistic
> - Evolutionary
> - Comparative
> - Qualitative
> - Focused on linkages
> - Focused on change
> - Based on fieldwork

and culture, the linkages between various parts of the human body, and the linkages between the various components of a culture. Biological anthropologists understand, for example, that walking upright efficiently is linked to changes in the skull, back, pelvis, legs, and feet. Cultural anthropologists may not know as much about human political systems as political scientists, nor as much about settlement patterns as human geographers, but they are likely best situated to understand the connection between politics, settlement, economics, religions, and other factors.

Anthropologists often focus on change. They understand that both human biology and human cultures are undergoing constant change, and this ties in with holistic and evolutionary perspectives and with focusing on linkages. Anthropologists are interested in how and why change occurs, both within groups and over time.

Another key element of anthropology is the focus on fieldwork. Anthropologists tend to collect their own data. Biological anthropologists want to find bones of early humans themselves or extract the DNA from bones already in collections. Archaeologists tend to want to find and excavate archaeological sites themselves. Linguistic anthropologists usually prefer to work directly with native speakers. Cultural anthropologists often immerse themselves in another culture to make their own observations and collect their own data. This sets anthropology apart from the many other disciplines that use data collected by governments, agencies, or other groups.

Other characteristics of anthropology that may be considered to fall within the anthropological perspective include the following:

- Anthropologists tend to be more interested in populations than individuals.
- Anthropologists are interested in big-picture things, including questions such as what makes us human? Why and how did we evolve the way we did? And how are some traits adaptive?
- Anthropologists are also interested in small things, such as how people greet each other.
- Anthropologists recognize that most traits, biological and cultural (but not all), are adaptive in some way.
- Anthropologists recognize that biological and cultural characteristics are not perfect.
- Anthropologists recognize that there are multiple ways of adapting, and one way is not necessarily better than another.
- Anthropologists recognize that similar problems can be solved in different ways.

History of Anthropology, Mostly in North America

Anthropology emerged globally as a widely recognized academic discipline in the 1800s, primarily in Europe. It emerged out of an interest in observations and interests, largely by Europeans, in cultural diversity around the world, as well as observations and interests in ancient archaeological sites and artifacts.

It wasn't until the late 1800s that anthropology took hold as a scholarly discipline in universities, but there was certainly considerable activity that could broadly be classified as anthropology before this. In the 1700s, for example, Thomas Jefferson (who would later go on to become the 3rd President of the United States) excavated one of the thousands of large earthen mounds that dotted the landscape of the eastern and central parts of the United States. His objective was to draw some conclusions about who had created the mounds, and he confirmed his hypothesis that it was the ancestors of the Indigenous peoples still living in the area.

Interest in the mounds continued throughout most of the 1800s, particularly in regard to studying them before they would be destroyed by colonial settlement, ranching, farming, and other activities. Almost all the mounds have since been

Table 1.1

History of Anthropology in North America

1700s	Little work that qualifies as anthropological. Notable exception includes Thomas Jefferson excavating to ascertain who created large earthen mounds.
1800s	Anthropology emerges in both Canada and the United States. Important developments include establishment of Bureau of American Ethnology and museum collections. Lewis Henry Morgan makes contributions in ethnography and theory. Salvage ethnography becomes common. Franz Boas begins to have impact on the development of anthropology throughout North America. Focus of anthropological interest almost entirely on Indigenous peoples of the continent.
Early 1900s	Influence of Boas significant, including development of four-field model and training many who would become influential, such as Alfred Kroeber and Margaret Mead. Cultural ecology developed as useful model by Julian Steward. Continued focus on Indigenous peoples in North America.
Late 1900s	Criticism of anthropology by Indigenous peoples in both Canada and the United States, largely accepted by anthropologists. Creation of heritage legislation protecting Indigenous heritage sites (restricting anthropologists and others from exploiting). Anthropology begins to break from focus on Indigenous peoples, instead focusing on other groups, within and beyond North American society. More women and minorities enter the profession.
2000s	Discipline continues to grow in membership numbers, diversity, and interest. More anthropologists, increasing diversity of anthropology, and more areas of interest, including food and sustainability. Many anthropologists becoming activists, including giving voice to the voiceless and disenfranchised and tackling issues of race and racism.

Figure 1.7
Totem Pole
Anthropologists often support Indigenous claims of cultural appropriation, including their art and symbols being appropriated by governments, the tourism and fashion industries, and sports teams.

Credit: Gillian Crowther

destroyed. A notable exception is **Cahokia**, near St. Louis, which is now a **World Heritage Site** (see Chapter 7). Much of the work on the mounds was funded by the American Ethnological Society and the Smithsonian Institution.

The beginning of pure scholarly or theoretical work in anthropology in North America is often associated with Lewis Henry Morgan (1818–1881). He made significant contributions to both ethnography and theory. His ethnography *League of the Iroquois* (1851) was the first scholarly ethnography of a Native American group. However, he is best known for developing the **unilinear theory** of cultural evolution, outlined in *Ancient Society, or Researches in the Lines of Progress from Savagery through Barbarism to Civilization* (1877). In this book Morgan proposed that every society in the world started as savages. Some progressed to barbarism, and others then progressed to civilization. Savagery and barbarism each had three stages, making for seven stages in total. Classification into any one stage was based primarily on subsistence strategy and technology. If a group did not have pottery, for example, they were savages. According to Morgan, cultural diversity around the world could be explained by some societies failing to progress as quickly as others. Although some anthropologists liked this theory, many did not support it, and it was largely discredited by anthropologists within a few decades. Many anthropologists knew then, and all know now, that there are usually multiple ways of adapting to environments and other groups, and no one way is necessarily better than another.

There were many other interesting developments for anthropology in North America beginning in the late 1800s. One such development included the

Figure 1.8
Indigenous Women Doing Archaeology
The profession of anthropology includes an increasing number of Indigenous peoples. Pictured here are two First Nations women from Canada working on an archaeology project.
Credit: Nadine Ryan

establishment of the Bureau of American Ethnology, which was created to collect information on the Indigenous peoples of the continent, and supported both archaeological and ethnographic research projects. The rapidly declining populations of Indigenous peoples (due largely to disease and conflict with those of European descent), and rapidly changing cultures (as traditional lifeways were changing in response to **colonialism**) gave rise to a sense of urgency to document these cultures. This created a kind of anthropology known as **salvage ethnography**, which became the most common kind of anthropology in the late 1800s and early 1900s. Another development with implications for North American anthropology was the golden age of museum collecting in North America, beginning in the late 1800s and continuing into the early 1900s. Anthropologists and others collected millions of objects from Indigenous peoples for museums in North America and Europe. Some were negotiated and paid for, others were not. Hundreds of thousands of human skeletons were included in the collections.

The most dominant figure in the history of North American anthropology is Franz Boas (1858–1942), who moved to the United States from Germany in the late 1800s. His own fieldwork focused on the Indigenous peoples of the continent, especially in the Pacific Northwest regions, but he made many other significant contributions. For example, he was an outspoken critic of Lewis Henry Morgan's notion of a unilinear model of cultural evolution. He developed the notion of **cultural relativism** and **historical particularism**, which became foundations of the discipline in North America and countered Morgan's theory. He is also widely

Box 1.3

The Indigenous Peoples of North America and Anthropology

Anthropology in North America has a long history of entanglement with Indigenous peoples of North America. From the late 1800s to the late 1900s, the overwhelming focus of anthropological study was on Indigenous groups in the territories now known as Canada and the United States. Anthropologists saw the rapid rate at which Indigenous populations were declining, traditional lifeways were changing, languages were disappearing, and archaeological sites were being destroyed. This led to many anthropologists undertaking what is known as salvage ethnography, recording as best they could what life was like before the influence of Europeans. There was some specialization, but many anthropologists were practicing four-field anthropology, meaning fieldwork for them usually included studying the Indigenous peoples in their own territories, undertaking ethnography (cultural anthropology), learning and recording languages (linguistic anthropology), measuring the physical attributes of the people (biological anthropology), and excavating archaeological sites.

Although there were certainly some good relationships between anthropologist and Indigenous peoples, it is justifiable to state that until the latter part of the twentieth century, the relationship was largely exploitative. Anthropologists would often take much from the Indigenous peoples in regard to their cultural knowledge and beliefs, as well as hundreds of thousands of human skeletons and millions of artifacts, while providing nothing or very little in exchange. Anthropologists were advancing their own careers, filling museums, and making contributions to the discipline of anthropology at the expense of Indigenous peoples. Anthropologists began to be called out by some Indigenous peoples in the 1960s. One of the most prominent voices, Vine Deloria Jr. (Dakota Sioux) published a scathing criticism in his book *Custer*

credited with many important developments in the field of anthropology, including the four-field approach in anthropology as it is practiced in North America. He became one of the first professors of anthropology and obtained significant funding for anthropology research projects. Boas also trained many of the most prominent North American anthropologists of the early 1900s (including Alfred Kroeber, Margaret Mead, and Edward Sapir), encouraged women to become anthropologists, and formally trained and collaborated with Indigenous peoples (including Ella Deloria and George Hunt).

The history of anthropology in North America has been intricately intertwined with the Indigenous peoples of the continent. Since the late 1800s some anthropologists have had good relations with Indigenous peoples, but for many the relationship can be characterized as exploitative on the part of anthropologists. Serious and widely published criticisms of anthropology in North America, by Indigenous people, began to become well known in the 1960s, and since that time, the relations can generally be characterized as better. Most anthropological work involving Indigenous peoples, for example, is now done only with the consent of

Died for Your Sins: An Indian Manifesto (1988:78–100), which includes the following excerpt:

> INTO EACH LIFE, it is said, some rain must fall. Some people have bad horoscopes; others take tips on the stock market ... but Indians have been cursed above all other people in history. Indians have anthropologists.... Over the years anthropologists have succeeded in burying the Indian communities so completely beneath the mass of irrelevant information that the total impact of the scholarly community on Indian people has become one of simple authority.... The implications of the anthropologist ... should be clear for the Indian. Compilation of useless knowledge "for knowledge's sake" should be utterly rejected by the Indian people.... In the meantime it would be wise for anthropologists to get down from their thrones of authority and PURE research and begin helping Indian tribes instead of preying on them.

The relationship between Indigenous peoples and anthropologists has significantly improved in recent decades. Many Indigenous people have entered the profession, and anthropologists who continue to work with Indigenous people in North America do so largely with their permission and on their behalf. Linguistic anthropologists often work with Indigenous groups in efforts to record and revitalize languages; archaeologists often work in support of claims of Indigenous rights and territories; and cultural anthropologist are often involved in assisting with documenting Traditional Use Studies (TUS) and Traditional Ecological Knowledge (TEK). Anthropologists are also often involved in supporting Indigenous peoples in addressing stereotypes, misconceptions, cultural appropriation, and commodification of their heritage. In many ways, the relationship that anthropologists have with Indigenous peoples can now be characterized as supportive, rather than exploitative.

the Indigenous peoples and with the anthropologist providing something of value, including knowledge, back to the Indigenous peoples.

Over the past few decades, anthropologists trained and working in North America have disentangled the relationship between the discipline and the Indigenous peoples of the continent. Indigenous peoples are not as central to North American anthropology as they once were. Anthropologists still work with Indigenous peoples in the traditional areas of research such as ethnography, archaeology, and linguistics, but their interests in Indigenous peoples also include many other areas, including Indigenous identity and **cultural appropriation**.

There are many other threads of interest in contemporary anthropology in early twenty-first-century North America, including but certainly not limited to corporate culture, youth culture, popular culture, militarization and warfare, terrorism, food, sustainability, disease, education, queer culture, gender, and much more. Many anthropologists now work among the voiceless and disenfranchised in North America, such as the homeless in urban areas and undocumented migrants, often challenging widely held misconceptions about their lives. Many anthropologists also address the concept of **race**, covered more fully in Chapters 4 and 8.

Over the last few decades there has also been a change in the makeup of those in the profession of anthropology. As in most academic disciplines, there has been a long history of white male dominance in North American anthropology. Male dominance has decreased in recent decades. Ethnic diversity is increasing, but it has a long way to go. Numbers of anthropologists may be roughly equitable in regard to gender, but in regards to ethnicity, people of European descent and light skin color remain a significant majority.

Situating Anthropology

Anthropology can be found in multiple contexts, including the academic world, the business world, and popular culture. Perhaps the most common perception of anthropology is that of an academic discipline, operating primarily out of colleges, universities, and museums. Indeed, most colleges and universities have anthropology departments with professors who teach, research, and write. Most commonly, it is the results of anthropological work done in the context of the academic world that make their way into mainstream media.

In most colleges and universities in North America, anthropology is considered to be part of the liberal arts or social sciences. In some educational institutions, though, especially those that focus on archaeology and biological anthropology, students may get a science credit, and the department itself may be aligned more closely with physics, chemistry, and biology than with any of the other humanities or social science areas.

Academic anthropologists, in addition to teaching, tend to focus on pure scholarly research. Typically a university professor or someone working toward a PhD applies for funding for research from a major funding agency, such as the National Endowment for the Humanities (NEH) or National Science Foundation (NSF) in the United States, or the Social Sciences and Humanities Research Council (SSHRC) in Canada. Once the research project is complete, he or she will often report the results at a professional conference (e.g., annual meetings of the American Anthropological Association, Society for American Archaeology, American Association of Physical Anthropologists, Canadian Anthropology Society, or Canadian Archaeological Association), and write an article for publication in a scholarly journal (e.g., *American Anthropologist*, *American Antiquity*, *American Journal of Physical Anthropology*, *Current Anthropology*, or one of dozens of more international, national, and regional journals). Presenting and publishing research releases it into the public domain, allowing other researchers to comment, critique, or build upon it.

Anthropology has found a home in many kinds of businesses. For example, some companies seek advice from anthropologists in order to better understand the dynamics of their own businesses. Other companies seek anthropological knowledge so as to better understand their clients or business partners and learn how not to offend those they do business with in other parts of the world. Others seek anthropological research and interest to better market to target groups.

Some examples of applied anthropology in business are included in Chapter 8, including those of anthropologists working for General Motors or collaborating with Ben and Jerry's Ice Cream. Another example of applied anthropology is the work of Robin Nagle, a professor at New York University, who is also the anthropologist-in-residence at the New York City Department of Sanitation. Her focus is on the labor and infrastructure necessary to deal with garbage. She wrote an ethnography of the Department of Sanitation, called *Picking Up* (2013).

Government agencies also hire anthropologists. The United States Army, for example, had a program (the Human Terrain System), which embedded anthropologists in combat units, reasoning that advice from anthropologists on local inhabitants and their customs may be a useful thing. This program, and the associated ethical dilemmas, is covered in Box 8.4. The program was discontinued in 2014.

Anthropology can also be considered in the context of **popular culture**. Anthropologists study popular culture, and both anthropologists and the discipline of anthropology are firmly embedded in popular culture. Of all the fields, archaeology seems to get most of the attention in popular culture, with archaeologists commonly portrayed as adventurers, and stories revolving around the past. Reports of discoveries of human fossils make their way into mainstream media quickly, and in recent years several successful television programs have been based on the work of forensic anthropologists. Box 1.4 considers both the study of popular culture and the portrayal of anthropology in it.

The Importance of Anthropology in an Increasingly Connected World

As the world becomes increasingly connected, the importance of anthropology also increases. For example, in recent times, anthropologists have been able to make important contributions to helping people suffering from epidemics, natural disasters, and conflict. They do this in multiple ways, including using their cultural knowledge to help those suffering as well as educating those seeking to provide aid. This is especially important, for example, in areas where Indigenous peoples may mistrust or not understand modern medicines and health facilities, and where the

Box 1.4

Anthropology and Popular Culture

Anthropology has an interesting relationship with **popular culture**. Anthropology and anthropologists are firmly embedded in popular culture, and popular culture is a topic of interest that anthropologists study.

Real anthropological work, featuring the work of real archaeologists, is often featured in semi-scholarly publications like *National Geographic*. Anthropological research, especially the work of palaeoanthropologists and archaeologists, often reaches mainstream media, albeit usually through the filters of journalists or social media, and often with lack of a critical perspective.

Anthropology has become firmly embedded in movies, television, and video games. Popular examples include the Indiana Jones series of movies and the Tomb Raider/Lara Croft video game and movie franchise. Fictional anthropologists have been portrayed in popular television series, including *Star Trek*, *Dr. Who*, *The Hitchhiker's Guide to the Galaxy*, and many more.

Figure 1.9 **Indiana Jones**
Fictional anthropologists are embedded in popular culture, including movies, television, novels, comic books, and video games. One of the best-known fictional anthropologists is Indiana Jones.

Credit: Courtesy of the Everett Collection

Anthropologists are occasionally involved in the creation of movies. Primatologist Michael Reid, for example, served as a consultant on ape behavior for the Hollywood production of *Rise of the Planet of the Apes* (2011), and linguistic anthropologist Christine Schreyer created the Kryptonian language for the Superman movie *Man of Steel* (2013). Keeping with the theme of artificially created languages, Schreyer also studies the community of contemporary speakers who have learned the Na'vi language created for the movie *Avatar* (2009).

Sometimes anthropology is associated with popular culture through its link with celebrities and politics. Ann Dunham and her work, for example, became popularized after the election of Barack Obama, the 44th President of the United States. Obama is the son of Dunham, who primarily practiced applied anthropology in Indonesia. In 2014, Ashraf Ghani, who achieved his PhD and taught anthropology in the United States, was elected president of Afghanistan, a fact that became well known in mainstream media.

Many anthropologists focus on popular culture as a scholarly area of interest. Anthropologist Shirley Fedorak (2009), for example, has authored a book called *Pop Culture: The Culture of Everyday Life*, in which she explores such topics as television, music, the Internet, folk and body art, sports, food, and wedding rituals through the lens of anthropology. There are also many other books offering critical perspectives on the portrayal of anthropology, especially archaeology, in popular culture. Examples include *Box Office Archaeology: Refining Hollywood's Portrayals of the Past* by Julie Schablitsky (2007); *Digging Holes in Popular Culture: Archaeology and Science Fiction* by Miles Russell (2002); *From Stonehenge to Las Vegas: Archaeology as Popular Culture* by Cornelius Holtorf (2005); and *Archaeology and the Media* by Timothy Clack and Marcus Brittain (2007).

people may have a general mistrust of governments or foreigners. Anthropologists can work in educating or serving as mediators between those providing and those receiving aid. Anthropologists can mitigate potential misunderstandings, and they also recognize, through the holistic perspective, that even emergency aid can have profound effects on other aspects of a culture.

Anthropologists have much to offer in discussions and planning for a sustainable future for people on the planet. They can use research on primate ecology, for example, to help sustain forest environments and support the people who live there. They can use examples from archaeology to demonstrate what has and has not worked in regard to the long-term sustainability of past societies. Importantly, by working with contemporary populations, cultural anthropologists develop both a local and a global view of deficiencies and successes in terms of sustainability.

Other areas where anthropologists make useful contributions are climate change and **food security**. Archaeologists, for example can cite multiple examples of how people have adapted to changing environments in the past, for instance by building smaller houses in colder times. The field of biological anthropology points to biological markers of stress or malnutrition in the diet resulting from dietary changes or food insecurity. Cultural anthropologists can cite examples of how various communities from around the world are able to maintain food security, or what factors impede it.

Anthropologists, perhaps more than most people, recognize the value of diversity, both biological and cultural. It is important that as the world becomes increasingly connected, both biological and cultural diversity be appreciated. Ultimately, it may ensure the survival of our species.

Summary

This chapter has provided an overview of anthropology. One objective has been to clarify the nature and scope of the discipline, including important terminology, concepts, and perspectives. Another objective has been to prepare students for what lies ahead in subsequent chapters. Mirroring the Learning Objectives stated in the chapter opening, the key points are:

- Anthropology is the scholarly study of humans. This includes human biology and human cultures, past and present. The perspectives, methods, theories, and research results of anthropology provide a good framework (or lens) in which to view and understand humans. The four major branches of anthropology include cultural anthropology, archaeology, biological anthropology, and linguistic anthropology. Each branch includes an applied component. The anthropological perspective includes holistic, evolutionary, comparative, and qualitative approaches. The perspective also recognizes the importance of examining links between various components of human biology and culture, collecting one's own data, and focusing on understanding how and why things change.

- Culture can be defined as the learned and shared things that people have, think, and do. The principal components of culture include subsistence strategies, diet, social and political systems, communication, technology, art, and ideology. Components are interrelated and influence each other. Cultures are constantly changing.

- The history of anthropology in North America has largely been focused on the Indigenous peoples of the continent, although anthropological interests have broadened significantly in recent decades. Franz Boas is widely recognized as a very influential figure in anthropology in North America for both his own research contributions and his training of future anthropologists.

- Anthropology may be considered in the contexts of the worlds of academia, business, and popular culture. Most pure research is undertaken by those in academia, although there are applied components (mostly in business applications in each of the subfields). Many corporations hire anthropologists to research and provide insight into their own employees as well as partners and clients. Anthropologists study popular culture and are embedded in it.

- Anthropology has important roles to play in an increasingly connected world. Anthropologists can make important contributions to helping those in need in times of disaster as well as offering examples and suggestions of how to cope with the problems of living in the twenty-first century, including issues related to food security, sustainability, and climate change.

REVIEW QUESTIONS

1. How do anthropologists define *anthropology*, *human*, and *culture*?
2. What are the main components of culture?
3. What are the key elements of the anthropological perspective?
4. What are the main branches of anthropology?
5. What is the history of anthropology in North America?
6. How is anthropology situated in the contexts of academia, the business world, and popular culture?
7. Why is anthropology important in an increasingly connected world?

DISCUSSION QUESTIONS

1. What might be some of the advantages of using an anthropological perspective to view and understand the world?
2. What might be some of the disadvantages of using an anthropological perspective to view and understand the world?

Visit **www.lensofanthropology.com** for the following additional resources:

| SELF-STUDY QUESTIONS | WEBLINKS | FURTHER READING |

PLACES MENTIONED IN CHAPTER 2

1 Southeast Asia
2 Costa Rica
3 Mediterranean

4 Madagascar
5 Congo River
6 Belgium

WE ARE PRIMATES: THE PRIMATE BACKGROUND

We are not alone. We share our taxonomic order with about 400 other species of mammals. #weareprimates

Learning Objectives

In this chapter students will learn:
- why it is important to understand humans as part of the primate world.
- the basics of primate taxonomy.
- key events in primate evolution.
- the basics of nonhuman primate behavior.

Introduction

To fully understand human biology and human culture, it is important to understand humans as primates. Anthropologists know that humans are not quite as unique as many believe we are. An anthropologist's comprehensive understanding of humans involves not only people from around the world today, but also those from the past. It also includes fundamental knowledge of how we are related to the other animals most like us, typically in the taxonomic order Primates. Anthropologists know that a comprehensive understanding of both human biology and human

Reasons Why It Is Important to Understand Humans as Primates

- Studying primates provides an understanding of our place in the world. Recognizing the similarities in biology and behavior is important to an understanding that humans are not quite as unique as many think they are.
- Understanding humans as primates allows anthropologists to make inferences about the conditions under which evolutionary changes occur.
- Understanding our common evolutionary history helps to explain the various ways of adapting to environments biologically. This includes understanding that there is not necessarily a single best way for adaptation to occur. Similar problems can be solved in different ways, biologically.
- It is important to see how various primates adapt to similar circumstances in different ways, behaviorally. This is important to understand how humans came to be, and the strategies they adopted.
- Studying contemporary primates is useful for providing models of how early humans may have lived. This includes such things as group size, subsistence and settlement strategies, diet, and social and political systems.
- Studying contemporary primates can provide models for understanding how human culture, including language and tool use, may have evolved.
- Studying primates is useful to other areas of inquiry, including evolutionary biology.
- Studying primates today is important for sustainability. Primates are integral to many natural ecosystems. With the knowledge obtained from studying primates, anthropologists may educate others and help maintain sustainability of natural environments where primates live.
- Studying primates is important for understanding issues related to diet. Anthropological knowledge of primate diets can be used to provide education about the relationships between diet and biology, and the correlation of biological changes with dietary changes.
- Studying primates is important for aiding the rehabilitation of primates that have been removed from their natural environments.
- Studying primates is important for aiding in the conservation of primates. Anthropologists know that diversity, both biological and cultural, is fundamentally important. Preserving primate diversity and their habitats is important.
- Studying primates is important for being able to critically evaluate popular, pseudo-scientific, and anti-scientific ideas about humans, other primates, and the past.

culture includes knowledge of the evolution of primates and the behavior of nonhuman primates.

Anthropologists recognize that there are problems with using primates as models for ancestral humans. Anthropologists are usually careful to explicitly recognize the limitations of their research in formulating models of how early humans may have been, but the research remains useful for suggesting possibilities. Basically, if behaviors are observed in contemporary populations or among groups of people from the recent past and similar behaviors are observed in our closest relatives, then there is a good chance that our human ancestors behaved in the same way as well.

Through the Lens of Anthropology: An Introduction to Human Evolution and Culture

Primate Taxonomy

Primates are a **taxonomic order**, belonging to the class Mammalia, commonly known as mammals. Biologists currently recognize about 5,500 different species of mammals, and divide them into more than a dozen orders, an order being a major subdivision of the class. Placement in the order Primates is dependent on having most or all of a specific set of characteristics, which distinguish it from the other orders.

Anthropologists generally accept that there are about 400 species of primates. Discrepancies occur as new species are identified, and distinctions between species and subspecies are often unclear. More than 100 new species and subspecies have been described since 1990.

The principal characteristics that distinguish the order Primates are outlined below. The characteristics are not necessarily unique to primates; and not all primates necessarily have all the characteristics listed. If an animal has most of the characteristics listed, however, it is almost certainly a primate. The characteristics listed are those that are most frequently used, but as with many things in the sciences, definitions are often fluid and subject to debate. Some scientists identify more than two dozen distinguishing criteria of primates (see, for example, Tuttle 2014).

Prehensibility (from **prehensile**) refers to the ability to grasp things with the digits of the hand and/or feet. Grasping is enhanced by flexibility in fingers and toes, allowing for them to separate and bend, and by opposability of our thumbs, and in many primates, toes.

Just as we have fingernails and toenails, so do the other approximately 400 species of primates. Primates have forward-facing eyes, which allow an overlapping field of vision from both eyes, which in turn provides for excellent depth perception. Primates tend to have large brains, especially in relation to the rest of their body. Although there are exceptions, with twins as the norm, most primate species have one offspring at a time, and there is a lengthy period of dependency on the mother. With rare exceptions (e.g., orangutans) primates are very social and live in groups, often with hierarchies, important family relationships, and friendships. The overwhelming majority of primates are diurnal (active during the day), although some species are most active during the night (nocturnal). Similarly, most primates are arboreal (spending most of their time in trees), although there are several exceptions, including, of course, humans.

Distinguishing Characteristics of Primates

- Prehensile hands and feet
- Nails instead of claws
- Forward-facing eyes/ stereoscopic vision
- Large brains (both in actual size and relative to the rest of the body)
- Single offspring
- Long period of infant dependency
- Diurnal
- Arboreal
- Movement in a variety of ways (quadrupedal, knuckle-walking, climbing, clinging/jumping, brachiation, bipedal)
- Social
- Nonspecialized diets

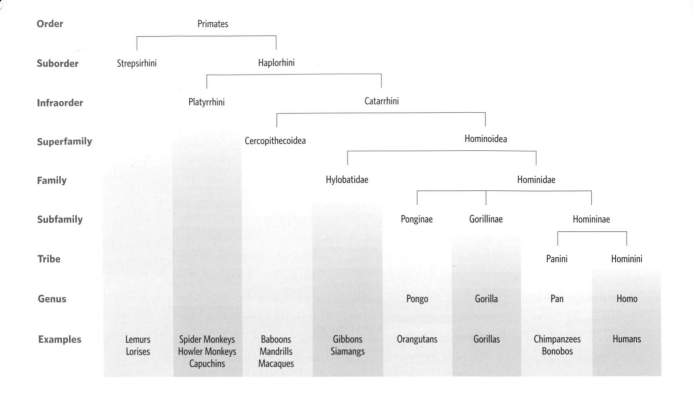

Order	Primates							
Suborder	Strepsirhini	Haplorhini						
Infraorder		Platyrrhini	Catarrhini					
Superfamily			Cercopithecoidea	Hominoidea				
Family				Hylobatidae	Hominidae			
Subfamily					Ponginae	Gorillinae	Homininae	
Tribe							Panini	Hominini
Genus					Pongo	Gorilla	Pan	Homo
Examples	Lemurs Lorises	Spider Monkeys Howler Monkeys Capuchins	Baboons Mandrills Macaques	Gibbons Siamangs	Orangutans	Gorillas	Chimpanzees Bonobos	Humans

Figure 2.1
Primate Taxonomy
This figure presents one of several ways of classifying primates, including humans. The diagram is simplified to focus on major categories of apes and humans.

Primate diets are diverse (See Box 2.1). As an order, primates may be considered to be omnivorous, but in practice particular **taxa** tend to specialize in fruit, leaves, or insects. Meat eating is rare but does occur among some ape and monkey populations.

Primates are often characterized as having a generalized body plan, which means they can do a lot of different things that many other animals can't. No other mammal, for example, has the flexibility of limbs seen in primates. With this flexibility, primates can run, jump, move sideways, move on two legs for at least short distances, climb, leap, swing, and **brachiate** (or swing from arm to arm).

Primate dentition is also considered generalized. Incisors, canines, premolars, and molars enable primates to eat a wide variety of foods, unlike other mammals, for example, that have teeth specialized for hunting and meat eating (e.g., carnivores) or grazing.

There are many categories within the order Primates, including suborders, infraorders, superfamilies, families, genera, and species. These are illustrated in Figure 2.1. Following is a brief overview of the various categories, focusing on the categories that include humans as a member.

There are two suborders of primates: **Strepsirhini** and **Haplorhini**. The distinguishing characteristics of each are mostly relative, as shown in Table 2.1. Most of the species that people would easily recognize as primates are members of the

Box 2.1
Primate Diets

Primates, as a taxonomic order, may be considered **omnivorous**. In practical terms, this means that primates eat a wide range of foods, including plants, insects, and in some cases, small mammals. It would be wrong to think, however, that all primate species or populations are omnivorous. Some species focus on fruits, some on rougher foliage, and others on insects.

The three principal dietary strategies of primates include **frugivory**, **folivory**, and **insectivory**. Frugivory (eating a diet focusing on fruits) is the most common, although it is not unusual for frugivorous primates to supplement their diet with leaves and insects. Folivory (eating a diet comprised mostly of leaves and other rough foliage) and insectivory (eating a diet of insects) tend to be linked to body size. Smaller primates, including many of the strepsirhines and some of the smaller haplorhines may be considered to be primarily insectivores, although they also eat plants. The larger primates, such as gorillas and orangutans tend to be, at least in some contexts, folivores. Orangutans, for example, tend to prefer fruit, but also eat leaves, bark, and insects. Likewise, gorillas often favor fruit, but often eat foliage. Chimpanzees also tend to prefer fruit, but also eat foliage, insects, and in some cases, small mammals they hunt.

Based on numerous primate studies on diet, Chapman and Chapman (1990) wrote an article called "Dietary Variability in Primate Populations," published in the journal *Primates*. They were able to demonstrate that primate populations often switch between frugivory, folivory, and insectivory. They note, for example, that orangutans had been observed to be primarily frugivorous one month (with 90 per cent of their feeding time spent on fruit, and the other 10 per cent split evenly between leaves and insects), and primarily folivorous in another month (with 75 per cent of their feeding time spent on leaves, 15 per cent on bark, and 10 per cent on fruit). In another example, they showed that a population of spider monkeys in Costa Rica switched strategies as well, one month eating only fruit, another month eating mostly leaves, and spending significant time in another month eating insects.

Primate diet is linked with biology. The teeth of primates that are primarily insectivores, for example, have molars with pointed cusps allowing the efficient piercing of insect exoskeletons. Teeth of folivorous primates are effective for slicing through leaves and other rough foliage, and the teeth of primates that are mostly frugivorous tend to have rounded cusps enabling effective crushing of fruit. Primates have differing kinds of microorganisms to aid in digestion, depending on diet. The features of their digestive tracts also differ, correlating with diet. Chimpanzees, for example, can digest foods that humans cannot, due to the different kinds of microbiota and length of intestines.

Other kinds of adaptations to accommodate diet include stomach size and the presence of cheek pouches. Some primates, such as baboons and macaques, have large cheek pouches, which allow them to store food temporarily. Chimpanzees, on the other hand, have relatively large stomachs.

In some areas, it isn't unusual for multiple species of primates to occupy the same environment. One of the reasons for this is that since they have different diets, there is little or no competition for food.

Figure 2.2
Capuchin
Capuchin monkey.
An example from the
infraorder Platyrrhini.
Credit: Michelle Malham

suborder Haplorhini, including all monkeys, apes, and humans. Strepsirhini include many different species, but the most common are known as lemurs.

Strepsirhini include those primates that are less obviously "primates" to non-specialists, meaning they may lack the full set of distinguishing characteristics or the characteristics are in less typical form. Compared to most other primates, Strepsirhini tend to have a greater reliance on **olfaction** (sense of smell). Associated with this, they tend to have a larger snout than other primates, and a **rhinarium**. Relatively few species of primates are nocturnal, but most of those that are belong to this suborder. Those primate species that retain a claw in addition to fingernails and toenails are strepsirhine. In general, compared to other primates, Strepsirhini

Table 2.1
Differences between Strepsirhini and Haplorhini

	Strepsirhini	Haplorhini
Sense of Smell	Better	Worse
Prognathism	More	Less
Rhinarium	Present	Absent
Sense of Vision	Worse	Better
Nocturnal	Some species	Rare
Multiple Births	Some species (twins)	Rare
Brain Size	Smaller	Larger

tend to have more limited prehensibility, and some lack color vision. Although some species of Strepsirhini inhabit regions of tropical Asia and mainland Africa, most species live on the island of Madagascar, off the southeast coast of Africa. One of the most well-known kinds of Strepsirhini is the ring-tailed lemur.

The Haplorhini, compared to Strepsirhini, have no rhinarium, worse olfaction, and better vision. Nocturnalism and multiple births occur among some species of Strepsirhini, but are rare among Haplorhini.

There are about 40 species of Strepsirhini, and several recognizable taxa, such as families, genera, and species. Some anthropologists focus their research among Strepsirhini, especially in Madagascar, but because humans belong to the suborder Haplorhini, there is more anthropological interest in Haplorhini than Strepsirhini.

There are two infraorders of Haplorhini that anthropologists study, the **Platyrrhini** and the **Catarrhini**. Major differences are outlined in Table 2.2. Platyrrhini is roughly synonymous with "New World monkeys," in practical terms meaning the monkeys of Central and South America. Catarrhini includes "Old World monkeys," meaning monkeys of Africa, Asia, and Europe, as well as apes and humans.

There are several distinguishing characteristics of Platyrrhini. The term *Platyrrhini* itself refers to the characteristics of the nose—basically flat, with nostrils flaring outwards. Their natural habitat includes the tropical and subtropical forested regions of Central and South America. All monkeys have tails, but it is only among some species of Platyrrhini that the tail is prehensile. If one observes a monkey hanging by its tail, it is a Platyrrhini. All Platyrrhini are primarily arboreal, tend to be smaller than monkeys of Africa, Asia, and Europe, and exhibit relatively little

Figure 2.3
Mandrill
Example of a member of Cercopithecoidea (Old World monkey). Mandrills were formerly thought to be a kind of baboon, but are now considered distinct.
Credit: Michelle Malham

Table 2.2
Differences between Platyrrhini and Catarrhini

	Platyrrhini	Catarrhini
Location	Central and South America	Africa, Asia, and Europe
Body Size	Smaller on average	Larger on average
Arboreal	All species	Most species
Prehensile Tails	Some species	No species
Dental Formula	2-1-3-3	2-1-2-3
Nostrils	Widely spaced, flaring outward	Closely spaced, facing down
Sexual Dimorphism	Relatively little	Often pronounced

sexual dimorphism. Widely known Platyrrhini include spider monkeys, squirrel monkeys, howler monkeys, and capuchins.

Catarrhini are distinguished from Platyrrhini in several ways. Catarrhini include the Old World monkeys (**Cercopithecoidea**), as well as all the apes and humans. Most Catarrhini are arboreal, but some, like baboons and gorillas, spend considerable time on the ground. Forests are the most common habitat, but some (e.g., baboons) occupy savannah-grassland environments as well. The term *Catarrhini* refers to the narrow nose, with closely spaced downward-facing nostrils.

Dental formula refers to the kind and number of teeth in the mouth. It is usually expressed as a series of numbers for each quarter of the mouth, going from front to back. All Catarrhini, including humans, have the same dental formula, commonly expressed 2–1–2–3, where the first "2" indicates incisors, the "1" represents canines; the second "2" represents premolars, and the "3" represents molars. Among Catarrhini, this dental formula is the same for each quarter of the mouth—upper right, upper left, lower right, lower left. In total, adult Catarrhini have 32 teeth. Many find it interesting that humans have the same dental formulas as chimpanzee, gorillas, baboons, and more than 100 other species of monkeys and apes from Africa, Asia, and Europe. The third molar is the tooth in humans commonly known in North America as the wisdom tooth. Many people now have the wisdom tooth removed before it erupts; sometimes it simply never grows. The lack of the third molar also occurs on occasion among other primates.

Catarrhini are comprised of two **superfamilies**: Cercopithecoidea and **Hominoidea**. Cercopithecoidea are the "Old World monkeys." Hominoidea includes apes and humans. Principal differences are listed in Table 2.3. Cercopithecoidea, or

Table 2.3
Differences between Cercopithecoidea and Hominoidea

	Cercopithecoidea	Hominoidea
Common Names	Old World monkeys	Apes and Humans
Tails	Present	Absent
Brain Size	Smaller (less developed)	Larger (more developed)
Body Size	Smaller	Larger
Ontogeny	Shorter	Longer
Shoulders	Less developed	More developed

Old World monkeys, have tails, but these are not prehensile. Old World monkeys also tend to be larger than their New World counterparts, and have more sexual dimorphism. Hominoidea are tailless, tend to be larger than Cercopithecoidea, and have extended **ontogeny** (i.e., increased length of dependency), larger and more developed brains, and more developed shoulders, enabling **brachiation**.

Since Hominoidea is the taxa to which humans belong, they are studied more than Cercopithecoidea. There is no consensus on the subdivision of the Hominoidea. One popular classification system recognizes three families of Hominoidea: (i) **Hylobatidae**, which includes gibbons and siamangs of southeast Asia, sometimes known as the "lesser apes"; (ii) **Pongidae**, which includes three genera—**Pongo** (the genus to which orangutans belong), Gorilla, and **Pan**. Pan includes two species: *Pan troglodytes* (chimpanzees) and *Pan paniscus* (bonobos); and (iii) Homininae, the family to which humans belong, as do all ancestors since the split from the common ancestor of chimpanzees about seven million years ago.

Another popular classification system recognizes recognizes two families of Hominoid—Hylobatidae (gibbons and siamangs) and Hominidae. Hominidae are divided into subfamilies of Pongidae (orangutans), Gorillinae (gorillas) and Homininae (chimpanzees, bonobos, and humans).

Since there is little consensus, understanding the biological classification of apes and humans can be confusing. In this book, we consider Homininae, and its informal name hominin, to equate with human and include the **genus** *Homo* and all other genera of bipedal primates descended from the common ancestor of humans, chimpanzees, and bonobos about seven million years ago. This means that there is only one genus of hominin today (i.e., *Homo*), but hominins also include genera of the past, such as *Australopithecus*, *Ardipithecus*, *Kenyanthropus*, *Sahelanthropus*, *Orrorin*, and *Paranthropus*.

Table 2.4

Alternate Classification Schemes for Hominoidea

A.

Superfamily	Family	Genus
Hominoidea	Hylobatidae	
		Hylobates (gibbons and siamangs)
	Pongidae	
		Pongo (orangutans)
		Gorilla (gorillas)
		Pan (chimpanzees and bonobos)
		Homo (and other now extinct genera)

B.

Superfamily	Family	Subfamily	Tribe	Genus
Hominoidea	Hylobatidae			
				Hylobates (gibbons and siamangs)
	Hominidae			
		Pongidae		
				Pongo (orangutans)
		Gorilla		
				Gorilla
		Homininae		
			Panini	
				Pan
			Hominini	
				Australopithecus
				Homo

Table 2.5
Human Taxonomy

Taxonomic Group	Includes	Examples
Class Mammalia	29 other orders, about 5,500 other species	Cats, dogs, bats, rats
Order Primates	About 400 other species	Monkeys, apes
Suborder Haplorhini	About 300 other species	Old and New World monkeys, apes
Infraorder Catarrhini	About 200 other species	Old World monkeys, apes
Superfamily Hominoidea	All apes and humans	Chimpanzees, bonobos, gorillas
Family Homininae	Only humans	Homo sapiens and ancestral humans

It is important for students to recognize that other classification systems do exist. When some refer to hominin, they may be referring to a form of classification that also includes chimpanzees and bonobos. Most biological classification systems simply use the categories of species, genus (a group of similar species), and family (a group of similar genera), but when describing humans and apes, some use categories such as subfamily (a subcategory of family), tribe (subcategory of subfamily), and subtribe (category of tribe). Table 2.4 provides examples of two systems of hominoid taxonomy. There are others.

Table 2.5 summarizes the place of humans in the primate world.

Primate Evolution

Primate evolution has occurred primarily, and perhaps entirely, in the Cenozoic, which began 65 million years ago and continues to the present. The Cenozoic is one of four geological eras, the others being the Mesozoic, from roughly 250 to 65 million years ago in the age of the dinosaurs; the Palaeozoic, from about 540 to 250 million years ago; and the Precambrian, from the origins of the earth about 4.5 billion years ago to 540 million years ago.

In the latter stage of the Mesozoic, mammals were in existence, but exhibiting nowhere near the diversity and abundance they would come to express in the Cenozoic. Conventional thinking is that when the dinosaurs became extinct about 65 million years ago, likely due to environmental change, the new environments and lack of dinosaurs opened up new ecological niches, which mammals quickly filled. This diversification is a good example of **adaptive radiation**. It is likely that many new kinds of mammals, including primates, evolved to fill these niches.

Table 2.6
Overview of Primate Evolution 65 Million Years Ago (MYA) to Present

Geological Epoch (Time Period)	Key Events
Palaeocene (65–55 MYA)	Probable emergence of primates
Eocene (55–34 MYA)	Proliferation of primates
Oligocene (34–24 MYA)	Establishment of Catarrhini and Platyrrhini
Miocene (24–5 MYA)	Probable emergence of Hominoidea and Homininae
Pliocene (5–1.8 MYA)	Multiple genera of Homininae, emergence of genus Homo
Pleistocene (1.8 MYA–10,000 YA)	Many species of humans
Holocene (10,000 YA–present)	*Homo sapiens* dominates

Those who identify early remains as belonging to the order Primates and the further subdivisions all the way down to **species**, necessarily make choices about which remains belong to what species. When assigning various remains to different species, we are making assumptions about the ability of different animals to mate and produce fertile offspring, based on bones that are sometimes tens of millions of years old. We really don't know the variability within various species, genera, and other categories. A relatively small sample size also affects our ability to classify.

Understanding and describing primate evolution is simplified through the use of time periods called epochs, created by geologists. Epochs are based in part by observable changes in the geological record, including the record of plants and animals. There has been discussion about naming a new epoch—the **Anthropocene**—based on the significance changes to the earth caused by humans in recent times, but the proposal is not widely accepted. The principal developments in primate evolution, by epochs of the Cenozoic, are outlined in Table 2.6.

The fossil record of primates in the Palaeocene is sketchy. There is some evidence of mammals that appear well suited for life in trees (e.g., features indicate climbing capabilities) and primate-like teeth, but whether this is enough to classify them as primates is debatable. One potential primate from this period is *Purgatorius*, discovered in Montana. Some suggest it may be ancestral to all later primates, but it should be remembered that its classification as a primate is itself dubious.

Primates were certainly well established by the Eocene. Dozens of primate species, at the least, lived during this time period; some suggest there may have

Box 2.2

Rafting Monkeys

One of the most intriguing areas of interest in the study of primate evolution has to do with the origin of the Platyrrhini, commonly known as the New World monkeys. They begin to appear in the fossil record of Central and South America about 26 million years ago, but their antecedents are unknown.

One common hypothesis suggests there was ongoing evolution from some of the earliest forms of primates existing in North America during the Eocene. A problem is the lack of supporting evidence in the fossil record. While there were animals best described as primates in the region during the Oligocene, there is no evidence of primates at all in the fossil record for at least 10 million years before the Platyrrhini, and those early forms did not resemble monkeys.

Another hypothesis is that the earliest Platyrrhini rafted over from Africa. The rafts were presumably floating islands of natural debris. To some it seems like a far-fetched idea, but it seems the most probable scenario for many. This hypothesis is covered by Alan de Queiroz (2014) in his book *The Monkey's Voyage: How Improbable Journeys Shaped the History of Life*. Several kinds of evidence are used in support of the hypothesis, including the knowledge that primates made it hundreds of miles from Africa to the island of Madagascar tens of millions of years ago (presumably by rafting on floating vegetation) and that, in more recent times, early populations of humans apparently traveled to some of the islands of Southeast Asia. Other support includes the observation of very large natural rafts, including one described as large as Belgium and another with living trees growing to a height of 30 feet. Such natural rafts have been observed to occur at the mouths of rivers, where fallen trees and other kinds of vegetation accumulate, and on occasion float into the ocean.

One of the biggest problems to deal with in accepting the hypothesis is the sheer size of the journey from Africa across the ocean to Central or South America. As pointed out by de Queiroz, while the distance today is about 1,800 miles, it was probably half that about 40 million years ago. It is also suggested that there were likely multiple islands in the ocean during the voyage.

Models factoring distance, currents, and winds suggest that the voyage could have been best measured in days rather than weeks. Further support is provided by the recognition of molecular studies suggesting that other animals also made the journey from Africa to the Americas via natural rafts, although these other animals were mostly lizards and snakes.

The fossil evidence may also be interpreted as supporting the rafting hypothesis. There are some primate fossils from the Oligocene in Africa that appear to be good candidates for being ancestral to both the Platyrrhini and Catarrhini, including, for example, having dental formula most commonly associated with Platyrrhini (2–1–3–3).

been as many as 200. Evident primate characteristics include those related to an emphasis on vision and prehensibility. The diversity of remains suggests that there was already an evolutionary split between Strepsirhini and Haplorhini, meaning the last common ancestor that monkeys, apes, and humans had with lemurs was more than 34 million years ago.

The Oligocene is the time period when Catarrhini and Platyrrhini become evident. Many believe that around 30 million years ago a population of a monkey

Figure 2.4
Young Gorilla
Gorillas are the largest living primates, with adults sometimes exceeding 400 pounds (180 kg.) They are a member of the superfamily Hominoidea.

Credit: Nadine Ryan

or monkey-like primate floated on a natural raft of vegetation from Africa to Central or South America and became the founding population of all subsequent primates there.

The Miocene is associated with the emergence and proliferation of Hominoidea. The last common ancestor of orangutans, gorillas, chimpanzees, and bonobos probably lived about 20 million years ago. The last common ancestor of gorillas, chimpanzees, bonobos, and humans probably lived about 10 million years ago. The last common ancestor of chimpanzees, bonobos, and humans probably lived about seven million years ago.

It is important to understand that all contemporary primates have evolved, and continue to do so. This includes humans. Humans did not evolve from chimpanzees, but they have a common ancestor with them. Chimpanzees (*Pan troglodytes*) and bonobos (*Pan paniscus*) have continued to evolve as well. The last common ancestor of chimpanzees and bonobos lived about one million years ago. It is likely that groups of the common ancestor to both became separated by the Congo River in Africa at about that time.

Primate Behavior

As outlined in the opening section of this chapter, there are many reasons for anthropologists to study nonhuman primate behavior. These include providing models of how early humans may have lived, an understanding of the advantages of certain kinds of behaviors exhibited by all primates, including humans, and investigating the various ways our closest relatives have of solving problems.

Methods

Like studying people, studying primates in the wild requires a long-term commitment on the part of anthropologists. The primates being studied need to be able to trust the human observers, and the observers need the primates to act as normally as possible—as if the observers were not there.

Most primatologists with a background in anthropology prefer to study primates in the wild, rather than in zoos or research facilities. This is mostly because anthropologists are interested primarily in how primates behave in the wild, without human interference. Also, primatologists trained in anthropology tend to be more interested in what primates actually do in the wild, rather than what they may be capable of, which is often the focus of zoo or lab-based studies. Anthropologists know, for example, that chimpanzees can be taught to use lighters to start fires, and to drive golf carts, but this has relatively little value to anthropology.

The primary method of primatology is direct observation of primate groups in the wild. Researchers make notes on specific behaviors for a specific period of time. Researchers try to be as unobtrusive as possible, observing the behavior of the primates and taking detailed notes. Those interested in primate diet also often collect samples of their dung, which is later subjected to analysis to determine the kinds and quantities of foods eaten. It was through analysis of bonobo dung, for example, that it was determined that bonobos ate meat (the digit of a monkey was found in bonobo dung).

> ## Principal Research Interests in Primatology
>
> - Communication (vocalizations, gestures, displays, expressions, other)
> - Social structure (how groups are formed, how dominance is achieved and maintained)
> - Aggressive and affiliative behaviors (conflict, grooming)
> - Subsistence and diet
> - Tool use

Principal Research Interests

Communication

Research on communication includes studying vocalizations, gestures, expressions, and language. Research reveals several reasons for vocalizations, or calls. Vocalizations may be used to identify information about the sender, such as individual identity, as well as the location of individuals and food sources, and potential threats (e.g., predators). Gestures include such activities as arm waving, hugging, and among gorillas, chest beating. Primate communication is also covered in Chapter 9.

Social Structure

Many studies focus on the social structure of primate groups. This includes the ways in which groups form, whether, for example, it is the males or females, or both, that

Figure 2.5
Chimpanzee
Chimpanzees
(*Pan troglodytes*)
are classified in
the superfamily
Hominoidea, and some
classification schemes
also place them in the
family Homininae, to
which humans also
belong.

Credit: Kjersti Joergensent/
Shutterstock

leave their home community to find or form a new group. Among groups of Central American monkeys, for example, capuchin males leave their home group upon maturity; among spider monkeys, it is the females that leave the home group; and among howler monkeys, both males and females leave their home group. Biologically, finding or forming a new group keeps the gene pool diverse and prevents inbreeding among families of primates.

Primate groups are often rigidly hierarchical. Females are equal to or dominant over males in about 40 per cent of primate groups. Research is often focused on how dominance is achieved and maintained, such as through strength, bluff, cleverness, and alliances. While males are dominant in most primate groups, in some, such as lemurs, females are dominant. This is usually explained as being adaptive to the environment. Female dominance ensures that mothers obtain enough food for the survival of the infants in seasons in which resources are depleted.

Aggressive and Affiliate Behaviors

Affiliative and aggressive behaviors are another area of research interest. One of the most common affiliative behaviors among primates is grooming. The hygienic aspect of grooming, such as removing bugs and dead skin, is usually understood to be a byproduct, while its real importance lies in socialization. Grooming is largely viewed as a social and political activity, reaffirming alliances, relationships, and group cohesion. Other affiliative behaviors seen among primates include hugging, patting, and kissing.

Among bonobos, sex can be viewed as an affiliative behavior. Most research indicates that bonobos are quite unlike chimpanzees and other primates. Where most primate groups have dominance structures, bonobos tend to be roughly **egalitarian**. Alpha females are often the highest ranked members of the group, leading to a much less violent society than chimp society, which is run by alpha males. Where other primates may fight or least make threats to resolve conflict, bonobos have sexual relations. Sex among bonobos is as common as a handshake or hug among humans. They are one of the few primates to have face-to-face intercourse occasionally. They commonly have male–female sex, female–female sex, and male–male sex.

Aggressive behaviors include physical displays, bluffs, gorilla chest beating, threats, and physical contact. Some primates do get aggressive, and some males have been observed to fight to the death in conflicts revolving around dominance.

One group of male chimpanzees has been observed to systematically hunt and kill males from another group, although this is certainly not a normal kind of behavior.

Differences in chimpanzee and bonobo behavior are of considerable interest to anthropologists. Why, many question, are chimpanzees so rigidly hierarchical, male-dominated, and aggressive to the point of killing adult members within their own as well as neighboring groups, whereas bonobos are much more egalitarian, have less conflict, and appear to use sex rather than aggression to prevent or resolve conflict? The basic question for many is: Was (sometimes lethal) aggression a trait of the common ancestor of chimpanzees, bonobos, and humans and then lost in bonobos? Or did (mostly male and sometimes lethal) aggression evolve separately in chimpanzees and humans? Of course, not all would agree that humans are innately aggressive at all (see, for example, the discussion of this issue in Chapter 12). The notion that innate aggressiveness is a driving force of human evolution is covered in Box 4.1.

Subsistence and Diet

Subsistence and diet are major areas of interest in primate studies. As described in Box 2.1, primate groups can be characterized as frugivorous, folivorous, or insectivorous, although the strategy may change from month to month. The diversity of foods in the diet is usually high. Studies of gorillas, for example, indicate they have about 150 different plants in their diet. Orangutans have been recorded as eating

Figure 2.6
Bonobo
Bonobos (*Pan paniscus*) were previously known as pygmy chimpanzees, but are now recognized as a distinct species. Studies indicate that they tend to be considerably less aggressive than chimpanzees.
Credit: Michelle Malham

over 400 different kinds of food, including over 200 different fruits. Many primates eat insects, but relatively few species eat mammals or other small animals.

Some monkeys have been observed hunting and eating meat, but most studies of hunting and meat eating focus on chimpanzees. Hunting and meat eating is very interesting to anthropologists because our human ancestors started focusing on hunting and meat eating more than one million years ago, and we are uncertain of how and why that occurred. Chimpanzee hunting and meat eating therefore provides a good model of similar events in human ancestry.

There are several important things to understand about hunting and meat eating among chimpanzees. It tends to be opportunistic, rather than planned beforehand. It is likely that a decision to capture a monkey or other small animal occurs only minutes or less before the capture begins. Hunting is usually a cooperative activity, which is unusual among nonhuman primates. In typical foraging, it is every individual for herself or himself, except for mothers looking after children. When it comes to hunting, however, chimpanzees often cooperate in capturing the prey. When an animal is captured, the meat is often shared. Sometimes the meat is shared only among those who participated in the hunt; other times it is shared with others in the group. Sharing does not occur like this in any other subsistence activity. It is also males that do the hunting. Females have been observed to participate, but it is most often the males. Interestingly, all these characteristics of hunting demonstrated by chimpanzees are also common among groups of modern human hunter-gatherers, except that hunting by humans is often planned.

Besides considering primate hunting and meat eating, anthropologists are also interested in primates as prey. Monkeys are often the prey of chimpanzees, but there are other predators to consider as well. Of course, the kind of predator depends on the region. Leopards and tigers are predators of primates in Asia, for example, and raptors and other large birds feed on primates as well. Primates are usually cautious around watering holes, since that is where many predators, including snakes and other reptiles, lie in wait. It is often the lower-ranking primates that will first come out of the trees to the water. Primates frequently will use alarm calls to warn others of predators, increasing the danger for the individual making the call. It should also not be forgotten that humans are predators of primates as well, hunting monkeys and apes for food, pets, and zoos.

Tool Use

Tool use is an interesting area of research among primates. Until the 1960s, it was widely thought that only humans made and used tools. Now there are several recognized instances of tool use among a variety of primates. Chimpanzees modify sticks to obtain termites in their mounds, monkeys and some apes use rocks to crack open nuts,

Primates in Crisis

Many primatologists start their field studies firmly embedded in an anthropological framework, with the ideal of contributing to the methods, theories, and discoveries of the discipline. Once in the field, however, it is not unusual for researchers to shift some of their focus toward additional objectives, including rehabilitation and conservation.

The Primate Specialist Group of the International Union for Conservation of Nature Species Survival Commission (IUCN/SSC PSG) is one of the key organizations keeping track of new primate groups discovered and primates in crisis, and frequently updating and publishing lists of endangered species. They report, for example, that all the great apes—orangutans, gorillas, chimpanzees, and bonobos—are endangered, some critically. They regularly identify the 25 most endangered primates to attract attention. The 2014 list included a variety of lemurs from Madagascar, monkeys from the Americas, and monkeys and apes from both Africa and Asia.

Stolen Apes—The Illicit Trade in Chimpanzees, Gorillas, Bonobos and Orangutans is a publication of the United Nations (Stiles, Cress, Nellemann, & Formo 2013:8) that documents the nature and severity of the primates in crisis due to trade. The document reads, in part,

> Great apes are trafficked in various ways. In many cases wild capture is opportunistic: farmers capture infant apes after having killed the mother during a crop-raid, or bushmeat hunters shoot or trap adults for food, and then collect babies to sell. However, organized illicit dealers increasingly target great apes as part of a far more sophisticated and systematic trade. They use trans-national criminal networks to supply a range of markets, including the tourist entertainment industry, disreputable zoos, and wealthy individuals who want exotic pets as status symbols. Great apes are used to attract tourists to entertainment facilities such as amusement parks and circuses. They are even used in tourist photo sessions on Mediterranean beaches and clumsy boxing matches in Asian safari parks.

Bushmeat is a term often used in the context of primates as food and, at least in North America, tends to have a negative connotation. In reality, however, it simply means wild animals. In some regions, including some places in North America, bushmeat from Africa is considered a delicacy. It is not unusual to see primates for sale as food in some markets in Africa. Because of the close biological relationship between apes and humans, there is some risk that eating apes may result in obtaining some of the pathogens causing diseases carried by the apes. Eating of apes has consequently been blamed, often incorrectly, for epidemics including the 2014 outbreak of Ebola in Africa (bats were a far more likely host). As noted in the UN document, however, it is those who butcher the apes that are at highest risk, since they are the ones to come in contact with the blood and organs of the apes.

One of the most egregious causes of orangutans being endangered is the transformation of their natural forest habitats of Southeast Asia to plantations for the production of palm oil, which in turn ends up in thousands of products including packaged foods, detergents, and cosmetics. With the reduction of the natural forest habitats, orangutans have difficulty surviving. Many starve to death, while others are killed to prevent them from eating parts of the newly planted palm trees.

Box 2.4

Assessing Bigfoot

Many people have reported seeing a large human-like ape in various parts of North America. Mostly it is known as Bigfoot, but there are many regional variations, including Sasquatch. There have been thousands of reported sightings over the past several decades. It is typically described as being quite large (8–10 feet tall and several hundred pounds), bipedal (walking on two legs), and hairy. It is almost always reported as being solitary, and many also report it as being omnivorous (e.g., eating stolen food from campsites and dumpsters) and nocturnal. It also typically flees when sighted. The name Bigfoot is derived from what many consider to be the most compelling physical evidence: very large, human-like footprints, usually in mud, often identified following an alleged sighting.

Most anthropologists doubt that such a creature really exists. Studies of nonhuman primate behavior simply do not support it. Of the approximately 400 species of primates, humans are the only one that is bipedal. Anthropologists have never found any kind of evidence of another primate that habitually walks upright. Reports of solitary behavior are troubling; being social is a characteristic of almost all primate groups. Orangutans are a rare exception, with males spending a significant amount of time alone, but even then the mother-and-child bond remains. In apes and humans, it is necessary for mothers to look after children for years, so we would expect that if Bigfoot did exist, it would be more likely that mothers with children, rather than solitary males, would be observed. Reports of Bigfoot being omnivorous are also troubling; large apes tend to be primarily folivorous (i.e., eating a diet of mainly leaves and other tough plant matter). Reports of being nocturnal are similarly problematic; most primate species are

diurnal, and those that are nocturnal tend to be small and are mostly classified as Strepsirhini—far removed from apes and humans.

There is no compelling biological evidence for the existence of Bigfoot. Claims that specimens contain Bigfoot DNA are occasionally reported, but when these are subjected to testing, they are invariably shown to be misidentified bears or other well-known animals, or hoaxes. No bones, teeth, or soft tissue have ever been discovered.

The knowledge that before the arrival of humans in North America, no other hominoid was ever here makes the notion that Bigfoot evolved here unlikely. There is virtually no fossil record of Bigfoot. Some believe that Bigfoot may be a remnant population of *Gigantopithecus*, a large ape that lived for a time in parts of Asia between about seven million and one million years ago. We have only mandibles (lower jaw) and teeth of *Gigantopithecus*, but based on these skeletal elements, it does appear to be a match in that it is a very large ape. We have no idea if *Gigantopithecus* was bipedal, though. Analysis of particles in the teeth suggest that *Gigantopithecus* ate a diet of plants, mostly bamboo.

Some who believe in Bigfoot suggest that the lack of a fossil record may be explained by Bigfoot deliberately burying their dead. This seems unlikely, however, because burial tends to improve preservation and archaeologists can often identify places where burials occur.

Believers should be aware that if they do sight Bigfoot, they should probably leave it alone. It probably isn't a large human-like ape. If it exists, it is probably a human who wants to be left alone. And nobody should do it harm. Recall that if a primate is bipedal, as Bigfoot is typically reported to be, it is classified as human.

and chimpanzees use sticks to poke small animals hiding in trees. Leaves are used as sponges, and gorillas have been observed using sticks to test the depth of water and to assist with walking. Before Jane Goodall first observed tool making among chimpanzees, the idea of "Man the Tool Maker" distinguished humans from other primates. When she reported seeing a chimp in her observation group stripping leaves from a twig to fashion a tool, her mentor Louis Leakey famously commented, "Now we must redefine tool, redefine Man, or accept chimpanzees as humans." Instead, we have accepted that many other primates also make and use tools, a fourth option.

Primates in Crisis: Ecological Stability and Critical Thinking

About half of the approximately 400 species of primates are endangered, some critically. The reasons for this include the destruction of primate habitats, the viewpoint that primates are pests to be eradicated, the illicit trade in primates for pets and zoos, and the idea that primates can be considered human food. This is more fully discussed in Box 2.3 (Primates in Crisis). This is the reason why so many primatologists work toward conserving primate habitats and rehabilitating rescued primates.

A Note on Primates and Ecological Sustainability

Nonhuman primates in the wild are integral to maintaining ecological sustainability. This is especially important in tropical and semitropical forests. Primates have an important role in seed dispersal, which promotes the ongoing growth and development of forests. Primates typically move from a few to several miles a day within their territory. They feed on the fruit of trees in one area and then, through their feces, deposit the seeds of those fruits in another. This is an important aspect of ecological sustainability that should not be overlooked. A reduction in numbers of primates can be devastating for ecological sustainability. This is particularly important to understand in light of the knowledge that thousands of primates are removed every year.

Using Knowledge of Primates to Think Critically

Knowledge of primate biology, primate evolution, and primate behavior can be used to deconstruct popular notions of primates and primate-like beings. A good example of this is applying knowledge about primates to reports about Bigfoot, as demonstrated in Box 2.4. Based on anthropological knowledge of primates past and present, most anthropologists doubt Bigfoot is real. Those who do believe in it usually suggest that it is a remnant population of *Gigantopithecus*, the largest primate that ever lived. *Gigantopithecus* lived in Asia, but some believe it may have migrated to North America, along with many other animals, including humans, during the latter stages of the last ice age.

Summary

This chapter has provided an overview of the primate world, and the place of humans in it. This includes an understanding of what makes primates different from other orders of mammals and the distinguishing criteria of the major taxa of interest to biological anthropologists. The chapter also provides an overview of primate evolution during the Cenozoic, with a particular focus on the emergence of primate taxa to which humans belong, and an overview of the major areas of research interest in the study on nonhuman primate behavior. Mirroring the Learning Objectives stated in the chapter opening, the key points are:

- There are many reasons why anthropologists study nonhuman primates. Most importantly, they provide models of how early humans may have adapted and evolved, both biologically and culturally.
- There are many subdivisions of primates. There is consensus that humans are members of the suborder Haplorhini, infraorder Catarrhini, and superfamily Hominoidea. There is no consensus, however, on how humans are classified within the superfamily Hominoidea. In this book, humans are considered to belong to the family Homininae, which includes all primates that are bipedal since the split with the common ancestor of humans, chimpanzees, and bonobos about seven million years ago.
- Primates have been around and evolving for about 65 million years. The biological family to which humans belong emerged about seven million years ago. Monkeys of the Americas probably rafted from Africa about 30 million years ago, and the split between the group that lead to contemporary monkeys of Africa, Asia, and Europe and the group that led to apes and humans probably occurred about 25 million years ago. It is important to remember that all primate species continue to evolve, although many are also critically endangered.
- Anthropological studies of nonhuman primate behavior focus on communication, social systems, aggressive and affiliative behaviors, subsistence and diet, and tool use. There are many different ways that primates organize themselves; most have rigid hierarchies, but some, like bonobos are relatively egalitarian. Some, but not all, primate species are aggressive, and all exhibit affiliative behaviors like grooming each other.

Primates eat mostly vegetation, although some specialize in insects. Some apes and monkeys also hunt and eat meat, but hunting is never a primary subsistence strategy among nonhuman primates.

REVIEW QUESTIONS

1. Why is it important to understand humans as primates?
2. What are the distinguishing characteristics of primates, Haplorhini, Catarrhini, and Hominoidea?
3. What were the key events in primate evolution occurring in each epoch of the Cenozoic?
4. What are the principal research interests in primatology and examples of discoveries for each?

DISCUSSION QUESTIONS

1. What might be some implications for anthropology if the loss of primates continues?
2. What may be some implications of using bonobos, rather than chimpanzees, as models of how early humans may have behaved?

Visit **www.lensofanthropology.com** for the following additional resources:

| SELF-STUDY QUESTIONS | WEBLINKS | FURTHER READING |

PLACES MENTIONED IN CHAPTER 3

1 Galapagos Islands
2 Middle East
3 Amazon River Valley
4 Indonesia

5 Europe
6 Africa
7 Czech Republic
8 London, England

CHAPTER 3
EVOLUTIONARY THOUGHT AND THEORY

Darwin was important, Mendel was genius, but I'd rather have a beer with Wallace #evolutionarythoughts

Learning Objectives

In this chapter students will learn:

- why it is important to understand evolutionary theory.
- the nature of science.
- the history of evolutionary thought.
- the basics of evolutionary theory.

Introduction

There are multiple reasons why an understanding of evolutionary theory is important in anthropology. Nothing really makes sense about human biology unless we understand evolutionary processes. We are far from the perfect creation, biologically speaking. Humans are more like an accumulation of quick fixes that serve a purpose. The biology that enables people to walk upright, for example, works well for a long time, but not necessarily into middle or old age. Ask an older person how their feet, knees, hips, and back are doing.

Box 3.1

Evolution in Action—Lactose Tolerance

A good example of human evolution in recent times is the ability for many people to effectively digest milk as adults, referred to as lactose tolerance. Genetic research indicates that lactose tolerance emerged independently among populations already using domestic cattle in various parts of the world (the Middle East, Europe, and Africa) over the last several thousand years. In each case a mutation occurred (not always the same mutation) that allowed people to digest milk without problems. This mutation became a favorable variation that was subsequently selected among populations, leading to many members of the descendant populations now being lactose tolerant.

Infants and young children are able to drink milk without ill effects due to the activity of a protein called lactase, which breaks down the lactose in milk making it easy to digest. As children mature, the ability to produce lactase is switched off for about two-thirds of the world's population. The inability to digest milk after childhood is common among mammals. Lactose tolerance in adulthood may be uniquely human. Due to a mutation that was passed on to subsequent generations, lactase continues to be active in the remaining one-third of the population, allowing them to continue drinking milk into adulthood. Rather than lactose tolerance, some people prefer to use "lactase persistence" to describe the condition, since it is the persistence of lactase that allows lactose tolerance.

Adults who are not lactose tolerant suffer many different kinds of unpleasantness if they drink milk. This includes severe cramps, diarrhea, bloating, and flatulence. Not a pleasant experience for those trying to digest milk, or for those around them. Without lactase persistence, drinking milk as an adult is simply not a viable option.

The majority of the 35 per cent of the world's population that are lactose tolerant have European ancestry, although there are small areas in Africa and Asia where it is common as well. For those in North America, a high proportion of people with European ancestry are lactose tolerant. A study of populations around the world indicates that in North America, more than 80 per cent of those with European ancestry are lactose tolerant. Fewer than 5 per cent of Native Americans and Asian Americans are lactose tolerant. The percentage of lactose tolerant African Americans and Hispanic Americans is about 30 per cent and 50 per cent, respectively. Most Europeans are lactose tolerant, but other than some cattle herding groups in Africa, elsewhere it is rare.

Figure 3.1 **Milk**
Lactose tolerance, including being able to drink a glass of milk without suffering, is a recent evolutionary phenomenon.
Credit: Shutterstock

Lactose tolerance evolved among cattle herders. It is clear that the herders were aware of the nutritional value of dairy products before becoming lactose tolerant. Considering that milk has protein and calcium, and provides a good source of vitamins, calories, carbohydrates, and milk fat, some have described it as a superfood of the times. Archaeological research indicates that herders accessed the nutrition of dairy by breaking down the lactose through fermentation, making cheese and yogurt that were easy to digest. The mutation leading to lactose tolerance simply sped up the process and allowed immediate nutrition by drinking.

It is also important to understand that evolution is a fact. We can see evolution happening. It is often difficult to see it happening in our lifetime with plants and animals we see every day, but it is happening. We see it in laboratories under controlled conditions, particularly with microorganisms and insects such as fruit flies. We see it in the fact that we need a new flu vaccine every year to protect us from evolving and changing viruses. We also see evolution happening as plant breeders create new varieties and animal breeders select for particular qualities or physical traits. If you have a pet, it is the result of evolution. One good example of recent evolution in humans has to do with the ability to digest milk—lactose tolerance—which is covered in Box 3.1.

It is important to recognize that one can both believe in evolution and hold onto religious beliefs. Many scientists and religious leaders attempt to convince followers that this is not possible, but for many, there is no problem. Stephen Jay Gould (1997) wrote an important essay called "Nonoverlapping Magisteria" in which he outlined how a belief in evolution and religion need not be incompatible, as long as one recognizes that science best covers the empirical world while religion best covers morals and values. Gould notes that even Pope Pius XII in 1950 and Pope John Paul II in 1996 accepted this notion of nonoverlapping magisteria (or separate and distinct) realms of authority. More recently, in 2014, Pope Francis also confirmed the compatibility of a belief in biological evolution with a belief in a divine creator.

Just as anthropology is a framework, so too is science. It is one of many frameworks scientists use, especially when dealing with biological anthropology and archaeology. It is especially important for understanding the biological evolution of humans, covered in Chapter 4. This chapter covers the nature of science, provides a brief overview of evolutionary thought, and outlines basic evolutionary concepts, especially those that are important for understanding the evolution of humans.

The Nature of Science

Science is a framework, consisting of principles, methods, and ways of evaluating explanations. It is often described as empirical, meaning it relies on things that can be observed, measured, and analyzed. It often requires experiments. Results from those experiments must be repeatable by others.

The principles and methods of science are listed in Table 3.1. The first basic principle is that there is a real and knowable universe. In simple terms, the universe is real, not in your or someone else's imagination. The more important part of this principle is that the universe is "knowable." In practical terms, this means that scientists accept that understanding something is not beyond their comprehension. It does not necessarily mean that it will be figured out in your lifetime. This is because most scientific advances are very small. But they accumulate. A particular scientist makes a small advance, then that advance is built upon by others, and on it goes. That is how most science works. Imagine, for example, space exploration. It wasn't so long ago that it was commonly thought that the earth was the center of the universe. We have gone from that belief 500 years ago to landing craft on Mars. Much of this work can be attributed to understanding that the universe is knowable. Similar kinds of advances apply to human biological evolution. Anthropologists accept that figuring out how and why humans emerged, how they evolved, and understanding the relationships between the various taxa of hominins is knowable. We work at it. Occasionally someone makes an important discovery and we build on that. We may not have human evolution entirely figured out in our lifetimes, but we accept that it is not beyond our capabilities.

The second and third principles are that the universe operates according to understandable laws, and that these laws are unchanging. These principles are linked to the notion that the universe is knowable. Scientists work toward understanding laws, which are as certain as we get about something in science. There are very few things that are so certain that they are called laws. One example is the law of gravity. Scientists also accept that these laws have stayed constant through time, meaning the laws that were active billions, or millions, or thousands of years ago are the same laws that are active today.

In science, we can start with a guess, which proceeds to a **hypothesis**. A hypothesis must be testable, meaning there must be some way to collect and analyze data to either support or reject the hypothesis.

Theory is usually as good as it gets in science. Outside of science, "theory" is often used to indicate a guess. One may often hear the phrase "It is just a theory," for example. When scientists use the word *theory*, however, it has different meaning, with a much more positive connotation. When one speaks of the theory of evolution, for example, it may mean one of two things. The term theory may be used to describe multiple well-supported hypotheses about evolution, including the role of natural selection, sexual selection, mutation, gene flow, genetic drift, and more. In other contexts, mostly historical, the "theory" in the "theory of evolution" refers to notions of how evolution occurs (e.g., such as by natural selection) rather than if it occurs. When one hears of the theory of human evolution, by comparison, it is not in the context of whether human evolution occurred. Rather, it refers to the multiple hypotheses and data that support the fact of human evolution.

The scientific method includes four primary stages. The first is to develop one or more hypotheses to explain an observation or answer a question. The next stage is to test the hypothesis, which requires the collection and analysis of data. For

Table 3.1
Principles and Methods of Science

Principles	Methods
There is a real and knowable universe	Create one or more testable hypotheses to explain observations or answer questions
The universe operates according to understandable laws	Test the hypothesis (or hypotheses)
These laws are unchanging	Accept, modify, or reject the hypothesis Continually reevaluate the hypothesis as new data become available and new hypotheses are created

example, in the study of human evolution, this may include collection and analysis of human remains. If anthropologists wanted to test the hypothesis that walking upright occurred before a significant increase in brain size, they would need to collect human skeletons of known antiquity. This would allow them to determine if walking upright preceded an increase in brain size. The third stage includes the acceptance, rejection, or modification of the hypothesis. The fourth stage involves the continual reevaluation of the hypothesis as new data becomes available.

In science, the best hypothesis is usually the hypothesis that fits the data today. We recognize that new research or a reevaluation of old research may bring new data, causing the rejection of a well accepted hypothesis. In the study of human biological evolution, for example, as new data emerge from ongoing research projects, hypotheses are continually reevaluated. Some may be strengthened by the new data, and some may lose support. The discovery of a new kind of human, an unusual bone, or a different kind of strand of **DNA**, for example, may cause anthropologists to reevaluate their ideas.

Ensuring that hypotheses are continually reevaluated is a key aspect of science. There is never certainty in science. Scientists always leave room for doubt. By continually retesting and reevaluating hypotheses, science is self-correcting. Some people find it frustrating that there is no certainty in science, but this is also one of its strengths. For example, we know much more about human evolution today than we did a few years ago. This is because we never accept a hypothesis, no matter how good it may seem, if it cannot be tested and/or does not explain the data.

Science also includes methods for evaluating competing explanations. These include ensuring the hypothesis is testable, assessing its compatibility with what we already know, how many phenomena the hypothesis can explain, and how simple the hypothesis is. These are discussed further in Chapter 7.

One of the characteristics of pseudoscience is developing a series of hypotheses and then accepting one by merely eliminating the others. This is a common ploy among nonscientists. It would be inappropriate, for example, to develop three hypotheses to explain the origin of an increase in brain size, test and reject the first two, and on this basis accept the third.

Figure 3.2
Charles Darwin
This portrait of Charles Darwin was done about 1840, during the time he was developing his theory of evolution by natural selection.

History of Evolutionary Thought and Theory

This section has two parts: (i) the history of evolutionary thought and theory to Darwin; and (ii) the contributions of Mendel.

History of Evolutionary Thought and Theory to Darwin

Charles Darwin is widely credited with developing the theory of evolution, upon which much of biology today is based. His book *On the Origin of Species by Means of Natural Selection, or the Preservation of Favoured Races in the Struggle for Life*, initially published in 1859, with five subsequent editions in years following, was certainly monumental. Many suggest it is one of the two or three most important books ever written.

We know a lot more about evolution now than we did in 1859, but Darwin laid the foundation in a very clear and comprehensive way. His ideas on how evolution occurred were articulated so clearly and he used so much evidence in support of them, that much of the generally educated public was quickly convinced not only that biological evolution occurred but also that it occurred through a process called natural selection.

Darwin (1859) summarized his ideas as follows:

As many more individuals of each species are born than can possibly survive; and as, consequently, there is a frequently recurring struggle of existence, it follows that any being, if it vary however slightly in any manner profitable to itself, under the complex and sometimes varying conditions of life, will have a better chance of surviving, and thus be naturally selected. From the strong principle of inheritance, any selected variety will tend to propagate its new and modified form.

Darwin scholar Joseph Carroll (2003:9) describes the importance of *On the Origin of Species*:

Darwin—In His Own Words

On the Origin of Species (retitled *The Origin of Species* at the sixth edition) has 14 chapters. The last is titled "Recapitulation and Conclusion," which includes the following excerpt:

> Therefore I cannot doubt that the theory of descent with modification embraces all members of the same class. I believe that animals have descended from at most only four or five progenitors, and plants from an equal or lesser number.... I should infer ... that probably all the organic beings which have ever lived on this earth have descended from one primordial form, into which life was first breathed.

Darwin makes few references to humans in *On the Origin of Species*, but he recognizes the implications. Near the end of the book, he writes, "In the distant future I see open fields for far more important researches.... Light will be thrown on the origin of man and his history."

The last paragraph of *On the Origin of Species* reads as follows:

> It is interesting to contemplate an entangled bank, clothed with many plants of many kinds, with birds singing on the bushes, with various insects flitting about, and with worms crawling about damp earth, and to reflect that these elaborately constructed forms, so different from each other, and dependent on each other in so complex a manner, have all been produced by laws acting around us.... Thus, from the war of nature, from famine and death, the most exalted object to which we are capable of conceiving, namely, the production of the higher animals, directly follows. There is grandeur in this view of life, with its several powers, having been originally breathed into a few forms or into one; and that, whilst this planet has gone cycling on according to the fixed law of gravity, from so simple a beginning endless forms most beautiful and most wonderful have been, are being, evolved.

In his autobiography, *The Autobiography of Charles Darwin*, Darwin writes of his interest in human evolution, "As soon as I had become, in the year 1837 or 1838, convinced that species were mutable productions, I could not avoid the belief that man must come under the same law" (Carroll 2003:441).

In *The Descent of Man* (1871), Darwin writes the following:

> The main conclusion ... is that man is descended from some less highly organised form. The grounds upon which this rests will never be shaken, for the close similarity between man and the lower animals ..., are facts which cannot be disputed.... The great principle of evolution stands up clear and firm, when these groups or facts are considered in connection with others.

On the Origin of Species has special claims on our attention. It is one of the two or three most significant scientific works of all time—one of those works that fundamentally and permanently alters our vision of the world. At the same time, it is one of the few great scientific works that is also a great literary classic. It is written for the generally educated reader and requires no specialized scientific training. It is argued with a singularly rigorous consistency, but it is also eloquent, imaginatively evocative, and rhetorically compelling.

There are several key elements or components of Darwin's theory of how biological evolution occurs. He observed that all species either do, or have the potential to, produce far more offspring than can survive. He also observed that there is variation within all species. From this he deduced that there must be some kind of competition for resources, and that some of the variability must be advantageous. He surmised that those with the variable variation would produce more offspring and the advantageous variations could be inherited. Over time, Darwin deduced, the accumulations of advantageous variations could lead to the evolution of a new species. The phrase "theory of evolution by natural selection" is based on the idea that it is nature that determines which variations are advantageous.

The theory is quite simple, but nobody had connected the pieces quite like Darwin. There are multiple reasons why he was able to develop the theory. These include his university education, especially in learning about geology and botany (even though he graduated with a degree in theology), his five-year voyage around the world making observations on the natural world, his passion for both describing and explaining the natural world, and his interest in reading widely. It was only after reading an essay written by an economist (Thomas Malthus), for example, that he realized that as with humans, there must be a struggle or a competition for existence among members of other species as well.

It is important to understand that Darwin did not develop his ideas in a vacuum. His theory was dependent both on the development of science in general and on the thoughts and research on the natural world of others before him, in particular those having to do with geology and biology. The framework of science, for example, out of which grew the fields of geology and biology, began about AD 1500. This is more than 300 years before Darwin developed his ideas.

There are many prominent researchers and thinkers who made important contributions to evolutionary thought, even though that was not the intention of all. In the late 1600s, for example, John Ray, an Anglican minister with an interest in the natural world, developed the concepts of genus and species. This idea was further developed in the early 1700s by Swedish botanist Carolus Linnaeus, who added the taxa of order and class to the classification system we still use today. It was Linnaeus, for example, who placed humans in the genus *Homo*, the order Primates, and class Mammalia. It was not the intention of Ray and Linnaeus to have their work used to support evolution, but indeed it has. For example, we now assume that placement of similar species in a genus, similar genera in an order, and similar orders in a class are a reflection of evolutionary relationships, and not just similar physical features.

Some French intellectuals had significant influence on evolutionary thought before Darwin. George-Louis Leclerc, Comte de Buffon, a very well-known scientist in the mid- and late 1700s, made some significant contributions. He recognized (and was perhaps the first to do so) that change within species could be an effect of environment. He publicly supported the idea of change, and refuted the need to resort to religious doctrine to explain things. He also speculated on an antiquity of the earth in the tens of thousands of years, rather than the 6,000 years many were claiming based on interpretations of the Bible.

Jean-Baptiste Lamarck is associated with an early nineteenth-century idea of how traits are passed on, known as the Theory of the **Inheritance of Acquired Characteristics**. Lamarck proposed that an individual that acquired specific traits could pass those traits on to its offspring. A classic example involves giraffes. The idea was that if a giraffe continually stretched its neck to reach higher leaves, its neck would become longer. Then, once the neck was longer and the giraffe mated, its offspring would have a long neck. We now know that this is not the way evolution works. The theory was never widely accepted, but it was an attempt, and led to further thought. It was one of those smaller steps that led to bigger discoveries.

A few people we would call geologists today were also influential in the development of evolutionary thought, primarily in establishing a long-time frame for life on earth, which was necessary for evolution to occur. In AD 1650, Archbishop James Ussher calculated the date of earth's origin as 4004 BC using a literary interpretation of Genesis in the Bible. (Some years later, another theologian declared more specifically that creation occurred on 23 October 4004 BC at 9:00 a.m.) In the late 1700s, James Hutton developed the principle of **uniformitarianism**, which essentially says the same geological processes active today were also the processes active in the past. The implication here is that since many of the processes were slow, the earth must be far greater than 6,000 years old. This idea was developed further and popularized by Charles Lyell in the early 1830s, suggesting the earth must be at least 100,000 years old. Importantly, Darwin's early readings included the writings of Lyell on this. We know now that the earth is much, much older.

Following graduation from university, Darwin obtained a position as the naturalist on the H.M.S. *Beagle*, a British ship on a five-year voyage of mapping and exploration (1831–1836). It was on this voyage that Darwin was introduced to extreme diversity and started formulating his ideas. One of the most significant stops was on the Galapagos Islands, off the west coast of South America. Here he observed that the tortoises and the finches on the islands were significantly different from those on the mainland. He further observed a significant diversity of finches within the islands. Each variety of finch had evidently evolved to suit its environment, making a connection in his mind between diversity and environment. Those living on islands with rocky beaches, for example, had short strong beaks suitable for overturning rocks. Those living in among trees had long thin beaks suitable for poking through bark.

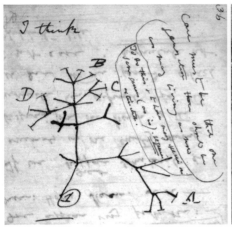

Figure 3.3
"Tree of Life"
Drawing by Darwin
This sketch is from one of the notebooks Darwin kept while he was developing his theory. The tips of the branches show living species, while the limbs and trunk illustrate evolutionary relationships.
Credit: Cambridge University Library

Figure 3.4
Statue of
Alfred Wallace
Wallace shared credit with Darwin for developing the theory of evolution.
Credit: Bob Muckle

Once back from the voyage, Darwin set to family life (marrying and having children) and academic work from his estate south of London. Darwin was from a wealthy family, so he was able to basically do what he wanted. Fortunately for the rest of the world, he wanted to describe and explain diversity. He started sketching his ideas about evolution but told few about them, fearing a backlash from the scientific community. The final piece of the puzzle for Darwin occurred in 1838 when he read the essay by the economist Thomas Malthus.

For 20 years Darwin occasionally worked on the manuscript that would eventually become *On the Origin of Species*. Then one day in 1858 he received a letter from Alfred Wallace, who had independently developed very similar ideas as Darwin had about how evolution worked. It created a quandary. Darwin had developed his ideas over 20 years but had told few. Wallace had developed his ideas quickly and shared them. It created a dilemma because in science, being the first to develop and publish an idea is important. An arrangement was made for both Wallace's and Darwin's papers to be read later that year at scientific meetings in London. Accordingly, they both are credited with coming up with the idea.

Darwin spent the next year polishing his manuscript and the book was released in 1859. Darwin preferred to avoid the use of the term "evolution." In its place he used "descent with modification" and "transmutation." The book does not deal with humans, but the implication was there. In 1871, he published his thoughts on human evolution in a book called *The Descent of Man*.

Darwin deservedly receives much credit for providing the foundation of evolutionary theory. Had he not developed it, however, we would probably still be in about the same place in terms of our scientific understandings, except the accolades would be going to Alfred Wallace rather than Charles Darwin.

Darwin and Wallace provide an interesting contrast. Darwin came from a wealthy family and didn't have to work, but followed his passions. Except for his five-year voyage at a relatively young age, he apparently mostly led a quiet life at home. Wallace, on the other hand, came from a lower-class family and had to work to get by. Nonetheless, he too followed his passion for describing and explaining the natural biological world. However, although most of the time he was collecting on behalf of institutions, he seems to have been much more adventurous. As a young man, Wallace spent a few years in the Amazon River valley in South America collecting specimens, only to lose his entire collection when the ship he was traveling home in caught fire and sank in the middle of the Atlantic Ocean. Luckily, after spending several days in a lifeboat, he was rescued. Undaunted, once back home he set his sights on Indonesia where he continued to make significant collections, and where he independently developed the theory of evolution by natural selection. According to some reports, he came up with the theory while hallucinating during a bout of malaria.

Contributions of Mendel

Neither Darwin nor Wallace knew about the mechanics of genetic inheritance at the time they published. The foundation of **genetics** is usually attributed to Gregor Mendel, a teaching monk with a background in mathematics and botany at a monastery in what is now the Czech Republic. His contributions on understanding genetics based on experiments in the 1850s and 1860s were significant, but his work was unappreciated, and he died in obscurity in 1884. The importance of his work was discovered in 1900, and combined with Darwin's theory of evolution by natural selection, provides the foundation for contemporary evolutionary theory.

Besides teaching, Mendel took it upon himself to study how inheritance works through a very careful and comprehensive program of breeding pea plants (*Pisum sativum*). He chose pea plants because they have several traits that appear in only one of two forms, as follows:

- color of flower: white or purple
- position of flower on stem: on stem (axil) or on top (terminal)
- length of stem: short or long
- shape of seed: round or wrinkled
- color of seed: yellow or green
- shape of pod: inflated or constricted
- color of pod: yellow or green

Mendel spent years studying the pea plants in the gardens of the monastery. He spent the first two years ensuring that he had true-breeding varieties, meaning those that had white flowers always had white flowers through multiple generations. He then spent several more years crossbreeding the plants and counting the occurrence of the various traits in each plant.

He found that when he crossbred plants with opposing traits (e.g., crossbreeding those that only produced round seeds with those that only produced wrinkled seeds), only one of the traits showed up in the offspring (i.e., all the plants produced only round seeds). When he then crossbred that generation, the trait that disappeared always appeared again, but in a 3:1 ratio (i.e., three round seeds for every wrinkled seed).

Part of the genius of Mendel was ensuring that he had true-breeding varieties to begin with. He also recognized the importance of large numbers. He examined approximately 30,000 pea plants over the years. Without these large numbers, it is unlikely the consistent ratio of 3:1 would be recognized. Others had used pea plants to investigate inheritance and noticed that some traits disappear and then reappear again, but they did not recognize the ratio.

From these observations Mendel was able to establish a very basic understanding of genetics. One of the things Mendel concluded was that traits are determined by specific units or factors in individuals, which are passed on to offspring. We now call these factors **genes**. Another thing Mendel concluded was that an individual inherits one unit from each parent. We now call these **alleles**. He further concluded that even though an individual has a specific trait, it may not be observable but can still be passed on. Besides understanding genes and alleles, Mendel is responsible for figuring out *dominant* and *recessive* alleles, and the differences between **genotype** (what the genes code for) and **phenotype** (the physical expression of the genes).

Relatively few human traits are passed on by simple Mendelian genetics; however, it laid the foundation for further work, which was important. Prior to the discovery of Mendel's work, there was really little understanding of how inheritance worked. Many thought that blending of traits was somehow occurring, but nobody knew how. The observations that some traits disappeared and then appeared again—rather than blending—were baffling. Most people had dismissed Lamarck's ideas, and when it came to humans, some went so far to suggest that children looked most like the parent who dominated during sex.

Modern Evolutionary Theory

Darwin's theory of evolution by natural selection and Mendel's pioneering work on genetics laid the foundation for evolutionary theory, but many advances have occurred since the late 1800s, which are outlined in this section.

Key concepts in evolutionary theory include mutation, natural selection, sexual selection, gene flow, genetic drift, and adaptive radiation. **Mutations**, which are errors in the replication of DNA, are the ultimate source of variation within populations. They can be neutral, beneficial, or harmful. We often hear about the bad mutations that are passed on via sperm or egg, since they can cause diseases, deformities, and death. DNA is complex and errors occur all the time. Your hair and fingernails grow, for example, by replication of cells. If you have a mutation in those cells, it is no concern. If, however, there is a mutation in the sperm or egg, it can be a big deal.

Mutations usually occur simply as copying errors. They can also occur, however, from exposure to radiation, chemicals, and viruses. All human variability ultimately derives from mutations. It is from mutations that our ancestors had variability from which bipedalism and larger brains emerged. It may have been a mutation, for example, that allowed one person to walk upright for a few meters farther than the average person could walk. Under specific conditions, that ability may have been favorable and may have led to that individual having more offspring, who also had the favorable trait. It is likely that the mutations that were selected for, since the split of our common ancestor with chimpanzees and bonobos, number in the millions.

Gene flow and **genetic drift** are important concepts. Gene flow is when genes move between populations that are members of the same species but who do not normally mate together. Because of separation, new alleles may have formed in one population that may be passed on to others. Regarding human evolution, for example, it was almost certainly the case that people moving out of Africa in the distant past mated with pre-existing populations in the Middle East and Asia. Gene flow would have occurred. Genetic drift is a random factor in evolution. It is when changes in **allele frequency** occur by chance, for instance, when a small group leaves its parent population and begins a new population elsewhere. The smaller the group, the larger the changes may be in allele frequency.

Adaptive radiation is when a species rapidly adapts to an ecological niche, often expanding its population quickly and diversifying into multiple species. A good example of adaptive radiation was when mammals adapted to new ecological niches following the extinction of dinosaurs. More recently, adaptive radiation likely occurred when humans first left Africa, quickly expanding across Asia and perhaps diversifying into different species.

Natural selection, as proposed by Darwin, remains an important concept in evolution. In regard to human evolution, for example, it is likely that it was natural selection that led to significant loss of body hair and changes in skin color (discussed in Chapter 4). Even Darwin recognized that there were likely other selection processes as well, such as **sexual selection**, which essentially means personal mate selection. For instance, a variety of male animals create colorful displays and performances to entice the female to have sex (consider the mating displays of fireflies or the architectural feats of the bower bird). Similar kinds of selection among humans, with mate selection having nothing to do with the potential for increased survival of the species, have likely been going on for millions of years. These mate choices may have been based on physical features, such as facial symmetry, or cultural factors, such as the ability to heal others.

On the Notion of Ape-Human Hybrids

It seems that we are becoming aware of an increasing number of hybrid animals—both in the wild and in captivity. A common example of a hybrid animal is a mule, the hybrid offspring of a horse and donkey. A horse-zebra hybrid is a zorse. Another example is the lion-tiger hybrid, known as a liger or tion.

There are no verifiable instances of ape-human hybrids, but apparently not for lack of trying. A Russian scientist in the 1920s apparently made multiple attempts at impregnating female chimpanzees with human sperm, presumably through artificial inseminations. No pregnancies were documented. He also apparently had plans to impregnate "volunteer" human females with ape sperm, but it is likely this never progressed beyond the planning stage.

It wasn't only Russians that were interested in ape-human hybrids. Russell Tuttle (2014) reports, for example, that besides the Russian attempts, American, Dutch, German, and French scientists have either encouraged or planned ape-human hybridization in the past. The ethical and legal dilemmas posed by such mating would presumably prevent such experiments and attempts from occurring in the twenty-first century, at least legally or in the court of public opinion. One never knows though. Perhaps in the eyes of some it would make good television.

In the 1970s a chimpanzee that looked to some people to have some human-like features was promoted as an ape-human hybrid, known as Oliver. DNA tests confirmed that he was 100 per cent chimpanzee. Many believe that such hybrids, known to believers as *humanzees* or *chumans*, exist, but there is no verified evidence of their existence.

In experiments, one researcher showed that human sperm could penetrate the egg of a gibbon, and presumably other apes, but not monkeys. Having the ability of human sperm to penetrate the egg of an ape is a long way from hybridization, however. It is possible that during the initial million years or so after the split of humans and chimpanzees with a common ancestor about seven million years ago, there may have been some hybrids, but it is very unlikely there have been any since.

Gradualism and **punctuated equilibrium** are models pertaining to the speed at which evolution occurs. Gradualism suggests a slow steady change, with a new species eventually emerging. Punctuated equilibrium suggests slow steady change occasionally interrupted by short periods of significant change. Punctuated equilibrium explains lack of transitional forms in the fossil record. Both models can be used to explain human evolution at various times. The transitions from *Australopithecus* to *Homo habilis* more than two million years ago for example, have left few fossils that can be described as transitional, so punctuated equilibrium best explains the transition. On the other hand, *Homo erectus* fossils show evidence of well over one million years of fairly slow, gradual change. These transitions are discussed in Chapter 4.

There are many working definitions of **species**. The definition used throughout this book is that a species is a population of individuals that can mate and produce fertile offspring in the wild. For instance, a horse and a donkey are different species. When they mate, they can produce a mule, but mules are almost always sterile.

Hybrids are known to occur in controlled conditions and increasingly in the wild as natural habitats decrease. In regard to human evolution, when anthropologists refer to different species of humans, the assumption is usually that they would not have been able to mate and produce fertile offspring. In recent years, DNA research is increasingly showing that different kinds of humans such as Neandertals and modern humans were indeed mating and producing fertile offspring, leading to the conclusion they were the same species.

Speciation is the process by which new species emerge. It can happen in numerous ways. Sometimes new species emerge from geographic isolation. It was likely the development of the Congo River in Africa 1.5 to 2 million years ago that separated the common ancestor of chimpanzees and bonobos, leading to those two separate species. Sometimes it is a single population of a species that evolves into another species, coexisting for a time with its ancestral species before the ancestral species become extinct. This is probably the more common situation in human biological evolution.

The concept of extinction is important. Sometimes an entire species evolves into another species; therefore, the originating species becomes extinct. In other cases, a species becomes extinct for other reasons, such as environmental change to which it cannot successfully adapt since it does not have enough variability from which to choose. This is likely what happened with the extinction of the dinosaurs 65 million years ago and the extinction of mammoths and mastodons about 10,000 years ago. In other situations species may become extinct because of the introduction of a new species that outcompetes them for resources. Extinction is normal, but occasionally extinction rates are extremely high. It is commonly accepted that there have been five periods of **mass extinctions**, when approximately half the species on earth became extinct. All previous mass extinctions occurred before the emergence of humans. Many believe we are on the verge of the sixth mass extinction, except this time humans appear to be the cause. Some biologists claim the rate of animal extinctions occurring in recent and contemporary times is 1,000 or more times above normal.

Terms that have appeared in recent years include **genome**, **genomics**, and **epigenetics**. Genetics tends to refer to the study of individual genes and their role in inheritance. Genome refers to the entire genetic makeup of an individual or species, including all the DNA and genes. Genomics is the study of genomes. Epigenetics is a new area of research that is still in its infancy. We realize that genes are the primary way traits are inherited, but that other factors, such as chemical reactions due to life events or stressors, may also have a role. Epigenetics essentially refers to the study of how factors other than DNA or genes may influence the occurrence of specific traits.

Box 3.4
Extinction and De-Extinction

Extinctions are part of the evolutionary process. It is likely that more than 99 per cent of all species that have ever lived are now extinct. Sometimes species evolve into one or more new species. Others simply have their populations dwindle until the population is too low to maintain a breeding population. Sometimes a species simply does not have the variability within its population to adapt to changing environments (i.e., not enough variability from which nature can choose favorable traits), the variability may be reduced by genetic drift, or the existence of a new species evolving in the regions or coming from elsewhere may outcompete the existing species.

There have been several mass extinctions in the past, where many taxonomic groups have become extinct. The last mass extinction occurred about 65 million years ago, causing many animals to become extinct, including the terrestrial dinosaurs. The consensus opinion is that an asteroid hitting earth caused significant climate change, which the dinosaurs could not effectively adapt to (not having the requisite variability). Small mammals had coexisted with dinosaurs, and many mammals likely became extinct as well. However, with the removal of dinosaurs and changing environments, some species of small mammals were able to quickly evolve, adapting to changing environments, occupying new ecological niches. Ultimately, one of these mammal species led to primates.

The primate fossil record is filled with now-extinct forms. Even the human fossil record is replete with species that have become extinct over the last several million years. One of the challenges for palaeoanthropologists is to figure out which of these early species are in the line that ultimately led to *Homo sapiens*.

De-extinction refers to the idea of bringing back extinct animals, in a kind of cloning. Some attempts have been made (e.g., unsuccessful attempts with a kind of goat), but the technology is very close to making it feasible. Some researchers have suggested it may be possible to bring back a Neandertal, although much more discussion revolves around bringing back mammoths. Complete genomes have been reconstructed for both Neandertals and mammoths.

For many, the advances in technology are such that we are very close—and perhaps already there—in regard to having the ability to clone mammoths, and Neandertals are not far off. The questions, therefore, are not so much "Can we do it?" as "Should we do it?"

Reasons for bringing back extinct species are varied. Some suggest that bringing back now-extinct species can be an effective way of recovering natural habitats. Introducing such animals to environments is often known as "re-wilding." Opponents suggest that introducing previously extinct animals to environments could wreak havoc on contemporary ecosystems.

Bringing back a mammoth would require gestation in a similar kind of animal, probably an elephant. Bringing back a Neandertal would presumably require a female chimpanzee or human. Legal and ethical issues would be tremendous. One American geneticist has already put word out that he is looking for a woman volunteer.

It is usually the ecology scientists that are front and center in the debate about bringing back mammoths and anthropologists front and center on the question of Neandertal de-extinction. Some anthropologists are keen for what they say they may learn about human evolution and that they may learn new cultural and biological adaptive strategies from Neandertals. Many, however, believe that little can be learned from bringing back a Neandertal, suggesting whatever we could learn from a Neandertal clone brought up and controlled by humans would have serious limitations and serious ethical considerations.

Summary

This chapter has provided overviews of the nature of science, the history of evolutionary thought, and the key concepts and vocabulary of contemporary evolutionary theory. Mirroring the Learning Objectives stated in the chapter opening, the key points are:

- Science is a framework with a specific set of principles and methods.
- Charles Darwin gets most of the credit for figuring out how evolution works, and deservedly so. However, he did not work in a vacuum, depending on the work of others who came before him. Alfred Wallace also had it figured out.
- Gregor Mendel pioneered genetics with his work on pea plants.
- Contemporary evolutionary theory has built on the work of Darwin and Mendel, and we have a far greater understanding of the variety of ways in which populations evolve.

REVIEW QUESTIONS

1. What are the principles and methods of science?
2. Who were the key people in the development of evolutionary theory before 1859, and what were their contributions?
3. What are the key elements of Darwin's Theory of Evolution by Natural Selection?
4. What was the contribution of Gregor Mendel to evolutionary theory?

DISCUSSION QUESTIONS

1. If you could go back in time, with whom would you rather have a conversation—Darwin, Wallace, or Mendel? Why?
2. What are some problems predicting how any kind of plant or animal species will continue to evolve biologically?

Visit **www.lensofanthropology.com** for the following additional resources:

SELF-STUDY QUESTIONS   **WEBLINKS**   **FURTHER READING**

PLACES MENTIONED IN CHAPTER 4

1   Great Rift Valley, Africa
2   South Africa
3   Zhoukoudian, China
4   Shanidar Cave, Iraq
5   Gibraltar

6   Siberia
7   Vietnam
8   Republic of Georgia
9   Neander Valley, Germany

HUMAN BIOLOGICAL EVOLUTION

Learning Objectives

In this chapter students will learn:

- the basic methods, concepts, and issues of palaeoanthropology.
- the nature of the human fossil record.
- ideas about why the bipedal adaptation may have emerged.
- the biological changes that occurred to allow efficient bipedalism.
- the genus and species of fossil humans over the last several million years.
- the general trends in human biological evolution.
- the fact that race is not a valid biological category.

Introduction

There are many thousands of human fossil remains, going back some several million years. Human evolution is not quite so simple as a linear evolution of one species evolving into another until *Homo sapiens* was reached. There is evidence that multiple genera of humans and at least a dozen species of humans have lived in the past, often coexisting at the same time in the same regions.

This chapter highlights the study of human biological evolution. It includes consideration of methods, why and how humans emerged several million years ago, and overviews of human evolution, including the major taxonomic groups and trends. The chapter also includes a section on the concept of race.

Palaeoanthropology—Methods, Concepts, and Issues

Finding Sites

There are several ways of finding palaeoanthropological sites. Researchers often return to the same general area year after year. There is good reason for this: the chances of researchers finding human remains in the same area where they have been found before is usually much better than finding them in areas where nobody has looked before.

Rarely do palaeoanthropologists dig blindly. Typically they search in areas where there are sediments exposed from the time period of interest. For example, a palaeoanthropologist interested in early humans in the time period of approximately two million years ago would look in an area where the sediments that were initially deposited two million years ago had been covered over and have now been reexposed. Thus, a palaeoanthropologist merely has to walk over the ground surface to see bones that were initially deposited two million years ago. Every year rains tend to remove fine layers of sediments and thus expose new remains. Palaeoanthropologists also want to search in areas that have good preservation of organic remains. When humans are found, they are usually only a very small percentage of the total assemblage of bones identified.

A very high proportion of all human remains over one million years old, and all of them over 1.8 million years old have been found in Africa, mostly in the **Great Rift Valley** of East Africa, running through Ethiopia, Kenya, and Tanzania, and in the country of South Africa. Most of the finds in East Africa have been discovered through the search process just described.

Sediments of the time period of interest are not always exposed or sometimes the preservation qualities are not very good, but fortunately there is another way of finding early humans, which involves looking in caves. Because they are in caves, bones are often protected from the normal elements leading to decomposition. It is important to understand that, although there are exceptions, most people did not live in caves (see Box 5.5). Many of the discoveries of early humans in South Africa have been in caves. There are many important palaeoanthropological cave sites outside of Africa as well. These include, but are certainly not limited to, Zhoukoudian in China (where 40 *Homo erectus* individuals were found), Shanidar Cave in Iraq (a purported Neandertal burial site), and Ling Bua on the island of Flores in Indonesia (where the remains of *Homo floresiensis*, popularly known as "the hobbits," were discovered).

Figure 4.1
Olorgesailie, Kenya
A *Homo erectus* site
in the Great Rift Valley
of Africa.
Credit: © Barry D. Kass/Images
of Anthropology

The Fossil Record

The word **fossil** is applied very loosely in anthropology. For some, it means the organic remains have turned into stone, or left an impression in stone, but this is not the case in anthropology. In anthropology, *fossil* is used to describe any preserved early human remains, no matter their condition. Thus, when one speaks of human fossil remains, it simply means they exist, and may be in an extremely soft or fragile state.

The human **fossil record** has multiple meanings. In one sense the fossil record may be taken to mean the interpretation of human evolution, based on the data of the collected remains. In another sense, the fossil record may be taken to simply mean the assemblage of bones collected.

The assemblage of human remains constituting the fossil record is substantial. More than a decade ago, popular writer Bill Bryson (2003) quoted well-known palaeontologist Ian Tattersall as saying the entire collection of early human remains could fit in the back of a pickup truck. Many fossils have been discovered since, adding thousands of bones and bone fragments to the assemblage. However, there are still unlikely to be enough to fill a dump truck and the total assemblage probably represents hundreds, rather than thousands, of individuals.

Preservation and Taphonomy

Not all human remains preserve equally. Teeth tend to preserve the best, followed by the bones of the skull. The mandible (lower jaw) is the thickest and most dense bone of the skeleton and thus preserves the best of all the bones, and is sometimes found with the teeth intact. All the bones beneath the head, commonly known as the post-cranial bones, are preserved less often. Except for the mandible, bones are rarely discovered complete. They are typically highly fragmented and pieces of bones are frequently missing. This is usually due to natural processes acting on the bone in the years since the individual died.

To make proper inferences from human remains, palaeoanthropologists are familiar with **taphonomy**, the study of what happens to organic remains after death. It is through taphonomy that anthropologists can identify the natural and cultural processes that may have acted upon the assemblage. For example, somebody familiar with taphonomy should be able to determine if bone breakage, marking on bones, the distance between bones, and what bones were present were due to specific kinds of natural or cultural causes.

The preservation of human remains before deliberate burial (probably about 50,000 years ago) is rare. In order for the remains to be preserved, the natural processes of scavenging and decomposition had to be impeded. Many animals, including humans, left on the ground surface will be eaten by other animals. Even without large-scale scavengers like wild dogs or hyenas it is only rarely that preservation occurs. Decomposition essentially occurs when millions of microorganisms and insects eat the body. Millions of these microorganisms are already inside humans while they are living, but the human body, while alive, prevents them from leaving those areas where they are most useful, such as the digestive tract. In addition animals such as flies may lay eggs on the corpse, which then hatch as maggots and eat the body.

In order for preservation to occur then, the remains almost always have to be removed quite quickly from the ground surface. This removes them from scavengers and also usually puts them in an environment not conducive to decomposition by microorganisms, such as in areas with low oxygen, like below the ground surface. Typically, for example, in order for early human remains to be preserved they were probably covered very soon after death, perhaps by sinking in soft sediments near the shore of a lake, being covered by sediments being washed down a slope, or slipping and falling into a subsurface cave system.

Osteology

Osteology is the study of the human skeleton. At a minimum, palaeoanthropologists must be able to identify very small bone fragments as human, as opposed to other kinds of animal remains. The human skeleton is illustrated in Figure 4.2., and Table 4.1 provides some basic information on the human skeleton. In addition to identifying bones as human, anthropologists also should be able to determine the age of the individual when they died. They can do this primarily by looking at how many adult teeth have erupted and the degree of bone fusion (e.g., the ends of long bones fuse to the shafts, and several of the bones of the skull fuse at certain times).

Table 4.1
Basic Osteology

Total Number of Bones in Adult Human Skeleton	206
Total Number of Teeth in Adult Human Skeleton	32
Human Dental Formula	2 incisors, 1 canine, 2 premolars, 3 molars

KEY BONES, BONE GROUPS, AND FEATURES	
Skull	Bones of the cranium and mandible
Cranium	Skull, minus the mandible
Mandible	Lower jaw
Maxilla	Upper jaw
Bones of the arm	Humerus, radius, ulna
Bones of the wrist	Carpals
Bones of the hand	Metacarpals
Hip bones	Pelvic bones
Leg bones	Femur, patella, tibia, fibula
Ankle bones	Tarsals
Foot bones	Metatarsals
Fingers and toes	Phalanges
Foramen magnum	Hole at the base of the skull through which the spinal column connects to the brain

Anthropologists also attempt to determine if the individual was male or female. They do this primarily by examining characteristic features of the pelvis (Figure 4.3).

Issues and Debates in Palaeoanthropology

Prominent debates among researchers involve the assignment of a particular genus or species to a particular assemblage of human remains. This is often framed as the "Lumpers vs. Splitters" debate. Lumpers tend to assume there is considerable variability within genera and species and therefore have relatively few taxonomic categories for the several million years of human evolution. Splitters, on the other hand, tend to assume there is relatively little variability within genera and species

Figure 4.2
The Human Skeleton
There are a total of 206 bones in the adult human skeleton.

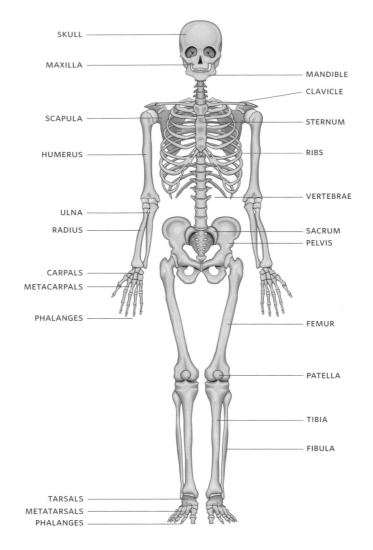

SKULL

MAXILLA

MANDIBLE

CLAVICLE

SCAPULA

STERNUM

HUMERUS

RIBS

VERTEBRAE

ULNA

RADIUS

SACRUM

PELVIS

CARPALS

METACARPALS

PHALANGES

FEMUR

PATELLA

TIBIA

FIBULA

TARSALS

METATARSALS

PHALANGES

Figure 4.3
Male and Female Human Pelvis
A female pelvis is typically wider, more basin-shaped, and has a wider subpubic angle than a male pelvis.

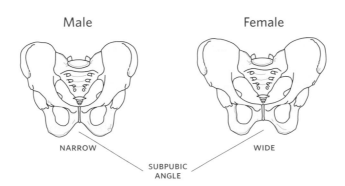

Male

Female

NARROW

WIDE

SUBPUBIC ANGLE

and therefore recognize many different genera and species over the millions of years. An extreme version of lumping for example would consider that over the past four million years there have only been two genera of humans—*Australopithecus* and *Homo*. Looking at the same assemblage, a splitter may see more genera (e.g., *Australopithecus, Paranthropus, Kenyanthropus, Homo*), and many more species of the genus *Homo* than suggested by lumpers.

Another prominent debate includes making the links between various populations. Most anthropologists accept that one population of species of *Australopithecus* (or maybe *Kenyanthropus*) evolved into the first members of the genus *Homo*. Early *Homo* was ancestral to *Homo erectus*, which was ancestral to *sapiens*, but the links between the many different species are debated. While there is general agreement that there have been many different species of hominins, which ones were something akin to evolutionary cousins (and eventually became extinct) and which ones are indeed ancestral to *Homo sapiens* is contested.

Problems arise in part because the taxonomic classification systems are essentially artificial constructs created by humans to make sense of their world. We assign assemblages of human remains into specific species, for example, but we do not know if all those assignments reflect what we commonly accept as a definition of species (ability to reproduce and produce fertile offspring). We often make guesses on the ability to reproduce and have fertile offspring based on skeletal features alone. However, this is problematic, since we do not know the variability with the populations. DNA studies are helping to clear up some of the debates, such as showing that many living people contain DNA at one time found only in Neandertal populations.

Another problem is that there is no consensus on what defines specific genera and species. There is no ultimate authority that decides upon the criteria for placing specimens in a specific genus or species. Thus, if palaeoanthropologists are using different sets of criteria, different assignments are likely to occur.

Dating Techniques

There are several ways of determining how long it has been since a fossil human died, or an archaeological site was created. The three most widely used include potassium argon dating, radiocarbon dating, and Dating by Association.

Potassium argon dating, often abbreviated K/Ar, is generally considered to be the best technique for determining the age of sites over 200,000 years. The basic principle of potassium argon dating is that when volcanic sediment (such as ash or lava) is hot (as it is when being expelled from the volcano), there is potassium, but no argon. As the sediments begin to cool, potassium begins to change into argon and we know what the rate of change is. It is therefore simply a matter of sending a small sample of the sediments to a lab to measure how much potassium and argon are in a particle of volcanic sediment, and then the dates when the sediments began to cool are determined. Since the process of changing from potassium into argon is very slow, this is not a useful technique for sediments more recent than a few hundred thousand years. How it is usually applied in palaeoanthropology is that volcanic sediments below and above the biological or cultural human remains are dated. The past several million years in East Africa was a time of intense volcanic activity. This area is where many of the early human remains and most important archaeological sites are found, so, fortunately, there are many volcanic layers which can be dated. Even when human remains are found on the ground surface it is usually still possible to use this technique by correlating volcanic layers on nearby hillsides.

For sites assumed to be less than 50,000 years old, the best technique for determining the antiquity of sites (assuming no written records exist) is generally considered to be **radiocarbon dating**, also known as Carbon 14 or C14 dating. The basic principle is that all living things contain carbon 14. At the instant of death, carbon 14 begins to decay at a known rate. Consequently, with lab analysis involving measuring the amount of carbon 14 left, the date at which the organism died can be inferred. Anything organic can be dated in this way, including human biological remains, but also other kinds of plant and animal remains. The reason this method is not reliable beyond about 50,000 years is that after that elapsed time there is not enough carbon 14 left to measure.

Sometimes there are no volcanic sediments or organic remains to date, or they fall outside the range of potassium argon and radiocarbon dating, so palaeoanthropologists use a technique known as Dating by Association. The basic premise of this technique is that if two things are found in the same stratigraphic layer, and the antiquity of one object is already known, then the other object is likely the same age. This technique is widely used in South Africa, where many of the most important early human remains have been discovered. For example, if human skeletal remains are discovered in the same deposit as bones of an extinct form of elephant that has been dated by potassium argon dating elsewhere, then the human remains are assumed to be the same age.

There are certainly many more techniques, but these three are by far the most common. When determining antiquity it is normal practice to use as many different kinds of dating techniques as possible and also to use as many samples as feasible.

Defining Hominins

As noted in Chapter 2, there is no consensus definition of human or hominin. Many, however, consider hominins to include all members of the genus *Homo* and other

Box 4.1

The Killer Ape Hypothesis

The killer ape hypothesis is based on the notion that aggression and violence are the driving force of human evolution and remains at the core of our being. Fans of the science fiction movie *2001: A Space Odyssey* may recall the opening several minutes of the movie depicts this scenario—one population of apes begins to become aggressive and violent, ultimately leading to the development of humans.

The killer ape hypothesis is used by some to rationalize violence, particularly male violence. The reasoning is that humans are essentially genetically programmed to be aggressive and violent. There is, however, no research that shows such behavior to be genetically based.

Support for the killer ape hypothesis is often based on observation of aggression and violence in other living primates, especially among male chimpanzees. Chimpanzees in the wild are usually quite social and demonstrate considerable friendly behavior within their groups, but they are also known to occasionally be aggressive and violent toward those within their group and to neighboring groups. One group of chimpanzees is known to have tracked down and killed several male members of a neighboring group.

Opponents of the hypothesis often look to bonobo groups that are just as close as chimpanzees are to us, but tend to be much less aggressive and violent. Some critics of the killer ape hypothesis also suggest that even though the male aggression and violence was witnessed among wild populations, those groups had been habituated by humans for some years, which may have altered their normal behavior.

Russell Tuttle (2014) explains how the popularization of the killer ape hypothesis changes with current events. He notes, for example, that it was following the horrors of World War I and World War II that the killer ape hypothesis first reached prominence; and then again in the 1960s and 1970s when North Americans were involved in Vietnam. There has been a revival of interest in North America in recent years, perhaps correlating to the ongoing violent international conflicts the United States has been involved with in the early twenty-first century. The reasoning here is that accepting that humans are innately aggressive and violent may serve to rationalize lethal violence.

The idea that aggression and violence was the driving force that led to becoming human has little support. Similarly, many anthropologists are skeptical that humans are innately aggressive. It would be a mistake to believe our ancestors lived in a perpetual state of bliss and harmony. We do see evidence of violence in ancient skeletons and wounds from battles as well as weapons. In general, however, it appears that aggression and violence in humans started to increase in significant ways only within the last several thousand years.

taxa with evidence of bipedalism that have emerged since the split from the common ancestor of humans, chimpanzees, and bonobos about seven million years ago.

The primary characteristic that distinguishes hominins from other hominoids (i.e., apes) is bipedalism. There are several other secondary characteristics that are used as well, although none as important as bipedalism. These secondary characteristics are often used in support of classifying fossils as hominins, but are not enough to make the distinction on their own.

These secondary characteristics focus on teeth and features of the skull. The **dental arcade** of hominins is usually parabolic (i.e., the rows of teeth widen as they go back), whereas the dental arcade of apes is usually u-shaped (i.e., all the molars on each side of the arcade are the same distance apart), although there are certainly exceptions. Hominins tend to have smaller canines than apes. Apes have **diastemas** to accommodate the large canines on the opposite jaw, which are rare in hominins. Hominins also tend to have thicker tooth enamel and reduced **prognathism.**

Becoming Bipedal

One of the most significant areas of interest in palaeoanthropology revolves around understanding the events surrounding the evolution of bipedalism. Why did bipedalism occur? What biological changes accommodated bipedalism? What was the biological variability that was selected for?

The transition to bipedalism wasn't all good. One of the negative consequences of walking on two legs is that it likely would have made our ancestors more vulnerable. They would have been easier to see by predators, for example. Moving on two limbs, rather than four, would have presumably made our ancestor slower. Walking on two legs also causes an enormous stress on the skeleton, caused by the entire weight of the human body being supported by two limbs instead of four. Just ask a middle-aged or older adult. Sore backs, sore hips, sore legs, sore knees, and sore feet are often caused by decades of supporting weight on two legs.

Yet, despite the negative impacts of bipedalism, our ancestors did make the transition. A few things to consider include (i) there had to be the necessary variability within the skeleton in order for the transition to be made; (ii) there must have been some advantages that outweighed the disadvantages; and (iii) just because it worked for our ancestors does not mean that an entire species became bipedal.

It was bipedalism that set us on a separate evolutionary tract, but it does not mean that even given the similar variability or circumstances that other populations would have necessarily done the same. Consider, for example, that other populations of our last common ancestor with chimpanzees continued to evolve as well without being bipedal. While bipedalism worked for our ancestors, it wasn't necessarily the only—or necessarily the best—option. Perhaps the variability in the skeletons that make bipedalism possible did not exist before several million years ago, or perhaps it did, but the advantages in the skeleton did not outweigh the disadvantages. We may never know.

Why Bipedalism?

There are multiple explanations for why humans became bipedal and for the changes that occurred to facilitate bipedalism (Table 4.2). Until the 1970s it was widely thought that bipedalism, a significant increase in brain size (and corresponding intelligence), and tool use were thought to have evolved together. If one was the trigger, it was probably the brain. A common line of thought was that a larger brain led to the intelligence required for making and using stone tools. Making and using stone tools was facilitated by standing and walking upright, freeing the hands. This made sense to many in light of the fact that many people like to believe that the principal thing that distinguishes humans from other primates is our intelligence. Discoveries in the 1970s indicating that bipedalism occurred at least a million years before significant increases in brain size and evidence for tool use caught many by surprise but were quickly accepted.

Throughout the 1970s and 1980s it was widely thought that bipedalism was probably an effective way to adapt to a **savannah**-grassland kind of environment. Many palaeoenvironmental reconstructions associated with finds of *Australopithecus* and early members of the genus *Homo* supported this idea. Consequently, hypotheses to explain the transition to bipedalism were commonly based on the assumption that it was an effective adaptation to living in the savannah-grassland environments. Examples include the hypothesis that by being bipedal, people were taller and thus exposed less of their body to direct sun and had better exposure to air currents above the grasses. Others suggested that being taller in the savannah-grasslands allowed people to look over the grasses, significantly increasing the areas in which people could search for food and predators. Some suggested that to be effective in the savannah-grasslands, our ancestors may have started scavenging animals killed by others. In this scenario, it is suggested that the primary advantage of bipedalism is that it provides greater endurance than using four limbs. Using four limbs may be faster, but it requires much more energy to power four limbs than two, and people likely had to walk long distances to scavenge.

Over the past few decades, there has been increasing research on both the early humans and the environments in which they lived. Evidence suggests that rather than the first humans living in an open savannah-grassland kind of environment, they were likely living in more of a mixed environment, perhaps with patches of open woodlands, forests, grasslands, and savannahs. The hypotheses that are based on the assumption that bipedalism was an adaptation to the open grasslands and savannahs now accordingly receive little attention.

For many, the best explanations for the transition to bipedalism are based on the assumption that the primary benefit was that it frees the hands. Not needing the forelimbs when moving around means that humans can carry things while standing and moving. In this vein, some believe that it may have been tools that were being carried. This would include tools yet to be discovered, but may include sticks and sharp rocks near impossible to identify millions of years later. It may have been useful, for example, for our early ancestors to be carrying rocks and sticks, to dig edible roots out of the ground, to scare off other scavengers from animal carcasses, or for protection.

Others suggest the principal advantage was to carry food. A common scenario is that our ancestors that were perhaps able to carry food would have an advantage. They could, for example, take advantage of a particularly productive kind of food that was in an otherwise dangerous area (such as a place frequented by lions or dangerous snakes) by gathering the food quickly and carrying it to a tree or other area of safety. Carrying food may also have been associated with food sharing. Some have hypothesized that it is the ability for males to provision females and children with food that was the driver of bipedalism, leading to monogamy. This hypothesis is certainly not without criticism, however, as we are aware that monogamy is not the favored form of marriage in most cultures of the world (see Chapter 11). Others have suggested that the primary advantage of free hands was carrying babies. Presumably being able to carry babies (rather than have them simply hold on to their mothers while moving as other primate babies do) was good for the babies and thus the population.

Some have suggested that the major advantage of bipedalism was for display. There are two aspects of this. For some, the primary advantage of bipedalism was that in threatening situations, standing and moving upright was an advantage. Many animals, including other primates, make themselves look larger as a show of dominance or aggression. Thus, those that could do this on a regular basis became dominant, leading to more sex and more babies who also carried the traits. Another view of the display hypothesis reasons that those that stood upright exposed their genitalia more, leading to more sex and babies that carried the trait. An interesting, but not likely, scenario.

Another hypothesis suggests that bipedalism occurred neither as an adaptation to living in the savannah-grassland, nor as an adaptation to spending significant amounts of time on the ground in a mixed environment. This hypothesis, commonly known as the walking-in-trees hypothesis, suggests that bipedalism evolved as a more efficient way of moving around in trees. It is suggested that our ancestors may have moved like orangutans that often walk along tree limbs in a bipedal way, but using their arms to hold onto branches above. This hypothesis was not given much serious consideration until the 2009 reports that *Ardipithecus ramidus*, which many accept as an early human, had opposable big toes, which would presumably have been an advantage for grasping onto tree limbs while walking.

Table 4.2

Bipedalism—Why and How

Explanations for Becoming Bipedal	Skeletal Changes Accommodating Bipedalism
Carrying model (food, children, rocks, sticks)	Repositioning of foramen magnum
Effective heat management (heat dissipation)	Changes to vertebral column (adding curves)
Greater endurance (energy efficiency)	Changes to the pelvis (widening, basin-shaped, stabilizing weight distribution)
Increasing height (for vision, more food, and display)	Lengthening of the femur (increased stride length)
Walking in trees (e.g., like orangutans)	Modification to knee (allowing full knee extension and locking in place)
	Angling of femur inward
	Changes in the foot (e.g., arch, realignment of big toe)

How to Become Efficiently Bipedal

There are several variations that were selected for to support bipedalism. To be efficiently bipedal, the **foramen magnum** has to be positioned centrally at the base of the skull. This is so the head is balanced properly on the vertebral column (spine). In other primates the foramen magnum is positioned further back in the skull since the vertebral column enters the head from the rear rather than directly below. Curvatures in the vertebral column are another change that likely occurred to facilitate bipedalism. Curves (an S-curve) are generally thought to have been selected for to facilitate the distribution of weight of the upper body and pelvis when upright. Similarly, a broader pelvis was likely selected for to deal with the weight of the upper body. In the lower body, skeletal changes occurring that are widely thought to correlate with bipedalism include angling of the femurs inward from the pelvis to the foot, once again to facilitate the distribution of weight; modifications to the femur and knees to allow a fuller extension; and structural changes in the foot. One change in the foot is the development of an arch, which is thought to help absorb weight as well as adding propulsion to walking. It was once widely thought that the loss of opposability in the big toe was related to bipedalism, but this has been called into question since the discovery of opposable toes in *Ardipithecus ramidus*.

The First Hominins

Sahelanthropus, *Orrorin*, *and* Ardipithecus

There is some uncertainty about which fossil assemblages represent the first hominins. The three primary candidates are genera *Sahelanthropus*, *Orrorin*, and *Ardipithecus*. All were discovered in the Great Rift Valley of East Africa, and collectively date from between seven and four million years ago. There is no consensus that any of these are absolutely hominins, but based on the current assemblages of fossils, these are the best contenders.

Sahelanthropus dates between seven and five million years ago. Hominin-like features include small teeth, no diastema, and the position of foramen magnum indicating bipedalism. Ape-like characteristics, on the other hand, include a relatively small brain, a u-shaped dental arcade, and thin enamel on the teeth.

Orrorin dates to approximately six million years ago. Hominin-like features include a femur indicative of bipedalism, a relatively large body, and small teeth with thick enamel. Ape-like characteristics include ape-like canine teeth in size and shape.

Ardipithecus has two species, and it is *Ardipithecus ramidus* that provides most evidence of being a hominin. Several features of both the cranial and post-cranial skeleton suggest bipedalism, and it has small canine teeth. One of the most interesting aspects of *Ardipithecus ramidus* is that it had opposable big toes, the only hominin or potential hominin in the human lineage with such a feature.

Australopithecus, *Paranthropus*, *and* Kenyanthropus

There is no ambiguity about the genus *Australopithecus*. There is consensus that it is hominin. Some generalizations about the genus include the view that its antiquity ranged from at least 4.2 million to about 1.0 million years ago. It was restricted to Africa, where there were several species with average bodies ranging in size from about 65 pounds and 3.5 feet tall to about 100 pounds and about 5 feet tall. At least some populations probably opportunistically hunted or scavenged. One population of one species of *Australopithecus* likely evolved into the first species of *Homo*, but which one remains debatable. The primary contenders are *afarensis* and *africanus*.

Three species of early hominins exhibit features that are relatively rugged, often termed robust. For lumpers, they are simply different species of *Australopithecus*. For splitters, they represent a different genus—*Paranthropus*. These species are clearly not ancestral to the genus *Homo*. They became extinct about one million years ago.

There is another assemblage that splitters term *Kenyanthropus*. It is quite *Homo*-like and some believe that it, rather than *Australopithecus*, may be ancestral to *Homo*. Lumpers consider it to be *Australopithecus*. The evidence consists of only one skull, and although based on physical characteristics, it does look like a potential *Homo* ancestor, it is difficult for many to support this claim based on such meager evidence.

Table 4.3

The Hominins (Splitter's View)

Genus/Species	Region	Approximate Dates (Range of Antiquity)
THE EARLY CONTENDERS		
Sahelanthropus	Africa	7.0–5.0 million years
Orrorin	Africa	6.0 million years
Ardipithecus	Africa	5.8–4.4 million years
THE AUSTRALOPITHECINES		
anamensis	Africa	4.2–3.9 million years
africanus	Africa	3.5–2.0 million years
afarensis	Africa	3.9–2.9 million years
garhi	Africa	2.5 million years
bahrelghazali	Africa	3.5–3.0 million years
sediba	Africa	2.0–1.8 million years
PARANTHROPUS		
robustus	Africa	2.0–1.0 million years
boisei	Africa	2.0–1.0 million years
aethiopecus	Africa	3.0–2.0 million years
KENYANTHROPUS		
platyops	Africa	3.5 million years
EARLY HOMO		
habilis	Africa	2.5–1.4 million years
rudolphensis	Africa	2.5–1.4 million years
naledi	Africa	not yet determined
MIDDLE HOMO		
erectus	Asia, Africa, Europe	1.7 million–200,000 years
ergaster	Africa	1.8 million–500,000 years
georgicus	Asia	1.7 million years
antecessor	Europe	1.2 million–700,00 years
heidelbergensis	Europe, Africa, Asia	700,000–200,000 years
LATE HOMO		
Neandertal	Europe, Asia	250,000–30,000 years
floresiensis	Asia	75,000–12,000 years
Denisovans	Asia	60,000 years
sapiens (modern)	Africa	200,000–present
	Asia	60,000–present
	Europe	40,000–present
	Americas	20,000–present

A Fossil Find Like No Other

In 2013, anthropologist Lee Berger was made aware of a potential find of early human bones in a narrow cave system in South Africa. Fortunately, Berger was able to enlist the aid of six women scientists with caving experience who could maneuver through the narrow passages. In 2015, the finds and the results of the analysis were made public. More than 1,500 human skeletal elements had been recovered. This is the largest single assemblage of early human fossils in Africa and one of the largest in the world. The specimens exhibit a mosaic of skeletal features, some australopithecine-like and others early *Homo*-like. The researchers interpreted the finds as representing a distinct and hitherto unknown species of human, *Homo naledi*. This species *may* be more than two million years old, but because of the nature of the sediments and lack of association with other animals of known age, determining the actual age is problematic. The people may have been ritually disposed of in the cave chamber, however, since deliberate burial is usually only associated with humans within the last 50,000 years, this too is problematic. It will take time to figure out the place of this assemblage in the story of human evolution—whether, for example, they are ancestral to *sapiens*, or perhaps a more recent group living alongside us tens of thousands of years ago.

The Genus *Homo*

The Emergence and Early Varieties of Homo *to One Million Years Ago*

Out of one population of *Australopithecus*, or perhaps, *Kenyanthropus*, evolved the first members of the genus *Homo*. This probably occurred between 2.5 and 3.0 million years ago. Some recent discoveries in Africa of bone and teeth dating to 2.8 million years ago have been tentatively categorized as *Homo*, but fossil evidence of *Homo* prior to 2.5 million years ago is not incontestable.

Compared to *Australopithecus*, *Homo* is usually characterized as having larger brains, smaller teeth, and a less prognathic face. Whereas the brain size of *Australopithecus* ranged between about 350 and 500 cubic centimeters (cc), the brain size of the first species of *Homo* ranged between about 500 and 800 cc.

These earliest members of *Homo* are referred to by lumpers as *Homo habilis*. Splitters see enough variability to suggest another species as well—*Homo rudolfensis*. The range of antiquity for these early *Homo* is from about 2.5 to 1.4 million years, and like their predecessors, they have only been found in Africa. As outlined in Chapter 5, these early species of *Homo* are the first undisputed makers of stone tools, which is probably associated with meat eating.

The lack of forms with a mosaic of *Australopithecus* and early *Homo* features suggests that the evolution into *Homo* was through punctuated equilibrium. A recently discovered species—*Homo naledi*—exhibits a mosaic of features, but it is known from only one site in Africa and the antiquity is yet to be reliably determined.

Figure 4.4
Reconstructed Head of *Homo erectus*
This reconstruction is based on fossil evidence of skulls and knowledge of primate anatomy. *Homo erectus* lived from about 1.7 million to 200,000 years ago.
Credit: Nadine Ryan

Another variety of human, referred to as *Homo erectus* by the lumpers (and *Homo erectus* and *Homo ergaster* by the splitters), emerged about 1.8 million years ago. They appear in Africa by about 1.8 million years ago and in eastern Asia by 1.6 million years ago. There are also some interesting finds from the Republic of Georgia, dating to about 1.7 million years ago, which some refer to as *Homo erectus*, but which splitters call *Homo georgicus*. *Homo erectus* was larger both in body size and brain size than their predecessors. The average height was likely over five feet tall, but some likely exceeded six feet. The average brain size averaged about 1,000 cc (compared to about 700 cc for the earlier species of *Homo* and the modern average of 1,350 cc). As described in Chapter 5, *Homo erectus* is associated with many cultural developments, including full-scale hunting, the control of fire, and cooking.

Varieties of Homo *over the Last Million Years*

Adaptive radiation of the genus *Homo* has continued over the past million years. Some finds from Spain, classified as *Homo antecessor*, may be ancestral to more recent species, but the evidence is too meager to have confidence. *Homo heidelbergensis* appears about 700,000 years ago, overlapping in time with *Homo erectus*, and may have evolved from *antecessor*.

The transition from *Homo erectus* to *Homo sapiens* is probably more a case of gradualism, rather than punctuated equilibrium. In Africa, Asia, and Europe there are individuals that appear to have a mosaic of features of both *Homo erectus* and *Homo sapiens*. Some anthropologists prefer to describe these individuals as "Archaic *Homo sapiens*," and they first appear about 800,000 years ago. Some prefer to describe some or all of these specimens as *Homo heidelbergensis*.

Neandertals likely evolved from a population of *Homo heidelbergensis* in Europe about 300,000 years ago. Their core territories appear to be focused in Europe but they also inhabited the Middle East until about 50,000 years ago and Asia as far east as Siberia until about 30,000 years ago.

There have been more than a hundred years of debates about whether Neandertals are *Homo sapiens* or a separate species, *Homo neanderthalensis*. Recent DNA research indicates that modern *Homo sapiens* living in Europe and Asia at the same time as Neandertals were able to mate and produce fertile offspring, lending support to the notion that they were simply a subpopulation of *Homo sapiens*.

Modern looking *Homo sapiens* evolved in Africa about 200,000 years ago. There are indications that populations of modern *Homo sapiens* moved into regions of Asia and Europe at least a few times before 50,000 years ago, sharing the lands and resources with others. DNA research indicates that the last significant wave of modern *Homo sapiens* moved out of Africa about 60,000 years ago, and overwhelmed the pre-existing population there, both genetically and culturally.

There have been a few recent discoveries that have challenged conventional thinking about human evolution over the last 50,000 years. One is the discovery of a previously unknown variety of human known as the Denisovans, so-named from the Denisova site in Siberia. Based only on DNA extracted from a finger and a tooth, researchers have identified a previously unknown kind of hominin living in the region between about 50,000 and 30,000 years ago, coexisting with Neandertals and modern *Homo sapiens*.

Another find that has challenged conventional thinking is the discovery of about a dozen very small individuals on Flores Island in Indonesia. These specimens are classified as *Homo floresiensis*, and are commonly referred to as "hobbits." They stood about three feet in height and had a cranial capacity of about 400 cc, smaller than most *australopithecines*, and a brain size roughly that of a chimpanzee. (They do not, however, as far as we can tell, have pointy ears or hairy feet like the hobbits of Middle Earth fame.) Some believe they may simply have been suffering from a disease that causes extreme dwarfism, but most accept they are a newly defined species of human that lived from about 75,000 to 12,000 years ago. Evidence of *Homo erectus* on the island dating to about 700,000 years ago suggests they may be ancestral.

The discovery of *Homo floresiensis* challenges conventional thought in multiple ways. First, a general trend, with few exceptions, in human evolution has been to get larger through time, both in body and brain size. If *Homo floresiensis* is indeed descended from *Homo erectus*, it is an interesting and important means of illustrating the variety of ways people can adapt. Second, there has been a widely held assumption that developments in culture parallel developments in the brain, including

Box 4.3
Neandertals

Neandertals (also spelled Neanderthals) are a very well-known variety of human that occupied much of Europe, the Middle East, and parts of Asia as far east as Siberia. The first evidence of Neandertal was discovered in 1856 in the Neander Valley in Germany, thus the name Neandertal. Although initially discovered in 1856 it was not immediately recognized as an early variety. Recall at this time there was little consideration of human evolution or that the earth had even existed for more than about 6,000 years.

Neandertals probably evolved from *Homo heidelbergensis* in Europe about 300,000 years ago. They lasted in the Middle East until about 50,000 years ago, when they probably could not effectively compete with modern humans there. They remained dominant in Europe until about 40,000 years ago when modern humans moved there. They probably could simply not compete with the modern humans effectively and the remnant populations were pushed to fringe areas, such as Gibraltar and Siberia. The last widely accepted Neandertal died about 27,000 years ago.

Neandertals were typically rugged, with prominent brow ridges, large noses, and powerful limbs. Their average cranial capacity, at 1,450 cc, is about 100 cc larger than the average among modern populations. Their body type is often described as being short and stocky, similar to that of contemporary Eskimos or Inuit. In a similar vein, the body type was probably an effective adaptation to the cold. It is estimated that when Neandertals were living in Europe, the temperature was an average of 10 degrees Celsius colder than present.

Neandertals were adept tool makers, had a diverse diet including many kinds of animals, used spears, and controlled fire. Numerous Neandertal skeletons have been found in caves, leading most to infer that they were deliberately buried, but some archaeologists remain skeptical the burials were deliberate. Similarly claims of Neandertal art, music, and jewelry remain contentious. Neandertals probably hunted effectively with throwing spears, cooked their food, wore clothing (not tailored) and used speech as their primary means of communications. Many believe that for the last 100,000 years they could probably speak as well as modern humans.

Figure 4.5 **Neandertal in a Business Suit**
While generally more rugged than contemporary humans, Neandertals are still clearly human. If one were living in a present-day large city, it might go unnoticed.
Credit: Neandertal Museum

Recent research indicates that although Neandertals were genetically and culturally overwhelmed by modern humans, their DNA lives on. DNA researchers have determined that modern looking *Homo sapiens*, probably arriving from Africa about 65,000 years ago, mated with Neandertals (a good example of gene flow), and some traces of Neandertal DNA remains in almost all people of European and Asian descent.

increases in brain size. Cultural evidence associated with *Homo floresiensis* suggest they were hunting and cooking large animals, including a kind of elephant and komodo dragons, which are deadly lizards that grow up to 10 feet in length and commonly weigh more than 100 pounds. Since the cranial capacity of *Homo flore-siensis* averages only about 400 cc, this poses a serious challenge to the notion that humans were only able to make tools when they achieved a brain size in the range of early *Homo* (i.e., closer to 700 cc).

Summary of Trends in Human Biological Evolution

There are several trends in human biological evolution over the past several million years. Our early ancestors became increasingly more proficient in bipedalism. While *Australopithecus* are properly described as being bipedal, for example, their skeleton was not as fully adapted as later members of the genus *Homo*. With some exceptions, humans have become larger in body size over time, and our brains have also become larger, both in real size and in proportion to the rest of our bodies. The shape of our skulls has changed, most notably with the development of vertical foreheads, and the widest part of our skull is now near the top. Our faces are now less prognathic and our teeth have become smaller.

We don't know for sure, but it is commonly thought that we lost most of our body hair at least a few million years ago as a way to regulate our body tempera-ture, as a response to being active in open areas, such as savannah-grasslands with direct sun, and/or simply spending considerable time being active on two legs, which creates body heat. The primary way of regulating our body temperature is by sweating. The thinking is that as people needed to regulate their body temperature more, either from being in the heat more, or becoming more active, thick body hair would have clogged the sweat glands. Thus, those with less hair were selected for. It isn't actually that people have lost their body hair. We have approximately the same number of hairs as apes. Rather than reducing the quantity of hair follicles, hominin hair got finer, lighter, and shorter.

Probably coincidently with the loss of body hair a million years or more ago, a darker pigmentation was selected for to protect the skin from the intense sun in Africa. As people moved northward into northern regions of Europe and Asia, it is likely that lighter skin was selected for. People need sunlight to create vitamin D in their bodies. Enough sunlight is able to penetrate dark skin in climates with lots of sun, but it becomes a problem in northern climates where there is less intense sun. A lighter skin is beneficial in these conditions.

Box 4.4
Statement on Race

Excerpts from the American Association of Physical Anthropologists Statement on Race

We offer the following points ...

1. All humans living today belong to a single species, *Homo sapiens*, and share a common descent. Although there are differences of opinion regarding how and where different human groups diverged or fused to form new ones from a common ancestral group, all living populations in each of the earth's geographic areas have evolved from that ancestral group over the same amount of time. Much of the biological variation among populations involves modest degrees of variation in the frequency of shared traits....

2. Biological differences between human beings reflect both hereditary factors and the influence of natural and social environments. In most cases, these differences are due to the interaction of both. The degree to which environment or heredity affects any particular trait varies greatly.

3. There is great genetic diversity within all human populations. Pure races, in the sense of genetically homogenous populations, do not exist in the human species today, nor is there any evidence that they have ever existed in the past.

4. There are obvious physical differences between populations living in different geographic areas of the world. Some of these differences are strongly inherited and others, such as body size and shape, are strongly influenced by nutrition, way of life, and other aspects of the environment....

5. For centuries, scholars have sought to comprehend patterns in nature by classifying living things. The only living species in the human family, Homo sapiens, has become a highly diversified global array of populations. The geographic pattern of genetic variation within this array is complex, and presents no major discontinuity....

6. In humankind as well as in other animals, the genetic composition of each population is subject over time to the modifying influence of diverse factors. These include natural selection, promoting adaptation of the population to the environment; mutations, involving modifications in genetic material; admixture, leading to the genetic exchange between local populations; and randomly changing frequencies of genetic characteristics from one generation to another....

7. The human species has a rich past in migration, in territorial expansions, and in contradictions. As a consequence, we are adapted to many of the earth's environments in general, but to none in particular ... Mating between members of different human groups tends to diminish differences between groups, and has played a very important role in human history....

8. Partly as a result of gene flow, the hereditary characteristics of human populations are in a state of perpetual flux....

9. The biological consequences of mating depend only on the individual genetic makeup of the couple, and not on their racial classifications....

10. There is no necessary concordance between biological characteristics and culturally defined groups....

11. Physical, cultural and social environments influence the behavioral differences among individuals in society.... The peoples of the world today appear to possess equal biological potential for assimilating any human culture. Racist political doctrines find no foundation in scientific knowledge concerning modern or past human populations.

The Concept of Race

Race is a term that is used widely in North America, but there is often a misunderstanding that it is a natural or biologically based category. It is not. The category was invented, suggesting race is something akin to a subspecies, identified by a combination of physical and behavioral characteristics.

Many have tried to validate the concept by using a variety of physical qualities to separate people around the globe, but all attempts have failed. There simply are no physical criteria that can separate humans into so-called races. Anthropologists that study human biological variability know that human variation is continuous; it does not cluster in racial categories.

The American Anthropological Association Statement on "Race" reads, in part:

> ..."race" was a mode of classification linked specifically to peoples in the colonial situation. It subsumed a growing ideology of inequality devised to rationalize European attitudes and treatment of the conquered and enslaved peoples. Proponents of slavery in particular during the 19th century used "race" to justify the retention of slavery ... and provided the rationalization that the inequality was natural or God-given.... The tragedy in the United States has been that the policies and practices stemming from this worldview succeeded all too well in constructing unequal populations among European, Native Americans, and peoples of African descent.

More on the concept of race is covered in Box 4.4 and in Chapter 8.

Summary

Mirroring the Learning Objectives stated in the chapter opening, the key points are:

- There are multiple important aspects of palaeoanthropology to understand. Researchers often revisit the same localities to look for sites. Principal dating techniques include potassium argon, radiocarbon, and Dating by Association. Palaeoanthropologists need to have a good understanding of osteology and taphonomy, and there are often debates about how best to classify various specimens.
- There are several reasons why bipedalism may have evolved, and several skeletal changes occurred to make it workable. Most anthropologists think the primary reason why bipedalism occurred was because it freed the hands to carry things while moving. Biological changes that occurred include

repositioning the foramen magnum, adding curves to the spinal column, widening the pelvis, and changes in the foot.

- There have been many varieties of hominins over the past several million years. Often there were multiple species coexisting at the same time. The precise ancestral line leading to modern humans is not known. It appears likely, however, that the first members of the genus *Homo* emerged from a population of one Australopithicus species. From the earliest members of the genus *Homo* multiple other varieties of humans evolved.

- There are exceptions, but the general trends in human biological evolution include becoming more efficiently bipedal, becoming larger, increasing brain size, and reducing prognathism.

- Race is not a valid biological concept.

REVIEW QUESTIONS

1. What are the basic methods, concepts, and issues in palaeoanthropology?
2. What are the principal explanations for becoming bipedal and skeletal changes that accommodated it?
3. What are the widely recognized genera and species of humans?
4. Why is "race" not a valid biological category?

DISCUSSION QUESTIONS

1. How can basic evolutionary concepts such as mutation, gene flow, genetic drift, and punctuated equilibrium be applied to human biological evolution?
2. What are some of the advantages and disadvantages of having no fixed criteria for assigning specimens to a specific genus or species?

Visit **www.lensofanthropology.com** for the following additional resources:

SELF-STUDY QUESTIONS   **WEBLINKS**   **FURTHER READING**

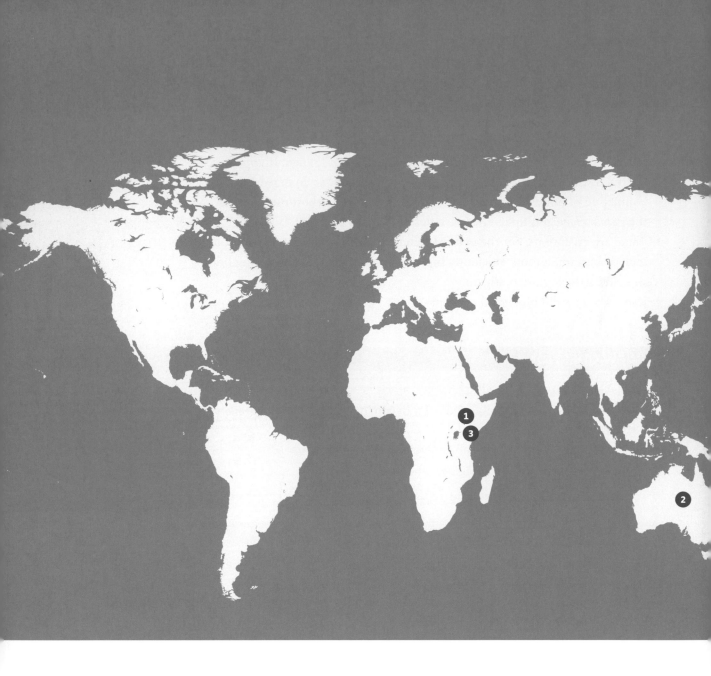

PLACES MENTIONED IN CHAPTER 5

1 Lomekwi, Kenya
2 Australia
3 Olorgesaillie, Kenya

HUMAN CULTURAL EVOLUTION FROM 2.5 MILLION TO 20,000 YEARS AGO

Our distant ancestors were cultural—
maybe not opera, but fire, tools, and art
for sure #humanculturalevolution

Learning Objectives

In this chapter students will learn:

- what constitutes the archaeological record.
- the problems with archaeological visibility and bias.
- the major cultural developments before 20,000 years ago.
- the sequence of territorial expansion.

Introduction

Chapter 4 outlined the last several million years of human biological evolution. This chapter focuses on the corresponding elements of culture associated with humans, from its first undisputed physical manifestation about 2.5 million years ago to 20,000 years ago. So, while Chapter 4 essentially provided an overview of evolution from a biological anthropological perspective, this chapter provides an overview from the perspective of archaeology. It is important to understand the nature of archaeology and potential problems associated with it, so the chapter begins with this coverage.

Figure 5.1
Projectile Points
Stone tools, such as these projectile points, are a common kind of artifact found throughout the world. People have been making stone tools for about 3 million years, although stone points usually date to within the last 100,000.

Credit: Nadine Ryan

The Archaeological Record

As with the fossil record, there is no consensus on precisely what is meant by the term **archaeological record**. At a minimum, it is taken to mean the actual physical remains of human activities that have been recorded by archaeologists. Some expand the definition to include, in addition to the recorded remains, all the records associated with archaeological investigations in the field and remains (e.g., catalogs, maps, photographs, reports on excavations). Others use the term *archaeological record* to refer to the basic facts about the past, based on the physical remains of human activity.

The primary database of archaeology is the physical remains of human activities. These may include, but are certainly not restricted to, human biological remains. The other major kinds of material remains investigated by archaeologists include **archaeological sites**, **artifacts**, **features**, **ecofacts**, and **cultural landscapes**.

An archaeological site can be broadly defined as any location with physical evidence of past human activity. In practical terms, archaeologists often narrow what will be described as an archaeological site based on a minimum age or number of artifacts. Major kinds of sites, recorded by archaeologists, especially in the time before 20,000 years ago, include **base camps**, **habitation sites**, **pictographs**, and **resource processing sites**.

Base camps are generally recognized by the presence of artifacts and ecofacts, often in specific patterns that can be identified as a feature. Some of the earliest archaeological sites, for example, appear to be base camps where people were carrying out butchering activities, reflected in discrete accumulations of lithic tools and butchered bones. In very early times, such as before about 500,000 years ago, it is difficult to ascertain if these camps where processing was occurring were also used for habitation.

The term *habitation site* is based on the inference that people were living at the site, at least on a temporary basis. As will be described in more detail in Chapter 6, people did not begin to live in permanent settlements until about 10,000 years ago, but it is very likely that they spent at least several days and perhaps weeks or months in the same camp for at least several hundred thousand years.

Rock art includes pictographs, which are paintings on immovable rock surfaces, such as boulders, cliff faces, or cave walls. Another kind of rock art is petroglyphs, which are engravings made on rock surfaces. Rock art begins appearing in the archaeological record about 40,000 years ago.

Resource processing sites include areas where the physical remains indicate people were harvesting resources (e.g., hunting, gathering, scavenging) and/or processing them, including butchering. It is also used to describe areas where people were obtaining raw materials such as stone for artifact manufacture (often referred to as a quarry), and/or where they made artifacts from the stone.

An artifact may be broadly defined as any object that has been manufactured or modified, or that shows evidence of being used by people. Many archaeologists, especially in North America, also make the distinction that it must be portable. As with the definition of an archaeological site, in practice archaeologists often use a more narrow definition. Some archaeologists, for example, may choose only to catalog an intended tool as an artifact and not the waste flakes removed from the original cobble of stone. Other archaeologists may choose to catalog the waste flakes as artifacts as well.

A feature is defined as a nonportable entity that has clearly been created by humans. Common examples include **hearths**, **lithic scatters**, **middens**, and shelter or house structures. A fire hearth indicates a discrete, contained fire. It does not necessarily have to have a ring of stone around it, but a fire hearth is usually about the size of a campfire. Evidence of fire is common in archaeological sites, but it is often difficult to be certain that fires were cultural rather than natural. Lithic scatters, meaning the accumulation of waste flakes created and left behind from the manufacture of lithic (stone) tools, are common. Middens are discrete accumulations of trash. It is apparent that people have never liked to live among their trash, so once people started to stay in one place for several days, they started to separate their trash from their living space. This is convenient for archaeologists, since it is easier to identify a midden than widely scattered trash. Shelters or house structures are often identified by depressions in the ground surface, which people created as a sort of foundation or to level the floor. They may also be identified by a pattern in the sediments, indicating posts from wooden poles were once there (known in archaeology as post-holes), or other alterations to the ground surface (including pathways, ditches, and sediments brought from elsewhere for flooring).

Ecofacts include plant and animal remains. Archaeologists are interested in ecofacts for two primary reasons. They are used to make inferences about (i) **palaeoenvironments** and (ii) diet. Plants and animals in archaeological sites, even if they occur naturally, provide indications of the kind of weather and climate people were adapting to. Of course, plants and animals also are important for determining what kinds of food people were eating. If ecofacts are to be used for reconstructing diet, however, it is important that they be in a good cultural context, such as a midden, or show use of modification by people, such as butchering marks on bone or evidence of cooking.

Plant remains in archaeological sites are commonly referred to as botanical remains or floral remains, and include seeds, nuts, pollen, **phytoliths**, and wood. Since they are organic, plant remains do not tend to preserve well, and therefore they are often rare or absent in archaeological sites. Charred wood, however, is often found where people had fires. Burning removes nutrients from wood, so the micro-organisms that contribute to decay tend to leave it alone. Plant remains, where they exist in sites older than 20,000 years, are often only visible microscopically.

Animal remains, also known as **faunal remains** in archaeology, may include any part of an animal, including bone, teeth, shell, hide, hair, fur, nails, claws, and internal soft tissue. Bones are easier to identify in archaeological sites than plant remains. This is at least partially due to the fact that bone preserves better than plant tissue, and archaeologists must be careful to recognize this bias when make inferences about diet (e.g., fewer plants at a site do not necessarily indicate few plants in the diet).

The Problems of Archaeological Visibility and Bias

When examining the archaeological record of human culture, one has to consider that it is vastly incomplete. Many aspects of human culture have what archaeologists describe as low archaeological visibility, meaning they are difficult to identify archaeologically. Archaeologists tend to focus on tangible (or material) aspects of culture: things that can be handled and photographed, such as tools, food, and structures. Reconstructing intangible aspects of culture is more difficult, requiring that one draw more inferences from the tangible. It is relatively easy, for example, for archaeologists to identify and draw inferences about technology and diet from stone tools and food remains. Using the same kinds of physical remains to draw inferences about social systems and what people were thinking about is more difficult. Archaeologists do it, but there are necessarily more inferences involved in getting from physical remains recognized as trash to making interpretations about belief systems.

Other things to consider include the fact that, in general, the further back in time one goes, the less visible evidence of culture will be. This is due to multiple reasons, including the fact that (i) the older a site is, the more likely it will be covered up; (ii) the older the site, the less likely organic remains will be preserved; (iii), the further one goes back in time, the fewer the number of humans there were to leave physical evidence; (iv) the further one goes back in time, the fewer the kinds of physical evidence of culture there were (e.g., first only tools, then shelters, etc.). Also, until about 10,000 years ago, most human groups were fairly mobile, moving within territories and peripheral areas, but not likely settling for months at a time in the same place, where trash could accumulate (making it more visible).

Archaeologists also recognize that most archaeological sites have already been destroyed by both natural and cultural processes. Archaeologists appreciate that the earth is a very dynamic system, ever changing the landscape, and often destroying or burying archaeological sites through a wide variety of processes, sometimes catastrophic (such as by glaciations, landslides, and tsunamis) and sometimes more gradual (such as through erosion). Archaeological sites near water are particularly susceptible, since sea levels have fluctuated widely in the past (only stabilizing in their current position about 5,000 years ago), lakes are often temporary, and rivers and streams often change course.

Humans, as well, lead to the loss of archaeological visibility. Many human activities lead to the loss of archaeological sites, both known and unknown. Every time landscapes are altered, there is a good chance archaeological sites are being destroyed or buried. Some archaeological sites remain intact but are no longer visible due to the modifications on the surface.

There are other kinds of biases to consider as well. Archaeologists recognize that there is a very strong bias toward inorganic materials, such as stone and ceramic artifacts, simply because they preserve better than inorganic materials. There is also a bias toward things recognized as trash and sites that were deliberately abandoned. Although there are exceptions, the overwhelming majority of artifacts recovered were recognized as trash by the people who left them. Similarly, most archaeological sites were deliberately abandoned. Like many disciplines, archaeology has suffered from a male bias, especially insofar as the history of the discipline has tended to be dominated by male archaeologists focusing on activities long thought of as primarily male activities, such as hunting. Fortunately, this male bias has diminished in recent decades, especially due to the significant increase in women becoming archaeologists.

Another important kind of bias to consider is that of place. Especially in regard to the time period before 20,000 years ago, there has been a strong bias toward archaeological research in East Africa and Europe. Much of what we know, for example, of the archaeology of early humans comes from the Great Rift Valley in Africa. This is understandable since so much research has been done there. However, it should be appreciated that there may be many other areas where early humans were active, but these areas simply have not been examined. There is also a strong Eurocentric bias in archaeology. This is not totally surprising, since archaeology itself developed in Europe. Nonetheless, we should be aware that although much of the focus in archaeology is on Europe, this is at least partially due to the interests in Europe, by Europeans. It is common, for example, to accept that many of the great cultural achievements, such as cave art, deliberate human burial, ceramic technology, spear throwers, and more, all developed in Europe. They may have, but we should not lose sight of the fact that not all areas have received as much attention by archaeologists as they have in Europe, especially during the period before 20,000 years ago.

Overview of Cultural Evolution to 20,000 Years Ago

Principal Cultural Periods

Archaeologists use frameworks when referring to prehistory. The most common for the period before 20,000 years ago are outlined in Table 5.1. Essentially, **Palaeolithic** means "Old Stone Age," with the prefix *Palaeo* meaning ancient or old, and *lithic* meaning stone. **Lower Palaeolithic** is used widely to describe the peoples and cultures associated with *Homo habilis* and *Homo erectus* (lumper's view); **Middle Palaeolithic** is often equated with the people and cultures associated with Archaic *Homo sapiens*, *Homo heidelbergensis*, and *Neandertals*; and **Upper Palaeolithic** (rarely used outside of Europe) primarily refers to the culture and peoples who replaced Neandertals in Europe beginning about 40,000 years ago. The range of antiquity is approximate, and varies among archaeologists and regions.

Table 5.1
Principal Cultural Periods 2.5 Million to 20,000 Years Ago

Period	Antiquity	Region
Lower Palaeolithic	c. 2.5 million–500,000 years ago	Africa, Asia, Europe
Middle Palaeolithic	c. 500,000–40,000 years ago	Africa, West Asia, Europe
Upper Palaeolithic	c. 40,000–12,000 years ago	Mostly Europe

Table 5.2
Principal Cultural Developments Prior to 20,000 Years Ago

Period	Cultural Developments
Lower Palaeolithic	First undisputed evidence of culture, in the form of stone tools, likely created and used by *Homo habilis*. Flakes of stone were chipped off one end of a cobble; the now sharp cobble was used as a tool, as were sometimes the flakes themselves. This technology is often referred to as Oldowan. *Homo erectus* made more complex tools, characterized by the Acheulean handax. *Homo erectus* likely controlled fire, had base camps and a division of labor. Hunting and meat eating was probably opportunistic or small-scale among early *Homo*, but a major part of the subsistence strategy among *Homo erectus*.
Middle Palaeolithic	Continued advances in lithic technology and evidence of finely crafted spears by 400,000 years ago. Some suggestion of deliberate burials, art, and jewelry, but the evidence is debatable. Peoples extended territories into northern latitudes.
Upper Palaeolithic	Continued advances in technology. Undisputed evidence of deliberate human burials and art. Invention of atlatl (spear thrower).

Table 5.2 provides an overview of the principal cultural developments in each period.

Subsistence and Diet

There are many ways to reconstruct prehistoric diets. These include finding plant and animal remains in good cultural context, examining residue left on artifacts, and examining isotopes in human skeletons. These are covered more fully in Box 5.1.

The earliest members of the genus *Homo* likely depended primarily on plant foods, but incorporated more meat in their diet than their australopithecine ancestors. Beginning about 2.5 million years ago, animal bones and stone tools indicate that meat eating became important. Accumulations of animal bones with evidence of butchery by stone tools appear, and many stone tools, presumably used for butchery, appear as well. These bones and tools are usually associated with *Homo habilis*. The significance of meat in the diet of early humans is debatable, but it is fairly clear that for at least some, meat became an important resource.

One of the biggest debates in the study of early human culture focuses on whether our ancestors transitioned to hunting via a period of scavenging. Many believe that scavenging animals killed by lions or other predators on the savannah would have made some sense. Presumably, early humans would not have been able to scare the large predators off a fresh kill, but they could have cleared scavengers such as wild dogs, hyenas, or vultures at least temporarily using rocks and sticks, which would have allowed some humans to move to the fresh kill and remove meat. There is relatively little evidence, however, for the scavenging hypothesis. Some

Box 5.1
Reconstructing Diet

Archaeologists have several ways of reconstructing the diet of people living in prehistoric times.

Major kinds of remains that archaeologists use include (i) plant and animal remains in cultural context, (ii) humans skeletal remains, (iii) coprolites, (iv) human soft tissue, and (v) residue on artifacts.

Plant and animal remains in good cultural context is one of the most common ways to study diet. However, archaeologists need to be confident that the remains represented food rather than naturally occurring plants and animals or those used for other cultural reasons. Some of the ways cultural context is inferred is if the remains show evidence of cooking, if they are in a discrete midden associated with other refuse, if they are in a distinct fire hearth, or if the bones show evidence of butchery with a tool.

An analysis of the bones and teeth of human skeletons provides good indications of major food groups. An analysis of specific kinds of carbon isotopes, for example, can indicate a diet based on different kinds of grasses, shrubs, or fruits. Isotope analysis can also indicate the amount of marine versus terrestrial resource in the diet. The amount of meat in the diet is reflected in trace elements. A diet rich in meat, for example, will usually include high levels of copper and zinc.

Coprolites, the word used by archaeologists to mean preserved human feces, are an excellent way of determining diet. Depending on the diet and health of the person, they may appear as cylinders, pellets, or pads. Some reports suggest that when remains are reconstituted for analysis, the smell sometimes comes back. Archaeologists examine the coprolites, trying to identify partially digested food fragments, such as seeds and small bones. The oldest reported human coprolites date to about one million years ago in Africa and 250,000 years ago in Asia, but whether these are human is in some doubt, and there are no reports of them being studied. The largest recorded coprolite came from a Viking; it measured 23 cm in length and indicated previous meals of meat and bread. The man also had intestinal worms.

Soft tissue and residue on artifacts are other ways of determining diet. When archaeologists find preserved bodies they are often able to determine diet by examining stomach contents, but since soft tissue does not preserve well, using this method is not common. Residue analysis includes a chemical analysis of food remains in or on artifacts. Residue in pottery, for example, also provides an indication of the kind of food or beverage stored in the pot. An analysis of residue on a projectile point or butchery tool can indicate the animal by its blood.

support is offered in the identification of large animal bones smashed in a particular way with a rock to extract marrow. Perhaps once the scavengers had left a kill, humans moved in to extract the marrow that scavengers could not.

Others think it unlikely that humans ever went through a scavenging phase. The reasoning is that while scavenging may occur among contemporary human foragers, it is rare and opportunistic, rather than a planned strategy. Those who dispute a scavenging phase also point to the knowledge that nonhuman primates that eat meat hunt rather than scavenge.

Box 5.2

Was Cooking the Driving Force of Human Evolution?

Anthropologists are often interested in the driving force of human evolution. One popular hypothesis is that the driving force was cooking. The hypothesis is valid, but is not widely accepted. It makes sense to many, but skepticism remains because of the lack of evidence in the archaeological record, including the lack of evidence for the control of fire close to two million years ago.

The person most often associated with the hypothesis that cooking was the driving force of human evolution is Richard Wrangham, who outlined his hypothesis in the book *Catching Fire: How Cooking Made Us Human*, published in 2009. He summarizes his idea as follows:

> I believe the transformative moment that gave rise to the genus *Homo*, one of the great transformations in the history of life, stemmed from the control of fire and the advent of cooked meals. Cooking increased the value of our food. It changed our bodies, our brains, our use of time, and our social lives. It made us consumers of external energy and thereby created an organism with a new relationship to nature, dependent on fuel. (p. 2)

Wrangham suggests that the initial change that made us human was increased meat eating about 2.5 million years ago (associated with *Homo habilis*), followed by cooking about 1.8 million years ago (associated with *Homo erectus*). He describes the value of cooking:

Cooked food does many familiar things. It makes our food safer, creates rich and delicious tastes, and reduces spoilage. Heating can allow us to open, cut, or mash tough foods. But none of these advantages is as important as a little-appreciated aspect: cooking increases the amount of energy our bodies obtain from our food.

The extra energy gave the first cooks biological advantages. They survived and reproduced better than before. Their genes spread. Their bodies responded by biologically adapting to cooked food, shaped by natural selection to take maximum advantage of the new diet. There were changes in anatomy, physiology, ecology, life history, psychology, and society. Fossil evidence indicates that this dependence arose not just some tens of thousands of years ago, or even a few hundred thousand, but right back at the beginning of our time on Earth, at the start of human evolution, by the habiline that become *Homo erectus*. (pp. 13–14)

In humans, because we have adapted to cooked food, its spontaneous advantages are complemented by evolutionary benefits. The evolutionary benefits stem from the fact that digestion is a costly process that can account for a high proportion of an individual's energy budget—often as much as locomotion does. After our ancestors started eating cooked food every day, natural selection favored those with small guts, because they were able to digest their food well, but at a lower cost than before. The result was increased energetic efficiency. (p. 40)

While it is widely accepted that early *Homo* incorporated some meat in their diet, the significance of meat and the adoption of hunting strategies clearly increased with the emergence of *Homo erectus*. The driving force may be linked with the use of fire for cooking, although this idea is controversial. (See Box 5.2.)

There is considerable evidence that hunting, at least for the past few hundred thousand years, included big game such as mammoths and mastodons. This would undoubtedly have required group cooperation, such as several people ambushing and targeting one specific animal. It is likely that hunting big game often occurred when the animals were most vulnerable, such as when crossing water. Hunting big game would have likely been a dangerous activity in early times, especially before the invention of throwing spears about half a million years ago. Prior to this, hunting even small and medium-size game likely depended on thrusting spears (i.e., held in the hands while thrusting into the animal). Some have suggested that hunting may have occurred by chasing animals until they died from exhaustion. This technique is called persistence hunting and essentially means that a small group of people would simply chase a selected animal, perhaps for days, until the animal died from exhaustion. This makes sense to some since, while most game animals are quite quick over short distances, they usually cannot maintain the quickness over long distances. Bipedalism in humans, on the other hand, leads to extended endurance. People may not be as quick as some animals over short distances, but they can outlast them over long distances.

Social Systems

Inferences about the number and organization of people living during the Palaeolithic is based on (i) analogy with nonhuman primates and human foragers of recent and contemporary times and (ii) archaeological evidence. Analogy with nonhuman primates and human foragers suggests that a group size of approximately 25 to 30 people was common. Membership would likely have been fluid (meaning that people could come and go), and groups would almost certainly have been exogamous (meaning that upon reaching mating age members would find partners from outside the group). Because of exogamy, no group lived in isolation. People from various bands would have known and interacted with neighboring bands.

There is little evidence of social stratification in the Palaeolithic, suggesting groups were mostly egalitarian. This is assumed by the fairly equitable distribution of resources within habitation sites. Stratification likely started in the Upper Palaeolithic.

There has likely been a division of labor based on sex for close to two million years. This is based on analogy with nonhuman primates that hunt and with human foragers. As mentioned in Chapter 2, when nonhuman primates hunt, it is mostly the males that are involved and meat is often shared, including with females. It is a similar situation when human foragers hunt. It is primarily a male activity, and the meat is shared. This is not to imply that males were more important than females in subsistence activities. For example, what we have learned from human foragers is that while meat obtained by men is shared, so are the plant foods collected by women, and it is often the plant foods that are more important for daily nutrition.

It should be recognized that this explanation of the division of labor is based primarily on inference; archaeological remains provide no incontrovertible evidence for it. Besides the analogies from nonhuman primates and contemporary human foragers, however, it makes sense to many that women were not usually involved in hunting, because it would have been difficult to hunt when pregnant or caring for a child. The division of labor also likely created the need for a home base, a place where both males and females could return to at the end of the day.

Controlling Fire

One of the most important achievements in the development of human culture was the ability to control fire. It is difficult to underestimate the importance of fire in human evolution. It provides warmth, light, protection, enhances diet, and provides a focus for social interaction.

Anthropologists are uncertain about when or why people started controlling fire, but archaeological evidence suggests that it has been common for at least tens of thousands of years, probably hundreds of thousands, and for perhaps almost two million years. Evidence comes from a variety of sources, including remnants of fires themselves, such as charred wood or ash, as well as things that have been heated, including bone, stone, and clay.

Problems for archaeologists include determining whether the remnants of fire they observe are natural or cultural. Similarly, determining whether a bone or stone in an archaeological deposit has been heated by a natural or culturally controlled fire is problematic. Even if heated bones are found in a cave with other cultural remains, there is often some uncertainty over whether the heated bones were cooked by people or whether perhaps some other animal scavenged a burned bone and brought it to the cave.

The ability to control fire was significant. It enabled more kinds of foods to be eaten, and increased the nutritional value of some. By providing light, it increased the practices that required or were enabled by light. By providing heat, it enabled the expansion into territories otherwise too cold. It also afforded protection from most animals, and provided a focus for social interaction. Eventually, it also enabled advances in technology, such as heating rocks to enable better fracturing qualities, making ceramics, and strengthening wooden spears and other artifacts. In recent times, fire has also been used in subsistence activities, such as lighting fires behind

Figure 5.2
Fire
Humans have probably been controlling fire for hundreds of thousands of years.
Credit: Dalourdumonde/ Shutterstock

herd animals to drive them, deliberately burning vegetation to speed the release of nutrients back into the soil, or providing a different kind of vegetation regrowth preferred by animals used in the diet.

Fire is also associated with religion and ritual. Anders Kaliff (2011:51) describes it in this context:

> The shaping of human culture is closely linked to the domestication of fire. The art of making fire has given humans the ability to survive in environments where it would not otherwise have been conceivable and has made it possible to cook food whose nutritional value could not otherwise have been fully utilized. This has formed us as people, shaping our conceptual world. Fire has been particularly significant for eschatology and the form taken by burial rituals, but also for cosmology as a whole and thus as a sacrificial medium.... It is therefore scarcely surprising that the enigmatic nature of fire has given it a divine character, that it has even been regarded as a divinity in itself.

Although some anthropologists believe humans started controlling fire almost two million years ago (see Box 5.2), most anthropologists are comfortable with claims ranging from a few hundred to several hundred thousand years ago. This comfort level usually comes from the quantity of evidence in cultural sites, even though some uncertainty remains, not so much in whether it is evidence of fire, but rather if it is evidence of natural or culturally controlled fire. Most archaeologists agree that the evidence of widespread control of fire by about 40,000 years ago is indisputable.

When people began to start fires is unknown, but it probably dates to the Upper Palaeolithic. The most common technique of starting fires in the distant past was likely by generating heat through the consistent friction of one stick against a stationary piece of wood, surrounded by some flammables such as dried botanical remains. However, the archaeological visibility of these items is very low, since they are unlikely to preserve, and if they did, they may be difficult to recognize. Another way of starting fire was by creating sparks by hitting certain types of rocks together. Archaeologists have found these kinds of rocks in European Upper Palaeolithic sites, showing evidence of repeated striking in the same place, something akin to an Upper Palaeolithic lighter.

Evolution of Technology

The evolution of technology during Palaeolithic times is profound. In particular, the differences in the levels of sophistication of lithic technology are astounding. Research on the average amount of cutting edge produced from a single pound of stone, for example, shows that the earliest members of the genus *Homo* (*habilis*/

rudolfensis) were able to create an average of 2 inches of cutting edge per pound of stone. *Homo erectus* was able to create an average of 8 inches of cutting edge. People living during the Middle Palaeolithic manufactured an average of 40 inches of cutting edge per pound of stone; and those of the Upper Palaeolithic (at least those in Europe) an astounding 120 inches of cutting edge per pound.

The early stone tools are often referred to as **Oldowan** or **Acheulean**. Oldowan are usually associated with *Homo habilis* and were typically made from a cobblestone with a few to several flakes struck off one side of one end, creating what is known as a unifacial tool (or unifacial chopper). These would have been quite effective for many purposes, including butchering animals, sharpening sticks, and perhaps even digging roots and cutting plants. In addition to the cobble itself with flakes removed, some of the larger flakes were also used, presumably for cutting.

In 2015, researchers reported discovering in Africa what may be the oldest known human tools, dating to 3.3 million years ago. Predating the Oldowan by several hundred thousand years, these apparent stone cobble and flake tools are different enough from Oldowan ones that the researchers suggest a new name for the tool-making industry or tradition: **Lomekwian**. Dating them to 3.3 million years is important insofar as they may provide the first evidence of tools created by *Australopithecus* or *Kenyanthropus*, or push back the origin of *Homo* to this time. Whether the finds truly represent a 3.3-million-year-old discovery of human tools remains debatable, however, and it may take some years before they are widely accepted or rejected.

Acheulean tools are associated with *Homo erectus*, and were typically bifacial, meaning flakes were taken off both sides. There are several recognizable kinds of Acheulean tools, but none receive as much interest as the Acheulean hand ax. Thousands of hand axes have been recorded but their function remains an enigma. Explanations range from the hand ax merely representing a core left behind after flakes for artifacts had been removed, to their being multifunctional tools, throwing weapons, and ways to express sexual fitness or goodwill. These notions are explained more fully in Box 5.3.

Anthropologists are not certain when projectiles may have first been used, but it is widely assumed that spear technology was in practice by at least several hundred thousand years ago. One of the problems, of course, is that spears are unlikely to be preserved; it seems probable to many that the first spears were sharpened sticks that were thrust rather than thrown. The first undisputed throwing spears are dated to 400,000 years ago and associated with *Homo heidelbergensis* in Germany. Attaching stone points to the ends of spears likely started about 100,000 years ago.

The first evidence of an **atlatl** (spear thrower) appears in Europe, about 30,000 years ago. An atlatl is essentially an extension of the arm. It requires shorter spears (commonly known as darts) and results in better distance, accuracy, and velocity

The Acheulean Hand Ax —Tool, Core, or Something Sexual?

The Acheulean hand ax (Figure 5.3) is an enigma. They are associated with *Homo erectus*, starting to appear in the archaeological record about 1.7 million years ago and continuing their basic form for more than one million years. Many are often found at the same site, such as at Olorgesailie (Figure 4.1).They are typically about the size of a human hand, tear-drop shaped, with flakes taken off both sides and usually the entire surface, pointed at one end, sharp around the entire circumference and weighted near the base, where it is also usually the thickest.

Their function remains unknown, but there are many ideas, some rather strange. Many suggest they may be multifunctional, to the extent that some refer to them as Swiss Army Rocks. In this view, they could variously be used for cutting, piercing, and scraping, for example. Others suggest the hand axes were merely the cores left behind after all the desired flakes had been removed. Some archaeologists believe they were thrown at animals as a hunting technique. Experiments with throwing them like a discus indicated this is certainly a possibility and would explain the weight distribution, shape, and cutting surface all around.

Figure 5.3 **Acheulean Hand Axes**
A characteristic tool of *Homo erectus*. Their precise function is unknown, but it is unlikely they were commonly held in the hand and used like an ax.
Credit: Nadine Ryan

Where it gets a bit strange is with the idea that the hand axes were created by men to influence women, leading to a kind of sexual selection process, with the women presumably favoring the men who made the best nonfunctional hand axes. A difficult hypothesis to test. An equally difficult hypothesis to test is that the hand axes were created as a show of trustworthiness or goodwill to others.

Most archaeologists reject the "sexy hand ax" and the "trustworthy" hypotheses and are more inclined to believe that they had a specific technological function, that they were some kind of tool or weapon. Despite their name, they were probably never used as a hand ax.

than by throwing by hand alone. Typically an atlatl was made of a piece of wood about one meter long, with a stopper at one end. A dart would be placed on the atlatl, with one end resting against the stopper. The thrower would move the atlatl much like a tennis racket in an overhand "serving" motion, releasing the dart (held between the fingers and thumb).

There is some suggestion that bow and arrow technology may have emerged as early as 65,000 years ago in Africa, but there is no consensus that the evidence is good enough to make the claim. There only exists a small point from that time period, of the size that may have been used on an arrow. Most archaeologists are more comfortable with bows and arrows emerging much more recently (no earlier than the Upper Palaeolithic, and probably more recent than that).

Art and Ideology

Art is an area of considerable interest in archaeology, especially considering its origins. Some believe that engravings on shell dating to about 500,000 years ago are evidence of art, but there is no consensus that they in fact represent art. The engravings were discovered in 2014 by a researcher analyzing shells collected from a *Homo erectus* site excavated in Asia about 100 years earlier. There is some question about the association of the shells with human remains, the dates the engravings were made, and whether the engravings are cultural or perhaps due to some taphonomic process. It is not uncommon to see reports of archaeologists making claim to evidence of art 100,000 years or more ago in Africa, or evidence of art among Neandertal, but there is likewise no consensus that the inferences are well supported. Disputes arise about the dating of the deposits and the inferences that the presence of ochre exists in a site, or that incised bone is in fact art.

The earliest undisputed evidence of art dates to about 40,000 years ago. Most of the art known around the world between about 40,000 and 20,000 years ago is found in caves in Europe. In 2014, some art reported to be 40,000 years old was also found in caves in Indonesia.

Art in the archaeological record, especially **cave art** or **rock art**, is often linked with religion and ritual. Cave art and rock art before 20,000 years ago is usually associated with shamanism, although it is not necessarily restricted to only shamans creating the art. Examples include paintings meant to manipulate supernatural powers, such as to ensure the ongoing fertility of animals or ensure success in hunting. This is supported by the fact that many of the paintings depict animals that were routinely hunted, or that were pregnant or had spears in them, and fertility symbols. As well, most of the paintings were done in the most remote parts of caves, and the images are often superimposed on each other. It is apparent to most that at least in some cases, it was the process of painting, rather than the product, that was most important.

Artifacts commonly referred to as Venus figurines are often categorized as art. They are associated with the European Upper Palaeolithic, and often described within the contexts of erotica (see Box 5.4).

Box 5.4

Upper Palaeolithic Figurines —Not Just Erotica

Approximately 200 small human-shaped figurines, mostly female, have been recovered from archaeological sites in Europe and Asia. They date to the Upper Palaeolithic time period; are constructed from stone, bone, ivory, and clay (Figure 5.5); and are commonly referred to as Venus figurines.

In both scholarly and mainstream media, the focus is often on the sexual characteristics, such as explicit genitalia and large breasts, and they are usually described in the context of being sexual objects. They are generally assumed to have something to do with sexuality, fertility, or gender. Some refer to them as goddess figures.

The notion that these figurines are best considered in the context of sexuality is critically examined by archeologists April Nowell and Melanie Chang (2014) in an article titled "Science, the Media, and Interpretations of Upper Palaeolithic Figurines." They challenge the common assumptions, for example, that

Figure 5.5

Upper Palaeolithic Figurine
Figurines such as this are usually described as art. Hundreds of figurines, made from stone, clay, and ivory, have been recovered from archaeological sites in Europe.
Credit: Nadine Ryan

they were made by men for men, that they are something like a prehistoric Barbie doll, that their function was to educate or titillate men, or that they may have been some kind of trophy commemorating acts of violence against women. The authors also challenge the assumptions that most are representing women specifically, showing that some represent men and others depict animals.

Nowell and Chang suggest that alternative contexts and hypothesis be examined, including how the figurines may have been created and used to maintain alliances, how they may have been used in rituals, or how they may have perhaps served as some kind of charm or totem. Alternatively, they could be considered in the context of art, including as self-portraits. Instead of focusing primarily on sexuality, the authors suggest, they should be studied in the same way as other artifacts from the period are: with the examination of material, technology, skill, modification, decoration, and reuse. They further suggest that the study of the figurines in the context of sexuality and the follow-up media reports say more about the archaeologists and media than they do about the figurines or life in the Palaeolithic.

Ideology is perhaps the most difficult aspect of prehistoric human culture to reconstruct. Art is one way to reconstruct ideology, and the treatment of the dead, primarily in the form of burials, is another. At a minimum, burials are usually taken as reverence for the dead. Often, they are used to infer a belief in an afterlife. The idea that they represent a belief in an afterlife is especially supported if there is evidence of an associated ritual or objects such as food or artifacts buried with the individual.

Box 5.5

Deconstructing Cave Men and Cave Women

Popular images and stereotypes of people living in the Palaeolithic are problematic, including gender bias and the idea that they lived in caves and were stupid and unkempt.

Living in Caves

Living in caves would not have been a common occurrence in the Palaeolithic. Certainly some caves were used for habitation, but it would be a mistake to think most people living in the distant past lived in caves. Living in caves doesn't make sense for an number of reasons, including (i) they are cold, dark, damp, and take a lot of wood to heat; (ii) other, often large and dangerous, animals such as bears like caves; (iii) because there is often only a single entrance, living in caves increases vulnerability for attack from other people or animals; (iv) caves are often difficult to access; and (v) caves are often away from water.

Caves are likely overemphasized because they have high archaeological visibility. Because they are protected, they usually have better preservation of organic remains, as well as evidence of art and ritual. We are more likely to find evidence of humans and human activity inside a cave than outside.

Being Stupid and Unkempt

Palaeolithic peoples are often depicted as lacking language and being fairly stupid and unkempt. Research indicates that the language of peoples living perhaps as long as 100,000 years ago was likely as complex as our own. The idea that they were stupid is ridiculous. Only a small percentage of people today would likely be able to make a stone tool like *Homo habilis* was doing more than 2 million years ago without instruction. Being unkempt is also problematic. In the article "Bad Hair Day in the Palaeolithic: Modern Reconstructions of the Cave Man," Judith Berman (1999) provides all kinds of

evidence, including the depiction of humans in prehistoric art, that people were well-groomed. Berman writes,

> ... the shaggy, grunting Cave Man, who fights dinosaurs, talks "rock," and woos prehistoric-bikini-clad Cave Women with a club, is firmly in place, and it is easy to see why ... over 150 Cave Man films, animated cartoons, and television shows.... These filmed images are supported and reified by other popular media. (p. 289)

Although we have never seen Palaeolithic humans in the flesh, we recognize them immediately in illustrations, art, cartoons, and museum displays. The familiar iconography of the "Cave Man" often depicts our early human ancestors with longish, unkempt hair. However, this conventionalized image is not congruent with available archaeological data on the appearance of Upper Palaeolithic humans.

Gender Bias

There is considerable gender bias in popular images of Palaeolithic peoples. Men are typically portrayed as the leaders and the providers, while women are largely featured in supporting roles and as sexual objects. An interesting popular article on this is "Paleohooters," written by Allen Abel (1997:16). The article includes many quotes from anthropologist Melanie Wiber, who responds to the idea that men were more important even in australopithecine times: "It's pandering to what we *want* to think our ancestors were doing. It's giving antiquity to what we do *now*." Wiber suggests that people have been programmed to believe that "females were secondary to the evolution of *Homo sapiens*, that light skin equals progress, and that woman exists to be domesticated and eroticized, even when she is a million-year-old, knuckle-walking, termite-eating ape." Anthropologists know that there is no reason to believe men had any more important role than women in the past. In fact, considerable research indicates that if anything, it was the women who were more important.

There is considerable debate among archaeologists about when people first began burying their dead. Some archaeologists believe they have evidence from hundreds of thousands of years ago, and most believe Neandertals started burying their dead by at least 40,000 years ago. The evidence that Neandertals deliberately dug pits into which they placed dead bodies remains contentious, however, and some archaeologists only accept that it was modern *Homo sapiens* that began burying their dead, about 30,000 years ago.

There is some suggestion that Neandertals may have carried a tune, and even played flutes, but the evidence of this is controversial. Many anthropologists accept that Neandertals and other varieties of humans dating as early as 100,000 years ago had the same language capabilities as modern humans, including speech. Whether they could sing, however, is disputable. There is a hollowed out and broken mammal bone discovered in Europe with puncture holes that some believe was a Neandertal flute. This interpretation is debatable. The bone has two complete holes and parts of what may be one or two others, and their placement resembles that of a modern flute. Some have even made reproductions of this so-called Neandertal flute and played music on them. However, some archaeologists believe the holes were likely made by an animal and the fact that their placement resembles that of a flute is probably coincidental. The bones also show evidence of gnawing by animals on both ends, suggesting to some that it was made naturally. Those who accept the bone as evidence of a flute suggest the animal gnawing came after its use as a flute.

Expanding Territories

There are a few things that most archaeologists agree upon. One is that the birthplace of humans and human culture was Africa. Another is that once humans had culture, it facilitated a kind of cultural adaptive radiation around the globe (Map 5.1).

It is clear that by almost two million years ago, early humans (probably *Homo erectus/ergaster*) had spread throughout much of Africa and the southern latitudes of Asia. By a million years ago, they had expanded westward into Europe. Eventually they started inhabiting northern areas. We know, for example, that they were in Siberia by at least 60,000 years ago.

People had been in Asia for more than one million years. From there they started colonizing southern areas. They reached Australia, likely using watercraft, by at least 50,000 years ago. People may have ventured into the Americas from Asia before 20,000 years ago, but all such claims are controversial.

The spread of humans during the Palaeolithic was clearly enhanced by culture. Unlike all other animals, humans were not dependent on biology for survival. They

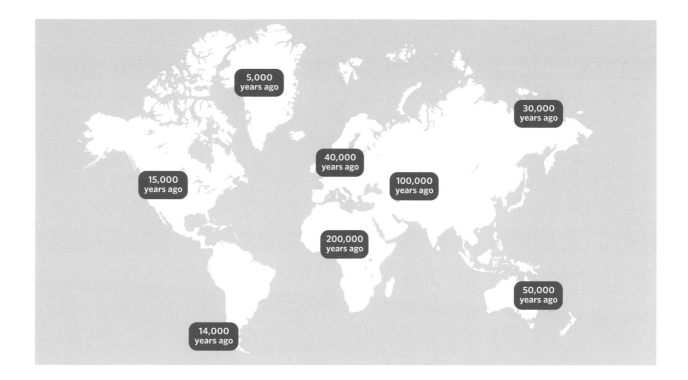

Map 5.1
Migrations and Expanding Territories around the Globe
This map illustrates the spread of modern *homo sapiens*.

could colonize colder environments for example, because they had fire and probably for at least a few hundred thousand years, clothing. Palaeolithic culture also allowed people to utilize a larger range of food, enhanced communication within and between groups, and made territorial expansion feasible.

Summary

This chapter introduces students to the archaeology of the period before 20,000 years ago. Mirroring the Learning Objectives stated in the chapter opening, the key points include:

- The archaeological record of the period before 20,000 years ago consists primarily of sites, artifacts, and features.
- The archaeological record is incomplete and biased.
- The first evidence of culture dates to 2.5 million years ago; hunting and meat eating was evident throughout the entire Palaeolithic; people have probably been controlling fire for at least a few hundred thousand years; organization in groups of about 30 was probably normal; and undisputed evidence of ideology and art begins about 40,000 years ago.
- Migrations and territorial expansions, including to northern environments and Australia, occurred during the Palaeolithic.

REVIEW QUESTIONS

1. What does the term *archaeological record* mean?

2. What are some biases in archaeology to be aware of?

3. What were the principal cultural developments in the Lower, Middle, and Upper Palaeolithic, respectively?

4. What is the timing for human expansion into Asia, Europe, Australia, and the Americas?

DISCUSSION QUESTIONS

1. How, using a holistic perspective, may changes in subsistence, diet, social systems, technology, ideology, and art be linked?

2. How, using a holistic perspective, may changes in culture identified in this chapter be linked with the changes in biology (described in Chapter 4)?

Visit **www.lensofanthropology.com** for the following additional resources:

SELF-STUDY QUESTIONS   **WEBLINKS**   **FURTHER READING**

PLACES MENTIONED IN CHAPTER 6

1 Beringia
2 Ice-Free Corridor
3 North Atlantic Ocean
4 Kenya
5 Yukon Territory, Canada
6 San Miguel Island, California

CHAPTER 6
CULTURAL EVOLUTION FROM 20,000 TO 5,000 YEARS AGO

(((Palaeo this, palaeo that. Mammoth eating here, drinking beer there, and farming yonder. #culture20,000to5,000yearsago

Learning Objectives

In this chapter students will learn:

- the principal cultural periods in North America and Europe.
- thoughts and evidence about North American prehistory.
- why and when people started developing new subsistence strategies.
- when new kinds of social and political systems emerged.
- how archaeologists reconstruct subsistence, settlement, and social systems.
- when and where civilizations and writing emerged.
- the conditions under which new technologies, such as pottery, were used.

Introduction

Many significant events and changes in cultures around the world occurred in the period from 20,000 to 5,000 years ago. These include the settling of the Americas as well as the development of new subsistence strategies, settlement patterns, technologies, and strategies of organization (social and political systems) around the world.

It was during this time that **food production** replaced food **foraging** as a primary subsistence strategy for many people around the world. Many believe that the

Box 6.1
Problems with "Palaeo"

There is a lot of interest in things "palaeo" these days. It is apparently a good marketing gimmick, feeding on people's sense of the "good old days," taken to the extreme. Thus, we hear of the palaeo lifestyle, the palaeo diet, palaeo exercise, palaeo sleeping patterns, palaeo medicine, palaeo this, and palaeo that. Some describe the interest as palaeo nostalgia. Anthropologists sometimes refer to it as palaeo fantasy.

There are problems with all things "palaeo." These include a misunderstanding of what humans were like in the past, both biologically and culturally, and how we have evolved. Another problem is that the past is misused to support assumptions, often incorrect, about some kind of natural state of humans, including how we should eat, sleep, have sex, and exercise. Many assume that if it is older, it must be better, but this isn't always true.

The very popular **Paleo Diet** provides a good example. The first edition of *The Paleo Diet: Lose Weight and Get Healthy by Eating the Foods You Were Designed to Eat* by Loren Cordain was first published in 2002 and by 2011 had already sold more than 200,000 copies. Cordain describes the diet as

> ... the diet to which our species is genetically adapted. This is the diet of our hunter-gatherer ancestors, the foods consumed by every human being on the planet until a mere 333 human generations ago, or about ten thousand years ago. Our ancestors' diets were uncomplicated by agriculture, animal husbandry, technology, and processed foods. Then, as today, our health is optimized when we eat lean meats, seafood, and fresh fruits and vegetables at the expense of grains, dairy, refined sugars, refined oils and processed foods. (p. xi)

Most anthropologists find this basic premise to be faulty. For archaeologists, the notion that there was a common diet in prehistory is absurd, and research shows evidence of grains in the diet long before 10,000 years ago. The notion that we have not evolved biologically with changes in our diet is also problematic. Lactose tolerance (the ability to drink milk without ill effects), for example, has evolved in different ways (from different mutations) at least three times in various parts of the world over the past several thousand years. And before this, people were able to enjoy the many nutritional benefits of dairy by processing milk into cheese and yogurt (see Box 3.1).

Those who take the palaeo diet a step further and eat only raw food often do not fully understand life in the past. Cooking food is a cultural universal, and probably has been for at least 30,000 years. Most archaeologists accept that cooking has been common for at least several hundred thousand years, and some suggest it may have originated about 2 million years ago (see Box 5.2). Cooking tends to enhance the nutrition of most foods, and makes digestion easier.

Marlene Zuk (2013), in *Paleofantasy: What Evolution Tells Us about Sex, Diet, and How We Live*, describes some of the problems, including how people often think that things were better in the past, and adherents to the palaeo lifestyle often do not know what life was really like:

> To think of ourselves as misfits in our own time and of our own making flatly contradicts what we now understand about the way evolution works.... The paleofantasy is a fantasy in part because it supposes that we humans, or at least our protohuman forebears, were at some point perfectly adapted to our environments. (pp. 6, 7)

Even assuming we could agree on a time to hark back to, there is the sticky issue of exactly what such an ancestral nirvana was like.

transition to food production and the changes in lifestyle that go with it—including diet, exercise, and sleep patterns—are not good for us humans. They harken back to the "days of old," which they generally perceive as better, and create diets and other fads to mimic life in Palaeo times. These fads are addressed in Box 6.1.

Principal Cultural Periods

There are several descriptive and analytical cultural periods used by archaeologists and others when considering the time period from 20,000 to 5,000 years ago. Some of the more popular ones are outlined in Table 6.1.

The use of these terms to describe cultural periods is in no way universal, and the start and end dates are very approximate. Not all archaeologists use this terminology, they are not applicable to all regions, and when they are used, the start and end dates may vary by locality.

In North America, PalaeoIndian and Archaic are two widely used frameworks. PalaeoIndian generally refers to the period in which people first arrived and settled, through to the end of the time in which they were hunting large animals such as mammoths and mastodons, about 9,000 years ago. Some archaeologists extend use of the term to include Central and South America as well, but it is never used outside of the Americas. The term Archaic is used to describe the period from about 9,000 to 5,000 years ago in much, but not all, of North America, which is characterized by an ongoing foraging adaptation.

Table 6.1
Cultural Periods 20,000 to 5,000 Years Ago

Period	Antiquity
NORTH AMERICA	
PalaeoIndian	14,000–9,000 years ago
Archaic	9,000–5,000 years ago
EUROPE	
Upper Palaeolithic	40,000–12,000 years ago
Mesolithic	12,000–10,000 years ago
Neolithic	10,000–5,000 years ago

Popular terms for cultural periods that are most applicable to Europe, but also used elsewhere, include the Upper Palaeolithic, Mesolithic, Neolithic, Bronze Age, and Iron Age. As mentioned in Chapter 5, *Palaeolithic* roughly translates into Old Stone Age. The Upper Palaeolithic is the most recent era, beginning about 40,000 years ago, correlating with the arrival of modern *Homo sapiens* in the area and ending about 12,000 years ago. The **Mesolithic**, from about 12,000 to 10,000 years ago, roughly translates as the Middle Stone Age. It correlates with climatic change in Europe (warming and deglaciation), advances in stone-tool technology and changes in diet, including more maritime resources. The **Neolithic**, from about 10,000 to 5,000 years ago, translates as the New Stone Age. Rather than being based on technology, it correlates with a shift to farming in Europe.

Metalworking provides the basis for labelling the Bronze Age and Iron Age in Europe. Natural copper began to be smelted about 6,000 years ago, but it was not widely used. Copper is much softer than stone and thus does not make durable tools. Approximately 5,000 years ago, people determined that by adding tin to copper they could create bronze, which required much hotter fires but was much more durable. A few thousand years later, people were able create sufficiently hotter fires to extract iron from ore, leading to what is popularly known as the Iron Age.

Table 6.2 provides an overview of some of the major cultural developments during the period from 20,000 to 5,000 years ago.

Table 6.2

Major Cultural Developments 20,000 to 5,000 Years Ago

Time Period	Cultural Developments
20,000–15,000 years ago	Domestication of dog occurs. People begin colonizing what is now known as the Americas. Continued expansion and increasing population growth
15,000–10,000 years ago	Transition in many parts of the world to food production rather than foraging. Megafauna (mammoth and mastodon) hunting in North America.
10,000–5,000 years ago	More people adopt food production as subsistence strategy. Significant population growth around the world. New forms of social and political organization emerge. Civilization and writing emerge.

Archaeology of North America from 20,000 to 5,000 Years Ago

Most archaeologists place the initial settlement of the Americas as occurring between 20,000 and 15,000 years ago. Some archaeologists suggest evidence at some sites indicates much earlier dates, but many archaeologists believe the very high standards of proof for claiming early archaeological sites in the Americas have not been met. According to these standards, (i) the evidence must be undisputedly cultural and (ii) the dating has to be undisputedly reliable. The purported evidence at some sites includes chipped stones that resemble stone tools, but many archaeologists are not fully convinced that those stones were not chipped naturally. At other sites, there is no question that artifacts were made by humans, but there are questions about the dating. Since carbon 14 dating is widely recognized as the best dating technique for early sites in North America (at least up until about 40,000 years ago), if a site is not dated by this technique, then the dates are usually questioned. Dates determined by carbon 14 are sometimes questioned as well, especially if they come from areas in proximity to sediments with carbon that could contaminate the results.

Timing and Routes

There is much interest in the questions of when and by which route people first came to the Americas (Map 6.1). Conventional archaeological thought indicates that the ancestry of contemporary Indigenous peoples in the Americas lies in Asia. This is supported primarily by biological similarities, with support from archaeology. It also makes sense in regard to the general patterns of prehistory, in which we have evidence of people in Siberia and other areas of northeast Asia for tens of thousands of years.

The route from Asia to the Americas was via **Beringia**, a large, ice-free area connecting northern Asia to northwest North America during the last ice age. There is no undisputed archaeological evidence of a human presence in the North American part of Beringia before about 14,000 years ago, but it still makes sense to most archaeologists that they were there. Explanations for the lack of evidence are linked with the ever-changing landscapes in the area, which have likely destroyed much of it. Also, the temporary nature of the settlements meant that little evidence was left, and there was probably a low population density, with a consequential low number of sites.

Prior to about 12,000 years ago, most of what is now Canada, as well as much of northern Asia and northern Europe was under ice. Beringia was an exception. Beginning about 14,000 years ago, however, undisputed archaeological sites dating to this time appear in the archaeological record of the United States. Somehow, the people who left these sites got around or through the glaciers covering Canada. The theory that has the most popular acceptance is that the people came down the coast of what is now Alaska and British Columbia in western Canada, using boats or walking along the coastline. This is often known as the **coastal migration route**. No sites clearly dating before 14,000 years have yet been discovered in these areas,

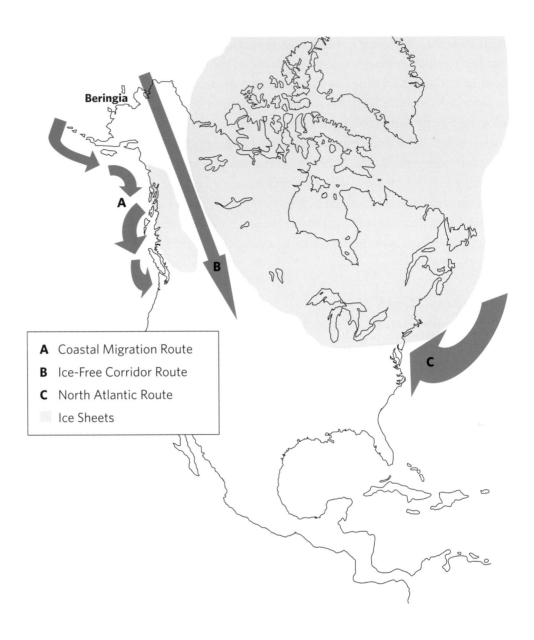

Map 6.1
Possible Entry Routes to the Americas during the Last Ice Age

Beringia

A Coastal Migration Route
B Ice-Free Corridor Route
C North Atlantic Route
  Ice Sheets

but palaeoenvironmental research indicates the coastal area was certainly inhabitable in the time period before 14,000 years ago. Archaeologists continue to look for sites along the coast, but as with Beringia, there are problems of both changing environments, including rising sea levels, and low archaeological visibility.

Another possible entry route from Beringia through the glaciers was through a corridor between the two large ice sheets covering most of Canada. During warming trends of the last ice age, the two glaciers separated, creating a corridor linking Beringia to the areas south. This is known as the **ice-free corridor route**.

A third possible entry route was from Europe, via the North Atlantic Ocean. This is often referred to as the Solutrean hypothesis, named after the peoples identified as being part of the Solutrean culture of Europe, about 20,000 years ago. This route would have necessitated boat travel across the North Atlantic and southward down the glacial environment of eastern Canada.

Once people traveled south of the ice sheets, they quickly spread throughout the region, with sites dating to about 14,000 years ago appearing in South America. It is likely that most Indigenous peoples of the Americas have ancestral ties to populations in Asia. Many probably are descended from those who first made their way around or through the glaciers before 12,000 years ago. Others may have come in subsequent migrations. Archaeologists remain uncertain about how many distinct migrations there were from Asia before 5,000 years ago, but there were probably at least several.

Cultures between 14,000 and 5,000 Years Ago

Despite the significant alterations to the landscapes, thousands of archaeological sites predating 5,000 years ago have been recorded in North America. Some of the most significant are described in Table 6.3. Their locations are shown on Map 6.2.

Although there are sites in North America that some archaeologists claim are older than 14,000 years, the claims are all contentious. Most archaeologists only accept an age of 14,000 years for the earliest reliable evidence of human occupation. Problems with finding sites older than 14,000 years are many. Since sea levels have risen since the last ice age, most coastal sites from that time would now be under water. Thousands of years of both natural processes and cultural activity have undoubtedly destroyed many thousands of sites, and the activities of the early migrants and settlers would undoubtedly have low archaeological visibility due to relatively low population densities and the temporary nature of their settlements.

It is clear that initial migrants and settlers of the continent adapted fairly quickly to the new ecological niches of the Americas. It is apparent that upon arriving south of the ice sheets, some populations—probably those arriving via the coastal migration route—continued a maritime adaptation, with settlement expanding along the Pacific Coast all the way to the southern tip of South America. Much of the evidence from the earliest sites on or near the west coast of North America indicates a maritime adaptation, including significant amounts of seafood in settlers' diets.

While some populations maintained a maritime adaptation, others adapted to inland resources. These may have been people who moved eastward once they got past the ice sheets along the coast. Perhaps they arrived through the ice-free corridor, preadapted to terrestrial resources.

Map 6.2
Significant Archaeological Sites in North America

Bluefish Caves

Kwayday Dan Ts'inchi

L'Anse aux Meadows

Charlie Lake Cave

Head-Smashed-In-Buffalo Jump

Ozette
Kennewick
Paisley Cave

Meadowcroft
Cahokia
Cactus Hill

Daisy Cave
Mesa Verde
Topper

Gault

Populations probably expanded fairly quickly beginning about 14,000 years ago, with essentially unlimited resources for the fairly small groups of migrants and early settlers. However, the overall population of North America remained relatively low for the first few thousand years of occupation. From perhaps hundreds of migrants traveling in small groups before 14,000 years ago, the population likely expanded to thousands by 12,000 years ago, when there was a population explosion of sorts.

Table 6.3

Significant Archaeological Sites in North America Older than 5,000 Years

Site Name	Description
Bluefish Caves	Located in present-day Yukon Territory, Bluefish Caves is significant because it provides evidence of people in Beringia during the last ice age. The site contains artifacts made of stone and bone as well as butchered animal remains. Most archaeologists accept dates between 15,000 and 12,000 years ago, although some suggest dates in the range of 25,000 years ago.
Cactus Hill	This site is located in Virginia. It is widely accepted as being older than 12,000 years, but the precise antiquity is uncertain. Some suggest that the site may be as old as 19,000 to 17,000 years, but these dates are contested.
Gault	This site, located in Texas, was a Clovis camp and was likely first occupied more than 12,000 years ago. The assemblage includes more than one million artifacts, including several hundred thousand that are more than 9,000 years old. The site is particularly significant for showing the diversity of diet, which, contrary to popular belief, indicates that mammoths and other large game were only a small part of the Clovis diet. The site is also significant in providing what may be the oldest art in North America, in the form of more than 100 incised stones.
Meadowcroft	Meadowcroft Rockshelter, located in Pennsylvania, is widely considered to contain deposits that are at least 12,000 years old. Some suggest the deposits may be as old as 19,000 years, but these dates are contested.
Paisley Caves	Located in Oregon, the oldest deposits in this site contain human coprolites dating to between 14,000 and 13,000 years ago.
Topper	This site, located in South Carolina, is widely considered to be at least 12,000 years old. Based on what appear to some to be artifacts below the 12,000-year-old layer, some believe the site to be older. Whether the so-called artifacts are really artifacts or naturally broken rocks remains debatable.
Charlie Lake Cave	This site, located in northern British Columbia, dates to almost 11,000 years ago and would have been in the ice-free corridor. The oldest levels contain a fluted point, a stone bead, and bones of several kinds of animals, including bison. DNA analysis of the bison and general similarities between artifacts here and in earlier sites in Montana suggest movement through the corridor at this time went from south to north.
Daisy Cave	Located on San Miguel Island, about 40 km off the coast of California, this site dates to almost 11,000 years ago. It is particularly significant insofar as it provides evidence of basketry and cordage, as well as circumstantial evidence of watercraft.
Kennewick	Located in Washington State, this is where the infamous Kennewick Man was discovered. Initially described as a Caucasian and subsequently dated to about 9,000 years ago, the remains created considerable debate, both about the initial classification as Caucasian and the following controversy about whether the remains should be turned over to local Native Americans or kept for study by scientists. Most anthropologists believe the initial classification as Caucasian was a mistake and the remains belong to an ancestral Native American.

The population explosion was likely triggered by the invention, about 12,000 years ago, of a new kind of projectile point, known as a fluted point. A fluted point is distinguished by its concave base, created by removing a flute (or channel) flake from one or both sides of the point. Well-known variants of the fluted points are known as Clovis and Folsom, and the people who used them are known by the same name (e.g., Clovis people). Fluted points were no longer used after about 9,000 years ago.

There is considerable evidence that the points enabled people to effectively kill large animals such as mammoths and mastodons. It is not unusual to find bones of these animals in sites of this time range, often showing evidence of butchery and in association with fluted points. There is some suggestion that overhunting may have caused the extinction of these and other large animals, but it is more commonly believed that they became extinct due to environmental change. In any case, both the points and the presence of mammoths and mastodons only appear in archaeological sites dating 12,000 to 9,000 years ago.

The purpose of the flute is uncertain. Popular ideas include (i) it may have led to more blood loss from the animal by creating a channel for it to flow along and (ii) it may have facilitated easier and quicker hafting to spear points. It is likely that the larger fluted points were hafted to spears thrown unaided by hand or perhaps thrust into the animals once they were wounded. Smaller fluted points were probably hafted to spears and thrown with an atlatl.

Sites with fluted points appear across the unglaciated parts of North America (i.e., mostly in what is now the "lower 48" United States) almost simultaneously about 12,000 years ago, and start appearing in what is now Canada shortly after deglaciation (i.e., between about 12,000 and 10,000 years ago). One scenario has one group inventing the point and then quickly expanding through the continent. Another, probably more accurate, scenario has many groups preexisting in unglaciated parts of the continent, then quickly adopting the new technology and incorporating large animals (often known as megafauna) into their diets. The reason for the numerous archaeological sites that start appearing around 12,000 years ago is probably due to a combination of (i) greater archaeological visibility and (ii) increased population. Megafauna hunting—particularly with large stone projectile points—has high archaeological visibility. Mammoth and mastodon bones, for example, are easily identifiable, as are the spear points. People before 12,000 years ago were likely hunting smaller animals, which leave far less trace, and using either smaller stone projectile points or simply sharpened bone or wood spears, which leave no trace at all.

It would be a mistake to believe that people necessarily depended on megafauna before 9,000 years ago. It was undoubtedly part of the diet of many, but we should always be aware of the bias of archaeological visibility. Research at the site of Gault in Texas, for example, indicates Clovis people had an extremely varied diet that included, but was probably not dependent on, mammoth.

Overall, diet was varied throughout the continent before 5,000 years ago, and the populations can be characterized as foragers. As everywhere, people used what was locally available in regard to both plants and animals, including maritime resources. Some of the best evidence of dietary diversity comes from coprolites (preserved human feces). The Hinds Cave site in Texas, for example, includes about 2,000 human coprolites spanning 8,000 years. In one coprolite alone, analysis revealed evidence of antelope, rabbit, squirrel, rat, and eight kinds of plants.

As was common with foragers elsewhere, people likely lived in groups of a few dozen or more, were familiar with and interacted with populations around them, and had significant population growth. It is likely that by 5,000 years ago, the population of North America was at least in the hundreds of thousands, and there were probably at least dozens of distinct ethnic groups, each with its own unique culture.

The Transition to Food Production

The transition to food production is certainly one of the most significant developments in culture in the period from 20,000 to 5,000 years ago. It is likely that before this, foragers around the world effectively managed their resources by, for example, doing some weeding before leaving a berry patch, or otherwise altering environments to make them more conducive to the cultivation of specific kinds of plant and animal foods. Beginning about 15,000 years ago, however, the manipulation of plants and animals got serious.

Ways of obtaining food began to start changing significantly between about 15,000 and 12,000 years ago. Many people around the world became **food producers**, meaning they began to manipulate plants and animals to increase their productivity, creating surplus. The process of food producing involves **domestication**, which means that the plants or animals are under the control of humans. Some people started to domesticate animals, which led to the subsistence strategy known as **pastoralism**. Others started to domesticate plants, which led to **horticulture**.

Archaeological research suggests domestication first developed in the Middle East and Asia, but was relatively quickly adopted by populations living in Europe and Africa as well. It developed independently in regions of the Americas. Early plant domesticates included rice, wheat, potatoes, and maize (corn). Early animal domesticates included sheep, goats, and cattle.

Why Domestication and Food Production?

Initially, it was likely that these new domestic plants and animals supplemented a diet of primarily wild food. However, by about 10,000 years ago, many people had become dependent on these newly domesticated plants and animals. And, with few exceptions, there was no going back. Domestication increased the **carrying capacity** of the regions which humans filled. Going back to subsistence based primarily on foraging would not support the increased numbers of people. Eventually, by

Box 6.2

Why Did People Domesticate Plants and Animals?

Why people started to domesticate and eventually depend on plants and animals is one of the principal areas of research interest in archaeology. Until the 1960s, it was widely assumed that domestication was a good thing, allowing access to more food with less risk, less work, and better health. Archaeological questions tended to focus on where the first domestication occurred and how the idea spread, all assuming that it made life better. Archaeological and ethnographic research in the late twentieth century, however, convinced many that the assumptions were not warranted; while some may have benefited from the transition to food production, many suffered from worse nutrition and less leisure time. The question then became, considering the negative effects of domestication, why many groups around the world would initiate the process of domestication, which led to pastoralism and horticulture.

Over the last few decades, popular explanations for the origins of domestication of both plants and animals have usually focused on ecological reasons. For example, many archaeologists reason that environmental changes reduced the number of people who could effectively forage in a region. Rather than reduce their population to match the now-reduced carrying capacity, move to another area, or resort to raiding others, people began to increasingly manage their resources to the point of domestication. The tendency to focus on ecological explanations may be tied in with contemporary concerns about changing environmental conditions.

Other popular, but not as widely accepted, ideas are that the reason for plant domestication may have been to produce alcohol, or perhaps to gain status. The notion that plants and animals may have been domesticated as prestige items, or luxury foods, to gain status and social and political advantages is the subject of an article by archaeologist Brian Hayden (2003) called "Were Luxury Foods the First Domesticates? Ethnoarchaeological Perspectives from Southeast Asia." Hayden suggests that certain animals and plants (including rice) were domesticated as luxury foods for feasting. He reasons, "... the primary force behind intensified subsistence production is not food shortage, but the desire to obtain social and political advantages—to obtain the most desirable mates, to create the most advantageous alliances, to wield the most political power."

In Hayden's view, domestication was initiated in societies where people were attempting to gain wealth and status, primarily by impressing others, and one way of accomplishing this was to have feasts with what he describes as luxury foods. Eventually these luxury foods became staples. For analogies of how early domestic foods like rice became staples, Hayden writes:

> Chocolate, once reserved for Mesoamerican elites, is now the bane of overfed multitudes. Oversized, out-of-season fruits and vegetables which once only graced the tables of kings and nobles have become everyday fare. Fat-rich meats, which formerly were used only for special occasions or for the highest ranks of society, are now commonplace.... Wines and spirits that played crucial roles in feasts for elites ... have now become the profane intoxicants of households throughout the industrial world. In short, our eating habits today largely are the result of, and reflect, the luxury foods of the past. (pp. 458, 459)

several thousand years ago, some **horticulturalists** took it a step further, which led to **agriculture**, sometimes known as intensive cultivation.

There is no consensus on why people started to become food producers. Historically, the domestication of plants and animals was envisioned by anthropologists as a great idea that made life easier, and most hypotheses to explain domestication began with notions of intelligence or keen observation. Now, however, it is clear that while the lives of some people got better, that certainly wasn't the case for all. Ethnographic research indicates that for most people, pastoralism and horticulture required more time spent on subsistence than a life based on foraging did. Analysis of skeletons also supports the notion that for many, health suffered as a result of domestication. Poor nutrition and diseases are reflected in the skeletons of early pastoralists and horticulturalists.

There were certainly trade-offs. One clear advantage of domestication was that it produced a food surplus, which could be used as a hedge against poor hunting or gathering, or turned into a trade item. Domestication was also associated with reduced mobility, which some viewed as an advantage. Staying in one place for longer periods, as one does when depending on domestic plants and animals, also meant people could accumulate more. Further domestication increased the carrying capacity of a region, meaning more people could live together. With large populations and more permanent settlements came more internal conflict, inevitable social inequality, and the emergence of more formal political systems.

Explanations for the emergence of food production are an area of considerable debate in archaeology. Many archaeologists recognize that since many people suffer from having to work more and being in worse health, a better explanation than food production simply being a good idea is required. After all, it isn't as if people in various parts of the world 15,000 to 12,000 years ago all woke up one morning and said, "We have too much leisure time and are too healthy, so let's change the way we get our food." Archaeologists examine the trade-offs.

What some researchers see as an advantage, others see as a disadvantage. Many in contemporary societies, for example, view being sedentary (living in permanent settlements) year round, as an advantage. Yet many foragers place a higher value on mobility. Many suggest the food surplus is a hedge against poor crops or hunting. On the other hand, domestication also ties up your resource base in fewer species, making people more susceptible to a disease or drought.

Most popular explanations for the emergence of food production are linked with changing environments. A basic idea is that changing environments may have reduced the carrying capacity of a region. Hypothetically, for example, an area that once maintained a human population of 1,000 may, due to environmental change, now only support a population of 900. The population has some choices.

Box 6.3
Was Alcohol a Driving Force of Human Evolution?

Probably not. But some people like to consider it.

In 2014 researchers suggested the ability to process alcohol was a driving force of becoming human. Their research, they claimed, indicated a mutation occurring in an ancestral human population about 10 million years ago made possible the ability to process alcohol, and thus, eat fermenting fruit. This, they suggested created a new food source—fermenting fruit left rotting on the ground. The mutation thus became favorable, was selected for, and spread. To effectively make use of this new food source, the researchers claim, the ancestral humans likely started spending increasingly more time on the ground, which in turn led to bipedalism. Thus, according to this very unlikely scenario, the ability to process alcohol led to humans. This is an interesting hypothesis, but only a real stretch of the imagination, perhaps under the influence of alcohol, would place it among the most realistic views of human evolution.

In *Uncorking the Past: The Quest for Wine, Beer, and Other Alcoholic Beverages*, archaeologist Patrick E. McGovern (2009:xi) describes the allure of alcohol:

> Humans throughout history have been astounded by alcohol's effects, whether it is imbibed as a beverage or applied to the skin. The health benefits are obvious—alcohol relieves pain, stops infection, and seems to cure diseases. Its psychological and social benefits are equally apparent—alcohol eases the difficulties of everyday life, lubricates social exchanges, and contributes to a joy in being alive.

Most archaeologists believe the origins of plant domestication are linked to food shortages, although some suggest it may have been more political (see Box 6.2). Some take another view: that the early domestic plants, such as wheat and barley, may have been cultivated to produce alcoholic beverages, particularly beer. It remains a minor, but interesting hypothesis—that the driving force of domestication was beer drinking.

Evidence for the production of beer begins appearing in the archaeological record about 10,000 years ago, predating wine by at least a thousand years. How or why people started making beer is uncertain, but it quickly caught on. Besides the fact that it made people feel good, other reasons that have been offered to explain the adoption of beer include that fermentation increased the nutritional value of wheat and barley, and that by killing the pathogens in water through the fermentation process, it was a safer and healthier option than drinking untreated water.

McGovern (2009:7) suggests some other reasons:

> Alcoholic beverages have other advantages. Alcohol spurs the appetite, and in liquid form, it also satiates feelings of hunger. The process of fermentation enhances the protein, vitamin, and nutritional content of the natural product, adds flavor and aroma, and contributes to preservation. Fermented foods and beverages cook faster because complex molecules have been broken down, saving time and fuel. Finally, as we have learned from numerous medical studies, moderate consumption of alcohol lowers cardiovascular and cancer risks.

Some breweries, with the aid of archaeologists, have begun recreating (and marketing) palaeo beers. The beers are typically based on a residue analysis on pots evidently used to store beer, which upon identification of the elements, are turned into a recipe. In more recent times, once writing began, the ancient recipes were recorded, and those recipes can be used today. Thus, some lucky drinkers have been able to drink beers as they would have been 9,000 years ago in China as well as in the ancient civilizations of Mesopotamia and Egypt.

Figure 6.1

Beer and Cultural Evolution

Beer was part of the diet of many people at least 10,000 years ago. It had many benefits and some suggest it was the driving force of cultural evolution including the domestication of plants.

Credit: Anders Nilsen

They could perhaps become aggressive and raid food from neighboring groups; they could migrate elsewhere; they could have fewer children; or they could simply start domesticating plants and animals to get the carrying capacity back up to 1,000. The big problem, of course, is that once domestication begins and food surplus is created, the populations keep increasing, and the cycle of increasing food production to keep up with demand continues.

There are, of course, other explanations for the transition to food production that are not based on environmental change. Archaeologist Brian Hayden, for example, suggests that at least some foods may have been domesticated to increase wealth and status (see Box 6.2). Others suggest that some plants may have been domesticated for the making of alcohol (see Box 6.3). This last idea, which has received considerable interest in recent years, has led to many jokes, including one explaining that the reason permanent settlements are associated with domestication is so that waiters know where to find us.

Transitioning from subsistence relying absolutely on wild foods to subsistence relying on domestication need not be considered a drastic event that developed in a vacuum. Food production can certainly be considered revolutionary, but it wasn't as if the change from depending on wild sources to domestication required special knowledge. It is very likely that people were already managing their resources in numerous ways. Archaeologists working in some coastal areas, for example, find archaeological evidence of people altering the landscape of beaches to make clams more productive. Similarly, there are indications that people in the past may have deliberately set fire to areas to manipulate the kinds of plants and animals that would repopulate. People have been smart for a very long time. It stands to reason that before leaving an area where they were gathering wild plants, for example, they may have done some clearing of unwanted plant material. Making the transition to domesticating plants and animals was likely a case of just doing more of what they were already doing in regard to managing the resources. And maybe doing it a bit differently.

Figure 6.2
Pastoralists
Pastoralism began more than 10,000 years ago. Pictured here is a Turkana woman in Kenya, watering livestock from a waterhole dug in the sand.

Credit: © John Warburton-Lee Photography/Alamy

Identifying Subsistence Strategies in the Archaeological Record

There are many ways of identifying subsistence strategies archaeologically. Foragers, for example, are usually distinguished in part by a wide variety of wild plants and animals as food refuse. Since foragers usually live in small groups, create temporary settlements, and are egalitarian, evidence of these factors can also be used to support inferences of foraging.

Because foragers are relatively mobile, archaeologists are often interested in determining in which season a site was used. The primary way of doing this is to look for the presence of seasonal plants in a site. The presence of migratory animals also allows for inferences.

Indications of pastoralism and horticulture are made by examining plant and animal remains and correlating them with other cultural elements, such as the size of settlements and populations.

Pastoralists, for example, usually have little diversity in the animals used for food, but retain a diversity in plants, which they often continue to gather. Horticulturalists, on the other hand, exhibit little diversity in plants but considerable diversity in animals. Since pastoralists and horticulturalists tend to live in larger and more permanent settlements, indications of these can also be used to make inferences about subsistence.

Of course, inferences of pastoralism and horticulture are aided by determining whether the plants and animals can be classified as "wild" or "domestic." Ways of making these determinations are covered in the next section.

Identifying Domestication in the Archaeological Record

Archaeologists have multiple ways of distinguishing between wild and domestic varieties of plants and animals. Table 6.4 lists some of the criteria for distinguishing wild from domestic varieties of the same species; there are several ways to do this, but few are visible in the archaeological record. The attribute most commonly used in archaeology is the size of the edible part of the plant. Frequently, as domestication continues, the size of the edible part continues to increase. In the earlier deposits in an archaeological site, for example, corncobs may be quite small, but as the deposits get younger, the size of the corncobs gets larger. This is a clear indication of domestication. Alternatively, if corncobs from the same time period are small in one area and large in another area, it may indicate that they are wild in the first and domestic in the other.

Table 6.4
Criteria for Distinguishing Domestic versus Wild Plants and Animals

Domestic Plants	Domestic Animals
The part of the plant that people use is usually larger.	The animals tend to be smaller (at least in early stage of domestication).
The plant may have lost its mechanism for natural dispersal.	There is a tendency to find more complete skeletons in the faunal assemblage.
The part of the plant that people use may have become clustered.	There is likely to be a high percentage of young, male animals in the assemblage.
There is often a genetic change.	There is likely to be a high percentage of old female animals in the assemblage.
There may be a loss of dormancy.	
The plants tend to ripen simultaneously.	
There is a tendency for less self-protection, such as thorns and toxins.	

The primary ways of identifying domestic animals are based on the size and completeness of skeletons, and the age and sex ratios of the butchered animals. At least in the early stages, domestic animals tend to be smaller than their wild counterparts. This may be due to the smaller animals being selected for domestication or nutritional deficiencies. Faunal assemblages with relatively complete skeletons are another way of identifying domestication. When hunting wild animals, some preliminary butchering is often done at the kill site, so the entire skeleton is not brought back to the settlement. Relatively high proportions of young males and old females in the assemblage are another indication of domestication. Young males are usually the most difficult to kill in the wild, but in captivity only one or a few need to be kept for breeding. Females are often kept for breeding and eaten only when their usefulness for breeding has passed.

Besides the plant and animal remains, domestication may also be identified by other kinds of evidence. Indications of plant domestication, for example, include the identification of garden plots and irrigation ditches. Indications of animal domestication may include large accumulations of animal dung close to a village, or evidence of fencing.

Settlement and Technology

Food production is strongly correlated with settlement patterns. When people started domesticating animals, for example, there was a necessary reduction in mobility. Pastoralists are typically semisedentary, meaning they move only a few times each year. They may graze their animals in a valley for several months of a year and at a higher altitude for the rest. This results in much more permanent structures. Knowing that they will be living in the same house for at least a few months each year, for example, leads to people spending more time building structures than if they were foragers spending relatively little time in the same location. The surplus created by pastoralism also means that more people can live together, leading to larger settlements than can usually be maintained by foragers.

Similarly, horticulture is correlated with increasing sedentism. Horticulturalists typically will build a settlement close to fields they have planted and only move once the nutrients are depleted, which is usually at least a few years. Consequently, like pastoralists, horticulturalists will put more time into building structures, knowing they will be there for at least a few years. Also, as in pastoralism, the surplus of food leads to larger population and settlement size.

Eventually, as food surplus increased, new kinds of settlements emerged. Villages and towns increased in number and size. The surplus of food led to many people not directly involved in food production, and even larger settlements, known as cities, emerged. A standard archaeological definition of **city** includes an assumption that there were at least 5,000 residents.

One of the most significant technological adaptations of the period was the use of **pottery**, which can basically be defined as **ceramics** (baked clay) used to contain something. Evidence from the Upper Palaeolithic in Europe indicates that people

Figure 6.3
Examples of Pottery
Widespread pottery use is correlated with settling down. Pictured here are coiled, pinched, and thrown pots. Each of these methods, as well as others, was in use before 5,000 years ago.
Credit: Nadine Ryan

had developed ceramic technology about 30,000 years ago (e.g., some of the figurines from the period were made from ceramics), but it wasn't until much later that people used the technology for containers. There is some suggestion that pottery may have been made in China as long as 20,000 years ago, and a recent discovery dates its use in Japan to about 15,000 years ago. Pottery did not become common in Africa, Asia, and Europe, however, until about 10,000 years ago. It did not become common in the Americas for another few thousand years.

It is likely that people had the ability to make pottery before 10,000 years ago, but it did not make sense to use it. Pottery has both advantages and disadvantages. One advantage is that it is easy to make. It is simply a matter of mixing clay and water and then heating. Another advantage is that, because clay and water are so common, nobody can control the resource, and it is therefore inexpensive. Pottery also makes excellent containers, including for liquids.

But there are also many disadvantages of using pottery. Reasons that probably led to it not being common before 10,000 years ago is that pottery is (i) bulky, (ii) heavy, and (iii) fragile. Foragers, being mobile, were unlikely to want the burden of carrying pots. It is likely that only when people started to settle down, at least temporarily, did using pottery make sense.

There were certainly other important inventions, innovations, and adaptations besides pottery during this period. The bow and arrow, for example, was likely widely used around the world by the latter part of this period. The wheel was likely invented for use in making pottery (i.e., the pottery wheel) about 5,500 years ago in Mesopotamia, and only adapted for transportation more recently. Metalworking began with smelting copper, leading eventually to bronze and iron working in more recent times. Beginning about 6,000 years ago, plows were used in farming. Technology was sufficient to build large monuments and cities.

Changes in Social and Political Systems

Changes in social and political systems are intricately linked with food production. Although some archaeologists believe that the significant changes in all aspects of culture during this period may have been triggered by social and political factors, many believe the driving force for change was food production, which in turn led to changes in social and political systems.

A basic idea is that the change to food production, perhaps triggered by an initial reduction in carrying capacity, led to larger populations, which in turn required new kinds of social and political structures in order to be effective. The reasoning essentially is that increasingly large numbers of people require leadership to coordinate activities within groups as well as create and maintain relations with other groups.

There is considerable evidence of the correlation of food production and social and political structures in the archaeological record. Pastoralists, for example, usually exhibit the beginnings of social stratification and leadership. They would typically be organized as a **tribe**, with some kind of leader (either official or unofficial), sometimes referred to as a **Big Man**. Tribes of pastoralists were usually divided into several villages with a total population of no more than a few thousand. Each village had its own Big Man, whose tasks included both maintaining order within the village and representing the village when interacting with others.

Horticulturalists are typically organized as either a tribe or a **chiefdom**. Small-scale horticulturalist groups, typically numbering a few to several thousand divided into several villages, typically organized as a tribe. Larger-scale horticultural groups, sometimes numbering in the tens of thousands, were organized as chiefdoms. Unlike tribes, chiefdoms were typically rigidly hierarchical, leadership was based on heredity, and there was taxation, which came in the form of goods or labor to the leaders.

Agriculture significantly increased the carrying capacity, leading to even more people—and to the problems associated with larger populations and agricultural activities. Populations based on agriculture are typically organized as a **state**, and even shortly after their emergence, about 6,000 years ago, could number in the hundreds of thousands.

There are multiple ways of identifying social and political systems archaeologically. The subsistence strategy often provides one good kind of evidence, correlating foraging with bands, pastoralists with tribes, horticulturalists with chiefdoms, and agriculturalists with states. In the absence of writing, archaeologists also look for

indications of social stratification through the size of houses and distribution of remains. Differences in the sizes of houses or the material used to construct them, for example, are often a good indication of social stratification. Similarly, if highly valued items are unevenly distributed within a site, it is probably an indication of stratification.

Civilizations, Writing, and Art

Civilization emerged a few hundred years before 5,000 years ago. The earliest civilization is commonly referred to as the Sumerian, and comprised 13 different city states in what is commonly known as Mesopotamia in ancient times. Today, it is Iraq. Many may have heard Iraq being referred to as the cradle of civilization, which indeed it was.

To qualify as a civilization, most archaeologists suggest, the society must have had at least most of the following: an agricultural base, a state level of political organization, monumental architecture, at least one city, and writing. For most societies making the transition to civilization, writing was the last requirement to be filled.

The earliest widely accepted form of writing is traced to Mesopotamia a little more than 5,000 years ago. It is written script on clay tablets, often referred to as

Figure 6.4
Turkana Village
The Turkana are pastoralists in Africa. Settlements of pastoralists and horticulturalists are usually larger than those of foragers. Indications of subsistence and social organizations can often be found by examining the kinds of plant and animal remains found in the settlement, the number and various sizes of the houses, and the distribution of remains within houses and the village.
Credit: Bob Muckle

Figure 6.5
Rock Art at Kakadu, Australia
Kakadu comprises one of the greatest concentrations of rock art in the world.
Credit: Gillian Crowther

cuneiform. Decipherment of some of the earliest tablets suggests that its primary function was as a form of record keeping. Prior to 5,000 years ago, the only known civilization and system of writing is that from Mesopotamia. Other systems of writing and civilizations soon followed, and are described in Chapter 7.

Art has been pervasive in cultures throughout the world for many thousands of years. As we get closer in time to the present, it becomes more visible. Rock art, for example, is known from around the world. One of the best-known pictograph sites from this period is Kakadu National Park in Australia, with one of the greatest concentrations of rock art in the world, with an estimated 15,000 sites ranging up to 20,000 years in age. (See Figure 6.5.)

Summary

This chapter has highlighted some of the key developments in culture around the world in the period from 20,000 to 5,000 years ago. Mirroring the Learning Objectives stated in the chapter opening, the key points include:

- The principal culture periods in North America are the PalaeoIndian and Archaic. The principal cultural periods during this time in Europe include the Upper Palaeolithic, the Mesolithic, and the Neolithic.
- People probably first came to North America, via Asia, between 20,000 and 15,000 years ago. For a few thousand years they incorporated megafauna in their diets.
- Between about 15,000 and 12,000 years ago, many populations began to domesticate plants and animals, which they ultimately became dependent upon.
- Associated with the emergence of food production, populations increased, settlements got larger and more numerous, and social stratification emerged.
- Archaeologists have multiple ways of determining subsistence, settlement, social, and political systems.
- Civilizations and writing emerged a little more than 5,000 years ago.
- Pottery became widely used only after people start settling down.

REVIEW QUESTIONS

1. What are the names and time ranges of the principal cultural periods in North America and Europe?
2. What were the major cultural developments occurring between 20,000 and 5,000 years ago?
3. What are the principal explanations for the emergence of food production?
4. How do archaeologists distinguish domestic plants and animals from wild ones?
5. How can archaeologists distinguish specific kinds of social and political systems?

DISCUSSION QUESTIONS

1. How may changes in subsistence, technology, settlements, and social and political systems be linked? Think holistically.
2. Do you think the development of new subsistence strategies, settlement patterns, social and political systems, and civilizations were beneficial for most people at the time they occurred?
3. If you could live any place on earth at any time between 20,000 and 5,000 years ago, where and when would that be? Why?

Visit **www.lensofanthropology.com** for the following additional resources:

| SELF-STUDY QUESTIONS | WEBLINKS | FURTHER READING |

PLACES MENTIONED IN CHAPTER 7

1 Mesopotamia
2 Egypt
3 Indus Valley, Pakistan
4 China
5 Mesoamerica
6 Canadian Arctic

7 New Zealand
8 Rapa Nui (Easter Island)
9 Hawaii
10 Stonehenge, England
11 Crete
12 Machu Picchu, Peru

ARCHAEOLOGY OF THE LAST 5,000 YEARS

Archaeology gives voice to the voiceless, provides balance, and helps solve problems of life in the twenty-first century #archaeologyofthelast5000years

Learning Objectives

In this chapter students will learn:

- the sequence of early civilizations around the world.
- explanations for the collapse of civilizations.
- North American prehistory from 5,000 years ago to AD 1500.
- that diversity in subsistence and political systems continues.
- why archaeologists work in areas for which written records exist.
- how archaeologists evaluate explanations.
- how archaeologists are involved with sustainability.

Introduction

Many significant changes occurred in the period from 2.5 million to 5,000 years ago. By 5,000 years ago, most people were dependent on domestic plants and animals, and several states as well as at least one civilization had emerged. Things did not slow down in regard to change, though.

This chapter provides an overview of ancient civilizations, including possible reasons for their collapse. This is followed by a section on population estimates, continued geographic expansion, and maintenance of diversity. Finally, the chapter provides an overview of the last 5,000 years of prehistory in North America, archaeology of the historic period, archaeology of the contemporary world, and pseudoarchaeology, including how archaeologists evaluate explanations.

Ancient Civilizations

There is no agreement on precisely what is meant by **civilization**. At a minimum, most archaeologists would accept that a society characterized as a civilization must have all, or almost all, of the following: at least one city, monumental architecture, subsistence based on agriculture, a state level of political organization, and a system of writing. In archaeology, city is usually defined as a settlement having at least 5,000 residents. Monumental architecture may include buildings, but it also often features other large structures like pyramids or megaliths. It is usually the addition of a system of writing that leads archaeologists to describe a society as a civilization. The other characteristics are generally already in place, and have been for a thousand years or more.

Civilizations are sometimes, but not always, equated with a state level of political organization. Often "civilization" is used to describe several distinct states in a region, with each one meeting the criteria of civilization. When one state dominates or exercises control over others, it is often referred to as an **empire**. Empires are often identified in the archaeological record by the comingling of cultural traditions and connecting road systems.

There were many civilizations in the ancient world. As mentioned in Chapter 6, the earliest known civilization was that of the Sumerians, in the region of modern-day Iraq. In reference to ancient times, this area is also known as **Mesopotamia**. It is the Sumerians who developed the world's earliest system of writing, known as cuneiform, about 5,100 years ago. Other major civilizations that followed in the region include the Akkadians, Babylonians, and Assyrians. In more recent times, the region was dominated by the Persian, Roman, and Islamic empires.

The world's second oldest civilization developed in ancient Egypt. It is generally accepted that the Egyptian civilization began 5,000 years ago, with the development of writing. The early writing is known as hieroglyphics, and was deciphered in the 1800s using the **Rosetta Stone**. It is in the earliest stages of the Egyptian civilizations that the famous pyramids were constructed. In more recent times, the region was dominated by the Roman and Islamic empires.

The Minoans were the first European civilization, centered in and around the Mediterranean, especially on the island of Crete. The civilization rose about 4,000

years ago, and its collapse was likely due to a tsunami that caused significant damage to the ports controlled by the Minoans. Many believe that the story of **Atlantis** is based on the collapse of the Minoan civilization. Subsequent civilizations in the area include the Hittites, Mycenaeans, and Etruscans. In more recent times the area was dominated by the Greek, Roman, and Byzantine empires.

Asia has many well-known ancient civilizations. The earliest is commonly known as the Indus Valley, or Harappan, civilization. This civilization, centered in the area now known as Pakistan, emerged about 4,400 years ago, and included well-planned cities of tens of thousands of people. It provides the first evidence of sewage infrastructure, with piping from inside houses joining to larger piping that carried waste out of the residential areas. In China, the Shang civilization emerged about 3,800 years ago. Subsequent civilizations in the region include the Zhou and Han. The well-known **terra cotta army** comprises about 8,000 life-size warriors deposited in formation near the tomb of the first emperor of the area.

There were many well-known civilizations of Central and South America in ancient times. The first civilization in **Mesoamerica** was the Olmec, which emerged about 3,500 years ago. Subsequent civilizations in the area include the Maya, Teotihuacan, Toltec, Zapotec, and Aztec. In South America, the first civilization to emerge is commonly accepted to be the Chavín, about 2,500 years ago. Subsequent to this were the Moche, Tiwanaku, Nasca, and Inka. Because of their territorial expansion and domination, the Maya, Aztec, and Inka civilizations are often referred to as empires.

All civilizations eventually collapse. In some cases, the explanation may be fairly obvious, such as the Aztec and Inka civilizations, which were decimated by Spanish invaders in the 1500s. For many other civilizations, however, explanations are not

Figure 7.1
Rosetta Stone
Discovered in 1799 in the town of Rosetta, Egypt, the stone repeats the same message in three scripts, providing the key for deciphering Egyptian hieroglyphics.
Credit: © The Trustees of the British Museum

Figure 7.2
Egyptian Pyramid
Pyramids symbolize the early stages of Egyptian civilization, known as the Old Kingdom.
Credit: Nadine Ryan

Figure 7.3
Terra Cotta Warriors
Eight thousand life-size terra cotta warriors guard the tomb of an emperor in China.

Credit: lapas77/Shutterstock

Figure 7.4
Machu Picchu, Peru
Machu Picchu is an Inka settlement, located high in the Andes Mountains.

Credit: © Barry D. Kass/Images of Anthropology

so clear, and there is considerable debate. Table 7.1 lists some of the most common explanations for the collapse of civilizations, which may be categorized as ecological, social/political, or ideological.

Ecological explanations vary. Most involve some environmental occurrence, which, in turn, makes it impossible to effectively feed the population and maintain the infrastructure. For example, climatic change may lead to reduced food supplies, resulting in abandonment of cities. Similarly, epidemic diseases among crops are suggested by some as a cause of reduced food production. Many suggest overuse of the soil for farming also leads to reduced food production, which can result in landslides, adding further difficulties. There is some evidence that some large sites have been abandoned due to overirrigation, which causes increased salinity of the soils, rendering them deficient for agriculture. Ecological catastrophe includes such things as earthquakes and tsunamis; the latter, for example, caused significant damage to Minoan sites, from which they could not recover.

Social or political explanations often invoke conflict as an important variable in the collapse of civilizations. Some archaeologists, for example, suggest that infighting likely led to too many resources supporting war or other forms of conflict, at the

Table 7.1
Explanations for the Collapse of Civilizations

Ecological	Ecological catastrophe · Climate change · Diseases to crops · Depletion of soil nutrients
Social/Political	Failure of trading networks · Internal conflict · Conflict with other groups
Ideological	Too many resources spent on religious activity

expense of other, perhaps more important aspects of the civilizations, such as maintaining enough food for all. Examples of this type of internal conflict include the continual fighting among the independent states of the Sumerians in Mesopotamia or the fighting among the various groups of Maya of Mesoamerica. Some archaeologists suggest civilizations collapse because of their failure to create or maintain trading alliances.

Box 7.1

The Collapse of the Maya

For about 2,000 years, the Mayan civilization dominated the region commonly referred to in anthropology as Mesoamerica (including what is now known as Mexico and other Central American countries). Then, approximately a thousand years ago, construction of monumental architecture and the writing of inscriptions ceased, populations of urban areas declined, and eventually the cities were abandoned. This is often described as a "collapse," but this term is loaded. The population of the urban areas certainly declined, the Mayan influence over other states stopped, and they ceased to be an empire, but Mayan civilization continued, and the Maya continue to exist today. In fact, the Indigenous people of the Yucatán area of Mexico are mostly Mayan.

The so-called collapse about a thousand years ago is an area of significant interest in archaeology, and many legitimate hypotheses have been put forward to explain this apparent event. The hypotheses can be grouped into the categories of ecological, social/political, and ideological.

Ecological hypotheses include (i) depletion of nutrients in soil necessary for farming due to overuse, (ii) landslides caused by deforestation, (iii) drought, and (iv) diseased crops. Social and political hypotheses for the collapse include devoting too many resources to conflict rather than to subsistence. This includes allocating resources toward conflict between Mayan states and kingdoms as well as allocating resources to conflicts with others such as Toltec invaders. This category also includes the failure to create or maintain sufficient trading alliances with other groups. Ideological explanations include suggestions that the collapse was caused by allocating too many resources to religion at the expense of either subsistence or maintenance of social and political harmony.

There is no consensus among archaeologists about why the collapse occurred. Anthropologist Richard Wilk (1985) wrote an interesting article on the collapse called "The Ancient Maya and the Political Present," illustrating how ideas about the cause of the Mayan collapse are biased by current events, at least by American archaeologists. Wilk notes, for example, that in the 1960s, most explanations for the Mayan collapse focused on warfare, which correlates with the US involvement in Vietnam. Presumably an American archaeologist hearing daily reports on the war in Vietnam may have been biased toward warfare as an explanation. It was in the 1970s that ecological explanations for the collapse became popular, which Wilk correlates with the emergence of the environmental movement. Wilk also correlates the popularity of ideological explanations with the rise of religious fundamentalism.

Religion has also been invoked as a cause of collapse. Some, for example, suggest that the collapse of the Maya may have been caused by religious leaders redirecting resources for religion and ritual at the expense of subsistence. One line of reasoning holds that leaders might blame a poor crop year on the failure of the people to devote enough resources, including time, to religion or ritual. Accordingly, the leaders demand more resources for religious purposes; this in turn leads to an even worse crop the following year, ultimately ending with the civilization's downfall.

Population Estimates, Continued Colonization, and Maintaining Diversity

Population Estimates and Growth

Estimating populations from prehistoric times is fraught with difficulties, but archaeologists are still able to make approximations. Principal difficulties include (i) many prehistoric sites for which no records exist or have been destroyed, and (ii) estimates that require many assumptions and analogies.

The primary method of estimating populations is to examine what are assumed to be residential structures in a settlement. If the group is assumed to move at least seasonally, archaeologists need to be aware that various settlement sites may be occupied by one group at different times of the year. Some researchers suggest, based on a wide range of ethnographies, that population size can be calculated by estimating 10 square meters (12 square yards) of floor space for every person. Archaeologists are aware, however, that without an indication of many other variables, such as environment, subsistence strategy, and social systems, using this average is not reliable. In many locales, house size is correlated with changing climates, such as smaller houses in colder times, because they are presumably easier to heat. People are likely to have larger living spaces, for example, when they spend more time indoors, as they do in areas with considerable rain. Archaeologists are also aware that in the past, much like today, people with higher status tend to live in larger places.

Archaeologists usually rely on ethnographic analogy when determining how many people occupied a site. If they determine foragers occupied a site, for example, they will use ethnographic data from foragers to make inferences about populations. If they determine pastoralists or horticulturalists occupied a site, they will use relevant ethnographic data collected from recent pastoralists and horticulturalists. Archaeologists are well aware of the problems with using ethnographic data, even if it is used for interpreting sites only a few thousand years old. Foragers, pastoralists, and horticulturalists are not simply living fossils of the past; over time, they have changed as well. And importantly, while foragers, pastoralists, and horticulturalists once occupied the prime habitats on earth, they are now largely in much more inhospitable environments, pushed out of the prime areas by agriculturalists and those interested in resource extraction.

There are many secondary methods of calculating prehistoric populations. Some archaeologists use ecological information to calculate the potential carrying capacity of an area, and then assume that numbers of people were at, or just below, that capacity. Some use cemetery information (e.g., counting graves), but this has many difficulties, including the identification of graves, determining contemporaneity, and assessing preservation. Some archaeologists estimate population based on the size of middens, number of fire hearths, and numbers of discarded cooking pots, but these too require many assumptions and are not reliable.

Because of these difficulties, estimates of prehistoric populations, even when calculated by archaeologists or demographers specializing in the past, should be considered only very approximate. Estimates from the historic period (i.e., when there are written records) tend to be more reliable, but it would be a mistake to consider that just because they were written down, they are accurate. Estimates of the Indigenous populations of North America calculated by Europeans, for example, fluctuate widely and were usually significantly lower than the probable population.

Despite the problems, many archaeologists have made estimates of population in the past. A review of estimates indicates that there were probably around 10 million people in the world about 10,000 years ago. By 5,000 years ago, the population had likely increased to about 100 million and, by 1,000 years ago, the population was probably close to 350 million. In 2015, the population was over seven billion, and climbing.

Continued Colonization

Most, but not all, of the major regions of the earth had been colonized before 5,000 years ago. Notable areas that have only been occupied within the last 5,000 years include the eastern region of the Canadian Arctic, and many islands and island groups of the Pacific Ocean.

The eastern Arctic was the last part of the Americas to be inhabited by humans. Settlement began about 4,000 years ago, and has included several different groups. Today's Inuit are descended from the Thule people, who migrated into the area from the west about 1,000 years ago, replacing the populations already there.

New Zealand and many of the Polynesian islands were among the last places on earth to be colonized. Despite its relatively large land mass and proximity to Australia, which has been occupied for about 50,000 years, New Zealand only appears to have been occupied for about the last 1,000 years. Some of the Polynesian islands, such as Fiji, Tonga, Samoa, and the Cook Islands were likely settled between

Figure 7.5
Statues of Rapa Nui (Easter Island)
Over the last thousand years, several hundred of these statues, called moai, have been made and positioned on the island. The precise reason is unclear, but archaeologists rule out pseudoarchaeological explanations, such as the theory that they were placed there by bored aliens awaiting rescue from the mother ship.
Credit: Nadine Ryan

about 3,500 and 2,500 years ago. It was only about 1,000 years ago that Rapa Nui (Easter Island) and Hawaii were settled.

Maintaining Diversity in Subsistence and Political Systems

There have been several significant changes in subsistence over the past few million years. As described in previous chapters, the first major change in human subsistence first occurred about two million years ago when people started incorporating significant amounts of meat into their diet. The second major change is associated with cooking, which increased the diversity of the plants and animals that could be eaten. The third major change in subsistence began between 15,000 and 12,000 years ago when people began domesticating plants and animals, creating a substantial food surplus. The surplus significantly increased several thousand years ago, when people began practicing intensive agriculture, including the use of plows, harnessing animal power (including animals to pull plows), and intensive irrigation. The surplus was enough that it enabled a large proportion of the population not to be directly involved in the collection or production of food. It is this surplus created by agriculture that basically allowed the population to expand to hundreds of millions worldwide.

The next major shift in subsistence occurred only a couple of hundred years ago. This involved relying on **industrialism** for food production. This essentially means that mechanized equipment, in many cases powered by fossil fuels, is involved in farming. This development significantly increased the food surplus once again, and it is likely that most people in North America eat food primarily produced by industrialization (see Chapter 10 for further discussion about food and industrialization).

The basic sequence of subsistence strategies starts with foraging and then moves through pastoralism and horticulture to intensive agriculture and then industrialization. It would be a mistake, however, to think these changes were necessarily progressive. It is important to remember that there are usually many ways of successfully adapting to environments, and other people and situations. What works for some people does not necessarily work for others.

Similarly, the basic sequence of political systems starts with bands and moves through tribes and chiefdoms to states and empires. Archaeologists know that subsistence and political systems are closely correlated and that no one system is necessarily better than another.

Thus, although many people now depend on food produced from industrialized farms and live in state level societies, it is important to understand that diversity in subsistence and social systems remain. Foraging, pastoralism, horticulture, and agriculture are not extinct strategies, nor are bands, tribes, and chiefdoms. Indeed, recent and contemporary examples of these systems are covered in the remaining chapters of this book.

In no way should groups that are not willing partners in industrialized states be considered inferior or primitive. In many ways, people that have resisted the changes have more leisure time and live a healthier life.

The Last 5,000 Years in North America

Hundreds of thousands of archaeological sites date from the period between 5,000 years ago to the arrival of Europeans in the United States and Canada beginning around AD 1500. Many of these are recognized as having "world heritage" status and are included in the United Nations list of world heritage sites. Some of the most significant and interesting sites dating to the last 5,000 years in the United States and Canada are described in Table 7.2 and shown in Map 6.2.

Groups occupying what is now the United States and Canada from 5,000 years ago to the arrival of Europeans were numerous and diverse. Scholarly estimates suggest a population of approximately five million people, speaking about 400 different languages. Many groups continued their generalized foraging lifestyles from

Table 7.2

Significant Archaeological Sites in North America Less than 5,000 Years Old

Site Name	Description
Cahokia	Cahokia, located near St. Louis, is a United Nations World Heritage Site. With an estimated population of about 20,000 people, it was probably the largest prehistoric settlement north of Mexico. The site is an excellent example of the mound-building peoples from the prehistoric period. Cahokia itself contains more than 100 distinct mounds. The largest is estimated to have covered 12 acres and to have been close to 100 feet in height.
Head-Smashed-In Buffalo Jump	This site, located in Alberta, is another United Nations World Heritage Site. It contains cultural deposits 10 meters thick, containing projectile points and buffalo bones. The site was used for several thousand years, and includes drive lanes to direct buffalo over the cliff. The site provides considerable evidence of technological and social evolution related to the communal hunting of buffalo, which was fundamentally important to the Indigenous peoples of the North American plains and prairies.
Kwaday Dan Ts'inchi	Located in the Pacific Northwest, close to the intersecting borders of Alaska, British Columbia, and the Yukon, this site yielded an extremely well-preserved body of an Indigenous man that was exposed by a melting glacier. The local Indigenous groups and archaeologists undertook studies of the body, after which the remains were returned to the land with ritual.
L'Anse aux Meadows	Located in Newfoundland, and a United Nations World Heritage Site, L'Anse aux Meadows is best known as a Viking settlement dating to about AD 1000. It is the oldest reliably dated site created by Europeans on the continent, but was probably only used a few years. The Vikings evidently did not have a good relationship with the local Indigenous peoples in Newfoundland and abandoned their settlement. Viking settlements have been found elsewhere in Arctic Canada and Greenland dating to approximately the same time. There is evidence of Indigenous occupation of the site up to 6,000 years ago.
Mesa Verde	Mesa Verde National Park is yet another United Nations World Heritage Site, representative of peoples and cultures of the American Southwest from several hundred to more than one thousand years ago. The park protects more than 4,000 archaeological sites, including 600 cliff dwellings constructed mostly with sandstone blocks and adobe mortar.
Ozette	Ozette is a village site, sometimes referred to as the "Pompeii of North America," due to the excellent preservation of remains caused by a mudslide burying the village. The site, located on the coast of Washington State, consists of several large multi-family houses and tens of thousands of wood and bone artifacts that do not normally preserve.

earlier times, since that is what likely made most ecological sense. Many others, however, developed new subsistence strategies. For example, several groups along the coastal areas of the northwest part of the continent developed into specialized foragers. They maintained a wide diversity of wild plants and animals in their diet, but specialized in salmon. Some groups in California became specialized foragers, focusing on acorns. Many groups practiced horticulture. This includes groups along the east coast and in the American Southwest. Primary crops included maize

Box 7.2

Contemporary North American Archaeology

Archaeology in North America is diverse—different archaeologists doing different kinds of things. Some archaeologists work in the academic world, some in business. Some focus on the prehistoric record in North America, some on the colonial and recent past, and others on the contemporary world. Some even focus on the archaeology of outer space. There are approximately 15,000 people making a career in archaeology in North America.

Academic, Commercial, Indigenous, and Amateur Archaeologies

Most of the archaeology that people hear about via mainstream media is academic archaeology. Archaeologists working out of universities usually undertake archaeological research with pure scholarly research objectives. Often the research is directed by professors, but some is also directed by students working on a master's degree or a PhD, to help prove their ability to undertake scholarly research. The results of the research are usually presented at a conference, and/or submitted as an article written for a scholarly journal. Sometimes a journalist attends the conference or reads an article and then turns the research into a story for media. Probably less than 1 per cent of archaeological research makes it to the mainstream media. Academic archaeology is ongoing throughout North America, but unless you are an archaeologist, or are directly involved in some way, you are unlikely to know about it.

Most people making a career in archaeology are doing what is broadly known as cultural resource management, or commercial archaeology. This is archaeology in the business world. It is likely that about 90 per cent of the people making a living in archaeology in North America are engaging in this kind of archaeology. Typically they are working in advance of development projects, assessing the potential damage to archaeological sites from the project. Sometimes, when highly significant sites are discovered, the project may be altered to avoid the site. Alternatively, the site is excavated.

Indigenous archaeology essentially means doing archaeology with, by, or for Native Americans or First Nations. In academic archaeology, it is the archaeologist that sets the agenda (determining goals and methods, etc.). In commercial archaeology, it is the government that sets the agenda. In Indigenous archaeology it is the Indigenous group that sets the agenda.

Amateur archaeology can be both good and bad. The good kind includes people not formally trained in archaeology who volunteer their time to work under the direction of archaeologists, following the methods and ethics of archaeology. The bad kind includes people who excavate archaeological sites without proper permits or permission and do not following established methods and ethics. These people are often referred to as "pothunters," which has nothing to do with searching for marijuana. Pothunter is a generic term applied to all looters of antiquities; it is based on those who once looted pottery from sites, but it now applies to all.

Prehistoric, Historic, and the Archaeology of the Contemporary World

The majority of archaeologists working in North America focus on prehistoric archaeology (i.e., before the arrival of Europeans) but there are many that focus on the historic period (since the arrival of Europeans). A recent area of interest is the use of methods and perspectives of archaeology to examine the contemporary world. Thus, we have archaeologists sifting through contemporary trash, archaeologists working among homeless people, archaeologists working in the aftermath of disasters, and archaeologists working in forensic investigations. Some archaeologists focus on documenting (and work toward preserving) human activity in outer space.

Figure 7.6
Stonehenge
The area around Stonehenge has been occupied for about 8,000 years, although the core parts of the stone structures were positioned at various times between about 5,000 and 3,000 years ago.

Credit: © Barry D. Kass/ Images of Anthropology

(corn), beans, and squash. The only animal likely domesticated for food was the turkey, although there is some suggestion that turkeys may also have been domesticated for their feathers. There were certainly domestic dogs, but it is unlikely they were domesticated for food.

When Europeans first arrived, most Indigenous groups could likely trace their ancestry to populations living in the same area for the previous several thousand years or more. There were certainly exceptions, though. The Apache and Navajo migrated from the subarctic region of northern Canada to the American Southwest about 1,000 years ago, and as mentioned earlier in the chapter, the ancestors of contemporary Inuit in Canada replaced other groups in the region about 1,000 years ago.

The Indigenous peoples of North America had a phenomenal understanding of plants for food and medicines. Archaeological and ethnographic research indicates that before the arrival of Europeans, more than 1,500 species of plants were used for food and more than 2,500 were used as medicines.

Archaeology of Recent Times, Excluding Civilizations

Much of the focus on the past 5,000 years is on ancient civilizations, and for those in North America, on the Indigenous populations there. It is important to understand that this is partly because of the high archaeological visibility of civilizations, and North Americans assume at least some ancestral connection with ancient civilizations.

Certainly there have been some great cultural achievements associated with civilizations, but it isn't as if they were, or are, necessarily superior. Stonehenge, for example, and many other similar monuments requiring advanced engineering skills were built by those living in chiefdoms. The settlement of some Pacific islands required seafaring skills at least equal to those of European explorers. We know they weren't simply blown off course accidentally, because they brought domestic plants and animals with them.

A major subfield of archaeology is historic archaeology, which essentially means that archaeologists are doing work in an area and focusing on a time period for which written records exist. Some non-anthropologists question why, when there is a written record, we would even bother, but archaeologists are aware that written records are usually incomplete and biased. The history of slavery, for example, is often written from the perspective of slave owners. The histories of Indigenous peoples and other minorities are usually written from the perspective of the majority, the oppressors. Archaeology provides balance. Archaeology gives voice to the voiceless.

In North America, the transition from prehistory (before written records) to history (with written records) occurs whenever Europeans entered an area. Thus, historic archaeology starts about 500 years ago on the east coast, but not until the late 1700s on the west coast of Canada. Major areas of interest in historic period archaeology in North America include the archaeology of colonialism, civil war archaeology, African American archaeology, and Asian American archaeology.

Figure 7.7
Excavating a Historic Site in North America
Historic archaeology often provides important information that was never written down or is biased. This site was a Japanese settlement in western Canada, for which no written records exist.
Credit: Emma Kimm-Jones

World Heritage

In 1972 the United Nations Educational, Scientific, and Cultural Organization, commonly known as UNESCO, created the Convention Concerning the Protection of the World Cultural and Natural Heritage, which led to the well-known World Heritage List. Sites included on the list have been determined to have outstanding universal value. There are currently more than a thousand sites on the list, with at least several being added each year. At least several hundred are in the "cultural" (as opposed to "natural") category.

A small sample of sites that fall within the time period of the last 5,000 years are included in Table 7.3.

The World Heritage List has many benefits, such as popularizing the importance of heritage, providing education about archaeology, providing some assistance and protection for the sites, and stimulating archaeo-tourism. Although there are strict criteria for nomination and inclusion on the list, it is not without bias. Even a quick look at the entire list provides evidence of bias toward specific countries (such as those in Europe and Central America), and bias toward sites from the historic period, especially with links to Europe or colonialism. The fact that a site is not on the list does not necessarily mean that it is not significant. Some countries simply choose to not nominate sites for inclusion.

Table 7.3

Selected World Heritage Sites from the Last 5,000 Years

Region	Sites
United States	Mesa Verde, Cahokia, Chaco Canyon, Pueblo de Taos, Independence Hall, Monticello and University of Virginia, Statue of Liberty
Canada	L'Anse aux Meadows, Head-Smashed-In Buffalo Jump, Historic district of Quebec City, Old Town Lunenberg, Anthony Island
Central America (including Mexico)	Tikal, Copán, Monte Albán, Chichen Itza, Palenque, Teotihuacan, Uxmal
South America	Tiwanaku, Rapa Nui, Machu Picchu, Lines and geoglyphs of Nasca
Europe	Acropolis of Athens, Pompeii, Stonehenge and Avebury
Asia	Angkor, Moenjo Daro, Terra cotta warriors, Bamiyan Valley
Africa	Pyramids at Giza, Great Zimbabwe
Australia	Kakadu

Archaeology of the Contemporary World

In the early twenty-first century many archaeologists have turned their archaeological lens toward the contemporary world. Areas of interest include contemporary household trash, nuclear waste, and trash in outer space. Archaeologists have developed new subfields such as forensic archaeology and disaster archaeology, as well as becoming advocates for the disenfranchised. They also like to contribute in practical ways to issues related to sustainability.

This trend toward shifting the focus of archaeology to contemporary society started in a serious way in the late twentieth century with the study of contemporary North American trash, commonly known as **garbology**. The guru in this regard was William Rathje (2002). He led archaeological projects focusing on trash at levels ranging from looking through individual household trash bins that were put out for collection to excavating landfill sites of large North American cities. Results in the late 1900s were surprising. They often showed a disconnect between what people said they did at the household level, and what they actually did, as indicated by their trash. (See Chapter 8 for a discussion of real culture versus ideal culture.) Similarly, popular perceptions of landfills were different from reality. One of the most important results of the landfill archaeology was the discovery that organic remains did not decompose very quickly. It was not unusual to find decades-old heads of lettuce and hot dogs. Research at both the household level and in landfills also indicates that North Americans are extremely wasteful, discarding a significant percentage of food, and that despite efforts to reduce trash, the average amount of trash thrown away by individuals continues to increase.

Many archaeologists have remained interested in contemporary waste in the twenty-first century, and they sometimes work alongside others from environmental geography, environmental science, discard studies, and sustainability studies, to help solve some of the problems of trash. Of course, the problems are many, and

Figure 7.8
Waste Audit Archaeology
Archaeology students put what they learn of archaeological method and theory into practice, sorting through campus trash. The university uses the results to effectively reduce waste.
Credit: Bob Muckle

include the sheer volume of trash, the danger of the chemicals and toxins within the trash, pollution, animals feeding on plastics, and the costs of packaging and recycling. Edward Humes (2012) provides an overview of some basic data associated with trash created by Americans. This includes the fact that Americans create 25 per cent of the world's total waste; the average American creates more than seven pounds of trash per day; there is more money spent on waste management than on fire protection, parks and recreation, libraries, and schoolbooks combined; there are about 60 million water bottles discarded daily; the amount of plastic wrap discarded each year could shrinkwrap Texas; and there is enough wood put into landfills each year to heat 50 million homes for 20 years.

Some archaeologists on campuses across North America are now tackling the problems of trash in a practical way. At Capilano University in North Vancouver, Canada, for example, archaeology students are involved in regular waste audits on campus. Waste is sorted and the resulting data are used to improve discard behaviors, reduce total waste, and increase campus sustainability.

Archaeologists have also been involved in studies of nuclear waste. The US government has consulted archaeologists since the 1980s on how to best mark nuclear waste sites so that people of the future will recognize the danger. Who better to consult than those that know what is likely to survive and be interpretable? Based on their experience and knowledge, archaeologists have made many recommendations, including that (i) multiple symbols, pictures, and languages should be used; (ii) structures should be made of natural materials such as earth or stone with no perceived value, for if there is a perceived value it will inevitably be looted; (iii) large monoliths should ring the site, so that a pattern will be visible; and (iv) subsurface markers, made of ceramic, should be included at various levels.

Archaeologists in the early twenty-first century are also interested in trash in outer space, including the tons of trash left on the moon and planets as well as the hundreds of thousands of pieces of space junk in orbit, also known as orbital debris. Archaeologists both remotely document the remains of human culture left on the moon and planets and advocate for their protection from space tourists, who will inevitably be making trips to the moon. Archaeologists also document and study the many thousands of pieces of orbital debris from satellites and other objects in space, which pose serious hazards to space travel.

Other ways archaeologists bring their lens and skills to the contemporary world is through the emergent subfields of forensic archaeology and disaster archaeology. Forensic archaeology is the application of archaeology in legal contexts, usually in regard to assisting criminal investigations. Forensic archaeologists offer skills of identifying, recovering, recording, and interpreting physical evidence of human activities. They also occasionally focus on human biological remains, but the focus

Archaeology and Sustainability

Archaeology has strong links to the environmental movement, including issues relating to sustainability. Archaeologists bring examples of how sustainability has failed to be maintained in the past in various ways, including how over-irrigation in some Mesopotamian communities led to oversalination, rendering the soils unsuitable for planting. They also use their knowledge to help people become more sustainable today, such as using their research on how people created and maintained raised fields in South America for thousands of years to recreate the same methods today, with great success.

Working toward reducing their own ecological imprint, many archaeologists are consciously going digital in fieldwork and lab work recording. Some archaeologists focus on studying contemporary waste to provide raw data which can be used to move forward in increasing sustainability.

The study of contemporary trash has been undertaken by archaeologists since the 1980s. Of the many important things they have learned, one of the most interesting and significant is that, at least in North America, the more opportunities there are to throw things away, the more things *will* be thrown away (rather than being reused or recycled).

on human biological remains is usually considered to fall under the umbrella of forensic anthropology.

Disaster anthropology emerged in the United States in the twenty-first century. It got its start with offers to help with the identification, recovery, and interpretation of human remains immediately after the 9/11 disaster in New York, in which thousands were killed after airplanes hit the Twin Towers. Since then, disaster archaeology has taken hold, and archaeologists are often on scene shortly after disasters, both natural and cultural, to aid in identification and recovery.

Pseudoarchaeology

Archaeologists are often faced with deciding which explanation is best for something that occurred in the past. There are often multiple explanations for a particular phenomenon, such as the origin of food production, or the collapse of civilizations, and archaeologists must choose for themselves which one is best. Likewise, there are often some rather bizarre explanations that include aliens and other strange phenomena that should be subjected to critical thinking.

Some of the criteria for evaluating explanations or hypothesis about the past are described in Table 7.4. Testability is paramount. If the hypothesis is not testable, then it should not be considered, especially within the framework of science or archaeology. This is where odd ideas involving extraterrestrials, supernatural forces, or other strange or bizarre explanations are discarded. We have no way of testing for the presence of an extraterrestrial or the supernatural. Archaeologists need empirical evidence, things that can be touched, weighed, drawn, photographed, and analyzed. People who maintain explanations involving aliens or supernatural phenomena often are characterized as practicing **pseudoarchaeology**. Popular notions about the Egyptian pyramids, statues of Rapa Nui, and Stonehenge, for example, having something to do with alien life forms, are pseudoscientific. They are not considered seriously since the hypotheses cannot be tested. In response to one such popular claim that aliens mated with ancient Egyptians, providing them knowledge to build the pyramids to specific criteria, well-known and highly respected scientist Carl Sagan (1979) stated:

> We are thinking beings. We are interested and excited in understanding how the world is put together. We seek out the extraordinary, and if you think of these claims, if only they were true they would be amazingly interesting—that we have been visited by beings from elsewhere who not only have created our civilizations for us, but mated with human beings. In my view it's much more likely to successfully mate with a petunia than an extraterrestrial.

Table 7.4
Criteria for Evaluating Explanations about the Past

Question	Action
Is the hypothesis testable?	If not, consider it no further.
Is the hypothesis compatible with our general understanding of the archaeological record?	If not, be cautious.
Occam's razor	The simplest explanation is usually the best. The simplest is the one that requires the fewest assumptions.
Have all competing explanations been considered equally?	Do not accept one hypothesis by merely rejecting the others.

When evaluating various hypotheses, it is important to consider how well it fits with our general understanding of the archaeological record. When considering the initial colonization of North America, for example, the route from Asia is usually considered the strongest hypothesis. This explanation best fits our basic understanding of world prehistory, insofar as archaeologists know people were already close by in Asia immediately before the first evidence in the Americas, and their subsistence and technology was similar.

An Archaeologist Eats a Shrew

One of the most interesting, some may say disgusting, stories about archaeology in recent years involves a bit of experimental archaeology. It concerns an archaeologist eating a small animal, followed by him and another archaeologist then sifting through feces of the eater, to see if all that went in also came out.

The experiments are described in an article called "Human Digestive Effects on a Micro-mammalian Skeleton" (Crandall & Stahl 1995). The objective was to be able to better interpret the assemblages of animal bones in archaeological sites, which is necessary to make proper interpretations of diet. The authors describe how they skinned, eviscerated, and cooked a shrew and then ate it without chewing.

After days of examining the feces of the one who ate it, the results were in. Of the 131 skeletal elements of the shrew that went in, only 28 were recovered from the feces. The authors are confident that the missing bones completely succumbed to the human digestive processes.

The research gained much publicity in 2013 when the archaeologists received an Ig Nobel Prize (a parody of the Nobel Prize), sponsored by the *Annals of Improbable Research*. As stated, the awards are to "honor achievements that make people LAUGH, and then THINK." In that regard, the award to the archaeologists is deserved. It may seem disgusting but the work is significant. Archaeologists interested in diet need to know what is likely to preserve and what isn't. Sometimes, apparently, for the good of archaeology, some will sift through the fresh feces of their own and of their colleagues.

Occam's razor is well known in science. Essentially, applying Occam's razor means that the simplest explanation is usually the best, with the simplest being the one that requires the fewest assumptions. Considering the initial colonization of the Americas again: the simplest explanation is that the ancestry of the initial migrants lay in Asia. The only assumption necessary to accept this hypothesis is that they expanded their territory. The idea that the migrants came from Europe, on the other hand, requires multiple significant assumptions, including the fact that the migrants had the ability to build boats able to navigate the often stormy North Atlantic; that they had the imperative to seek distant lands they probably knew nothing about; that they were able to travel by boat for very long distances in glacial environments; that they were able to adapt to resources substantially different from those in Europe; and that they left behind the significant artistic traditions common in Europe at a time the voyages are assumed to have occurred.

It is important that all explanations be considered equally, and that we not simply accept one explanation by elimination of the others. Accepting one hypothesis by eliminating the others is a common ruse of pseudoarchaeologists. A pseudarchae-ologist, for example, may generate four hypotheses, systematically reject the first three and then proclaim the fourth explanation, one that involves aliens, as the only possible explanation. This is very bad science.

Summary

This chapter has provided an overview of the archaeology of the last 5,000 years. Mirroring the Learning Objectives stated in the chapter opening, the key points include:

- Ancient civilizations were many, and they all collapsed. There are multiple explanations why.
- A significant recent development is industrialization, beginning only a couple hundred years ago.
- Foraging, pastoralist, and horticultural groups still exist, as do the forms of political organization known as bands, tribes, and chiefdoms. They are not inferior or primitive. In many cases they provide a better life.
- North American prehistory over the past 5,000 years was highly developed, and some groups practiced horticulture.
- Many archaeologists focus on the time period for which written records also exist, providing balance and new kinds of information.
- Some archaeologists focus on the contemporary world, using the methods and theories of archaeology.
- The World Heritage List is important, but biased.
- Pseudoarchaeological claims can be evaluated and debunked by using established criteria.

REVIEW QUESTIONS

1. What is the history of early civilizations around the world?
2. What are the principal explanations for the collapse of civilizations?
3. How do archaeologists make population estimates, and what are the estimates?
4. What are the principal cultural developments around the world over the last 5,000 years?
5. What are some examples of the archaeology of the contemporary world?
6. What is the World Heritage List?
7. How do archaeologists evaluate competing explanations?

DISCUSSION QUESTIONS

1. Why do you think there are so few prehistoric world heritage sites in North America? Do you think it is the result of Eurocentric bias, historic bias, lack of significant sites, lack of features with high archaeological visibility, or something else?
2. Assume North American civilization collapses and all cities are abandoned within the next 100 years. What kinds of evidence will archaeologists have of twenty-first-century North America 5,000 years from now, and what might their interpretations be?

Visit **www.lensofanthropology.com** for the following additional resources:

| SELF-STUDY QUESTIONS | WEBLINKS | FURTHER READING |

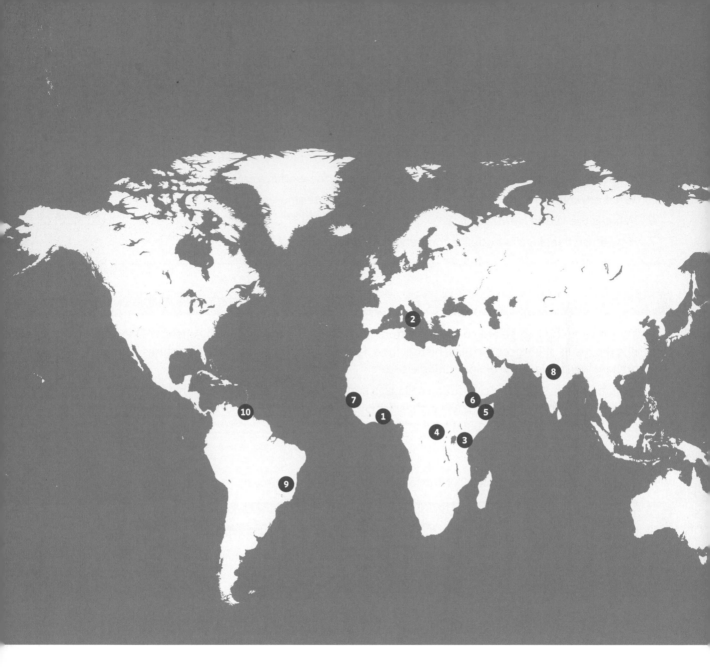

PLACES MENTIONED IN CHAPTER 8

1 Ghana
2 Italy
3 Tanzania
4 Ituri Forest, DRC
5 Somalia

6 Djibouti
7 Guinea
8 India
9 Brazil
10 Venezuela

STUDYING CULTURE

Learning Objectives

In this chapter students will learn:

- what anthropologists mean by culture.
- the usefulness of using the approach of cultural relativism over ethnocentrism.
- how to evaluate whether cultural practices are adaptive or maladaptive.
- the functions of culture.
- how personality and culture are linked.
- how anthropologists study culture in the field.

Introduction

This book introduces the perspective of anthropology as a kind of lens through which one sees the world. In particular, the lens focuses on each society's intricate web of knowledge, beliefs, and practices—a web that we must understand as a whole. In addition, the anthropological lens sees every culture as valid and complex, a magnificent puzzle that the anthropologist attempts to piece together.

Similarly, culture can be thought of as a kind of lens, although no special skills or knowledge are needed to look through it. All humans use their own cultural lenses to understand and interpret their surroundings. The cultural lens guides our behavior and interactions with others.

We're not born with one particular lens, or cultural perspective, but all humans have the capacity for culture. That is, we are born ready to learn culture, but nothing in our genes or biology determines what culture we learn. For example, an infant born to a Ghanaian mother and father will learn Ghanaian culture. Equally, an infant born to an Italian mother and a Polish father living in Ghana will learn Ghanaian culture. She'll likely wear Kente cloth and enjoy *fufu* (a Ghanaian staple food) in her school lunches. Of course, she will also be exposed to aspects of her parents' upbringing as well (and may also enjoy the occasional linguini or kielbasa), but she doesn't receive "Italian DNA" or "Polish DNA" that translates directly into culture or language. In other words, she acquires her culture based on experience.

Understanding culture allows us to behave appropriately when we interact with others. When a baby is born in a hospital in the United States, nurses provide a little blue cap or a little pink cap to mark the baby's gender. Is this so the baby learns to act properly? No, because of course, the baby doesn't understand yet. It's for others, so they can behave appropriately in relation to the infant. To the baby in the pink cap, a family member may coo, "Hello, beautiful princess." On the other hand, the baby in the blue cap will more likely elicit comments about the strong kicks that the little "future soccer player" is making in his bassinet. Expectations of how people behave based on their sex are an essential part of culture.

All human groups have culture (and some animal groups too, although to a lesser extent). Sharing culture means people understand what goes on around them in approximately the same ways. They can read their surroundings as if social interaction were a text. Another helpful way to think about culture is to imagine members connected by threads of a web. These webs of meaning are invisible and usually unspoken. But the unwritten rules are there, guiding our behavior, as we choose which threads to take along the way.

Since culture can't be measured, held in your hands, or shown on a map, how do anthropologists understand it? We learn about culture by getting in the thick of it. Ethnographers go and live among the people that they aim to learn about, and slowly, over time, come to understand their world.

Practicing cultural anthropology means that field-workers participate in people's lives at the same time that they are observing and analyzing behavior. We call the process of studying culture **ethnographic research** and the written or visual product of that research an **ethnography**. Importantly, the lens of anthropology shapes how **ethnographers** approach their subjects and what questions they ask. In particular, ethnographers seek to understand the **emic**—or cultural insider's—view as well as the **etic**—or outside observer's—view.

Practicing Cultural Anthropology

Carole Counihan is a cultural anthropologist, professor, and author interested in food, culture, and gender. She began as a graduate student at the University of Massachusetts at Amherst, where she was inspired to pursue food studies after taking a course in food and culture. Her fieldwork led to six years studying, living, and eating in Italy; first, on the island of Sardinia in a town called Bosa for her doctoral dissertation, then in Tuscany, in the city of Florence.

In Florence, Counihan collected life histories of 15 female and 10 male members of a single family to discover their attitudes and behaviors regarding food. In particular, she wanted to learn about how gender expectations affect food preparation as well as the giving and receiving of food items. Traditionally, women's identities and power centered on their roles as the makers and givers of food. Today, more women must work outside the home in jobs or careers that do not allow them to fulfill these roles in the ways their mothers and grandmothers did. Therefore, Counihan found that women experienced a deep and frustrating identity conflict, wanting to succeed in both the domestic and external spheres. This is the subject of her book *Around the Tuscan Table: Food, Family, and Gender in Twentieth-Century Florence* (2004).

Figure 8.1 **Carole Counihan**
Carole Counihan in Cagliari, Sardinia, Italy.
Credit: Photo by James Taggart. Reproduced by permission of Carole Counihan

Like many anthropologists, Counihan joined a college faculty to be able to teach and continue her research. She is currently a professor of anthropology at Millersville University, where she also teaches in the Women's and Latino Studies departments. She has authored several additional books on food, gender, and culture, including *A Tortilla Is Like Life: Food and Culture in the San Luis Valley of Colorado* (2009), and *The Anthropology of Food and Body: Gender, Meaning, and Power* (1999). Counihan has also edited several volumes on food and culture, and has been the editor-in-chief of the interdisciplinary academic journal *Food and Foodways* for several decades. She is currently living and working in Cagliari, Sardinia, Italy where she is studying food activism.

Every cultural anthropologist has a story about how their interest in anthropology developed, which field sites attracted and hosted them, and what issues called to them over the course of their career. Box 8.1 introduces Carole Counihan, a cultural anthropologist whose interest in food led her to Italy.

The Culture Concept

A basic way to define culture is as the shared understandings that shape thought and guide behavior. That is to say, members of a culture share a set of beliefs, customs, values, and knowledge. These shared understandings allow us to act in ways that make sense to others.

Symbolic anthropologist Clifford Geertz (1973) emphasizes the idea that culture is a set of functions, and not simply a list of attributes or behaviors. He argues that culture works like a computer program, in that it has the rules and instructions for behavior. This prescient definition, written before computers were an integral part of our everyday lives, makes sense now more than ever. In other words, cultural practices can be observed, but what anthropologists really want to get at is what causes those behaviors. Anthropologists want to know how culture functions like an "app" that "writes" our behavior. At the same time, depending upon their framework, anthropologists are also interested in how biology (such as genetics) and environmental influences affect the thoughts and behaviors of people in society.

What Are the Parts of Culture?

Culture has three basic parts: what we think (cognition), what we do (behavior), and what we have (artifacts).

First, what we think: The values we learn from our parents and the symbols we understand in our environment are cognitive. This includes the information and understandings that allow us to relate to other members of our culture.

Second, what we do: Actions and interactions with others are behavioral. How a person eats, works, and plays are all products of this shared knowledge. Shared culture guides behaviors in ways that allow people to understand and act appropriately with each other.

Finally, what we have: The material products of our society are artifacts (portable items) and features (non-portable items). This includes things like pottery and clothing (portable) to buildings and roads (non-portable). Artifacts and features are also referred to as material culture: the things that people make, alter, and use.

Four Characteristics of Culture

Culture has certain important features that make it different from biological instincts or personality traits. Instincts are something people are born with. That is, instincts are coded in their DNA as part of the legacy of *Homo sapiens*. Personality traits arise in individuals due to their unique development or experience. Culture differs from genetics or personality because it is learned, based on symbols, holistic and shared.

Humans are not born with knowledge of their culture. They learn it actively and acquire it passively from the people around them. The process of learning begins with an infant's interactions with primary caregivers and family; then, the process extends in childhood to friends, schoolteachers, the media, and other influences.

When we talk about culture being based on symbols, we are not only referring to peace signs and happy faces. Although these and other graphic representations of ideas are symbols, a **symbol** can be anything that stands for something else and carries meaning. Symbols are generally arbitrary, that is, there does not need to be any connection between the symbol and the idea.

For instance, you may not have thought of language as symbolic. But what else is it besides a set of sounds (speech) or a set of squiggles (writing) that stand for ideas? What makes language symbolic is that it is conventional. In other words, members of a culture agree upon the meaning of the sounds and squiggles. Humans are the only species to have developed full-blown, symbolic natural language. We can scheme, imagine, and analyze—things that non-human animals don't seem to be able to do, at least not to the extent to which we can. (You will learn more about symbolic language in Chapter 9.)

Culture is holistic, or integrated. Anthropologists approach the study of culture with the knowledge that all aspects of a society are linked. If one aspect is altered, then the others will be affected as well. For instance, in a colonial situation, the dominant society may impose new religious practices on a traditional or smaller society. With the loss of familiar ritual, the rites performed to ensure a good harvest may be lost, farming practices may change, and even family life may be altered. This is why some compare anthropology to conducting an orchestra: the fieldworker must listen to the strings, winds, horns, and percussion to understand the whole musical piece.

Finally, because the idea of culture involves more than just one individual, culture must be shared. A personality feature that isn't shared by others could be called a quirk or unique attribute. For example, if one person wears earrings made of tomatoes, it is a quirk. If that person carries some status, such as being a celebrity, and others join in, then it may become a cultural fad (albeit a very strange one). The shared nature of culture allows people to understand each other's words and actions.

Culture as Community

In this book, several different terms are used to talk about people and their cultures. Depending on the context, people may be referred to as a community, group, or society. When people share a geographical space, they are referred to here as a **community**. A community of people lives, works, and plays together. **Group** is a looser term, referring to people who share culture. Members of a group generally live in the same region. Finally, **society** is used somewhat interchangeably with the term group, to refer to a large number of people with social connections.

Sometimes there is confusion over the differences between culture and society. For instance, Vietnamese society shares a culture. In other words, Vietnamese people

Figure 8.2
Steampunk Cosplay
Participants in the Steampunk subculture share an interest in creative re-imaginings of a Victorian/Wild West past inspired by authors like Jules Verne and H.G. Wells.

Credit: Angel Piedad /Chapter One Photography

learn the roles and expectations of their culture. Of course, this is a broad generalization, since not all members of a culture know everything about it! Every culture has variation: generally the larger the culture, the more variation exists.

Ants and bees also may be said to have a society. However, in the insect world, society refers to their instinctual organization and roles. Some bees are born drones and some are born queens. They don't get to decide. Young teenage bees don't suffer angst about what they are going to be when they grow up. They just know, because they're born with impulses that drive their behavior. Human society, on the other hand, is predicated on cultural values and expectations, not on biological imperative.

Within any culture, we can find many communities based on **identity markers**. Markers may include ethnicity, socio-economic class, religious beliefs, age, gender, and interest. These sub-groups, or **subcultures**, are made up of people connected by similarities. Subcultures may reflect ethnic heritage, such as Mexican-Americans. Or they may denote common interests, such as Steampunk cosplay in which people dress in futuristic Victorian-era clothing and hold events where they interact in character.

If a group shares many identity markers, it is referred to as **homogeneous** (*homo* = same). An example of people who share homogeneous culture is the Hadza people of Tanzania. The Hadza have a close-knit community and remain primarily hunter-gatherers in the twenty-first century. They largely reject outsiders joining their social group and marry within it. Therefore, although of course there are individual differences among Hadza people, they share many of the same beliefs, values, and behaviors.

Groups that share few identity markers are described as **heterogeneous** (*hetero* = different). An example of people who share heterogeneous culture is in the United States. It has been described as a "melting pot" or "tossed salad," referring to the mixture of people of different ancestry who are all residents. There are many languages, religious beliefs, values, and ethnicities, but all share a set of understandings (i.e., culture).

Cultures can be large or small; they can be concentrated, or **diasporic** (spread across the world). A culture is not a fixed entity, especially when so many migrants have left their birthplaces to live in another region, state, or country. Many people today are first- or second-generation citizens of a country to which their parents or grandparents have emigrated. Often people whose families have left their home countries and now reside in a different one are bi-cultural or multicultural. They share values and practices of the culture of their parents and the culture of where they currently live.

Even though the term *culture* is used in this book and others to refer to a set of understandings that guide people's behavior, it is important to recognize that culture is not static. It is always changing. Some changes may be slow, such as the goals of gender or racial equality. Other changes may be fast as lightning, such as the adoption of smart phones and social media. Nonetheless, every society adapts and evolves. No group is fossilized as if their culture were a museum exhibit.

Learning Culture

Since culture is learned, people are not born with instincts about what to do to be a fully functioning member of that culture. They don't yet know what and how to eat, how to behave as a girl or boy, or what is right and wrong. Because members of a group share culture, the knowledge and understandings that make up that culture must be passed on from member to member. Culture is transmitted from one generation to the next, from parents and other adults to children, through the process of **enculturation**.

People who have the most contact with infants and young children act as the primary transmitters of culture. While this is usually a child's mother and father, it may also be his grandparents or another close adult. As the child gets older, he comes into contact with many other people outside his family. His peers also play a role in the enculturation process. As kids play together they learn from each other, practicing cultural roles they will later step into, such as dad, mom, warrior, healer, or teacher.

Figure 8.3
Girl with Braided Hair, Runaway Bay, Jamaica
Children in every culture learn the appropriate ways to behave as boys or girls. This young girl from Runaway Bay, Jamaica, has been enculturated into her community from a very young age.
Credit. © Barry D. Kass/Images of Anthropology

In North America, little girls rarely play with trucks as their first toys. Little boys rarely play with tea sets. Girls are given dolls to prepare them for motherhood, a nurturing role that society considers appropriate for females. Boys play soldiers, spies, or superheroes, which prepares them for more aggressive masculine roles. All this play is also considered enculturation. Enculturation combines all the formal teaching ("no, we don't eat dirt," "don't pull your sister's hair," "clean your room") with the informal acquisition of culture that comes with everyday life.

Race and Ethnicity

Chapter 4 discussed the reasons why anthropologists agree with biologists and geneticists that biological **race** doesn't exist for the human species. Since all humans, no matter where they live on the globe, share about 99 per cent of their DNA, there are no meaningful divisions in their biology. Even if two people share skin tone, they may speak different languages, have different family histories, and come from entirely different places. Of course, humans recognize that we have differences. What an utterly boring world it would be if we were all the same! But those differences don't stem from an inherent or biologically based distinction; they come from culture and society.

So, how did the term *race* become such a common part of our vocabulary? The sixteenth century was a time of exploration for our species. In a bold move, the pope had decreed that all lands west of Brazil would belong to Spain. Europeans came to the Americas (the New World) to discover they were not the only people with fully developed social organization and community living. However, since the Europeans could not understand the language or ways of the Indigenous peoples living in the Americas, they considered them to be primitive and savage.

Furthermore, since the European goal was ultimately to conquer land and colonize people, an argument ensued in Spain as to whether the natives were actually humans, or some type of lower being. If sub-human, they could be treated with no more thought than animals. If human, it meant they had souls, and would require baptizing. In 1551, in the court of the Spanish city of Valladolid, a trial argued this issue. The eventual result was the baptism and conversion of Indigenous peoples of the New World to Catholicism, and the establishment of an order from the pope forbidding their enslavement.

Two hundred years later, the field of science was developing. The Swedish naturalist Carolus Linnaeus (sometimes referred to as Carl, the Swedish variant of the Latin *Carolus*) set to the task of assigning Latin names for all observable species in nature, as was explained in Chapter 3. In 1758, he added humans to the great taxonomy of living things, after analyzing the reports of those who had sailed across the seas.

Table 8.1

Linnaeus's Four "Varieties" of Humans

Homo sapiens americanus	Red, choleric [angry], upright. Hair black … obstinate, content free … ruled by habit.
Homo sapiens europaeus	White, sanguine [cheerful], muscular. Hair yellow, brown, flowing … gentle, acute, inventive … ruled by custom or law.
Homo sapiens asiaticus	Pale-yellow, melancholy, stiff. Hair black … severe, haughty … ruled by belief [opinions].
Homo sapiens afer	Black, phlegmatic [sluggish], relaxed. Hair black, fizzled … crafty, indolent, negligent … ruled by caprice [impulse].

However, looking at Linnaeus's "varieties" of humans, it's clear that they were based on biased observations and skewed positively toward Europeans. Besides the bizarre *Homo sapiens ferus* (four-footed, mute, hairy wild men) and *Homo sapiens monstruosus* (giants, dwarves, and misshapen individuals), the other four varieties that can be identified more clearly as people are described in Table 8.1.

For the next several hundred years, these categories—based on reports from explorers and those involved in the slave trade—came to represent a pseudoscientific basis for different biological races of humans. It laid the foundation for centuries of slavery and oppression of non-white peoples based on "God-given" traits that were unalterable. Racial classification played a role in the horrific extermination of people during the ethnic cleansing of World War II under the guise of **eugenics**, a pseudoscientific plan to "purify" the human race. More recently, it has led to forced abortion and sterilization, laws against marriage, and anti-immigration policies.

After several hundred years of misunderstanding and misuse of "race," Darwin's theories of natural selection and an understanding of genetics began to shed light on how evolution by natural selection works. In the twentieth century, scientists began to apply those principles to the study of human variation. We now know that people's DNA differs by no more than 0.14 per cent anywhere in the world.

Of course, humans have differences! But although we may refer to differences among groups of people as "racial," clearly those differences are not biological. The differences attributed to race are only meaningful as a set of categories based on social and cultural experience. The bottom line is this: race is a cultural category in humans, not a biological one.

The term **ethnicity** more accurately expresses all those aspects of a person that might otherwise be glossed as "race." Ethnicity includes heritage, geography, and language. It incorporates aspects of where a person's family originates (their heritage) with cultural features (such as their staple foods). For instance, ethnicity can tell us whether a person is more likely to enjoy rice, tortillas, noodles, or bread.

Figure 8.4
Roasted Guinea Pig
Food is one way that our ethnocentrisms are expressed. This Peruvian meal features *cuy*, or guinea pig, which is often raised in rural homes as we might raise chickens. However, most North Americans could never imagine eating guinea pig. What is the difference? What is the North American rule about the difference between food/not food that this ethnocentrism brings to light?

Credit: © Barry D. Kass/Images of Anthropology

How is ethnic identity different from **cultural identity**? While culture plays a part in ethnicity, we can also identify aspects of our lives that are cultural, without their being linked to one particular ethnicity. For instance, while a person's ethnic identity may be Ukrainian-American, her cultural identity would include her gender, level of education, and socio-economic status. Cultural identity also includes the subcultures one belongs to based on interests, such as membership in a subculture of car enthusiasts, bloggers, or triathletes.

For example, a triathlon subculture may contain people of many different ethnic backgrounds. A person's membership in the subculture is marked by an understanding of the unspoken rules of triathlete behavior and knowledge of the special language that triathletes speak. For instance, a member of this subculture would know how to respond to the comment, "I bonked on the fartlek today." It takes time to learn the expectations, norms, and values of any group. Eventually, a member will learn to fluently "speak" the language of the subculture.

Ethnocentrism and Cultural Relativism

Consider a group of people with a very different set of beliefs and behaviors from mainstream North American ones, such as the Efe people of the Ituri Forest, who regularly eat fat, squiggly grubs for protein, or Peruvians who farm raise guinea pigs for meat. Initial reactions might be "how weird" or "that's gross!" It is normal to feel that the way *we* do things is normal, and the way *others* do things is not. This idea—that our own customs are normal while others' customs are strange, wrong, or

Do You Eat Bugs?

The idea of eating insects (called **entomophagy**) may sound strange to most North Americans, but it may be the wave of the future. With nine billion people expected to inhabit the earth by 2050, food production will need to double. Farming insects is one way to ensure there will be adequate protein for more people in the same amount of space.

Insects are an excellent source of nutrition. Over two billion people in more than 80 countries in the world eat a variety of insects regularly. The types of edible insects range widely; however, the most consumed species are beetles (and their larvae), caterpillars, bees, wasps, and ants. Bugs are an excellent source of protein, with less fat per gram than most meats. Mealworms, for example, have about as much protein, vitamins, and minerals as the same amount of fish or chicken. And, from this author's personal experience, they taste like roasted almonds.

While people who live in forests, deserts, and jungles have easy access to insects through gathering, urban people can benefit from eating bugs as well. In urban areas, eating protein-rich culinary insects decreases the pressure to create more and faster factory-farmed meat. Industrial meat production is one of the largest contributors to greenhouse gases, especially considering the tons of methane produced by gassy cows. Just as much protein could be farm raised using a fraction of the land and water.

Western culture has not yet embraced the culinary potential of insects. An ethnocentric feeling of disgust (the "yuck" factor) prevents most people from seeking out this alternative, sustainable source of protein. Ironically, all industrial consumers in North America ingest a percentage of insect parts on a regular basis, since the US Food and Drug Administration (FDA) and Canadian Food Inspection Agency (CFIA) set similar allowable levels according to the food item. Somehow, it is more palatable to eat marine animals with exoskeletons, such as shrimp and lobster, than those on land. But the benefits for the world's growing population are becoming clear.

even disgusting—is the notion of **ethnocentrism**. Ethnocentrism allows people to feel superior to others by denigrating differences in their behavior, ideas, or values.

A little bit of ethnocentrism is instilled in children at a young age. Members of a group are taught to love their country, identify with their city and state, and support their community. In San Diego, California, the motto of the city police department is "America's Finest." These words are written on every patrol car on the streets. In a mildly ethnocentric way, San Diegans are proud of their city, their people, and especially their weather.

Pride in people and origins isn't a bad thing. It becomes a problem when ethnocentric ideas about the value of other people's beliefs and behaviors turn into hateful words or misguided actions. Thinking ethnocentrically doesn't allow people to fully understand other cultures because it blinds them to the intrinsic value in every way of life.

When undertaking research, anthropologists reject an ethnocentric mindset in order to understand people in the most objective way possible. Even if one doesn't agree with certain behaviors or values personally, it is the anthropologist's responsibility to observe, describe, and interpret those behaviors objectively. Anthropologists have a particularly important duty to keep ethnocentrism in check when studying other cultures, no matter how foreign those cultures are to our own.

In addition, it is important to remember that most of our behavior is learned. Therefore, the study of cultures around the world also reminds us that were we to be born in societies with those "abnormal" or "bizarre" practices, we would likely practice them ourselves. This includes all aspects of culture, from marriage patterns, to religious beliefs, to what is and what is not acceptable to eat. (See Box 8.2.)

In contrast to ethnocentrism, anthropologists use a model called **cultural relativism**. This is the idea that all cultures are equally valid, and that culture can only be understood and interpreted in its own context. This perspective allows anthropologists to study people's beliefs and behaviors without judgment. Because culture is integrated, anthropologists can understand any one aspect of culture only if we understand the whole.

Although all anthropologists take cultural relativism to heart as an essential tenet of their practice, not all anthropologists agree to what extent this should be done. It is easy to maintain objectivity when analyzing something relatively neutral, like language use. On the other hand, some think that extreme cultural relativism goes too far, for example, when human rights are violated or abusive behavior occurs toward children. When ethnographers witness violence while in the field, they may have a hard time maintaining objectivity on a personal level. Some anthropologists may feel compelled to get involved, to expose the practice or stop it, even when the practice is culturally accepted in the region of study.

Cultural Adaptation and Maladaptation

One important quality of humans is that we are able to adapt. In fact, our ability to adapt to changing circumstances is likely the reason that *Homo sapiens* is still here today. Although humans are still evolving biologically, it is the cultural adaptations that have not only allowed us to survive, but to thrive, as the dominant species on earth. We have been able to expand across the globe into every environment possible: the desert, the tropical rainforest, or the snowy tundra. In more recent times, we've even been able to live in submarines under water and on the International Space Station! Our early *Homo* ancestors could never have dreamed as much.

Biological adaptations allow an organism to better survive in its present conditions, or to live successfully and reproduce in a variety of habitats. A good example is the hummingbird's long, thin beak and the wings that beat so rapidly that it can

hover. These physical adaptations allow it to extract nectar from deep within a flower, finding nutrition where other birds cannot. Other easily recognizable examples of evolutionary fitness through adaptation include the buoyant, hollow fur of the otter, which allows it to float; the long neck of the giraffe, allowing it to eat acacia leaves off the tops of trees; or the double-layered fur coats of polar bears. While humans have some very useful biological adaptations (including bipedalism and a vocal tract that allows speech), we are unique in developing advanced cultural adaptations.

Cultural adaptations include all the ways that humans use cultural knowledge to better adapt and succeed in their surroundings. Since humans have language, we pass on knowledge orally or in writing. We use language to record, test, and develop knowledge. Rather than having to reinvent the wheel every generation, we compile and share our knowledge. The development of science and technology, including medicine, are products of culture. We can start a fire, use a blanket, buy a parka, or turn on the heat when we are cold, rather than having to evolve a fur coat.

There are cultural practices, however, which do not benefit a society. Any behavior that leads to a decrease in well-being of the members of a culture or to the culture itself is not adaptive. These practices are known as **maladaptive** since they may lead to harmful results. Practices that harm women's reproductive health are maladaptive, such as female genital mutilation (FGM), even when the practices have existed in the society for as long as anyone can remember. (See Box 8.3.)

Figure 8.5
Slender Blue-Winged Grasshopper (*Sphingonotus caerulans*)
This Slender Blue-Winged Grasshopper (*Sphingonotus caerulans*) has adapted biologically to its environment with a brown-banded camouflage. This adaptation allows it to hide from predators in its typically dry, bare, and sandy environment.
Credit: Christian Ferrer. Reprinted under CC-BY-SA 4.0.

Female Genital Mutilation (FGM)

Female genital mutilation (FGM)—also called female genital cutting or circumcision—is widely practiced as part of a young girl's entry into the community and preparation for marriage. The practice involves surgical removal of the clitoris, labia majora, and/or labia minora for non-medical reasons. In more extreme cases, it involves "infibulation," the sewing together or cauterization of the labia minora, leaving only a small opening for urination.

Currently, FGM is common in 29 countries in Africa and the Middle East. Ninety per cent of women from 15 to 49 years old have undergone the practice in four countries: Somalia, Guinea, Djibouti, and Egypt (UNICEF). Migrant communities often continue the practice after they have left their natal countries.

Although many women willingly subject their daughters to this traditional practice, it is not seen as an adaptive one. Some advocates for cultural freedom argue that having undergone the practice is a form of cultural identity and social belonging. If a girl is not cut, then others in the social group may view her as "dirty," "rejecting tradition," or "unfit for marriage." Nonetheless, there are many reasons why FGM is seen as a maladaptive practice by the world's health and human rights organizations.

Primarily, the practice is maladaptive because it leads to often-severe health problems. Immediate risks include hemorrhaging, bacterial infection, shock, and death. Long-term complications can lead to recurrent bladder or urinary tract infections, cysts, infertility, childbirth complications, and newborn deaths (WHO 2014). Another argument against FGM is that it represents a severe form of gender discrimination against women and girls. It violates the fundamental rights of human beings to be free from cruel and degrading treatment. FGM has been denounced by feminist scholars in Africa and around the world as a dangerous and traumatic means of controlling women (UNICEF 2014).

Today, some maladaptive practices are attractive to young people, leading to long-term health issues. For instance, smoking cigarettes raises a person's risk of lung cancer by 25 per cent. Yet the US Centers for Disease Control and Prevention reports that in each day of 2014, more than 3,200 new smokers under the age of 18 had their first cigarette (CDC Office on Smoking and Health 2014). Another example is the trend of artificial tanning. According to the American Cancer Society (2014), people under the age of 35 who use tanning beds increase their risk of malignant melanoma 75 per cent. Melanoma kills over 10,000 people in North America each year. Unfortunately, artificial tanning is still popular among teens and young adults.

The Functions of Culture

Culture, beyond providing the shared understandings that guide people's behavior, has certain functions. In any society, the culture should provide for the basic needs of the group. Specifically, aspects of culture (beliefs and behaviors) should serve to support the health and well-being of members and the survival of the culture itself. In this view, aspects of culture can "work" or not.

Since anthropologists take the perspective of cultural relativism, they avoid judging cultures based on their own set of values. Doing this would be ethnocentric and misguided. However, people who study culture can examine in an objective way whether aspects of a culture are adaptive or maladaptive. That is, if aspects of culture are adaptive, they should support the health and well-being of members. If maladaptive, they may lead to ill effects for the people or the longevity of the culture itself. To answer this question, an anthropologist might examine the kinds of issues listed in Table 8.2.

Of course, not everyone experiences the same level of satisfaction with his or her culture. Consider two families, one who lives in a mansion in a posh neighborhood, and another that occupies a room in a homeless shelter downtown. Clearly, different circumstances lead to one family getting their needs met better than the other.

For example, the Penobscot Indians of Maine have traditionally relied on fish from the Penobscot River as the main staple of their diet. In the twentieth century, industrial paper mills were built abutting the river. Unfortunately, the runoff from the paper mills polluted the river with dioxins creating a toxic environment for fish and the humans who eat that fish (Bisulca 1996). Dioxin is a carcinogen that poses severe hazards to the human reproductive and immune systems. The tribe has been proactive in trying to preserve their traditional food source and environment. They have successfully taken steps to work with the EPA to better monitor and filter the waste from the mills, which has substantially increased the health of the river. This case shows a maladaptive practice resulting from culture contact and competing values that was turned into a more adaptive solution.

Table 8.2

Assessing the Adaptiveness of Culture

Health	How is the physical and mental health of members? Do women get prenatal care to support infant health?
Demographics	What do birth and mortality rates say about the longevity of members?
Goods and services	Can people get what they need when they need it? Is there access to clean, safe food and water?
Order	Do people feel safe? Are there systems in place for effectively dealing with violence?
Enculturation	How well does the culture get passed down to the next generation?

Personality Development

We might imagine **personality** as the sole property of the field of psychology, since it represents the unique way an individual thinks, feels, and acts. Actually, anthropology also has something to say about how personality develops. Culture plays a big role. In fact, we can think of personality as what happens when your specific set of genes comes into contact with your culture and social environment. It's a product of culture coming smack up against the individual.

Child Rearing

Essential to the way culture and personality interact are the values regarding how children are raised in any society. Anthropologists who have studied child rearing around the world have found two general patterns of enculturation, which we refer to as dependence training and independence training. Each type of child rearing contributes to a different set of cultural values and different types of social structure. This is one way in which the integrated nature of culture can be seen clearly.

Dependence training is the set of child-rearing practices that supports the family unit over the individual. In societies with dependence training, children learn the importance of compliance to the family group. Typically, dependence training is taught in societies that value extended (or joint) families, that is, in which multiple generations live together with the spouses and children of adult siblings. Family members may work together in a family business or they may pool resources. In horticultural or agricultural communities, this may mean that all members of the family work on the farm. Children are doted upon and indulged but learn quickly that they are part of a unit. Their sense of self develops as essentially linked to the group.

Independence training refers to the set of child-rearing practices that foster a child's self-reliance. It is found in industrial societies, like our own, and in societies in which earning an income requires moving to where the jobs are. The family unit in independence training societies is typically a nuclear family; that is, only two generations living together (parents and children). The individual is seen as an actor who can shape his or her own destiny. Competition is fostered, especially in boys. Emphasis is placed on developing the talents and skills of each child so they can be competitive and successful in life. The sense of self is strongly linked to the individual.

Anthropologist Susan Seymour (1999) studied changing family life in the state of Orissa, India, focusing on the roles of women in child care. At the time of her fieldwork, some residents of the Old Town (a traditional village) of Bhubaneswar had resettled into the New Capital (a more Westernized part of town with secular schools and administrative careers). The division of the community into two separate socio-cultural environments had direct consequences on family life. While residents of the Old Town held fast to traditional dependence-training methods and values, residents of the New Capital adjusted to new opportunities, especially for women's advancement. Women's educational and employment opportunities resulted in a shift to more nuclear, rather than joint (extended) families. This trend is seen in many societies as modernization occurs.

Personality Norms

There is a wide variety of what can be considered "normal" personalities in any culture. Even though people are very different, cultural norms dictate appropriate and inappropriate ways to behave. We have a clear sense, when confronted by someone on the street, for example, if that person is behaving appropriately or not.

Each culture has its own norms, which help guide appropriate versus non-appropriate behavior. For example, in some societies, no word exists for "privacy." Clearly this suggests a regular social environment that is very different from our modern industrial lives. In a village where the emphasis is on community and many people live in a group house, privacy doesn't occur, nor is it desired. Therefore, being surrounded by others at all times may be completely acceptable.

CULTURE-BOUND DISORDER

Of course, in any society there will be individuals who deviate from the norm. Nonetheless, even those people who opt out of society, or rebel against it, are still behaving in ways that are understandable. In extreme cases, when an individual deviates from cultural and social norms, the behavior may be due to mental illness, such as psychosis or neurosis.

When a person develops a biochemical brain disorder, he or she acts in ways that are considered deviant by the non-ill members of society. Even these behaviors, however, may be shaped by culture. When a person develops schizophrenia, for example, his or her delusions will be dictated by culture. In Western industrial societies, paranoid schizophrenics may believe government agents are spying on them. They may experience delusions of persecution, believing that powerful organizations such as the police or military have caused them some injustice.

A schizophrenic in another society may not share the same delusions. Although the biochemical disorder may be the same physiologically, delusions are guided by culture. A mental disorder specific to particular ethnic groups is known as a **culture-bound disorder**.

For instance, Algonquian-speaking native populations of the eastern and northern United States and neighboring parts of Canada recognized the existence of cannibalistic half-monsters called *wendigos*. When individuals developed psychosis, they believed they were turning into cannibals, fearing they would eat the people around them. The syndrome was common enough to merit its own name: Wendigo psychosis. This is the same type of mental disorder in both cases, but it is expressed in culturally specific ways. Many culture-bound disorders that exist throughout the world are valid expressions of mental illness.

Fieldwork Methods and Ethics

Cultural anthropologists study culture "in the field." That is, they live with another group of people for an extended period to learn firsthand how the group views the world and behaves within it. They immerse themselves in the culture and daily patterns of life such that they begin to understand how members think, feel, and act.

The process begins with a research question: Why do people do that? The anthropologist seeks funding to support the months or years of field study, and spends time preparing for her entry by reading all of the available material on the topic and area. She may learn the language, or work with a translator.

Being in the field allows an anthropologist to produce an ethnography. Ethnography is both the process and the product, which is most often a document, book, or film. Producing an ethnography is an artistic endeavor, because it must be written in a way that evokes the reality of the culture. It is also a scientific endeavor, because it must produce an authentic, rigorously researched representation of people and their behavior in a wider cultural context.

Participant Observation

In the field, an ethnographer uses a variety of methods to understand another group's way of life. The main method is called **participant observation**, a process in which a researcher lives with a people and observes their regular activities, often for a year or more. The ethnographer participates in daily life while at the same time maintaining some observational distance to be able to reflect and analyze.

Anthropologists believe there is no substitute for witnessing firsthand how people think and what they do. This is why they look forward to submerging themselves in a new environment with all the messiness of life, and trying to make sense of it. Sometimes it feels as if learning a new set of cultural norms is like a code, with language and behavior no more than beeps and blips. The ethnographer's role is to observe, describe, interpret, and analyze so this "code" makes sense. This is why anthropology relies more heavily on fieldwork than on surveys and statistics, which can provide a bit of the story, but maybe only the bit that people want to share.

While doing participant observation, an ethnographer seeks to understand a full picture of the culture. One can approach this goal by asking three different kinds of questions. First, how do people think they should behave? (What are the norms and values in the society?) Second, how do people say they behave? (Do they say they conform to these standards or not?) And lastly, how do people actually behave? (This can only be discovered by long-term fieldwork and by establishing trusting relationships with the people involved in the study.) We can think of the difference between what people say and what they do as the contrast between **ideal behavior** and **real behavior**. The fieldworker, of course, is most interested in real behavior.

For participant observation to produce the desired goals, the ethnographer needs to talk to trusted members of the community. These important individuals in the field study may be called **informants**, collaborators, or associates, depending on the anthropologist's choice of terms. They are often people with particularly deep knowledge about the issues the ethnographer is interested in. They can very often become close friends, with whom the fieldworker continues to correspond and collaborate with beyond the field study.

Figure 8.6
Kikuyu Dancer with Makeup
Without any context of the culture, an observer of the event in which this Kikuyu dancer is participating would be completely lost. Anthropologists attempt to get a full picture of a culture to analyze any one part of it accurately.

Credit: © Barry D. Kass/Images of Anthropology

Choosing Informants

Depending on the circumstances and the study goals, the ethnographer may choose one or more methods of approaching informants. In a **random sample**, the ethnographer's goal is to allow everyone an equal chance to be interviewed, which is done by selecting people randomly. This might best be employed in a small, homogeneous community, or when an average is desired. A **judgment sample**, on the other hand, selects informants based on skills, knowledge, insight, and/or sensitivity to cultural issues. The fieldworker will usually develop close ties to one or more informants who are chosen for these reasons and will spend a lot time with them. These crucial members of the community are referred to as **key informants**. Finally, a **snowball sample**, in which one informant introduces the ethnographer to other informants, can be very helpful.

Within participant observation, many different methods may be used, depending on the circumstances. The fieldworker must be flexible and reflective enough to assess which techniques might work best, whether a technique is working or not, and if the approach must be modified. One can never anticipate what will happen in the field, and a good fieldworker is open to all possibilities. Learning all the relevant information about the culture before departing for the field is crucial, and an ethnographer will often spend several years doing research before leaving.

Beyond the everyday task of participant observation, other specific fieldwork methods may be employed with success. These include:

- formal interviews (in which the same set of questions are given to multiple informants)
- informal interviews (in which the fieldworker seizes an opportunity to ask questions)
- life histories or other oral histories
- case studies, in which a particular event is examined from multiple perspectives
- kinship data (a family tree or village genealogy)
- mapmaking
- photography

These methods each lend themselves to a certain type of data gathering. Depending on the circumstances and the study goals, one or more techniques may be used at the ethnographer's discretion.

Code of Ethics

Some people imagine that doing fieldwork among people is like being "a fly on the wall." In other words, the ethnographer would hang around unobtrusively, watching people go about their daily business, while writing notes on a notepad. In fact, the situation is generally the opposite, in which the ethnographer gets a job or takes on an apprenticeship in the midst of something they want to learn about. They learn by doing, getting in the mix of daily life and relationships with people who live there.

It is clear that there is no such thing as a "fly on the wall" in terms of ethnographic research. The ethnographer's presence is keenly felt, especially in the beginning, and may be distracting. The informants among whom one is working may not trust that this is an academic study—the anthropologist could just as easily be a government agent, come to spy on them! In fact, anthropologist Napoleon Chagnon recalls that due to their suspicion of his motives, his Yanomamö informants in the rainforests of Brazil and Venezuela told him lies about their relationships with family members. In the film *A Man Called Bee*, he admits to having had to throw out nearly all of the data gathered on kinship in the first year of his fieldwork (Asch & Chagnon 1974).

Once trust is gained, other interpersonal problems may arise. For instance, intercultural communication is not always perfect, even if one knows the language. That is, the anthropologist's intentions may not always be clear, and they may read others' intentions wrong as well. There are plenty of possibilities for errors in judgment and poor decision making in the process of fieldwork. Therefore, it is crucially important to have a set of guidelines that lay the foundation for interactions with others while in the field.

The largest North American organization of anthropologists, the American Anthropological Association (AAA), created such a set of guidelines called the Code of Ethics (2014). The Code of Ethics may be applied to anthropologists in any field, and it seeks to provide a set of guidelines for proper conduct. It primarily protects those with whom they interact in the field and those who may be affected by their work.

Box 8.4

The Human Terrain System— Ethical Dilemmas in Anthropology

For soldiers going to war, wouldn't cultural knowledge of the region and its people help your mission? This question led to the development of a program in 2007 in the United States Army called the Human Terrain System (HTS). The goals of the program are to embed a team of academically trained social scientists within an army brigade, to provide knowledge of the local population and increase the army's effectiveness (US Army 2014). The program began in 2007 with two Human Terrain Teams (HTTs) and grew to 14 teams by 2013. The progam was phased out and discontinued in 2014.

Montgomery McFate, a Yale-trained military anthropologist, was one of the key developers of the program. McFate and other proponents of the project argued that providing a team of people with regional, linguistic, geographic, and anthropological knowledge would greatly reduce misunderstandings and misguided actions in the military theater. This program claimed to decrease the number of deaths due to misinterpretation of actions on both sides.

However, the American Anthropological Association is not one of those proponents. In fact, the AAA found that the use of anthropologists in a war zone was disturbing and ethically challenging. Drawing upon a history of anthropological research being used against native and oppressed peoples in wartime, the association chose to publicly state their opposition to the program.

In late 2007, the AAA published a statement explaining that they opposed the HTS program for several reasons. The most important reason is that participation in the program directly violates the AAA Code of Ethics. In particular, embedded anthropologists cannot ensure that their information will "Do No Harm" to the subjects of study, since those subjects are also often being targeted by the military. In addition, since HTT members wear fatigues and carry weapons, their information-gathering goals may be misinterpreted. Finally, voluntary informed consent of informants may be difficult or impossible.

The first and foremost item in the Code is to "Do No Harm." Like a physician who has taken the Hippocratic Oath, anthropologists also are bound to act ethically toward others in the course of their work. In particular, anthropologists must weigh the possible impacts of their actions on the dignity, health, and material well-being of those among whom they work.

The Code of Ethics makes it clear that anthropologists' responsibilities are primarily to the people and animals with which they work, and then to scholarship and science. Translated into practical decision making, this means that if the anthropologist's work or the outcome of that work may harm the community of informants (in cultural anthropology), or the primates in a study (in the field of biological anthropology), then the anthropologist must choose to put the well-being of these individuals ahead of completion or success of their own research.

This seems clear enough on the page, but situations can arise in which it isn't clear to the anthropologist what the repercussions of a decision might be. Alternatively, there may be pros and cons that must be carefully weighed. It isn't always easy to navigate these potential problems in the field. This can lead to some controversies over whether anthropologists should be involved in certain endeavors at all. (See Box 8.4.) Nonetheless, field research is a valuable and satisfying undertaking.

Digital Ethnography

Wherever there is human culture, there will be anthropologists. This means that anthropologists are also online, studying virtual communities. Anything that exists in person today also has a digital component. Therefore, the Internet becomes a virtual location for learning about identity in the digital age, as well as communities such as fandoms or underground subcultures. Because new modes of research must be adapted for use online, this type of research is sometimes referred to as netnography.

While online ethnographic research may sometimes be conducted anonymously (as a so-called lurker), the digital anthropology community largely rejects this method. This is due to its clear conflict with the AAA Code of Ethics, which states that it is necessary to provide full disclosure to study participants. Therefore, many anthropologists use a similar method to traditional participant observation, in which they become full participants in the online community.

Tom Boellstorff, professor of anthropology at the University of California, Irvine, conducted two years of virtual research in the online universe of Second Life. In this virtual world, he examined topics such as race, sex and gender, antisocial behavior, place and time, and personhood. He achieved traditional participant-observation goals in an online environment, just as anthropologists do in face-to-face communities.

Of course, digital technology is an essential part of nearly all anthropological endeavors today. In fact, for many anthropologists working today, it's hard to imagine the pre-digital world, in which research, communication, writing, and publishing were done without the Internet. The Internet has become an essential tool for ethnographic research.

Applied Anthropology

Finally, it is important to note that anthropologists are not only researchers and teachers. Many working anthropologists apply their knowledge of anthropological methods, theory, and perspectives to solve human problems. This field is called **applied anthropology**. Applied anthropologists work to find solutions for problems in the real world, rather than focusing entirely on contributing to the body of research in the discipline. Some applied anthropologists may also teach in universities, and some may work outside of academia entirely.

Applied, or practicing, anthropologists may work in corporate settings, for governments, or for non-governmental organizations (NGOs). They may work in any field, as consultants who are trained in participant–observation techniques, to seek solutions to problems. Often these anthropologists consult with organizations that are developing sustainable practices in countries in the process of modernization. They work toward solutions for drought or famine, such as helping provide clean water, or in medical clinics to bridge the cultural gap between Western and traditional medicine. There are many cultural obstacles to overcome in the process of modernization. Applied anthropologists help with surmounting those obstacles while remaining sensitive to a people's traditional values and identity.

Figure 8.7
North African Nomads Drawing Water from a Well, Southern Sahara, Niger
Applied anthropologists often work on projects to increase people's access to fresh water. These nomads in North Africa are drawing water from a well in the desert.

Credit: © Barry D. Kass/Image of Anthropology

Practicing anthropologists may work for a corporation interested in streamlining aspects of its organization. For instance, Elizabeth Briody, an applied anthropologist, works for General Motors in the research and development sector. In an interview with the AAA, Briody explains in very basic terms what her job entails: "I conduct studies of GM culture. My role is to come up with ways to

improve GM's effectiveness. In my research, I try to understand the issues that people face in doing the work they have been asked to do, and then offer suggestions to make their work lives better" (Fiske 2007: 44). One recent project required Briody to examine the different corporate cultural norms and values when GM entered a formal partnership deal with the Italian car company Fiat. Briody's work allowed collaborations to go more smoothly, with each group understanding the other's assumptions about corporate decision making.

One of the more delicious collaborations between practicing anthropologists and a for-profit company resulted in the Ben and Jerry's ice cream flavor Rainforest Crunch (Ben & Jerry's n.d.). Rainforest Crunch is a vanilla ice cream with pieces of cashew and Brazil nut "butter crunch." The flavor was developed by Ben Cohen (the "Ben" of Ben & Jerry) with the anthropologists of Cultural Survival (2014), a non-profit advocacy group for the survival and autonomy of native peoples. Working with Amazonians, the ice cream company provided steady income for sustainably harvesting tree nuts and vanilla for a large market, as an alternative to clear cutting and drilling. Unfortunately, the flavor has since gone to Ben & Jerry's "flavor graveyard."

Applied anthropologists use a model of field research and implementation that is referred to as **participatory action research**. Because their goals are to effect change in a community, the research prioritizes the needs and concerns of the people who desire change. As outsiders, the anthropologists can often bring to the table their understandings about the global conditions that may limit change. This provides a larger framework within which to understand the problem and seek potential solutions. Most importantly, applied anthropologists partner with community members throughout the process, to bring the rewards directly back to the community.

Summary

This chapter has explored cultural anthropology. It is the study of culture, or the shared understandings that people use to guide their behavior. Mirroring the Learning Objectives stated in the chapter opening, the key points are:

- Culture is shared, learned, integrated, and based on symbols; therefore, it is not instinctive or biologically based. In fact, even though people are different all over the world, biologically there is not enough difference for the human species to be separated into races. Therefore, race is actually better identified as ethnicity, which includes all of the aspects of a person's culture.

- When anthropologists study culture, they take a culturally relative perspective, avoiding the biases of ethnocentrism and attempting to learn about people in an objective way.
- Cultural anthropologists may evaluate cultural practices to determine whether they are adaptive or maladaptive for the long-term health and well-being of the members of that society.
- Anthropologists may look at the functions of culture: how culture provides for its members such that people who share that culture get their basic needs met.
- Anthropologists may examine how culture is expressed through the beliefs and behaviors associated with mental disorders.
- When ethnographers go into the field to study any aspect of culture, there are a variety of methods that can be used. All must be done with an eye toward ethical practices, including any sub-field such as digital or applied anthropology.

REVIEW QUESTIONS

1. What makes anthropologists' study of culture different from that in other fields?
2. What are the differences between an ethnocentric and culturally relative approach to culture?
3. What are the criteria for adaptive aspects of culture?
4. How do different child-rearing practices affect the development of personality and culture?
5. How should anthropologists in the field (whether face-to-face or virtually) ensure they are acting ethically?
6. How can anthropological understandings and perspectives help solve real-world problems?

DISCUSSION QUESTIONS

1. What aspects of your culture are maladaptive? Use the criteria in Table 8.2 to make your assessment.
2. How might an applied anthropologist help solve a particular problem in your community?

Visit **www.lensofanthropology.com** for the following additional resources:

| SELF-STUDY QUESTIONS | WEBLINKS | FURTHER READING |

PLACES MENTIONED IN CHAPTER 9

1. Vancouver, Canada
2. Quebec, Canada
3. Georgia, United States
4. Zambia
5. El Salvador
6. Papua New Guinea
7. Tasmania
8. Hokkaido
9. Aotearoa (New Zealand)
10. Nunavut Territory, Canada

LANGUAGE AND CULTURE

Hello there! Yo, what's up? Have you eaten rice yet? Language encodes culture, says more about us than we might imagine. #languageandculture

Learning Objectives

In this chapter students will learn:

- the differences between human language and primate communication.
- different hypotheses for the origin of human language.
- the steps a linguistic anthropologist would take to understand the components of a language.
- what the components are that make meaning beyond just words.
- the types of language that an ethnolinguist would study.
- how language is changing in the digital age.
- how languages go extinct.

Introduction

This chapter explores one of the most essential aspects of human culture: language. It is through language that humans are able to pass down oral and written knowledge, something no other species on the planet can do. Storing cumulative knowledge allows the development of advanced science and technology. In essence, language has allowed humans to become who we are today.

This chapter examines the unique qualities of human language, as well as what makes our communication similar to that of other primate species. It covers how

Figure 9.1
Bean Sellers, Batak Toba Society, Sumatra, Indonesia
These bean vendors on the island of Sumatra send and receive a vast amount of cultural information as they talk, using gestures and movements learned in the local context.
Credit: © Avena Matondang/ Images of Anthropology

anthropologists approach the origins and study of language, since they are sometimes the first people to write down an oral language. The intimate connection between language and culture can be seen in the many ways humans express themselves, modifying language use in different social, cultural, or political contexts.

Definition of Language

Human culture is heavily reliant on a system of communication that allows people to interact with one another in socially meaningful ways through voice, gestures, and written words. It is more than simply communication based on pure emotion. **Language** is a symbolic system expressing meaning through sounds or gestures. It is symbolic because, through words, we refer to things that are not physically in front of us. We ponder ideas and concepts. We talk about things that have happened in the past or may happen in the future.

There is a huge amount of information that any person must process and produce to function fully in human society. This includes all of the components of language that accompany our conversations, such as our tone of voice or hand movements, which also express meaning. Whether by sounds, gestures, or writing, language allows us to live with others in a cooperative and communicative environment.

A person's **speech** is influenced by multiple factors: biological, cultural, social, and political. Language is biological in that we use our mouth and throat to produce sound. Socio-cultural factors such as gender, socio-economic status, level

Greetings! Have You Eaten?

When a Thai friend stops by, he may greet you by asking *Gin khao reu yung?* In other words, "Have you eaten rice yet?" The speaker isn't really inquiring whether you've had lunch, but the phrase is used to mean "Hello" or "How are you?" In English, we similarly use phrases to greet one another that have other literal meanings, such as "What's up?" A non-native speaker unfamiliar with the informal greeting might wonder if something is actually "up." Even our mainstay greeting "How are you?" isn't supposed to elicit a list of maladies. It is just another way to say "Hi."

Several languages use a similar inquiry when greeting others. For instance, in South India, Malayalam speakers ask *Chorruntu?* ("Have you eaten rice?") In Mandarin, *Chī le ma?* translates literally to "Have you eaten?" It's the same in Nepali with *Khana khannu bhaiyo?*

Why would so many languages ask whether someone has eaten as a greeting? The history of how greetings develop is different for every language and cultural context. For some, it's because asking whether someone has eaten and asking after their well-being is essentially the same. For other languages, the practice may have developed during times of food scarcity, when neighbors would inquire about how others were getting along by asking if they had a supply of a staple food. In every culture, there are norms of hospitality that make the exchange of food and drink customary when visiting.

The rituals of hospitality may be the biggest influence in the development of this greeting. Offering food and drink and a place to sit are very common, as are the culturally appropriate ways to accept them. In Western countries, accepting a glass of water when offered one is seen as appropriate. In others, the norms of behavior require a respectful interchange of polite denial and insistence. For instance, in Iran, the custom called *taarof* requires that a guest accept the first serving of food or drink, but refuse a second helping several times. The number of times and the level of insistence, depend on the relationship between the host and guest.

Food is central to welcoming visitors into one's home. A combination of cultural context and history, along with norms of hospitality, has brought the question "Have you eaten?" into so many languages as a way to greet others.

of education, and geographic region influence the way we speak and provide additional information to listeners, who use all available information to pick up meaning. Language is also political because it is bound up in relationships in which power is constantly negotiated.

Because so much of what we say and how we say it is based on our cultural environment, it is clear that culture deeply influences language. In other words, who we are and where we come from shapes our speech and the way we interact with others. Even the way we greet one another carries meaning about history and values, as explored in Box 9.1.

The inverse is also true in that language shapes culture, by reflecting the changes in society. Consider the rapid changes made by digital social media in the realm of language alone. Texting shorthand, the use of hash tags, and words like "selfie" or "unfriend" quickly entered into an entire generation's daily conversations.

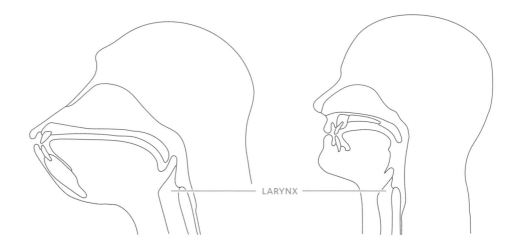

Figure 9.2
Throat Anatomy with Emphasis on Differences in Larynx in Chimps and Humans
The larynx of chimpanzees sits higher in the throat than that of humans. A lower larynx allowed our human ancestors to develop the kind of control over sound that led to language.

LARYNX

Nonhuman Primate Language

Many people want to know why, if humans are related to apes, apes can't speak. One part of the answer has to do with the brain. Nonhuman primates have structures in the brain that are similar—though not as developed—to those of humans. However, primate brains lack the strong neural connections that the human brain has, linking the areas to one another.

The second part of the answer has to do with mouth and throat anatomy. Nonhuman primates' mouths and throats lack the intricate musculature that humans have. Sometime before 50,000 years ago in human development, our tongue descended, our mouth got smaller, our larynx dropped, and our neck elongated. These changes allowed humans to develop an incredible amount of control over their breath and their ability to produce sound.

The changes leading to human vocal physiology had an evolutionary advantage as well. Controlling sounds meant that an individual could be better understood in social situations, leading to a higher level of cooperation and, therefore, survival. The advantages of speech came at some risk for humans, however: because our larynx sits so low in the throat, we are at risk of choking on food as it reaches the esophagus, whereas other nonhuman primates are not. In evolutionary terms, the advantages of speech were more important for human survival than the risk of choking.

Humans are the only primates who are born with fully developed brain structures for acquiring and processing language. Three structures in particular help the human brain process language. Wernicke's Area is thought to be where the brain primarily processes spoken language. Broca's Area produces language. A third zone called Geschwind's Territory allows the brain to understand different qualities of language simultaneously (spoken and written), which may help to classify sounds and words. Neurologists are still studying the ways in which these three areas are linked to one other. An interesting fact is that these structures are the same in both hearing and deaf people, demonstrating that the same brain processes are at work in people speaking and signing.

Language and Communication: Signs and Symbols

Signs

Communication is based on **signs**, that is, something that stands for something else. In spoken language, there are two basic types of signs used in communication: index and symbol. Animals in the wild mainly communicate using an **index sign**, that is, an emotional expression that carries meaning directly related to the response. For example, when a pygmy marmoset feels fear, it emits a high-pitched scream. A chimpanzee that has hunted and caught a monkey to eat will hoot loudly with excitement.

Certain monkeys have developed more predator-specific signs. For example, a group of putty-nosed monkeys (*Cercopithecus nictitans*) studied in Nigeria emit two specific sounds, transliterated as *pyow* and *hack*, to communicate. When alarmed, these monkeys will emit a series of hack calls to alert others in the group. In the absence of other context clues (such as the sound of a tree falling or other noise), the monkeys will look up and search the sky for an incoming eagle. In this case, the putty-nosed monkeys have learned to associate a specific call with their most-likely predator (Arnold & Zuberbühler 2013).

Symbols

Like an index sign, a **symbol** also stands for something else, but it has no apparent or natural connection to the meaning. For instance, when we see a peace sign, we understand it to symbolize the concept of peace. The shape of the image doesn't reflect peace in a natural way, since peace is an abstract concept.

Language itself is symbolic. When we use sounds to speak, the sounds stand for the meaning of the words. When I say the word *peace*, the sounds themselves do not inherently capture the idea of peace, but refer to it. It is also true with gestures in sign language and lines on a page in writing.

Humans have expanded the system of symbolic communication in ways that nonhuman primates cannot. Nonetheless, interesting research over the last several decades appears to show that the human and nonhuman uses of symbolic language are not completely distinct from one another; rather, the differences between them are a matter of degree. Here are some comparisons of human and chimpanzee use of symbolic language:

1. Humans use symbols freely. The first way in which human language distinguishes itself from animal communication is that we have the ability to talk about something in a symbolic way, or in a time besides the present. Without spoken language, this capacity is severely limited in nonhuman animals, although a few

recent events have demonstrated an ability to plan—as in the case of Santino, a chimpanzee in a Swedish zoo that, before the zoo opened, stockpiled rocks to throw at visitors. Planning is one of the brain's executive functions, along with abstract thought.

2. Humans use words to deceive. Another feature of human language is that we possess the ability to say something that isn't true. Animals are generally bound by instinct to respond to stimuli. For instance, as discussed above, when a putty-nosed monkey sees a predator, it lets out a call as a signal to the other monkeys in the group. This is a stimulus-based response; in other words, seeing the predator (stimulus) requires the monkey to call (response). Stimulus-based responses are also emotional ones; in this case, the stimulus produces fear.

   Nonetheless, there are some examples of deceptive behaviors in nonhuman primates, both in captivity and in the wild. These behaviors appear to be based on social, rather than biological, stimuli. For instance, Franz de Waal (1992) of Emory University describes the behaviors of chimpanzees that can deliberately hide instinctive signals or direct others' attention to something that isn't happening.

3. Human language is infinitely creative. A third important feature of human language is the ability to create new phrases and sentences in nearly infinite forms. People can talk about things today that they have never talked about before. Every year, new words are added to the dictionaries of the world. One modern example is the use of the prefix *e* or *i* (as in eBay or iPhone) to identify something digital or computer-related.

   Certain captive apes have shown an aptitude for this type of creativity with language, putting words together, for instance, to describe something for which they don't already know the word. Washoe was a female captive chimp born in the wild but reared in a human environment in which her researchers only spoke ASL. She produced strings of words by the age of two and is said to have coined several creative word phrases. Upon seeing swans for the first time, she signed "water bird." Eating her first Brazil nut produced the phrase "rock-berry."

Documented instances of nonhuman primates achieving certain aspects of symbolic language are intriguing. More research will surely produce more interesting findings. Nonetheless, the three abilities stated above are part of the acquisition of language for humans and will come naturally during a child's development.

Language Origins

How did language begin? Evidence suggests that human language likely began as a system of gestures. Many primatologists see the origins of language early in our primate lineage, in primates who do not have the ability for verbal speech but do use gestures and calls to express meaning to one another.

Among chimpanzees, gestures and vocalizations may be combined in various ways. Therefore, these meaningful actions can be said to have syntax and semantics (grammar that affects meaning). In addition, the choice of what gestures and calls are used, and at what times, is shaped by the relationship between the two individuals. Therefore, these forms of communication also contain essential aspects of pragmatics (contextual meaning). It is likely that nonhuman primates have the same protolinkages among multiple areas of the brain as humans do.

All nonhuman primates are quadrupeds and use their front limbs for locomotion. When our hominin ancestors adopted an upright, bipedal gait, it freed up their arms and hands when they were standing and moving. They could therefore communicate silently through gestures while walking, even over long distances, which would have conferred on them a selective advantage and may have been one of the driving forces that led to bipedalism, as discussed in Chapter 4. The advantage would be even greater if vocalizations could be made more specific, so that the two individuals wouldn't need to be in visual contact to pass information between them. Sounds that are distinguishable and carry different meanings can be called words.

There are other ideas about how humans moved from gestural to vocal language. Some argue that the need to make and use tools with the hands forced hominins to verbalize their needs. Others see cooperative work as the starting point for vocal speech. There is ethnographic evidence that many societies used song or chants to coordinate movements while rowing, building, or doing other group work that required accurate timing.

One thing that most researchers can agree upon is the level of trust necessary for the shift from gestures to words. Why trust? Primate communication is largely based on signals that are hard to fake, such as facial expressions of anxiety or cries of fear. In contrast, words are symbolic; they represent something in a nonphysical and arbitrary way. Trust must be present for communication based on words rather than signals, since words may relate to something that is not immediately present. If gestures and sounds were made simultaneously, it is possible that the sound alone eventually became a trustworthy marker of meaning.

It was likely a combination of many factors that led to verbal communication. Social pressures made it beneficial for hominins to be able to multitask (e.g., carry food while alerting the group vocally to a particular type of predator). The migration of our hominin ancestors out of the dense forests resulted in bipedalism being advantageous. The resulting evolutionary changes in anatomy laid the biological framework for full-blown language.

Studying Language through the Lens of Anthropology

What Does a Linguistic Anthropologist Do?

While a linguist (a scholar who studies language) may focus on the units of construction of a particular language, a linguistic anthropologist is most interested in the social context in which it is used. Linguistic anthropology studies the ways in which language, social life, and culture are intertwined. Linguistic anthropologists are interested in the different ways that people talk in various situations, how language helps define a group's worldview, and whether males and female speak or are spoken to differently. Since language is also one of the main ways that people assert power over others, language is also political. Speech becomes coded with meanings that are negotiated by participants in a conversation. Linguistic anthropologists attempt to tease out and understand these meanings as part of the overall process of practicing culture.

Recording a Language

Imagine you are the first anthropologist to study a small, traditional society. To understand their culture you must first learn their language. But with no textbooks or dictionaries, how do you begin? The first step would be to break down the language into components.

The first thing you would do is to listen to the sounds of the language. This is called **phonetics**, or the study of the sounds in human speech. Learning the sounds of the language allows you to understand which sounds are possible. For instance, the sound *-tl* is a sound used in the ancient Aztec language, Nahuatl, as in *tlatoani* (political leader) or *tomatl* (tomato). This sound combination is not found in English. Distinguishing which basic sounds are used and which are not is a good starting point.

Once you know the sounds of a language, you would want to know how those sounds convey meaning by understanding the **phonemics**. A phoneme is the smallest unit of sound that confers meaning. For instance, the word *ox* refers to one specific thing (in this case, a particular type of animal). If a *b* is added, as in the word *box*, it changes the meaning of the word. Therefore, *b* is also a phoneme. Furthermore, adding *-es* to the end, as in *boxes*, changes the word's meaning so that it is plural (*-es* = phoneme). In contrast, another plural ending might render the word unintelligible, such as *-en* for *oxen* but not *boxen*. Knowing what doesn't make sense in a language is as important as knowing what does.

Then, you would want to learn about how words are structured to make meaning. A **morpheme** is the smallest part of a word that conveys meaning. For instance, the word *textbooks* contains three morphemes: *text* (a book used for instructional purposes), *book* (that which is read), and *s* (a marker to show it is plural). Morphemes differ from phonemes in that a single morpheme may contain several sounds.

Next you would decipher the **syntax**, or how units of speech are put together to create sentences. Grammatical rules govern speech in all languages, both spoken and signed. Statements are often organized differently from questions, for example. In French, a statement places the subject (*vous*) before the verb: *Vous allez au marché*. A question reverses the order of the subject and verb, placing the verb first (*allez*): *Allez-vous au marché?* Knowing the grammar rules of a language allows a person to be understood by others.

Semantics is important to understand how words and phrases are put together in meaningful ways. It won't do much good in the field if you can say single words but don't know how to put them together to make meaning. Semantics studies signs (things that represent something else, such as male and female figures on restroom doors), and symbols (things that stand for an idea or belief, such as a peace sign). Semantics also includes meaning derived from body language, facial expressions, and other nonverbal means of communication. If one doesn't understand these other clues, words become empty of most meaning and often impossible to interpret accurately.

As an anthropologist, you would ultimately want to understand the **pragmatics**, or context, of a language. Every **utterance** depends on the context within which it is spoken. If someone says, "I love you," context is crucial for interpreting that statement. Who is the speaker? What is the listener's relationship to the speaker? What is the time and place of the utterance? All of this extra information is included when we listen and analyze another's speech. It is essential for a correct interpretation of the meaning. Understanding this background information fully in another language may take some time, however. It's a good thing your fieldwork grant money will last for at least a year.

Nonverbal Communication

Paralanguage

Human language goes far beyond just the words we speak. We use the term **paralanguage** to refer to all of the ways we express meaning through sounds beyond words

Figure 9.3
Radio DJ
Radio disc jockeys (DJs) will sometimes train themselves to speak in a standard—nondialect—form of their native language to be marketable to a wider audience.
Credit: © Corbis Super RF/ Alamy

alone. Paralanguage is a subset of semantics, since it gives us information about meaning. The way someone speaks can give clues about the identity of the speaker within the first few utterances. This includes information about regional background or socio-economic class. Of course, the sounds of a person's speech don't always reflect their histories so simply. For example, a person with bilingual parents may display a mixture of speech habits; and a person wanting to work in a job that requires a more "standard" form of mainstream speech, such as a radio DJ or newscaster, may have deliberately worked to erase a certain accent.

There are two main types of paralanguage. First, speech contains **voice qualities**. These are the background characteristics of a person's voice, including its pitch (how high or low a person speaks), rhythm of speech, articulation of words, and types of lip movements. An angry person who says "I'm happy you're here" with pinched lips and little change in inflection sounds very different from a person with a wide smile and variable pitch who is genuinely happy. The same sentence said two different ways carries completely different meanings that we interpret using our understanding of paralanguage.

The second type of paralanguage is called **vocalizations**. These are intentional sounds humans make to express themselves, but that are not actually words. For instance, when an English speaker says "Uh-oh," it signifies a problem. Just "Oh!" can mean surprise. "Ahh" lets someone know we understand, especially when accompanied by a nod of the head. "Eee!" with knitted brows likely means we've been frightened but with open eyes and wide lips means we are happy.

Voice qualities and vocalizations are culturally variable. Each language has its own set of meanings attached to its paralanguage. Even dialects of the same language can be extremely variable. Consider the differences in voice qualities and vocalizations between an English speaker from Vancouver and one from Quebec, or a Southerner from Georgia and a New Yorker. One variant of American English, African American Vernacular English (AAVE), may have its roots in the exposure of early American slaves to a variety of British dialects. Although some may mischaracterize it as "sloppy" English, it has a set of consistent grammatical, lexical, and pronunciation rules that is widely shared among speakers.

Silent Language

Making meaning in a language involves more than words, and even more than sounds. The nonverbal cues that accompany speech, known as **silent language**, also contribute to meaning. Silent language refers to the very specific set of nonverbal cues such as gestures, body movements, and facial expressions that is acquired by speakers of a language.

While paralanguage tends to develop based on a person's experiences (such as gender, education or occupation), members of a culture share silent language. The hand gestures or eyebrow movements used by members of a community convey certain meanings. For instance, North Americans nod their heads to mean yes, and shake their heads from left to right to mean no. In contrast, Indians shake their heads on a horizontal axis to agree, or simply for emphasis. One mustn't assume that even the most basic movements have the same meaning across cultures.

Because silent language can be entirely different, it can easily be misunderstood if used incorrectly. A gesture with a positive connotation in one region of the world may mean something offensive in another. World leaders are not immune to these kinds of mistakes. For example, in the early nineties, US President George Bush Sr. was touring Canberra, Australia. He meant to show solidarity with protesting farmers by flashing a "peace" or "V for Victory" sign, with two fingers in the air. Unfortunately, he made the mistake of turning his palm backward, which communicated to the farmers that he wanted them to go "screw themselves." He later apologized for the error. Similarly, British Prime Minister Margaret Thatcher made the same gesture to her constituents upon winning the 1979 election.

SPACE

Several features of silent language are especially important for understanding meaning in a cultural context. One of these is **proxemics**, or the cultural use of space. This field looks at how close members of a culture stand to one another based on their relationship. How far away do friends normally stand from one another? When strangers approach one another to speak, are they close enough to touch? It also examines how space is organized in homes and cities. Does household space assume members want privacy or that most interaction will be done together? Does the

Table 9.1

Proxemic Zones for People in the United States

Intimate	6"
Personal	1½'–4'
Social	4'–7'
Public distance	12'–25'

Source: Hall 1990

community landscape offer places for people to gather, or is it structured for efficiency in getting to work and coming home?

One of the pioneers of the study of proxemics, Edward T. Hall, first classified the informal zones of personal space, as shown in Table 9.1. Public space is the largest zone that extends the farthest away from a person. In this large space, activities are felt to be relatively anonymous. Closer in, social space is where a person conducts regular business with strangers and acquaintances, and then closer still, personal space into which friends may pass. Closest of all is intimate space, in which only the closest friends and family may enter comfortably.

These comfort zones will vary widely between cultures. The North American comfort level for distance between people is quite far compared to that of some other cultures. In the United States and Canada, strangers in an elevator will move to opposite sides and generally attempt to avoid eye contact. On a sparsely occupied train, people tend to put several rows between themselves and others.

In contrast, North Americans used to a wide zone of social space may find themselves in very close proximity to strangers if getting on a train in Japan, especially at rush hour. This can cause anxiety for people who are out of their comfort zone. Conversely, this may also cause some foreign visitors to North American cities to feel that people are "cold" or "unfriendly," because we tend to stand at a distance. This perception is generally a matter of different cultural expectations.

MOVEMENTS

Another aspect of silent language is **kinesics**, or cultural use of body movements. In Mexico, touching one's elbow is a way to call someone stingy, since the word for "elbow" (*codo*) and "stingy" (*codo*) are the same. In Puerto Rico, people in conversation will crinkle their noses at one another. This gesture is shorthand for "What do you mean?"

Although the meanings of some gestures, such as smiling, are nearly universal, people of different cultures use different gestures to signify different things. Gestures like the "thumbs up" or "OK" sign, which are positive affirmations to North Americans, are severe insults in other regions of the world. One must not assume that the meanings of kinesic gestures are the same across cultures.

TOUCH

Related to kinesics is the cultural use of touch. Social life requires greeting others in culturally appropriate ways. North Americans often shake hands or hug (depending on age, gender, and status), Latin Americans often kiss on the cheek once, and

Table 9.2
Categories of Touch

Functional/professional	Touching another in the course of one's work, such as that of a doctor or manicurist.
Social/polite	Touch that is part of a greeting or hospitality, such as shaking hands.
Friendship/warmth	Touch between friends to express mutual appreciation or support.
Love/intimacy	Touching another to express nonsexual love and affection.
Sexual/arousal	Touching in an intimate context.

Source: Heslin 1974

the Swiss kiss three times. In Eastern Europe (e.g., Serbia) or the Middle East (e.g., Turkey or Lebanon), men may kiss each other's cheeks in greeting, although this same-sex greeting may carry sexual connotations in other parts of the world. Table 9.2 summarizes the categories of touch.

These categories vary widely cross-culturally, especially in ethnic groups where a high value is placed on women's modesty, such as Arab cultures. Certain religious groups, such as Orthodox Jews, prohibit all touch between men and women who are not married or blood relatives. In personal interactions, differences in the type and frequency of touch may be examined for cultural and gender distinctions. For instance, in the United States, women tend to touch one another more frequently than men do.

TIME

A fourth component of silent language is the perception of time. Time is experienced differently based on cultural norms. For instance, certain cultures value punctuality as a sign of respect. Other cultures believe it is disrespectful to arrive too early while the host may still be preparing. In some countries, open-ended social gatherings or parties may last for days, while in others, revelers adhere to a strict timetable. As with other features of silent language, the cultural use of time needs to be understood in order to place people's behaviors and expectations in the correct context.

Ethnolinguistics

Ethnolinguistics is the study of the relationship between language and culture. It is generally considered a subset of linguistic anthropology. An ethnolinguist would be interested in how people's cultural environments shape their language

Figure 9.4

"100 Words for Lawn" by Speed Bump

Many anthropology students hear that the Inuit know over 100 words for snow, as an oft-cited example of linguistic determinism. This comic reverses the ethnographic gaze in a humorous way to refer to stereotypes of North American culture.

Credit: © Dave Coverly

use, or how language shapes the way they organize and classify the world. Sociolinguistics is a similar field of study; in particular, it focuses primarily on the effects of social and cultural norms on language. Some linguistic anthropologists argue that these fields may be too similar to differentiate.

It is well understood that culture directly influences language. At the most basic level, a person is born into a given culture and acquires the language(s) necessary to interact with others. Because humans are born with the capacity for language, but not instinctively knowing any particular one, language is essentially a by-product of culture.

An interesting and controversial question is "To what degree does the language we speak shape our perception of the world?" One of the first linguists to research this question was Benjamin Lee Whorf, under the guidance of his academic mentor, Edward Sapir, in the 1930s. Although many people today refer to this idea as the Sapir-Whorf Hypothesis, Whorf himself referred to it as the **linguistic relativity principle**.

The principle considers language to be intimately connected to culture, such that people who speak different languages may in fact experience the world in distinct ways. An extreme version of this argument asserts that one's language directly determines one's worldview. That is, the structures of a language lock people into seeing the world in certain ways. Few linguists today would argue for this type of total linguistic determinism. Nonetheless, the close correlation of language and culture for which Whorf argued clearly exists.

Consider the Nuer (who call themselves *Naath*), a pastoral people living in the Nile Valley of Sudan and Ethiopia. Their main mode of life for thousands of years has centered on their herds of cattle. Cattle are essential to the Nuer economy, with people's wealth and status measured in the size of their herds. The herds also provide sustenance: Nuer people drink milk, and eat whey or cheese from their cows. In addition, young men and women take on "cattle names" which identify them with their favorite animals, gifts of cattle are given upon marriage from the groom's family to the bride's family, and family relationships in general revolve around pasture and water access for the herd.

It follows that the Nuer language has many detailed ways to talk about their cows and oxen. For instance, anthropologist E.E. Evans-Pritchard (1940) recorded 10 general color terms for the hide, several dozen more for markings combined with the color white, and dozens more for the location of those markings on the body.

Figure 9.5
Rainbow over Beach
All humans can see the varying colors of the rainbow, but many languages do not distinguish the same seven colors that we do in English.
Credit: © Barry D. Kass/Images of Anthropology

He recorded over a hundred descriptive color terms for cattle. Even more detailed vocabulary is used to talk about the size and shape of the horns, and the age and sex of the animal.

Nuer cattle vocabulary illustrates how language is deeply correlated with the cultural environment. I invite you to think of even 20 words to describe the color of a cow in English! Granted, if you grew up on a ranch, you might be able to accomplish this. But for the majority of us, it would be difficult.

Color Categories

Most English speakers take the rainbow for granted. When one appears in the sky, seven colors are clearly distinguishable. Schoolchildren often learn a mnemonic to recall the seven colors, such as ROY G. BIV, each letter standing for a color of the spectrum in order.

When anthropologist Victor Turner (1967) did fieldwork among speakers of the Ndembu language of Zambia, he found that they used only three primary color terms: white, black and red. Other colors are either derivative (i.e., gray = "darker white") or descriptive (green = "water of sweet potato leaves" or yellow = "like beeswax"). Many languages, like Vietnamese, specify more color terms than three, but have only one term to refer to blue and green (*xanh*). Speakers define the color they want to identify by association. Is it *xanh* like the ocean, or *xanh* like the grass?

What does this mean? Does language shape reality so much that because the Ndembu have only three terms to talk about color they visually see only three colors? No. Physiologically, their vision is the same as ours. They use one term for related colors because their cultural environment doesn't demand it. The use of metaphor and description fills in any gaps.

Cultural Models

Language contains a set of **cultural models** that reflect our thought patterns and guide our behavior. These models are widely shared understandings about the world that help us organize our experience in it. It follows that the models also determine the metaphors we use to talk about our experience. In this case, metaphor is not merely decorative, but is a fundamental aspect of the way we understand our world.

For example, a cultural model that guides English speakers is the notion that anger is like heat. Metaphors expressing this connection can be found throughout the language: "You make my blood boil"; "Leave him alone; he needs to let off some steam"; and "They were having a heated argument." The underlying model is that "anger is heat" which, contained in the body, may impair normal body function, or even explode. In a consistent model, the opposite is also true. To release anger one would need to "cool off" or "simmer down" (Lakoff & Kovecses 1987:3–6).

In the realm of health, we often talk about illness as war against our own bodies: we *build defenses* against illness, and we get sick because our *resistance* was low. We *fight* a cold, *combat* disease, *wage war* on cancer, and have heart *attacks* (Atkins & Rundell 2008). The importance of cultural models for anthropologists lies in understanding the worldview of others. Another ethnic group, speaking a different language, may have developed an entirely different set of cultural models.

In contrast to the idea of illness as war, the Diné (to whom we commonly refer as Navajo), approach healing differently. When a Diné person falls ill, it is evidence of a disruption in the harmony of the universe. With the support of family and community, a healer creates sandpaintings for a healing ceremony. Diné people believe that their gods, the Holy People, are attracted to the painting. When the sick person sits on the completed sandpainting, the Holy People absorb illness and provide healing. The person's health becomes reconnected to the Holy People and thus realigned with life forces. In this case, we might argue for a "musical" cultural model of health among the Diné with ideas of being "out of tune" with the "harmony" of the universe. The two different models reflect an entirely different cultural approach to medicine.

Gendered Speech

Sex and gender also shape language use. This area of study is known as **gendered speech**. Men and women learn to use different speech patterns based on the cultural expectations of each sex. Sometimes this leads to misunderstandings between men and women that are more about gendered speech patterns than about the individuals in conversation (see Box. 9.2).

During the second wave of the Women's Rights movement in the United States in the 1960s to 1970s, Robin Lakoff (1973) wrote about the apparent sexism inherent in the English language. She argued that discrimination—mostly unconscious—against women was embedded in vocabulary choice, sentence construction and speech practices. Consider the following two sentences Lakoff uses to illustrate this point: "Oh dear, you've put the peanut butter in the refrigerator again." "Shit, you've put the peanut butter in the refrigerator again" (p. 50). Lakoff argues that we would identify the first sentence as spoken by a woman, while attributing the second one to a man due to the degree of expletive. She argued that women are generally expected to speak in a "ladylike" manner.

While this is still true to a certain degree more than 40 years later, Lakoff saw that, even at the time, it was becoming more acceptable for women to use stronger language in public. These changes correlate with women moving into public positions of employment that are traditionally held by men. The reverse is not true, however. It is acceptable for the less-powerful group (women) to take on both language and behaviors of the more powerful group (men), but not vice-versa. Diminished power or status is not desirable.

Another aspect of gendered speech that Lakoff addresses is women's frequent use of tag questions. A tag is added to the end of a statement. The tag turns it into a question, decreasing its forcefulness. For instance, "The weather is terrible, isn't it?" Or "Your sister seems happy, doesn't she?" By including the tag question, the utterance comes across as more accommodating. The tag asks for confirmation that this is a valid opinion. Women's speech often uses tag questions, while men's speech more often does not. (Note: This type of tag question is different from the Canadian "eh?" used to confirm agreement or understanding.)

Speech Communities

A **speech community** is a group that shares language patterns. It can map directly onto a geographic location, since people who live in the same area may also share language patterns and vocabularies. However, speech communities also form in subcultures of people who share the same interests without necessarily living in the same area. Speech communities both occur naturally as part of membership in a given social group, but also may be manipulated consciously to signal one's membership to the group or to others.

For instance, *lavender linguistics* is a term used to refer to the speech patterns of members of the lesbian, gay, or queer community. Gender and sexual orientation are essential to social identity, and therefore can become important in the formation of language patterns.

"Why Don't You Understand Me?"—Gender and Speech

Georgetown University linguist and popular author Deborah Tannen (2007) studies the reasons why people of the same culture, even of the same family, sometimes feel that they are not understood. In her book *You Just Don't Understand: Women and Men in Conversation*, she argues that men and women's conversational styles are different. Because each gender has different goals and expectations in a conversation, talk between men and women can be challenging.

Tannen studied the speech patterns of men and women on videos to understand the differences in cross-gendered communication. She concludes that female speech emphasizes rapport. "Rapport-talk" focuses on how a speaker is feeling, shows empathy and understanding, and tends toward self-disclosure.

Male speech, on the other hand, is more of a report style, in which information is stressed rather than emotion. "Report-talk" establishes power and status among speakers, and tends to be task oriented.

These different speech patterns develop as part of the socialization process of boys and girls. Since boys and girls "grow up in what are essentially different cultures ... talk between women and men is cross-cultural communication" (Tannen 2007:14). This results in the frustration that men and women may experience in a relationship when they try to communicate.

Men may think their girlfriends or wives are "demanding and needy." Women may feel their boyfriends or husbands "never tell them anything" or that they "don't listen." Tannen wants you to know that it's not you—it all just comes down to different styles of talking.

Linguists conclude that most gay speech patterns are not natural in a biological sense, but are socially constructed. Because gay subcultures are very diverse, certain features of language may be used to signal membership to others inside the larger gay community. In other words, gendered language and behavior may be "performed," in what researchers call "doing gender" (West & Zimmerman 1987). For gay men, clues signifying membership may include intonation, certain vowel and consonant modifications, or slang vocabulary. For lesbians, it may include not only slang but also forms of nonverbal communication, such as style of dress and hair.

Code Switching

Participants in two or more speech communities can move easily between them when the context calls for it. This is called **code switching**, because it switches between speech styles known to each group. For instance, a professional may use a more neutral "General American" dialect at work. When visiting family in Boston, he may slide easily into a Bostonian accent. Similarly, when students address their professors, they often use more formalized speech patterns and vocabulary. After class, at the cafeteria with friends, their style of speaking and use of vocabulary fall into more informal and relaxed patterns.

Different styles of speaking are called **language registers**. Many people use multiple registers in social interactions daily. Generally, languages have a formal and an informal register. In Spanish, for example, a speaker uses the formal *Usted* when addressing a teacher, doctor, or other professional, as well as strangers they have just met who are older than the speaker. The informal *tú* is used to speak to friends, family members, and children. Rules can change based on the country of origin. For instance, in El Salvador, children address their parents as *Usted* as a form of respect. The use of registers may also be used deliberately in social situations in ways that are typically incorrect, to invoke sarcasm or change the meaning of an utterance.

Code switching also occurs between different languages when multilingual speakers talk together. Words or phrases may be switched from one language to another in a single sentence. An interesting feature of code switching is that it is grammatically correct according to the rules of the dominant language of the sentence.

For example in the question, "This dress, *es muy largo*, isn't it?" the speaker switches effortlessly from English to Spanish, then back again. The word *largo* is an adjective modifying the masculine Spanish word for dress, *vestido*. Even though the English word "dress" was used in the sentence instead of *vestido*, the ending of the adjective *largo* (with an "o") correlates to the masculine noun *vestido*.

This is done unconsciously; that is, the speaker seamlessly switches when it makes sense in the sentence to switch. Don Kulick, who studies language in Papua New Guinea, asked a Papuan informant about why speakers switch from one language to another. His informant answered simply "If *Tok Pisin* comes to your mouth, you use *Tok Pisin*. If *Taiap* comes to your mouth, you use *Taiap*" (Verhaar 1990:206). In other words, a speaker doesn't think about code switching; it just happens.

Language in the Digital Age

Digital Language

The widespread use of personal digital devices, such as smartphones and tablets, has created a host of new ways to communicate. In fact, it has become more and more common to write to one another (through email, instant messaging, or texting) than to talk on the phone or face to face. Due to this, writing has undergone a radical transformation in the past 20 years. Users of electronically mediated communication (EMC) in languages all over the world have developed creative new ways to write and talk.

A topic of interest to anthropological linguistics is the widespread use of text messaging. Users text as if they were having a conversation, constantly inventing

Table 9.3
Laughing Online around the World

Thai	55555	the Thai word for 5 sounds like "ha," so 555 sounds like "hahaha"
Japanese	www	warai = "laughing"
French	mdr	mort de rire = "dying of laughter"
Spanish	jajaja	the letter j sounds like an h, so jajaja sounds like "hahaha"
Korean	kkkkk	keukeukeu = "laughing"
Swedish	asg	asgarv = "intense laughter"
Nigeria	LWKMD	"laugh wan kill me dead"
Brazilian Portuguese	rsrsrs	risos = "laughter"

Sources: Megan Garber 2013; McCann and Brandom 2012

innovative ways to use "fingered speech" (McWhorter 2013). For instance, shorthand and abbreviations allow users to text rapidly. In English, *SMH, IDK, AFK,* and *LMAO* are just a few examples. Since users perceive texting as an extension of speech, these same abbreviations also find their way into spoken language. The shorthand becomes a word in its own right, and thus enriches the language. *OMG* (or *oh-em-gee*) as a single word now carries a different meaning than its original referent, "Oh my God."

Texting lacks the nonverbal features that are essential to speaking face to face. Therefore, challenges arise in expressing one's intent clearly. The use of emoticons, smileys, capital letters, and varied punctuation allow users to express complex levels of meaning. Consider the difference in meaning between "going to dinner with cousins ☺" and "going to dinner with cousins ☹."

As with any other words in a language, meanings change over time and may be used in creative new ways. The abbreviation for "laughing out loud" as *LOL* (spoken as *el-oh-el*) began as an authentic response to something funny. Now, after years of use, it has evolved into *lol* (*lahl*) or *lolz* (*lahls*) to express irony, sarcasm, or just as a written placeholder to let the other person know that you're (sort of) paying attention. Table 9.3 lists some of the ways that users express laughter (whether authentically or sarcastically) in different languages.

Research finds that students have clear rules for EMC, including levels of formality and appropriateness. Just as in spoken language, students use a different register when writing emails to friends than they would when emailing a professor. While "c u in class lolz" might be appropriate for friends, students know to use the more formalized register with teachers: "See you in class, Professor." There appears to be little support for complaints that texting is "ruining" language or preventing students from learning to spell. On the contrary, it is an exciting avenue for studying language change.

Language Change and Loss

Language Change

How do languages change? As culture changes, so does language—as we see in the texting example above. Moreover, large-scale social changes can have broad impacts on language use. The results of contact, colonization, and assimilation force new modes of communication on speakers, especially in the subordinate language. Often languages will merge to some degree.

When communication relies on understanding between speakers of two or more languages, they require a **lingua franca**. This is a language used for business transactions and is the most likely to be known by multiple ethnic groups. Examples include the use of French for countries of Northwest Africa, Swahili for East Africa, and Hindi for India. On the Internet, a virtual location for business and communication, English is the lingua franca.

Pidgin languages develop when culture contact is sustained and there is no common language to serve as a lingua franca. A pidgin language uses two or more languages for communication by mixing certain features together. The dominant language often supplies most of the vocabulary, while the subordinate language maintains features of its grammar. This particular mix is likely because pidgins develop quickly, out of necessity for communication. Words are more important for meaning, and generally easier to incorporate than syntax changes.

When a pidgin language remains relevant and, in the next generation, becomes the dominant language of a group, then we refer to it as a **creole** language. *Tok Pisin* is a language that first developed as a pidgin due to sustained contact with North Americans in Papua New Guinea. Today, it is one of the official languages of Papua New Guinea, with millions of speakers.

Language Extinction

According to *Ethnologue* (Lewis 2013), just under seven thousand languages are currently spoken in the world. About two thousand of them are listed at the time of this writing as "in danger." Because 90 per cent of those languages already in danger have fewer than 100,000 speakers, the twenty-first century may see a severe increase in language extinction.

Figure 9.6
Truganini
Truganini is widely believed to be the last Tasmanian Aboriginal woman. It is hard to imagine what she might have seen and experienced in her lifetime.

Why do languages die? In practical terms, a language dies when children are no longer taught to speak it. Many forces contribute to the extinction of a language, just as there are complex reasons for the extinction of animal or plant species in nature.

One tragic possibility is that a language is left with no living speakers due to genocide. This occurred when the English colonized the island of Tasmania, off the coast of Australia, at the turn of the nineteenth century. Disease and attacks on the native population left few survivors. The last remaining Tasmanian Aboriginal woman, named Truganini, died in 1876. All the native languages of Tasmania are extinct.

Another, less violent, cause of language extinction is that some languages evolve completely into other languages. The sacred language used to write ancient Zoroastrian religious texts, Avestan, had already gone extinct in an oral form before the development of its written language in AD 3. Original spoken Avestan had become several languages, including Old Persian and probably also Pashto, spoken in Afghanistan. The language was re-created in a written form to preserve the ancient prayers.

Another way a language may disappear is due to deliberate suppression by a dominant culture after contact. The Ainu of Japan are an ethnic group who live on the Japanese island of Hokkaido. They have experienced severe discrimination by non-Ainu Japanese, beginning in the fifteenth century with invasion and enslavement. Brutal treatment of the Ainu decreased their numbers considerably. In the mid-twentieth century, the Japanese claimed Ainu land, prohibiting hunting and fishing. The use of Ainu language in schools was prohibited, and children were forced to learn Japanese instead. Estimates of remaining Ainu speakers today range from just 20 to 30 individuals.

These violent language suppression tactics occurred close to home as well. Starting in the 1800s and continuing until the late 1900s in some regions, the governments of the United States and Canada made attendance at special schools (called "boarding schools" in the United States and "residential schools" in Canada) for Native American/First Nations children mandatory. The children were forbidden to speak their native languages under threat of punishment. They suffered terrible abuses and even death at the hands of boarding school staff, who were infamously told to "kill the Indian in the child." These oppressive practices caused the decline of not only Native languages but also Native culture.

Box 9.3

Saving Disappearing Languages

A language is of such critical importance because it encodes all of a culture's information. For instance, there are many words and phrases that cannot accurately and fully be translated into another language without a lengthy description. Even then, native speakers will say that the translated description does not capture the essence of the original term.

In an effort to appeal to young language learners, some advocates for Native American languages are pushing for more online use and visibility. For instance, the Winnebago (Ho-Chunk) tribe of Nebraska is developing language apps and games for the Ho-Chunk language, making language learning fun and flexible with today's technological devices, including a game based on the show *Who Wants to Be a Millionaire?* (Rindels 2013).

Another way that Native languages adapt as culture changes is by rejecting English loan words. In particular, words having to do with technology often are borrowed from English as the dominant language of the Internet. Some speakers, however, resist the intrusion of external words, and instead choose to develop their own.

For instance, the Language Commissioner of Nunavut (Canada's northernmost territory) chose the word *ikiaqqivik* to represent the word Internet in the Inuktitut language (Soukup 2006). This phrase translates to "traveling through layers," which is the way Inuktitut shamans describe their experiences of traveling through space and time on a quest. In a similar way, an Internet user travels through multiple locations (sites) with information written in and about the past, present, and future. This is an example of how traditional concepts can integrate into modern ones, preserving original cultural elements.

Tribal leaders are also working to translate Internet interfaces into their native languages. While several Native languages have websites, YouTube videos, or apps devoted to learning them, Cherokee is the first that has successfully partnered with Google to create an entire Google interface. Speakers or learners of the language can now search on Google and send Gmail entirely in Cherokee. Young Cherokee speakers can Facebook and text with the virtual Cherokee keyboard. It joins the more than 140 Native languages that are quickly gaining their place on the Web alongside English. Languages with a major online presence may be best situated to engage younger speakers.

Linguistic diversity is similar to biodiversity. In the natural world, it is important to prevent the extinction of flora and fauna because ecosystems are healthier and more resilient when they contain diverse species. Cultures are healthier too, in a sense, when their native languages are spoken. This is because assimilation and cultural loss are much more likely to happen when speakers adopt an external dominant language.

Figure 9.7

Google Interface with Cherokee Characters

Using the Internet and social media in one's native language is an excellent way to support language learning and use.

Credit: Google and the Google logo are registered trademarks of Google Inc. Used by permission.

There is some good news, however. Some languages that were critically endangered are being actively revitalized. Linguists and anthropologists all over the world are working to maintain the viability of dying languages. Some communities are using the popularity of the Internet and digital media to reach younger speakers, a topic explored in Box 9.3.

One example that shows a reversal is from the Māori people of Aotearoa (New Zealand). English settlers outlawed the Māori language (*reo Māori*) in schools by 1867. A hundred years later, it was clear that the language was dying out. Only about 18 per cent of the Māori population could speak it in the 1970s, and most of those individuals were over 50 years old (Tsunoda 2006).

With the awareness that *reo Māori* was a dying language, school programs known as "language nests" were established beginning in the 1980s. These programs provide an early childhood foundation in Māori language, values, and culture for children ages zero to six years old. The success of the language nests led to a demand for Māori-language primary and secondary schools. Today, there is revitalized interest in traditional Māori language, and the number of speakers is increasing.

Summary

This chapter discussed language as one of the main characteristics of human culture. Mirroring the Learning Objectives stated in the chapter opening, the key points are:

- Although nonhuman primates (and some other species) can communicate with rudimentary forms of symbolic language, humans are the only species to have developed full-blown natural language.
- How human language began is a question that has been addressed in many ways. Some ideas emphasize the role of trust and the need for people to trust that a sound means the same as a recognized gesture.
- In order to be able to record an oral language they are studying, linguistic anthropologists break it down into components, including the units that comprise sound, grammar, and meaning.
- Linguistic anthropologists are interested in the associated body language, facial expressions, and other silent language that lend meaning to an utterance.
- When looking at speech patterns from an anthropological perspective, the communities and cultural contexts (such as gender) provide rich cultural data.

- Although some may fret that languages used today on the Internet and for social media are being irreparably damaged, anthropologists actually find EMC an exciting area of creative language change.
- Unfortunately, some languages have been lost forever due to severe cultural oppression. Nonetheless, today many languages are in a state of active revitalization.

REVIEW QUESTIONS

1. Do other primates or animals use the same kind of symbolic language that humans do?
2. Why do anthropologists argue that language is much more than speech?
3. To what degree do anthropologists believe in the validity of the linguistic relativity principle today?
4. Why do languages die?
5. How can we slow down or stop the extinction of languages?

DISCUSSION QUESTIONS

1. Do you think that texting is ruining the language? In your experience, how has texting changed the way you talk or write?
2. Have you had experiences while traveling in which others had different zones of kinesics, proxemics, or touch?

Visit **www.lensofanthropology.com** for the following additional resources:

| SELF-STUDY QUESTIONS | WEBLINKS | FURTHER READING |

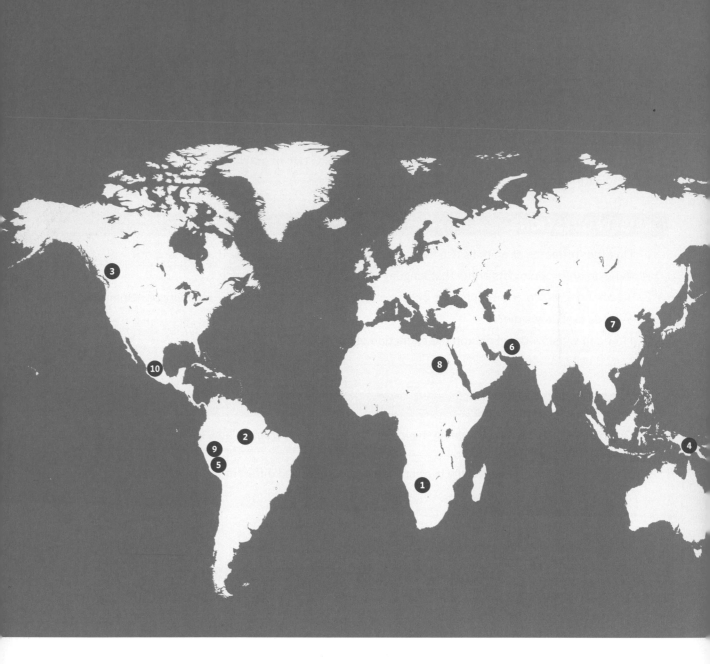

PLACES MENTIONED IN CHAPTER 10

1 Kalahari Desert
2 Amazon rainforest
3 British Columbia
4 Papua New Guinea
5 Peru

6 Southern Iran
7 Yellow River Valley
8 Nile River Valley
9 Andes Mountains
10 Mexico City, Mexico

FOOD-GETTING AND ECONOMICS

(((Seeking? Planting? Shopping? How you get your food is fundamental to how you live your life. #foodgettingandeconomics

Learning Objectives

In this chapter students will learn:

- the connections between how people get their food, how they organize themselves socially, and how they distribute their resources.
- the differences between food foragers and food producers.
- about distinct types of foraging based on the resources of a given area.
- which forms of economic production, distribution, and consumption are found in different types of societies.
- the characteristics of food-producing societies, including horticulturalists, pastoralists, intensive agriculturalists, and industrialists.
- many diverse diets based on nutrient-rich foods can be healthy for the human body.

Introduction

How do people get the resources they need to survive? Do they grow or raise their own food, forage for it in the local area, or purchase it at the grocery store? Each of these different food-getting strategies lays the foundation for a very different type of society. The ways people get their food dictate their daily schedules, interactions with the environment, modes of cooperation and competition, and the expectation of division of labor between genders.

Food-getting strategies also provide a foundation for the **economics** of a society, or how goods and services are produced, distributed, and consumed. Economics examines how food is found, grown, or harvested; how people get that food; and how it is eaten. Anthropologists also look at how material goods are made and by whom, how they get into the hands of people other than the producers, and how those items are used. In addition, economics looks at resources such as land and water. How are those natural resources used?

Anthropologists divide the many different types of food and resource-getting strategies into general categories. The largest division is between food foragers (those who find food) and food producers (those who grow food). Within this broad division, procurement strategies are separated into categories: foragers are in one category, while the category of food producers includes horticulturalists, pastoralists, intensive agriculturalists, and industrialists. Often a society will practice one or more of these strategies. Each will be explained in detail in this chapter.

Technological "Tool Kit"

When we talk about how people get their food, we are looking at their technology. In this case, technology doesn't mean whether they can use their laptops to order takeout on the Internet (although in many societies, it could!). **Technology** in a more general sense refers to the tools, skills, and knowledge used by people to survive. Anthropologists may refer to the tool kit as **traditional ecological knowledge (TEK)**, or the collective and cumulative knowledge that a group of people has gained from living in their particular ecosystem over many generations.

For example, the technological tool kit of a desert dweller would be very different from that of an inhabitant of the rainforest. Desert **subsistence** relies on knowledge of water-storing plants. Knowledge of how to access these water sources is crucial. On the other hand, people of the rainforest have a relatively constant supply of water, but need to know how to distinguish between other things, such as edible or poisonous fruit, or between harmless or dangerous insects and animals. In each case, group members develop an extensive tool kit over time according to their needs. Each generation uses the skills necessary to procure food essential for survival in their environment.

Adaptive Strategies: Food Foragers and Food Producers

When anthropologists examine different food-getting strategies, we find it useful to distinguish between those who use what the land produces and those who deliberately manipulate the environment to produce food. Those who seek their food

supply among available resources are called **food foragers** or **hunter-gatherers**. Groups that farm, keep food animals for their own use, or otherwise transform the environment with the goal of **food production** are referred to as **food producers**. Depending on the means by which the food is produced, they may practice horticultural or agricultural techniques, engage in animal herding, and/or rely on others to produce, distribute, and make food products available. A culture's **foodways** are fundamental to the structure and functioning of its society.

Food-getting strategies are flexible and nonexclusive. No society is locked into one settlement or economic pattern, and all societies have a dynamic relationship with their environment and with other societies with whom they come into contact. Several strategies may be used at one time, with one generally being dominant. For instance, a pastoral herding society may also plant crops part of the year and trade or purchase certain food items at a local store.

Food-procurement methods are subject to change from internal pressures and external sources. These range from environmental change, the invention or adoption of new technology, peaceful trade, or violent conquest. Furthermore, as new resources make themselves available, groups can and will make use of them, if it means they can make a better living. Even today, small-scale Indigenous communities are involved in global processes of change. They are linked to regional, national, or international economies by selling their products or services to production or manufacturing industries.

Figure 10.1

Foragers

Foraging peoples represent a way of life that humans have practiced in varying forms since the beginning of our species. In other words, we became human while living in small foraging groups.

Credit: © Ariadne Van Zandenbergen/Alamy

Food Foragers

It is estimated that humans have spent 99 per cent of their existence hunting and gathering for survival. It's important to look at the traits of foragers to understand not only techniques of food procurement but also the types of social networks upon which human society is built. Even though most humans on earth no longer forage for a living, our basic humanness is defined by the cooperation and social connections between people that foraging fostered.

While the lifestyles of various foraging peoples share many traits, there are also major differences. The environments, gender roles, supernatural belief systems, and other features of foraging groups may be distinct. Food-getting strategies are always embedded within a set of unique cultural values, beliefs, and practices. Sometimes these cultural values override the mere quest for calories, a topic explored in Box 10.1. To get a sense of some of these differences, this book examines several different foraging lifestyles among the Hadza of Northern Tanzania; Ju/'hoansi (pronounced *zhut-wasi*) of the South African Kalahari Desert; and the **Inuit** of the Canadian Arctic.

Forager Foodways

Depending on the ecosystem, foragers' daily food may consist of wild plants, animals, or fish. The types of wild plants are highly variable, and certainly more than just "nuts and berries." Land-based plant foods include a wide variety of wild fruit and vegetables, roots, seeds, tree sap, and nuts. For those groups with access to lakes, rivers, or the ocean, aquatic plants provide excellent nutrition, including algae and seaweed. Hunting brings in local game, including small and large mammals, reptiles, amphibians, and birds. Insects can be gathered for an easy source of protein. Animal products such as honey and eggs may also be gathered. In marine environments, foragers' daily meals may consist primarily of fish, marine mammals, and crustaceans. For instance, the Inuit of the Canadian Arctic hunt caribou, seal, and sea birds in the winter, and supplement with a variety of fish and whale in summer months when the ice thaws.

While hunting is often portrayed in popular films as the primary source of food, in fact ethnographic and archaeological studies show it was the opposite in certain areas. Living among the Ju/'hoansi, anthropologist Richard Lee discovered that the group could identify over 90 different plant foods in the desert environment of the Kalahari, which provided them with a wide range of vitamins and minerals, including fat and protein from plant sources. Hunting brought in only about 20 per cent of the group's calories, while gathering of plant materials and insects supplied the

Optimal Foraging Theory

Evolutionary ecologists developed the **optimal foraging theory** to understand the relationship between predator and prey in the natural world. It has also been used to describe human food-getting strategies, especially hunting and gathering. The concept predicts that individuals are driven to maximize the benefits and minimize the costs of food procurement. This can be broken down simply into calories: the calories an individual forager takes in must be more than the calories expended. The larger this gap, the more efficient the foraging strategy is.

Critics of optimal foraging theory in anthropology argue that human choice cannot be narrowed down to calorie optimization. This is due to the ramifications of culture and human social relations. They argue that cultural rules, not strict biological needs, dictate why certain high-calorie foods are chosen and some calorie-dense foods are never eaten at all. Intergroup relations, religious beliefs, and political considerations such as status may guide food-getting practices.

The optimal foraging theory model suggests that maximizing short-term gains is more important than the long-term preservation of food species. However, some foraging groups do consciously choose to preserve their environmental resources when they become unstable. For instance, William Balée (1994) documents the choices that Amazonian Ka'apor people make to protect their main food resource. They consciously choose to move camp when the numbers of the yellow-footed tortoise are running low. In another example, the Makah of Neah Bay, Washington, in the Pacific Northwest chose to cease hunting whale in the 1920s when the numbers of gray and humpback whales were dangerously low, even though there were no laws prohibiting them from hunting (Gottlieb 2012).

It's clear that optimal foraging theory may be applied to human food-getting strategies in certain cases, where calorie optimization is the most important goal. However, human society is embedded within a dense network of social expectations and cultural values. Sometimes it's more important to choose food sources that may be low in calories but high in status. In these cases, optimal foraging theory is only one of several theoretical models that can be applied.

bulk of their diet. Although we tend to think of hunting and gathering as eking out a meager living at subsistence level, their diet was undoubtedly more nutrient dense than our limited diets today.

The Hadza of Northern Tanzania are one of the remaining groups on earth in which up to 40 per cent of members still hunt and gather exclusively as their main food-getting strategy. Approximately 1,000 Hadza remain in their ancestral homeland in the area of Lake Eyasi, bordering the Serengeti National Park. The Hadza primarily hunt game that comes to their water holes to drink, and forage for tubers, berries, and baobab fruit. They also trade for foodstuffs such as maize (corn), millet, and beer. Like many other foraging peoples across the world, the Hadza especially prize honey as a source of energy.

Why do Hadza still forage for their main living? Anthropologist Frank Marlowe argues that it is mainly due to poor ecological conditions for farming and pastoralism. The soil is largely unsuitable for agriculture, and infestations of the tsetse fly prevent the successful herding of animals. Therefore, Hadza people stay isolated as foragers as a choice. They know that they cannot survive by farming the depleted soil, and choose not to work for others. Because they don't want to give up their autonomy, they continue hunting and gathering in a close-knit community.

SOCIAL ORGANIZATION

Foragers live and travel together in small groups that anthropologists call **bands**. These groups could vary in size based on seasons. For instance, among the Hadza, band size has varied little over the past 100 years, with the average around 30 people. During berry season, band membership can temporarily grow to 100 people. The Ju/'hoansi lived in bands of 30 to 40 people moving across the landscape before being settled into camps in the 1970s. The Inuit live in extended families, from a dozen to over 50 people, depending on the geography of the area.

What are the advantages of staying in small bands? In a harsh environment where survival depends on cooperation, it is important to minimize problems and stay together. Fewer interactions cause fewer opportunities for conflict and division. The measure of these interpersonal conflicts is referred to as the **social density**, or the frequency and intensity of interactions among group members. Maintaining small numbers minimizes the density, making social life easier than if there were several hundred individuals living together. Nonetheless, where there are people, there is conflict. An often-used solution to interpersonal conflict is for individual members to join another group, either temporarily or permanently. This causes the numbers in a band to fluctuate occasionally. It also keeps the bands from breaking apart.

In general, men's and women's tasks are divided by gender. Although a **sexual division of labor** predominates, it doesn't mean that men are necessarily restricted from gathering or women from hunting. However, due to women's role in pregnancy and child care, along with a multitude of tasks they perform at the campsite, it is more efficient for men to hunt. Hunting requires stealth, something that would be nearly impossible with infants or toddlers along. Some tasks are open to all group members. Among the Hadza, men, women, and children gather honey, their most prized food item.

Bands have no social classes. Life in an **egalitarian** society means every member gets immediate rewards from **foraging**. Sharing the same access to resources limits status differences. In addition, being nomadic requires that everyone carry all their possessions on their backs when moving from camp to camp. This limits the number of belongings a person can have to what he or she can carry.

How does everyone get approximately the same amount of resources if some families have more able-bodied members, or certain hunters are more skilled than

Figure 10.2
Fishtraps in the Huahine Lagoon, Tahiti
A foraging lifestyle includes hunting and fishing, where accessible. These fish traps are set in the Huahine Lagoon, Tahiti, to lure fish inside. Once the trap is closed, the fish mature in the ponds and will be eaten.
Credit: © Barry D. Kass/Images of Anthropology

others? Bands are **cooperative societies**, in which sharing is a key strategy for survival. When groups of hunters return with game, or women return from gathering, the food is divided among members of the group. This specialized sharing ensures that everyone eats. It also creates a social and economic bond between the people engaged in the sharing process. Once food has been shared, a recipient must reciprocate the next time he or she has a surplus. Among the Ju/'hoansi, an individual member may have 10 or more sharing partners in a network that may be called upon when needed. This reciprocity network creates a safety net in times of hardship. According to Marjorie Shostak (1981), when Ju/'hoansi people are angry with one another, they may call someone stingy—a terrible insult in a band society.

Bands are homogeneous societies, meaning members share culture, religion, and ethnicity. All members also share collective rights over the land, the potential to heal others, and knowledge about how to find and process food. Because of the high level of sharing of responsibilities and experience, there is a lack of **specialization** in the tasks performed by individuals. All adults have some say in making decisions that affect the group, as there is no formal leadership beyond the respect afforded to the wise. This lack of specialization supports and maintains their egalitarian nature.

FORAGERS AND THE ENVIRONMENT

Foragers are **nomadic**, meaning they move frequently. The Hadza and Ju/'hoansi are examples of foragers: they move frequently and process food on site. In contrast, the Inuit are collectors: they bring their fishing catch or other marine foodstuffs back to their base camp for processing. Because the Inuit generally live in tundra environments, they use domesticated husky dogs (or, today, snowmobiles) to pull sleds for transportation to these sites.

Each group is well acquainted with its home territory, over which it walks annually to locate seasonal foods. Each band has some historical connection to its route, and some rights over it, although they do not have the conception of owning land or water as we might today. Once food resources in a given area are sufficiently used, the group moves to the next site. Collectors, such as the Inuit, may have winter and summer base camps, moving between them twice a year as the seasons change.

Until the twentieth century, foraging territory was very large. Therefore, by the time a group returned to any previous site, the food resources would be plentiful again. With all the land available up to several hundred years ago, this was a truly sustainable way to procure food. Today, land is in short supply. Foraging as a primary means of sustenance is possible for only a tiny percentage of people in the world.

Most foraging peoples today have mixed diets, with foods coming from many different sources, including local commodity stores. Nearly all people everywhere take part in the global industrial economy. Inevitably, commodity stores introduce processed foods, which are lower in nutrients. For instance, anthropologist Polly Wiessner found that store-bought items from the Ju/'hoansi village at Xamsa from 1996 to 1998 included sugar, flour, bread, soup, candy, chips, and beer. Nevertheless, most of the store-bought items are shared among camp members, in an extension of the traditional economy (2002).

Economic Resources: Who Gets What and How?

A major part of understanding food-getting strategies has to do with how that food gets distributed to others. The economic practices of a society provide guidelines for how food and other resources get spread among group members. There are three basic processes, which will be discussed in this section:

1) Reciprocity
2) Redistribution
3) Market Exchange

Reciprocity is practiced in all types of societies. Redistribution is found specifically in societies with central governing authorities, such as farming, pastoral, or industrial societies with official leaders. Market exchange is found in agricultural and industrial societies in which surpluses are produced.

Reciprocity

Reciprocity is a set of social rules that govern the specialized sharing of food and other items. Early sociologist Marcel Mauss originally referred to these items as gifts, including the gift of one's time or effort in addition to actual physical items.

Box 10.2

Talking about Hunting

In the ethnography *"We Are Still Didene": Stories of Hunting and History from Northern British Columbia*, anthropologist Thomas (Tad) McIlwraith (2012) examines talk about hunting among the Iskut people. His study is primarily interested in how language is embedded in social contexts. By looking at everyday speech, he concludes, "hunting is the central metaphor that informs Iskut culture" (p. 12).

Iskut villagers are *didene* (Native) and have ancestry in the area dating back thousands of years. Because the village is of recent, twentieth-century construction, not all villagers have the same backgrounds, experiences, or dialects. However, the one thing that all Iskut people have in common is their reliance on and identification with hunting.

In focusing on communication among hunters primarily, McIlwraith found that hunting was rarely spoken about openly and directly. Nonetheless, the use of hunting metaphor and allusion in everyday speech allows Iskut people to establish personal connections between hunters through shared experience, uniting the community. Hunters from different areas even use common structural elements while retelling stories about their hunting experiences. Talking about hunting affirms the relevance of traditional Iskut life in the modern context. Further, it allows them to assert their difference from non-Native outsiders, such as government workers or anthropologists, who may claim ownership over their histories or Traditional Ecological Knowledge (TEK; see Chapter 14).

Figure 10.3

Didini Kime, "Young Caribou Camp"
This typical Tahltan hunting camp is used by multiple generations of people from the same family. Occupied as a base for caribou- and moose-hunting expeditions in the late summer and fall, this camp is visited throughout the year.
Credit: Thomas McIlwraith, 2012

Cultural models at work in Iskut life establish the idea that animals, nature, and people are connected in a closely knit web. Animals should not be spoken of poorly or treated with disrespect. Similarly, the land should also be treated well; otherwise, punishment may follow. For this reason, Iskut villagers have stood their ground in an ongoing political battle to protect their native area from government-sanctioned mining exploration and development. As McIlwraith discovered, talking about hunting privileges personal relationships over economics and stewardship of the land over exploitation. In this way, talking about hunting is essential to Iskut identity.

However, gifts are not given in a vacuum. Strict social rules dictate the requirements of sharing among members of a group, especially when the group relies on reciprocity to survive.

Parties involved in a reciprocal exchange enter into a social and economic bond. Once a gift is given, the two parties are now connected in an ongoing relationship.

If one side of this relationship doesn't reciprocate with a gift of some type that is roughly equal in value, then the bond between them is damaged. Failing to reciprocate can destroy social, political, or economic relationships between individuals, families, or entire communities.

RESOURCE DISTRIBUTION: GENERALIZED RECIPROCITY

Friends and family often practice a loose form of reciprocity we call **generalized**. The value of a gift is not specified at the time of exchange, nor is the time of repayment. However, the parties involved have the responsibility to reciprocate at some time and in some roughly equal way. Because every society has a circle of people they trust, generalized reciprocity can be found in every type of society.

For example, Ju/'hoansi hunting is governed by the rules of generalized reciprocity. Hunters begin preparations by equipping their quivers with others' arrows. Killing a large animal such as a giraffe takes multiple arrows, likely from each member of the hunting party, who must track and follow the animal for days as the poison debilitates its system. Therefore, responsibility for the kill is already shared from the moment the hunters set out. If the hunt is successful, the hunters will divide the animal in such a way that all members of the band receive some. Contrary to what we might imagine, only a small portion goes to the hunters and their families. However, by entering into a relationship of sharing with each member of the group to whom they have given meat, the hunters have solidified an ongoing bond. The debt of food will be repaid to those hunters at a later time, when others have brought home meat.

Foraging groups include nature in their reciprocal networks of giving and sharing. Living intimately with the natural world, foragers have an ongoing reciprocal relationship with their environment. They believe that as long as people care for their environment, nature will provide.

Food Producers

Horticulturalists

The last 15,000 years have seen a human population explosion. As numbers of people grew, land became scarcer and resources decreased. Some foraging groups with lands suitable for planting began supplementing their foraging lifestyle with small-scale farms or gardens. As was explained in Chapter 6, there may have also been social and political reasons for the changes. Anthropologists refer to these groups as **horticulturalists**.

Because small-scale farming requires daily maintenance, groups who plant must settle in one area. Their villages are often small and occupied year-round. Hunting and gathering trips fan out from this central location. Small-scale farming is done with the use of simple hand tools, such as digging sticks and other garden tools fashioned from objects in the environment. These groups rely on rainfall for water.

HORTICULTURALIST FOODWAYS

Horticulturalists are food producers. While they may practice some hunting and gathering, they get a substantial percentage of their calories from crops they have planted, tended, and harvested. Crops vary widely, depending on the demands of the environment. Often there is some reliance on roots and tubers, possibly grains, and a selection of appropriate fruits and vegetables for the region.

How does a major change in food-getting strategies occur, such as the change from foraging to planting? Economic anthropologists see the answer to this question in the relation between group size and the food items available at any given location. The number of people that can be sustained with the existing resources of a given area is called the **carrying capacity** of the land. Among foragers, a group will remain in one place until the resources needed to feed and shelter all members of the group are used. Then, they move on to the next campsite. If the human population in the area is so large that available food items are never enough, a group will be forced to seek a new strategy to feed its members. In other words, if the labor needed to forage and hunt becomes greater than the labor needed to plant crops, people will plant. This process appears to be the origin of most **horticulture**.

The Kaluli people are horticulturalists who live in the tropical rainforest in Papua New Guinea. They occupy communal homes called longhouses. They refer to their longhouses and their social group with the name of their land, signifying a deep connection to their physical environment. The Kaluli mainly gather wild sago, a starch, from the sago palm. Sago is supplemented with produce from small family-maintained gardens, including bananas, breadfruit, sugarcane, sweet potatoes, and some green vegetables. Small game and fish add animal protein to the diet. Kaluli food procurement strategies are largely cooperative, even though men and women pursue separate activities. Men clear the land for swidden farming and plant crops. Women tend gardens, gather small game for extra protein, process food, and look after the village's pigs.

SOCIAL ORGANIZATION

Among horticulturalists, food-getting tasks are most often divided between men and women. For instance, among the Yanomamö of the Venezuelan and Brazilian rainforest, men clear and prepare fields, and plant and harvest crops, including plantain, sweet potatoes, cotton, and tobacco. They also hunt and fish, controlling the group's food resources. Women's work among the Yanomamö is entirely domestic. In contrast, among the Jivaro of Peru, women are responsible for planting, tending, and harvesting crops, including the sweet potato, manioc, and squash that provide the bulk of the Jivaro diet. Men supplement the diet by providing animal protein from hunting and fishing. While the division of labor is most often by gender, there are variations that can be found in different horticultural groups throughout the world.

Moving from a nomadic life of foraging to a sedentary village life of tending gardens rearranges the most basic patterns of social life. No longer are people keeping only what they can carry on their backs, but can accumulate goods and store them in their homes. This fundamental shift in behavior brings with it a challenge to the traditional egalitarian values of the group. Where sharing and cooperating was the most essential practice, now inevitably some individuals and families will have more than others, based on the location and production of their gardens. No longer are all possessions in the open for the community to see; people can store their things inside, out of view. The tensions created by these new practices need to be reconciled, as sharing is an intrinsic part of their value system.

To maintain the equal level of status among all members of the group, a society will practice some sort of **leveling mechanism**. This is a social and economic obligation to distribute wealth so no one accumulates more than anyone else. Horticultural societies develop rules for how and when goods get distributed, with the wealthiest members of the group experiencing the most pressure to share with others.

Between individuals, leveling may take the form of "demand sharing," in which members of the group may request items on demand. Among the Ju/'hoansi, it is perfectly appropriate to demand or take meat or other food items when hungry. The leveling practices between individual members in horticultural societies help distribute the wealth in culturally resonant ways.

There are also social institutions that more formally distribute wealth. An example of this type of leveling mechanism is the **cargo system** found in Maya villages and towns from Mexico through Central America. In this political and religious system, men living in the village must serve a volunteer position as a town laborer or official for at least one year. Since this is obligatory volunteer service, a man's family must pay for whatever expenses are incurred during his tenure. The more years one serves the community, using one's personal wealth to support local needs and events, the more prestige an individual is given. Ideally, leveling mechanisms such as the cargo system help to keep the socio-economic system of a horticultural society aligned with the traditional values of a foraging one.

HORTICULTURALISTS AND THE ENVIRONMENT

A sustainable method of farming when there is plenty of available land is known as **swidden** (also **shifting**) **cultivation**. This is the primary technique used in many different locations around the world, to grow crops ranging from bananas to rice. Using swidden cultivation, farmers prepare a plot of land by clearing fast-growth trees and other plant material from an area and burning the debris directly in the plot. Ash from the fire acts as a soil conditioner and fertilizer, containing high levels of potassium, calcium, and magnesium. Gardens are planted in the nutrient-rich ash. After harvesting crops from that plot for a time, farmers move to another area and begin again.

The movement from place to place on large areas of land allows the used plot to lie fallow and "rest." Wild plant material eventually regrows. Depending on the amount of land available, a group can farm many plots in this way before returning to the first, allowing land to lie fallow for up to 10 years or more.

Done correctly, swidden farming works with an area's natural ecosystem. The swidden technique mimics what happens after fires burn a landscape: after several years, plant life flourishes again. Done poorly, however, it can erode the soil. This is the result when plots are not left to lie fallow, but are used continually without the micronutrients in the soil being replenished.

An example of large-scale swidden farming is the use of millions of acres to raise food animals. Some multinational corporations providing beef to North American markets have created vast wastelands in the world's tropical rainforests to keep high densities of cattle on millions of burned acres. The forest is cut and burned, but the cattle farms remain on the same land year after year. On a small scale, this can be a very sustainable method. On the fast-food scale, not so much.

RESOURCE DISTRIBUTION: BALANCED RECIPROCITY

Because, like foragers, horticulturalists live in small-scale societies, they also practice reciprocity. Their main methods of distributing food within the village are generalized reciprocity (in which they share with family and close friends) and **balanced reciprocity** (in which they trade with others outside their trusted circle). Balanced reciprocity is an exchange in which both the value of goods and the time frame of repayment are specified. Trading partners who need to ensure that items or payment will be delivered on time use this type of exchange. Because the value of the items is known, as is the delivery time, failing to come through is a major social transgression.

Off the coast of Papua New Guinea, a system of balanced reciprocity exists, called the **Kula Ring**. This involves the circulation of gifts among trading partners in the archipelago of the Trobriand Islands. As a man travels from island to island, he meets his trading partners and gives gifts of red shell necklaces (*soulava*) or white

Figure 10.4
Blue-Veiled Tuareg Nomads, North Africa
These Tuareg men, notable for their blue veils, live a pastoral lifestyle in the Sahara desert of North Africa. They ride and herd camels, moving across national borders to access pasture lands.
Credit: © Barry D. Kass/Images of Anthropology

shell armbands (*mwali*). He also receives the same items from his partner. He does not keep the items but must continue to trade them with other partners on different islands. The necklaces move in one direction around the islands and the armbands in another. It may take up to a decade before the items return to this same person. Having the items in one's possession gives a man status, but more importantly, the history of each object remains with it. The man who has at one time owned, and then given away, many Kula items enjoys a great amount of prestige.

Pastoralists

Not all foragers find it most efficient to settle in villages and plant gardens. In some regions, it makes more sense to develop their food-getting strategies around domesticated animals. Herding pasture animals is most successful in areas where the ecological conditions are poor for farming, such as in desert environments. The way of life that revolves around herding animals is called **pastoralism**. Depending upon the region, animals suited for herding include goats, sheep, camels, yaks, llamas, reindeer, or cattle. Social and political motivations may also contribute to adopting livelihoods that shift from foraging to pastoralism.

PASTORALIST FOODWAYS

In pastoralist societies, **animal husbandry** is the main mode of sustenance. Animal herds provide food staples such as milk, blood, butter, yogurt, or cheese. Occasionally an animal may be slaughtered for symbolic or ritual purposes, but the utility of live animals far outweighs the benefits of slaughtering animals for meat. Although pastoralists generally don't farm, some groups may practice a more diversified economy that includes some cultivation. They also trade with neighboring groups for food and other items.

There are several hypotheses as to how and why pastoral lifestyles developed. One suggests that farming communities developed a secondary reliance on animal husbandry that provided the bulk of their protein and other nutrients. This idea suggests that **agriculture** and pastoralism developed concurrently. The second suggests that hunters in foraging societies learned the habits of the animals they pursued. Thus, they developed successful techniques to graze their animals, keeping them alive for food and other material products. Both hypotheses may be valid in different regions of the world.

The Basseri are pastoralists who live in Southern Iran. Today, there are approximately 16,000 Basseri occupying 3,000 tents in a region that extends from mountains to desert. The group is divided into networks of families who migrate together (occupying a handful of tents in the winter and up to 40 in the summer). They are nomadic, moving their herds of sheep and goats along a route called the *il-rah* (tribal road). The road is the property of each tribe at a specific time of year, allowing full access for all groups.

Men generally ride horses while migrating along the route, while donkeys and camels carry women, children, and possessions. To maintain an adequate standard of living, each household strives to keep at least 100 sheep and goats; some may have up to 400. Milk and milk products (buttermilk, butter, and cheese) make up the bulk of the Basseri diet, supplemented with meat. They occasionally forage, hunt, and cultivate for additional dietary items, although the majority of external items comes from trade or purchase at the marketplace.

SOCIAL ORGANIZATION

Pastoralists are nomadic, since herding animals requires going to where the grazing is good. Therefore, male herders may leave their families at the home base and be away for months at a time, tending animals. Most pastoralists, such as the Basseri, use horses as their main vehicles, to cover larger territory and aid in herding the animals. Therefore their livelihoods depend not only on the herds but also on the horses. During the warm months, the group may move anywhere from once every three days to as often as once a day. During the cold season, the base camp may remain stationery for longer, with herders making forays out to pasture.

Each tent houses an individual family that is relatively autonomous, although the larger social group consists of all families who migrate together. The division of labor requires that, generally, men and boys herd animals, haul wood or water, and roast meat back at the tent. Women generally take care of the majority of food production, and other domestic duties such as washing and sewing. Again, while these divisions are common, there are exceptions.

Figure 10.5
Plowing the Rice Paddies, Madagascar
Draft animals, such as these cattle, are used to plow the wet rice paddies in Madagascar.

Credit: © Lee Hunter/Images of Anthropology

PASTORALISTS AND THE ENVIRONMENT

Nomadic pastoralism is sustainable in environments that are unsuited to farming. Land that may be unproductive for cultivation can serve as excellent grazing lands for herd animals. Pastoralists may move back and forth over long distances to productive pastures seasonally, a migration movement known as **transhumance**. In addition, grazing may actually help the environment in that it encourages the biodiversity of native plants.

Pastoralists attempt to utilize every part of the animal and minimize waste. Beyond food products, animals also provide material goods. For example, animals' hair or wool and hides can be woven into clothes, shoes, and tents. Organs, such as stomachs, can be used to carry water. The manure of grazers is highly fibrous, allowing animal dung to be used as fuel for fires.

RESOURCE DISTRIBUTION: RECIPROCITY

Like foragers and horticulturalists, pastoralists practice reciprocity. Their economic exchanges are on the individual level, between family, friends, and associates such as trading partners. When people know one another well, the **social distance** is minimal. Thus, they are likely to practice generalized reciprocity. When items are traded between lesser-known or unknown members of different communities, the greater social distance requires the use of balanced reciprocity. In this case, items are generally exchanged on the spot for an agreed-upon value.

Intensive Agriculturalists

Large populations that can produce more than just the amount of food required for a subsistence economy practice what we call **intensive agriculture**. This type of planting is intensive because the land has a short (or no) fallow period, meaning fields are planted year-round with different crops. The intensity of this planting may deplete the soil more rapidly than horticultural methods, which typically allow fields to lie fallow for a time. Therefore, agriculture requires more preparation and maintenance of the soil through natural fertilizers, crop rotation, and water management. This type of intensive cultivation generally also requires more highly developed tools, such as plows, irrigation, and draft animals. All these inputs cost more in human labor, but also make agriculture more productive per acre than horticulture.

INTENSIVE AGRICULTURAL FOODWAYS

The earliest evidence of agriculture is from approximately 9,000 years ago in the Middle East. Populations living between the Tigris and Euphrates Rivers in Mesopotamia settled on the rivers' flood plains to make use of fertile land and water resources. They dug irrigation canals to bring water to their crops, relying heavily on grains such as wheat and barley. Over the next several thousand years, agriculture appeared independently in other locations across the globe: the Indus valley (Pakistan), the Yellow River valley (China), the Nile valley (Egypt), the Andes (Peru), and Mexico.

Where agriculture arose, populations grew with a steady supply of food from crops. We may assume that since agriculture led to population growth, farming supported better nutrition. In fact, the opposite is true. Studies of the bones and teeth of people in farming societies, compared to those in foraging societies, show that health suffered under an agricultural lifestyle. This is because most agricultural societies depend heavily on just a handful of crops, especially grains, reducing the variety of vitamins and minerals.

Decreased nutrient intake can have other effects. For instance, it may lead to susceptibility to infectious disease, seen in the archaeological record. Low nutrition levels and susceptibility to disease, coupled with the physical stress of agricultural labor, raises the mortality rate. Therefore, while there are many benefits resulting from the agricultural revolution, it is clear that human bodies suffered during this shift.

There is also evidence for **domestication** of animals such as cattle, goats, and sheep in the same time period. Animal domestication refers to the process of shaping the evolution of a species for human use. This is done through choosing the traits most suited to human needs and breeding animals for those traits. Domestication shapes companion animals to accompany hunters and working animals for the farms, as well as providing alternate sources of nutrition from animal products.

The ancient Aztec Empire was built on intensive agriculture. However, it began with the migration of nomadic peoples called the Mexica (me-SHEE-ka) into the Valley of Mexico. Settling on an island in today's Mexico City, the Aztecs founded Tenochtitlán in AD 1325. By the time of the Spanish conquest of Mexico City in 1521,

Figure 10.6
Diversity of Maize, Peru
Although we see only a few varieties of corn (maize) in North American stores, many types are grown across Mesoamerica. Peru has a wide diversity of individual crops, including over 50 varieties of maize and over 2,000 varieties of potato. These cobs are for sale at an outdoor market in Pisac.

Credit: © Barry D. Kass/Images of Anthropology

approximately 200,000 Aztecs inhabited a series of islands linked by waterways and canals (drained by the Spanish as part of their conquest strategy). Agriculture laid the foundation for the growth of the Aztec population, although they still supplemented their diet with foraging, hunting, fishing, and swidden farming.

Maize (*Zea mays*) was the staple crop and played a revered symbolic role in Aztec political and religious life. Other important crops included beans (*Phaseolus vulgaris*) and squash (*Cucurbita* varieties). The Aztecs planted these crops, called the Three Sisters, in close proximity. This type of companion planting can produce high quantities of calories per acre. The maize stalks provide support for bean vines, and squash plants, growing low to the ground, suppress weeds. In addition, beans are "nitrogen-fixing" plants, which replace the nitrogen in the soil used by the maize. These three staple crops support soil sustainability and still provide nutrition for millions in the Americas today.

In addition to practicing traditional agriculture, the Aztecs employed an ingenious method of increasing farming acreage using the waterways surrounding their islands. They developed floating gardens, called *chinampas*. The chinampas were built by piling mud into a shallow area of water, and planting willow trees in the corners. The roots of the trees would anchor the garden to the bottom of the lake, creating a man-made farming platform.

New World native crops such as maize and beans are well suited to varying climates, from tropical lowlands to high elevations. When people began crossing oceans to settle in the New World, foodstuffs from Europe and the Americas also began crossing oceans in a process we call the Columbian Exchange. Important nonfood items were exchanged as well, including raw materials such as latex and cotton. Table 10.1 provides an overview.

Table 10.1
New World Crops

Food Crops

Maize (corn)	Potatoes	Chocolate (cacao bean)	Sunflower seeds
Beans	Sweet potatoes	Avocado	Papaya
Squash	Peanuts	Pineapple	Pecan
Chili peppers	Tomato	Vanilla	Guava

Nonfood Crops

Tobacco	Cotton	Sisal (fiber)	Latex/Rubber

SOCIAL ORGANIZATION

Intensive agricultural cultivation requires a fully settled population, who can work the land throughout the year. Because a shift to grains as the staple crop can feed a large number of people, agriculture allowed populations to grow and settlements to expand over wide areas of land. Large populations result in more complex social, economic, and political systems. This complexity is reflected in the way settlements expand into a tiered structure, with high-status people living in the central area and lower-status people living in villages on the periphery. Because the central settlement is heavily populated, it is referred to as a **city**.

No longer is farming a way of life for everyone, as in smaller-scale societies. Therefore, occupational specialization begins. Agricultural laborers do not own their farms, but work for others. Owners of the land reap the benefits of their labor, as well as the wealth produced from selling the crop surplus at the marketplace. Others pursue a multitude of occupations, such as artisan, trader, merchant, soldier, or scribe. Some occupations are more highly valued than others, as reflected in a social and economic hierarchy.

This type of complex society requires the control of a centralized governing body, with the power of officially recognized politico-religious leadership. A class of **nobles** develops, which is able to harness the labor of workers to farm, build, or fight. The **peasant** class supports the growth of the settlement by providing labor, generally under threat of punishment. Agricultural societies force the development of a social hierarchy in which those who control resources have power over those who do not.

INTENSIVE AGRICULTURE AND THE ENVIRONMENT

Agricultural production leads to an entirely different relationship between people and land. While small-scale cultivation generally conserves future resources, the

Figure 10.7

Onion Field, India

Agriculture requires many different kinds of human inputs, before planting, during the farming process, and post-harvest. In this photo, South Indian women are sorting onions to sell at the market.

Credit: © Serena Nanda/ Images of Anthropology

goal of large-scale agriculture is to maximize production. The intensity of year-round cultivation requires the use of more advanced tools. Draft animals suited to the area (such as oxen, zebu, or yaks) are used to pull plows to till the soil and create trenches for planting.

Agriculture takes many forms, based on the needs of different crops. The most common of these include maize, wheat, rice, millet, sorghum, and barley. Rice, first domesticated in China approximately 9,000 years ago, is one of the world's most commonly cultivated staple grains. Different varieties of rice are suited to different methods—such as dry rice cultivation, wet rice cultivation, and deep-water rice cultivation—depending on the ecology of the area. Highland areas may be **terraced** to accommodate the irrigation needs of rice or other crops on mountainsides.

RESOURCE DISTRIBUTION: REDISTRIBUTION AND MARKET ECONOMY

Societies that have developed central authorities, such as religious or political leaders, have more control of resources. They can demand taxes or tribute or hold festivals for religious deities that require donations of food or money. Two ways that societies with centralized governing bodies can get food and other resources to its members are through redistribution or the market economy.

REDISTRIBUTION

Redistribution is the process by which goods and money flow into a central entity, such as a governmental authority or a religious institution. These goods are counted, sorted, and allocated back to the citizens. Taxes and tribute are forms

Box 10.3

The Potlatch

The potlatch is a ceremony common to Indigenous peoples living in the coastal areas of the northwest part of the North American continent, extending southward from Alaska through British Columbia, Washington, and Oregon. The basic elements of the potlatch include a host group (a kinship group) inviting guests to witness an event of significance. The potlatch typically includes the reciting of oral history, feasting, dancing, and gift giving. The acceptance of gifts following the event signifies the acceptance of the event.

Prior to the arrival of Europeans in the region, it was likely that potlatches were quite rare for any particular group to host, being reserved for such events as a person's formal assumption as chief. Neighboring groups would be invited, and the potlatch would last weeks or even months.

In 1885, the Canadian government imposed a legal ban on potlatches, with imprisonment as punishment. They saw the potlatch as wasteful, harmful to economic growth, and an impediment to social progress. As a result, thousands of items—many of them sacred—used in the ceremonies were confiscated and ended up in private and museum collections Even more detrimental was the disruption of an essential aspect of coastal First Nations life, with an entire generation unable to participate unless the ceremonies were underground. The ban on potlatches in Canada was lifted in 1954.

Potlatches continue in contemporary times, and today are much more common than in precolonial times. In addition to being organized to validate a person's assumption of the position of chief, for example, potlatches may be held today for a variety of reasons, including marking a person's obtaining an Indigenous name (and all the rights and responsibilities that go with that), celebrating a marriage, or mourning the loss of a community member. Acceptance of gifts signifies that guests agree that the host has the right to the position, rights, and responsibilities.

While the explicit function of potlatches was, and continues to be, to validate an event of significance, there are other functions as well. They give visiting guests opportunities to put on public record events that have occurred within their own community, and they also provide opportunities to recite and validate oral history, validate myths and other stories through performance, affirm identity and status, and maintain alliances.

Potlatches also have an economic function, primarily in regard to redistribution of wealth. The host group typically spends years accumulating things to give away, including jewelry, blankets, ceremonial items, and food. In many Indigenous groups, such as those in this region, status is achieved and maintained by how much one gives away rather than how much one accumulates. This serves as a form of redistribution, now and in the past. The redistribution of food and other items occurs in addition to feeding the guests for the duration of the potlatch.

This redistribution means that most groups in the area remain relatively equal in regard to the distribution of resources. No one group monopolizes the resources, nor will any group be devastated by a particularly bad year. It also serves to keep the production of items steady.

of redistributive processes. For instance, modern industrial societies require that citizens pay taxes annually. The monies collected are then redistributed through public works such as road repaving, brush clearing on public land, or other infrastructure upgrades.

Redistribution is also used in religious practices when offerings for gods or ancestors are brought to a place of worship. After the items are made sacred in a ceremony in which the gods are thought to partake of them in a nonearthly way, they may be divided among the worshippers. The Hindu *puja* is a form of worship in which members of the religious community bring offerings to the temple. After the ritual, food may be divided and shared with members.

MARKET ECONOMY

Large and complex populations develop a **market economy**, which is a more formal and bureaucratic system. The laws of supply and demand set market rates for food and other goods, which must be traded or purchased according to a set price. The price remains the same for all consumers, some bargaining notwithstanding, since most buyers and sellers no longer know one another personally. However, informal economic exchanges also persist in market economies. People make reciprocal exchanges between family and friends. In order to participate as members of society, they pay taxes to the government, which then redistributes them in public works, such as infrastructure improvement.

Intensive agricultural and industrial economies are built in the marketplace, or the buying and selling of goods and services. Because farmers are producing a surplus, a central location for exchange draws people to negotiate the cost of items. In general, the laws of supply and demand set prices. In other words, when there is a lot of something, it will fetch a small price, but when there is little of something that many people want, it will fetch a high price. Staples such as grain will be accessible to all, even the lower social classes. Only the upper classes will be able to afford exotic goods.

The market economy is based on the use of **money** for buying and selling goods and labor. Today, we think of money in terms of dollars and cents. However, throughout history, money has taken many forms. It can be anything that is used to measure and pay for the value of goods and services. Money must be portable, so it can be brought to the marketplace for transactions. It must also be divisible, such that it can be measured to the appropriate amount, and change can be given. Trading land for a cow is fine if the value of the plot of land equals that of the entire cow. Change can't easily be given though, unless the cow is butchered (which can be messy). It is much easier to weigh out bags of salt or yams to the exact amount.

Other examples of items that have been used as money throughout history, and that are more easily divisible, are shells, teeth, jaguar pelts, bones, beads, tobacco, and metals. Foodstuffs such as salt, rice, cacao beans, peppercorns, and alcohol have also been commonly used as money. Teeth, bones, and shells are referred to as

special-purpose money, in that these items were used only to measure the value of things in the marketplace and lacked another use.

In contrast, salt and cacao beans are **multipurpose money** (also called commodity money) in that the commodity can be used for other purposes besides simply as money. In other words, the item has value in itself. For instance, salt is an essential mineral for human bodies and is used to preserve and flavor foods.

Ancient Aztecs and Maya greatly valued cacao beans and used them to make a sacred drink used in religious rituals by the elite. Cacao beans were so valued that they were included in the list of tribute that Aztec-controlled regions paid annually to the empire. Mesoamericanist Michael Coe (2013) found that the Aztecs demanded a total of 980 loads of cacao beans annually, each load weighing 50 pounds.

Early Spanish settlers to the area were even tricked by counterfeit cacao beans. The beans were actually removed from the pod, which was then stuffed with dirt to give the right weight and feel before their use as money! This would be an example of **negative reciprocity**, in which the seller is deceiving the buyer as to the real value of the object. With dirt inside the cacao pod, buyers are certainly not getting what they paid for.

Industrialism

Industrialism is a way of life in which highly mechanized industry produces food. This is the second major shift in food-getting technology. The first shift was working the land, rather than simply relying on its bounty. The second shift took agriculture out of the hands of many workers, and placed it in the hands of fewer people, using advanced technology. The productiveness of a farming operation on a massive industrial scale relies on organization and management, the power of machinery, the effectiveness of **chemical inputs** into the soil, and information provided by the Internet. At no other time in human history have farm managers been able to harness real-time data instantly about climate patterns, weather changes, soil analysis, and crop price fluctuations. The main goal of using technology to produce food is to create a viable product at the lowest cost possible.

Around 1800, a slow but steady Industrial Revolution began changing the way people in Western countries did their work. New machinery took over small-scale or home-based production, completing products much faster and more efficiently. Steam-powered engines fed by coal were put into wide use for transportation and power generation. Larger-scale wind- and water-powered technology, such as windmills and water wheels, allowed farms to grow in size and to produce more food for more people at a lower cost. Since the last decades of the twentieth century, mechanized production has moved toward tractors and combines that are powered by

Figure 10.8
Industrial Factory Farm

Factory farms and confined animal feeding operations have drastically changed the way people produce food. Farmers are now managers of a largely unskilled workforce in which profit maximization is the goal. Even with government subsidies, it is hard to make a good living as a farmer in the United States today.

Credit: MENATU/Shutterstock

gasoline. Agriculture is now also heavily reliant on biochemicals such as pesticides, herbicides, and fungicides to help manage the success of crops on such a large scale.

Fields with thousands of acres may today be planted with a single crop, such as corn or soy, to maximize profit. **Monocultured** crops are more susceptible to loss from a single type of soil-borne illness or insect pest than are naturally resilient mixed ecosystems. Monocropping also depletes certain nutrients from the soil, especially when done year after year. Companies who produce and control the seeds, fertilizers, and chemicals are constantly seeking new technologies to make their products more attractive than those of others. Unfortunately, agricultural products are consolidated into just a handful of global multinational companies, who tend to make a profit at the expense of farmers.

An example of one country's challenges with industrial agriculture is India's "Green Revolution." In the 1960s and 1970s, this movement sought to provide farmers with new technology to increase their yields and feed India's massive population. Farmers in the Indian state of Punjab were the first to adopt the new technologies to increase yields, using high-yield seed varieties, chemical fertilizers, mechanized irrigation, and later, **genetically modified (GMO)** seed. In short, methods were transplanted that had worked to increase crop yields in North America.

At first, these technological advances in agricultural methods had several significant and positive effects. Yields greatly increased, and fewer rural people lived under the poverty line. Nutrition improved because more people could afford a diverse range of foods. Furthermore, the economy was stimulated due to demands for farm equipment and transportation.

Unfortunately, these gains were not sustainable. Farmers who adopted the intensive input technologies found that their soils suffered from the monoculture planting of high-yield seeds, which stripped the soil of its nutrients. To maintain the productivity of soils, more and more chemical fertilizers had to be used. Purchasing seed and fertilizers annually became a major burden for rural farmers. In addition, heavy water requirements ended up tapping the fields dry. Farmers have found it necessary in the last decade to drill deeper wells to access water, draining the groundwater and lowering the water table.

In some places, the losses are catastrophic. Now reliant on agribusinesses, farmers must find additional sources of income or lapse into abject poverty. In tragic worst-case scenarios, farmers will take their own lives in order that their families can receive insurance money to live on. This occurs with alarming regularity, with official reports of 14,000 farmers committing suicide in 2011 alone (Stephenson 2013).

SOCIAL ORGANIZATION

For examples of an industrial society, all we need to do is to look around us. Industrial food production operates in our cities and towns, and links food producers and consumers on a global scale. Ironically, the ability to feed millions through mechanized and digital technology has created a situation in which fewer people than at any time in our history are involved in the production of their food.

The process of food distribution in industrial societies is complex. Conventionally produced food goes on a long journey from "farm to fork," traveling an average of 1,500 miles (Pirog, Van Pelt, Enshayan, & Cook 2001). Produce must be picked before it is ripe and transported to several different distribution centers before arriving at the store to be sold. Shipping produce long distances requires that varieties be selected for color and durability rather than solely for taste. Food products are highly processed and require preservatives to ensure a long shelf life.

Most food production takes place in rural areas on private lands owned by corporations. These farming operations can stretch over thousands or hundreds of thousands of acres. The general public is not allowed on these private lands, so consumers don't see crop or meat production. Food animals are raised in **Confined Animal Feeding Operations (CAFOs)**, which operate differently than farms of the past did. In CAFOs, thousands, or even millions, of animals are fenced or crated to create maximum profit in a minimum of space. Because these conditions are often unhealthy, conventional production demands that antibiotics be given to food animals at every meal to prevent illness.

Industrial food production creates several environmental concerns. Most of these relate to pollution of the area surrounding farming operations, and beyond. Pollution may be caused by animal waste or biochemical inputs such as pesticides or herbicides.

Since factory farms concentrate an enormous number of animals in a very small area, the farms generate far too much manure to be absorbed by the land. Excess manure is stored in huge holding tanks or manure lagoons, and is often overapplied to fields. The manure creates an overwhelming stench, and releases hazardous gases into the air. It often contaminates local groundwater and surrounding waterways with pathogens and excess nutrients. According to the Environmental Protection Agency, agricultural practices are responsible for 70 per cent of all pollution in US rivers and streams.

Pesticides are also responsible for illness in people who are exposed to them through farm labor, spraying around the home, or in food. Even when pesticides are used correctly on farms, they still end up in the air and in the bodies of farm workers. Pesticide exposure is associated with dizziness, headaches, nausea, vomiting, as well as skin and eye problems. Long-term exposure is associated with more severe health problems such as respiratory problems, memory disorders, miscarriages, birth defects, and several types of cancer.

The Human Diet

With all of these different methods of food procurement and production, it follows that human diets are widely diverse. The Maasai and Samburu (*Lokop*) people of Kenya and Tanzania can live mainly on blood, milk, and occasionally meat from their cattle; Hindus eat a vegetarian diet of mostly grains, pulses, and vegetables; and Inuit can mostly subsist on fish, seal, whale and other marine life. How can all these populations be healthy?

The human body has the incredible ability to get the nutrients it needs from many different sources of carbohydrates, fats, proteins, and a range of vitamins and minerals. The environment can also help nutrient synthesis. An equatorial climate helps the skin synthesize vitamin D, which is essential for growth and development, and may compensate for a lack of vitamin D–rich foods.

One thing that seems to occur with regularity is a decrease in the level of nutrition when people shift from a diet based on locally sourced and home-prepared foods to one that is heavily based on store-bought and processed foods. Local foods offer a diverse array of nutrients, while processed foods rely heavily on white flours, processed soy, and chemicals. Sources of sugar in the local environment, such as fruit or honey, often provide better nutrition and a lower **glycemic index** than processed sugars.

This shift in diet and the associated health problems, including obesity, is referred to as the **Nutrition Transition**. It has occurred all over the world where people adopt a lifestyle that is connected to the modern global economy. For some Indigenous groups, such as the Pima and Tohono O'odham of Arizona, the transition has taken a debilitating toll on their health. Obesity is common and the incidence of diabetes is 15 times higher than in the rest of the non-Native population. A community-wide initiative to return to local foods (such as tepary beans, cholla buds, and cactus fruit) has been successful in some areas where people have committed to changing their lifestyle, and in fact has restored Native people's health (Nabhan 2002).

Industrial food production in the developed world today provides consumers with a mind-boggling variety of choices. There is so much food choice that consumers can adopt a specific diet based on personal goals. Cultural trends and a quest for health may cause us to limit our choices and take on a label for our eating style, such as vegetarian, vegan, pescatarian, palaeo, or raw-foodist.

While the bounty of food available allows us to make these choices, certain diets over a long period can actually cause more harm than good to the functioning of our bodies. For instance, a long-term study of raw-food diets found that the long-term intake of 70 per cent or more raw foods resulted in a lower than normal **Body Mass Index (BMI)**, interrupted female menstrual cycles, and reduced male fertility.

Studying human diets throughout the past several hundred thousand years has made it clear to anthropologists that humans evolved as omnivores. The bulk of our human diet has come from plant material and wild animal protein. Of course, the ratio of plant to animal food items was dependent on what the environment offered. It appears to be most adaptive for humans to eat foods that are as close to the forms in which they grow as possible, avoiding highly processed food products.

Conventional food production, with its focus on high yields, results in lower levels of nutrition today than in the past. Conventional production has other risks as well: unsanitary factory or factory farm conditions and environmental degradation. Although the human diet evolved as omnivorous, nonetheless, the negative aspects of industrial production and processed food products cause some individuals to choose alternative diets.

Summary

This chapter has examined the different ways in which people procure their food and access the resources they need to survive. Mirroring the Learning Objectives stated in the chapter opening, the key points are:

- Depending on the limitations of the environment, the society's technology (including knowledge and skills) will be different.
- The largest difference in technologies is between those people who seek their food (food foragers) and those who manipulate the environment (food producers) to grow and raise it. Not only are the food procurement techniques different, but the social structures are different as well.
- The population size and complexity of societies tend to grow as people move from foraging to horticulture or pastoralism. Intensive agriculture allows a society to support an even larger population. The mechanization and digitization of industrial agriculture can feed people all over the globe.
- Different types of economic systems—including reciprocity, redistribution, and market economy—are used in societies with different population sizes and levels of complexity.
- Each of these food-getting techniques creates a different relationship between people and their ecosystems, with some of the most aggressive practices occurring on a large scale today with the use of monocropping in agriculture.
- Nevertheless, it seems clear that as long as humans eat a diet based on whole foods, they can be healthy and thrive on a wide variety of foods.

REVIEW QUESTIONS

1. What characteristics distinguish food foragers?
2. What characteristics tend to correlate with the five basic subsistence types?
3. What are the three basic types of economic systems?
4. What are some of the major changes that have accompanied industrial farming?
5. Since humans everywhere eat different kinds of foods, what seems to be the requirement for a healthy diet?

DISCUSSION QUESTIONS

1. What type of "tool kit" does a modern industrial eater need to survive?
2. Do alternative food movements today have any similarities to any of the traditional foodways?

Visit **www.lensofanthropology.com** for the following additional resources:

SELF-STUDY QUESTIONS   **WEBLINKS**   **FURTHER READING**

PLACES MENTIONED IN CHAPTER 11

1 Tibet
2 Nepal
3 Pakistan
4 Ethiopia
5 Sudan

6 Burma/Myanmar
7 Finland
8 Saudi Arabia
9 Greece

MARRIAGE, FAMILY, AND GENDER

Culture, not biology, dictates the social norms and expectations of women and men in society.
#marriagefamilyandgender

Learning Objectives

In this chapter, students will learn:

- about the variety of stable marriage and family patterns across cultures.
- about different rules for taking one or multiple spouses.
- the correlates of different kinds of family and residence patterns.
- about marriage as an economic exchange between families, requiring compensation.
- how different societies trace their family lineages.
- that gender is a cultural construction while sex is a biological one.
- that a variety of gender identities exist on a spectrum and have existed across cultures.

Introduction

One of the most basic ways that social life is organized is through the relations of men and women within the family. The roles and responsibilities of parents and children, siblings, marriage partners, and extended family members provide structure for other aspects of society, such as food procurement, the availability of resources, and reciprocity. In addition, expectations about how men and women should behave in society are shaped by culture.

Although North Americans may be most familiar with a particular type of family structure—that is, parents and children living together in a single-family home—this is not the most common arrangement. In fact, the small, two-generation family unit is a relatively new development in cooperative living. Anthropologists studying marriage and family patterns around the world recognize that there are diverse family arrangements that lay the foundation for a stable society.

Furthermore, the male/female gender divide that North Americans take for granted is not universal. In the two-gender system, males are "masculine" and females are "feminine" (according to Western concepts of gender). However, gender roles vary widely across cultures in many different and accepted ways. Culture, not biology, dictates the social norms and expectations of men and women across the **gender spectrum** in society.

Marriage

While marriage and family are found in some form in nearly all cultures of the world, practices differ widely. How do we identify marriage with all of these variables? To recognize **marriage** across cultures, anthropologists look for three main characteristics: (1) sexual access between marriage partners, (2) regulation of the sexual division of labor, and (3) support and legitimacy of children in society.

(1) Sex: Sexual relations within a marriage partnership are sanctioned by society. This doesn't mean that extramarital affairs are not expected. In fact, in some societies it is understood that husbands and wives will take lovers outside of their marriage. Among the Ju/'hoansi, for instance, taking lovers is a common practice as long as it is discreet.

(2) Division of labor: Marriage regulates the tasks that women and men are expected to perform in society. Some of these are biological, such as childbirth and nursing of infants. However, most of the expectations about what work that men and women will do are based on cultural values of what is appropriate. This sexual division of labor contributes to the group's survival because although men and women perform different tasks, resources will be shared.

(3) Children: Children need care and support to grow up physically and emotionally stable. Socially sanctioned marriage and family structure—in whatever form it may take—help provide the kind of environment that supports child development. In addition, children born from a marriage union are considered to be legitimate heirs to family property. They will take on the benefits and responsibilities that come with inheritance.

Figure 11.1
Catholic Wedding Ceremony in Manila
This couple is getting married in a Catholic church in Manila, Philippines. Marriage is set within a complex set of traditions that include expectations regarding religious practices, family patterns, and social life.
Credit: © Barry D. Kass/Images of Anthropology

Spouses: How Many and Who Is Eligible?

All societies have clear rules for marriage, though they may differ greatly. We can think about marriage in human society as a partnership between families, who join together in a relationship that is based on an exchange of partners. This way of thinking may not be familiar, though, to modern Western people who choose partners based on love and trust. However, it makes sense when we consider economic patterns of exchange. Family bonds can contribute to survival and mutual support by sharing resources such as land, food, and money, or non-tangibles such as child care, time, and labor.

Family roles will differ based on whether members are related by marriage or by blood. A bride and groom joined in marriage create a web of economic and social relationships between their **families of orientation**, including their blood-related parents, siblings, grandparents, and relatives. When the pair has its own children, we refer to this as the **family of procreation**. Each of these family members has a role based on his or her position in the social group.

Monogamy

Marriage between two people is referred to as **monogamy**. Marriages that are most common in the world are opposite-sex unions, between one woman and one man. Societies with high divorce rates practice **serial monogamy**. This is marriage to one partner at a time in a succession of partners.

Why do we see monogamy most in industrial Western nations? First, European colonizers imposed strict religious rules wherever they conquered native peoples. Catholicism requires monogamy, based on a series of laws established in the fourth

century AD. The Church created a series of prohibitions against multiple spouses, divorce, and adoption. Childless couples, having no other recourse, were then forced to bequeath their land to the Church. For this reason, the Roman Catholic Church became the largest landowner in Europe.

Second, monogamy works best in countries that rely on independence training to raise their children, such as in Western countries. One of the results of independence training in formative childhood years is that children will grow to be individualistic adults with a drive to act in their own best interest. Therefore, choosing one's own spouse is a natural result of this kind of upbringing.

Although monogamy is most often practiced between one man and one woman, many societies in the world and throughout history have supported and accepted same-sex unions. While heterosexual partnerships clearly support the biological reproduction of the species, the successful rearing of children can result from a multitude of different family types. Anthropologists responded to this very issue when the George W. Bush administration introduced a constitutional amendment banning same-sex marriage, as discussed in Box 11.1.

Polygamy

The marriage practice of having two or more spouses is called **polygamy**. This is a gender-neutral term that can refer to either multiple wives or husbands. Polygamous marriages have social, economic, and political functions, including benefits for producing and raising children, keeping land holdings together, and labor distribution. This is different from the more rarely found **group marriage**, in which there are multiple spouses of each sex.

AAA Response to Proposed Constitutional Amendment

In February 2004, US President George W. Bush (2004) called for a constitutional amendment banning same-sex marriage. His speech, reproduced on CNN.com, claimed that "millennia of human experience" made it "natural" that marriage should be limited to one man and one woman as "the most fundamental institution of civilization." Several days later, the American Anthropological Association (AAA), the largest organization of anthropologists in the world, released the following statement in response:

> The results of more than a century of anthropological research on households, kinship relationships, and families, across cultures and through time, provide no support whatsoever for the view that either civilization or viable social orders depend upon marriage as an exclusively heterosexual institution. Rather, anthropological research supports the conclusion that a vast array of family types, including families built upon same-sex partnerships, can contribute to stable and humane societies. (American Anthropological Association Executive Board, 2004)

The AAA strongly opposed a constitutional amendment restricting marriage to heterosexual couples since successful partnerships and stable families come in many forms around the world. Claiming that monogamy between one man and one woman is the only "natural" or correct way to marry is a severely limited view. Anthropologist Laura Nader at the University of California, Berkeley, called President Bush's proposal one that "serves the views of the religious right" (Burress 2004).

In 2013, the US Supreme Court agreed that such an amendment limited people's rights as citizens in the landmark case *United States v. Windsor*. Citizens' rights, including marriage equality, are preserved under the Fifth Amendment's guarantee of equal protection of personal liberty. After this decision was reached, the United States joined a growing list of other countries that legally recognize same-sex marriages, including Canada, France, Spain, England, Scotland, the Republic of Ireland, Belgium, Sweden, Norway, Iceland, Argentina, Brazil, Uruguay, and South Africa. Challenges persist for marriage equality in the United States, however, since not all states accept this ruling.

POLYGYNY

The most common type of polygamous marriage arrangement is **polygyny**, or having two or more wives at the same time. Most societies in the world accept polygynous marriages; however, not all men in those societies have the wealth to take on more than one wife. (A clarification: the fact that a great many societies, including small societies, accept polygyny does not mean that most of the world's nations or most people practice polygyny.) Expensive gifts, such as animals or food items (and today, modern appliances, cars, or gold) are often required to be given to the bride's family upon marriage. Not all men can afford the expense or the maintenance of a larger household.

From a biocultural perspective, it makes sense that polygyny is popular for the survival of the species. Multiple wives allow families to grow rapidly, whereas having multiple husbands doesn't afford the same benefit. There may be a surplus of women in any given society since more men die of violence than women in raids and wars. In addition, women's life expectancy tends to be longer in places where women and men enjoy equal access to health care.

In the Maasai tribe in Kenya, East Africa, wealthy men marry multiple wives to keep up with growing herds of goats and cattle. It's important for the success of a man's family to have multiple adult women to watch the different herds as well as take care of domestic responsibilities: building the huts, preparing food, and caring for children. While we might imagine that women do not want to share their household with other wives, Maasai women accept the help. In fact, in many polygynous societies, a woman can divorce her husband if she can prove he has the resources to take on a second wife, and refuses.

Polygyny also exists in small numbers in North America, as practiced by members of the Fundamentalist Church of Jesus Christ of Latter Day Saints (FLDS) and offshoot groups. One such group lives in the settlement of Bountiful, British Columbia. Consisting of approximately 1,000 members, the Bountiful population practices polygyny according to Mormon Fundamentalist values. While members assert their rights to practice polygyny due to religious freedom, court cases have also confirmed the rights of members, especially women and children, to be free from abuse in these and other settlements.

As alluded to above, there are downsides and dangers for women in polygynous marriages. Many polygynous societies don't afford women the same rights as men. Women may be treated as property and essentially sold to husbands who can be more than twice their age. Because they often move far from their families of orientation, wives who suffer mistreatment have little recourse. Tragic circumstances may ensue for women who are forced into marriages where they are abused. Under the best circumstances, co-wives can live together as sisters in a household where all adults respect one another. Under the worst, women may be killed, abused, or may commit suicide rather than be forced to exist under oppressive conditions.

POLYANDRY

Polyandry, the custom in which a woman takes two or more husbands, is less common but is still practiced in a smaller number of the world's societies. From a biocultural perspective, it limits the number of offspring of each husband, passing on fewer genes. Furthermore, it is unlikely that a society will have a surplus of men, due to shorter life expectancy or war casualties.

Polyandrous marriage may be beneficial in places where limits on population growth aid survival. In Tibet and Nepal, women may marry brothers (called **fraternal polyandry**) to keep their land holdings intact. The scarcity of land available in

Figure 11.3
Orthodox Jewish Women Praying at the Western Wall
These Jewish women are praying at the Western Wall in Jerusalem. They pray in a separate location from the men. Orthodox Judaism is found in a homogeneous community in Jerusalem with social rules, such as endogamy, that support the continuation of their culture.

Credit: © Janet Kass/Images of Anthropology

the Himalayan Mountains makes this a better choice than splitting the land into smaller, unsustainable parcels at marriage. Brothers and their wife who remain in the same household continue to share access to crucial family resources.

Exogamy

Further rules exist to narrow down the eligible pool of potential spouses. **Exogamy** is the practice in which marriage partners must come from different groups. Depending on the cultural norms, a person's choice of marriage partners may be required to be from outside one's clan or lineage. Socially, this practice links families from different communities together, creating alliances. Bioculturally, it acts to broaden the gene pool of any intermarrying group. This limits the possibility for inbreeding and leads to more genetic diversity.

For instance, Pacific Northwest Tlingit society is divided into two large categories. These are called **moieties** by anthropologists, but referred to in Tlingit social life as **clans**. Women who belong to the Raven (*Yeil*) Clan seek partners from the Eagle (*Ch'aak'*), also called Wolf (*Ghooch*), Clan. Members of the same clan address one another as "brother" and "sister." Therefore it would not be appropriate to marry someone from one's own clan, since they are classified as siblings.

Endogamy

In contrast to exogamy, some societies require that marriage partners come from the same group in society. This is called **endogamy**. Endogamous marriage can be seen in societies with strong ethnic, religious, or socio-economic class divisions in which individuals tend to marry within their groups. This may be due to social or geographic isolation. Some religions, such as Orthodox Judaism, practice endogamy as a religious law, forbidding marriage to a non-Jewish partner. This practice supports the survival of the group into the future.

One of the best-known endogamous marriage patterns is the **caste system** of India. All Hindus are born into one of four major castes, with membership in a subcaste, or into a category outside the system as a Dalit or "untouchable." Castes are unlike social classes because membership is based on descent; there is no movement from one caste to another. Until very recently in India, marriage partners were only chosen from within the same caste, often the same community, or even the same extended family (such as first cousins).

Several societies have practiced sibling endogamy, especially among the ruling classes. Historically, sisters and brothers married to preserve the royal bloodlines of ruling families. The Egyptian pharaoh Cleopatra was married to her brother Ptolemy XIV, and pharaoh Hatshepsut was married to her half-brother, Thutmose II. Sibling marriages keep the ruling power within the family. Similarly, ancient **Inkan** royalty believed that they were direct descendants of Inti, the sun god. Brothers and sisters would marry so that their pure-blooded heirs would retain divine authority.

However, close endogamy reduces genetic diversity. This increases the risk of the expression of harmful recessive genes. With severe inbreeding, genetic diseases become hard to escape, such as the hemophilia passed from Queen Victoria through European royalty in the Hapsburg line.

INCEST TABOO

Incest in royal families is the exception, as sexual relations within the immediate family are taboo in societies throughout the world. That is, even in cases in which closely related royalty marry one another, the larger society does not share those tendencies. The **incest taboo** is an example of a cultural universal, that is, a cultural practice that meets universal human needs. How cultures define kinship and relatedness affects how the taboo operates. Nonetheless, there are several reasons that societies everywhere shun this practice.

The first reason the incest taboo is universal is psychological, in that children raised together develop sexual aversion toward one another. This is referred to as the "Westermarck effect," based on the work of early Finnish researcher Edward Westermarck. Evidence for this hypothesis includes the very rare chance that unrelated children raised together on Israeli *kibbutzim* will develop sexual relationships or marry.

The second reason is social, due to the need for clear-cut roles in society. If a woman marries her son and they have a child, is the infant her son or her grandson? How do people involved in and related to these partners behave around one another if each person has multiple roles? The "role confusion" that results undermines successful social interaction.

Box 11.2
Comfort Food and the Family

Memories and positive associations with food from our childhood connect us to our families, communities, and ethnicities. Ethnic heritage often dictates the kinds of foods that are served in the home, and therefore the kinds of foods that are linked to childhood and family. While North Americans may agree that a warm chocolate chip cookie satisfies their cravings, a person of Greek ethnicity may argue that a honeyed *baklava* pastry is best.

Comfort foods are those foods eaten for emotional reasons. Brian Wansink and Cynthia Sangerman (2000) of the Cornell University Food Brand Lab write that foods become comforting for two main reasons: positive memories and expression of identity. Foods in the first category elicit feelings of "safety, love, homecoming, appreciation, control, victory or empowerment" (p. 66). Examples of these types of foods might be a kind of soup routinely served with compassion during bouts of childhood illness, or a Thanksgiving turkey. Identity-expressing foods in the second category may include steak for men or fermented Kombucha tea for "hipsters."

Speaking to people about their comfort foods reveals a clear connection to items prepared by family members, especially during childhood. Love for people translates into love for foods made and offered by those people. Foods that represent ethnically diverse family backgrounds may fall into either or both of the categories above; they may be connected to positive memories of family and to expressions of ethnic identity.

Figure 11.4
Kuai Tiao Noodles, Bangkok
Comfort foods are often warm, such as this bowl of Kuai Tiao noodles enjoyed in Bangkok, Thailand.
Credit: Sashur Henninger

Soup is one dish that many people eat for comfort. Often this is because a parent or other caregiver prepares it when a child is sick. For example, a Filipino woman may prefer *Sinigang* as her comfort food. Sinigang is a meat and vegetable soup in a sour and savory broth flavored with tamarind. Ashkenazi or American Jews may turn to matzoh ball soup, a chicken broth with vegetables and a large breaded dumpling. A Japanese college student may crave miso soup with tofu and green onion while away from home.

While all of these examples describe warm, savory meals, the soups are not interchangeable. Comfort foods have a strong connection to personal experience and memory. Sometimes nothing else will do besides Mom's minestrone.

The third reason is political, because marrying outside one's own family creates relationships with others. Inter- and intra-group alliances contribute to the stability of the larger society. Forcing people to seek partners outside their family leads to the benefits of exogamy, including building power alliances and expanding one's economic base.

Finally, the fourth reason the incest taboo exists universally is biological. Reducing the gene pool for generation after generation causes a loss in genetic diversity. This loss leads to a higher potential for genetic diseases and a risk to the longevity of the species. These risks occur because more deleterious conditions emerge fully when both mother and father pass on an afflicted **allele** to offspring. It is likely, as in many human behaviors, that the biological threat to survival lies at the heart of the taboo, with social and psychological reasons developing to support it in human society.

Family Residence Patterns

Where does a newly married couple live? Do they move into the bride's or the groom's parents' home? Do they set up their own residence? To examine these questions, let's begin with the definition of a **household** as a domestic unit of residence. In a household, members contribute to child rearing, inheritance, and the production and consumption of goods. Members of a household do not need to physically live under the same roof, yet they still contribute to the needs of the whole family.

A household is most commonly synonymous with a family unit, but not always. For instance, in the Brazilian rainforest, members of Mundurucú communities send their sons to live in the village Men's House (*eksa*) at around 13 years old. From then on, they become contributing members to the residential unit of teen and adult males, rather than to the house of their mothers and sisters. Living among older males teaches the boys men's knowledge, such as hunting, mythology, and men's religious rituals. The Men's House is not a family per se, but it fits our definition of a household.

Nuclear Family

In industrial societies such as our own, a bride and groom are generally eager to start a new household after marriage, away from their household of orientation. They are more likely to reside in an independent household in a **nuclear family**, with two generations living together (i.e., parents and children). We refer to this type of residence as **neolocal**. There are many variations on the nuclear model, since sometimes grandparents or a single parent cares for children in their own household.

Independence training is practiced in industrial societies, which stress self-fulfillment and ambition. Living in nuclear families makes sense, since adults can pursue jobs with relatively easy mobility. In other words, it's easier to move four people than it is to move 15. Moving to where the jobs are ensures food security, since city dwellers rarely produce their own food (save for backyard gardens). Although neolocal residence is familiar to us in North America, it is actually the least common residence type in the world's societies.

Extended Family

The type of family structure that is most common across cultures is the **extended family**. In an extended family, blood-related members will bring their spouses to live with their family of orientation. This creates a household that is a mix of people related by marriage (**affinal** kin) and by blood (**consanguineal** kin). Depending upon the custom, wives may live with their husbands' families, or husbands may join their wives' families. Until recently in human history, all people lived in extended families for cooperation and protection. This family model may be most advantageous for the constant care of children, with many role models of both sexes.

There are several different residence patterns for extended families. Here, we will concentrate on the two most common. When husbands join their wives' families of orientation after marriage, it is referred to as **matrilocal** residence. The extended family in this type of household includes sisters, their parents, husbands, and children. When men marry, they move to their wives' homes. The Hopi, an Indigenous nation that lives in the American Southwest, practices matrilocality. Therefore, a Hopi groom will leave his family of orientation upon marriage and take up residence with his wife's family of orientation.

Matrilocal residence is common under conditions in which land is held by the woman's family line. Women remain in the home of their family of orientation so land doesn't get divided upon marriage. In these societies, women's cooperation in subsistence is crucial, such as in horticultural societies where women do the bulk of the labor. And of course, in polyandrous societies, multiple husbands would require residence at the wife's household.

When wives join their husbands' families of orientation after marriage, it is called **patrilocal** residence. This is the most common type of residence pattern in the world's societies, in which extended families are made up of brothers and their wives, their children, and the brothers' parents. When women marry, they move to their husbands' homes. This is the traditional arrangement, for instance, for Han Chinese families. The Han are the majority ethnic group in China. Therefore, most Chinese brides will leave their own home of orientation to live with their husband's family of orientation.

In societies where men play the predominant role in subsistence, such as pastoralist or intensive agricultural societies, patrilocal residence is common. This way property may be accumulated and passed down through the men's line. It is also found in societies in which men's cooperation in central government and warfare is important. As well, polygyny requires patrilocal residence so multiple wives can live together in their husband's household of origin.

Marriage as Economic Exchange

Fundamentally, the union of individuals from two different families is an economic exchange. Not only is the bride or groom "given" to the other family, but a series of gifts is also given between families to cement their bond. This is most true for extended families in which rules for residence after marriage are clearly delineated. **Marriage compensation** depends upon the cultural context: Who is losing a family member and who is gaining one?

Bride Price and Bride Service

If the bride leaves her family's household of origin and becomes a resident in her husband's household of origin, the husband's family compensates the bride's family. The compensation is called **bride price**, which refers to the valuables that a groom and his family are required to present to the bride's family. The young bride is not only an additional resource for support and labor in her new household, but is also expected to bear children that will extend the husband's family line (and provide more potential resources and labor). Among the Maasai herders of Kenya and Tanzania, bride price is paid in cattle, the most valuable goods owned by Maasai families.

Bride price is often paid in a series of gifts, such as those required upon marriage by the Trobriand people of the Kiriwana Islands in Papua New Guinea (see Table 11.1). The gift giving begins before marriage and continues until sometime after the actual ceremony, sometimes annually, sometimes longer. Complying with the exchange on time and correctly signals each family's responsibility and commitment to one another. Partaking of the gifts (in the Trobriand case, eating the first gift of cooked yams) begins a social and economic bond between them.

Another way in which compensation may be given to the bride's family for the loss of their daughter is to offer **bride service** to her family. Rather than the gift of goods or money, the groom spends a period of time working for her family. Among the Ju/'hoansi, early marriage of children ensures a long period of bride service in which the young husband hunts for his bride's family.

Dowry

Societies in which the groom goes to live with the bride's family of origin have the opposite form of compensation. **Dowry** is the gift of money or goods from the bride's family to the groom's family to compensate for the loss of their son. This dowry is essentially the portion of the bride's inheritance given early, to ensure the new couple will have some financial resources.

Dowry can also be seen in societies in which neolocal residence occurs. These goods help the new couple begin their life together once they separate from their

Table 11.1
Trobriand Islanders' Exchange of Marriage Gifts

Marriage Gift (in the order that it must be given)	Consisting of . . .
(1) Katuvila	Cooked yams, brought in baskets by the girl's parents to the boy's family.
(2) Pepe'i	Several baskets of uncooked yams, one given by each of the girl's relatives to the boy's parents.
(3) Kaykaboma	Cooked vegetables, each member of the girl's family bringing one platter to the boy's house.
(4) Mapula Kaykaboma	Repayment of gift (3), given in exactly the same form and material by the boy's relatives to the girl's family.
(5) Takwalela pepe'i	Valuables given by the boy's father in repayment of gift (2) to the girl's father.
(6) Vilakuria	A large quantity of yam-food offered at the first harvest after the marriage to the boy by the girl's family.
(7) Saykwala	Gift of fish brought by the boy to his wife's father in repayment.
(8) Takwalela vilakuria	A gift of valuables handed by the boy's father to the girl's father in payment of (6).

Source: Malinowski 1929

parents. It is considered the girl's family's gift to the newlyweds, or their share of the bride's family's inheritance. In the colonial United States, dowry consisted of goods the girl sewed or crafted throughout her young life, collected in a *trousseau*. While there is an expectation of neolocal marriage in modern North America, the pressure to provide a dowry has considerably lessened. The parents of the bride may still pay for wedding expenses as a legacy of this practice.

Perhaps surprisingly, we also see dowry in societies that practice patrilocality. This is due to cultural values that encourage families to marry their daughters into the same or higher class (or caste, in Hindu India) as their own. The focus on "marrying up" forces the bride's family to promise expensive gifts to ensure a good marriage for their daughter. When families have multiple daughters, dowry gifts can be extremely taxing on the family's resources.

Promised but undelivered dowry gifts can cause major problems for a girl in her husband's household. In some circumstances, an unscrupulous family-in-law can extort gifts or money from the bride's family. In severe circumstances, young women die due to unmet dowry demands, a result known as **dowry death**.

Each year, thousands of women in India and Pakistan commit suicide or are killed over dowry. The news often reports the death and disfigurement of women from acid or kerosene burning. Both India and Pakistan have passed laws officially outlawing the request, payment, or receipt of a dowry. Yet the practice still exists across these countries, embedded in cultural patterns of marriage and family life.

Arranged Marriage

Throughout time and across cultures, the most common way to ensure a suitable union takes place has been for parents to arrange the marriages of their children. Marriage based on romance and love is a relatively recent development. In an **arranged marriage**, parents will generally seek a match for their son or daughter from the same (or a higher) community, socio-economic class, and/or religion. This ensures they will pass down their values to the next generation while joining together in a multifamily arrangement that will be mutually beneficial.

Arranged marriage may sound strange or even terrifying to those raised in independence training societies. However, modern arrangements for this practice generally take into consideration the wishes of the young people involved, especially among more educated families (see Box 11.3). For instance, a son or daughter may have the power to refuse a particular match. The arrangement is not the same as **forced marriage**, in which a young person has no say, or **child marriage**, in which young girls are betrothed to older men.

Kinship Descent Patterns

All human groups face certain problems: how to regulate sexual activity, raise children, and divide the labor necessary for subsistence. **Kinship**, or family relations, provides a structure for solving these problems. Since all societies recognize kin, rules linked to family and household organization are common. Dividing labor along gender lines is one way to ensure that labor is distributed. Another way is through family descent groups, or lineages.

Although kinship implies the relatedness of people through blood or marriage, there are forms of kinship that extend beyond these boundaries. The practice of adoption brings individuals who are not biologically related into a kinship relation. Adoptive families (and their variants such as step-, foster, or surrogate families) generally experience the same social norms and expectations as biologically related families.

Fictive kinship is the term sometimes used to refer to a constructed "family" of unrelated individuals, such as an urban gang who rely on each other for social support, economic resources, and protection. Relationships built upon mutual caring and attachment may be called **nurture kinship**, such as between a mentor and mentee. Both fictive and nurture kinship may exist in the relationship created by

Arranged Marriage in Mumbai

Arranged marriage is still an option among young, educated, middle-class women in India's biggest city. However, arrangements happen in very different ways today. Today, girls meet prospective partners through social events called Marriage Meets, community registries (called marriage bureaus), and online matrimonial sites. More liberal parents may even accept matches that are initiated by the girls and boys themselves—once condemned as "love matches." (Indians refer to unmarried people as "girls" and "boys" independent of age.)

Until the mid-twentieth century—the generation of these girls' parents—nearly all Indian marriages were arranged by extended family connections. This included marriages made by educated, middle-class families. Traditionally, a matchmaker, who may have been a family friend or relative, would solicit possible matches on behalf of the family. After photos and background information were exchanged, a potential match would be identified. The boy's family would be invited to the girl's house for a "bride viewing." While parents talked, the girl would enter dressed in a sari and would serve tea, speaking only when addressed, and would not make eye contact with the boy. After this initial meeting, the girl and boy might not see each other again before the wedding day, depending on what parents allow.

One might wonder how it's possible for modern, educated young men and women to accept a marriage arranged by their parents. Nonetheless, there are several reasons why the system is still desirable, even with the possibility of dowry problems. First, the bride-viewing model is no longer used formally in most cases. Second, contemporary arranged marriage in Mumbai allows some "dating," which gives the young couple a chance to get to know one another. The shift toward the development of romantic feelings is connected to modern urban life. In addition, young people know clearly what their family's expectations are for their future marriage partners, and have internalized these guidelines. In her fieldwork, Serena Nanda (2000) found this is because Indian girls trust their parents to make good decisions for their future.

Today, it is less likely for a marriage to be strictly self-initiated and self-managed until the wedding and beyond. It is also less likely for a marriage today to be strictly arranged with no sense of individual needs being met. A hybrid set of practices exists today in which urban middle-class girls in Mumbai negotiate the traditional social expectations of extended Indian families, and the modern tensions of urban life with its focus on self-fulfillment and female empowerment (Gonzalez 2013).

the *compadrazgo* system in Mexico. Parents of infants choose a set of godparents (*compadres* and *comadres*) to help support the child's financial needs. Compadres are also expected to care for children should their parents unexpectedly pass away. Some compadres provide little more than financial support, while others are deeply involved in the child's life, providing emotional support and care.

A **descent group** is a social group of people who trace their descent from a particular ancestor. Descent groups form connections from parents to children, tracing their lineage through their father, mother, or both parents. Dividing the extended family in this way allows different rights and responsibilities to be assigned

Figure 11.5
Agate-Mays Family
Jory Agate and Jeb Mays foster a loving and supportive environment for their two daughters, Katy and Mica. Katy was adopted internationally, while Mica has a donor father and was carried by Jory. Jory and Jeb were legally married in the Unitarian Universalist Church in Cambridge, Massachusetts, in 2004.

Credit: Reproduced by permission of the Agate-Mays family.

to different family members. Certain members of the descent group might act as godparents to newborn children, or be responsible for harvesting crops when they ripen. A descent group may share a mythological ancestor, called a **totem**.

Some societies trace their genealogy through both the mother's and father's line, called **bilateral descent**. The English language underscores this equality: we use the same term to refer to the same relatives on our mother's side and on our father's side (aunts, uncles, or grandparents). These kinship terms represent generally equal expectations of both our father's and mother's families.

In some societies, descent is reckoned along one family line. This form of descent is called **unilineal**. There are two types of unilineal descent. **Patrilineal** descent is traced through the father's bloodline. **Matrilineal** descent is traced through the mother's. One lineage is responsible for the continuation of the family's name and possessions, such as landholdings or other inherited items. One lineage may be responsible for giving certain gifts, or assistance during rites of passage.

Societies with unilineal descent encode differences in social roles with different terms for the same relations on either side of the family. For instance, in Farsi, the official language of Iran, *khaleh* refers to one's mother's sister, and *ammeh* refers to one's father's sister. Some languages in which respect is given to eldest members of the family use different terms for those who are older than one's parent, and those who are younger. Both lineages have clearly defined, and different, roles and expectations that are marked with different terminology. The languages listed in Table 11.2 are just a few of the many that use different terms to refer to these different family relationships.

Gender Roles: Patterned by Culture

Every culture has norms regarding how men and women should act and interact with others. This especially plays out in the family, where both men and women share resources and raise children. However, social expectations extend to all aspects of society, differing widely from culture to culture.

Table 11.2

Talking about Families

Language	Aunt (Maternal)	Aunt (Paternal)
Arabic	Khalto	Amto
Farsi	Khaleh	Ammeh
Hindi-Jain	Mosi	Bua
Mandarin	Yí	Guu
Cantonese	Yee (if older than mother) Yee Ma (if younger than mother)	Lerng (if older than father) Sum (if younger than father)
Urdu	Badi Khaala (if older than mother) Choti Khaala (if younger than mother)	Badi P'hupoo (if older than mother) Choti P'hupoo (if younger than mother)

Defining Gender and Sexuality

Although in English we tend to use the two terms interchangeably, sex and gender refer to different aspects of a person. **Sex** refers to our biological and physiological differences, including sex chromosomes, hormones, reproductive structures, and external genitalia. On the other hand, the set of social meanings assigned by culture is referred to as **gender**. Gender is a person's internal experience of their identity as male, female, both, or neither, as well as the expression of that identity in social behavior.

Human men and women have certain differences in their physiology, anatomy, and sex hormones. The most obvious external sex difference is seen in male and female genitalia, even though the male penis and female clitoris grow from the same undifferentiated fetal tissue. Human male and female bodies may also exhibit different susceptibility to disease. For instance, females are much more likely to suffer from breast cancer and osteoporosis, and males are more likely to develop hemophilia and Duchenne muscular dystrophy.

Approximately 1 person in every 2,000 is born **intersex**. They have a combination of physiological or morphological elements that place them on the gender spectrum in a way that does not allow simple definition of male or female. As one might expect, cultural responses to intersex infants are widely variable. In some cases, doctors decide to manipulate the external appearance of genitalia and assign a child's sex. These choices are not always in the best interest of the individual in the long term, as sex consists of more than simply genitalia. As more awareness is created regarding intersex issues, parents are instead guided toward medical counseling and allow the child to choose his or her gender upon reaching puberty.

Gender Roles

Gender roles are the culturally appropriate roles of individuals in society. They express the cultural norms expected of a person of each sex. For instance, a female infant born in North America who grows up to play with dolls exhibits "feminine" (girl-like) gender characteristics. This is generally thought of as the normative behavior for a young girl. However, if she prefers toy guns, society may deem her "masculine" (boy-like). In this case, her gender expression does not fit neatly with social expectations of female behavior.

Different societies value very different traits in men and women. For example, many Native American societies, such as the Yuma (*Quechan*) from Arizona and California, valued women with upper body strength. The woman of the Quechan household was expected to perform daily manual labor, including grinding dried corn to a fine powder for use in cooking. When looking for a wife, a man would be much more likely to seek a woman with a large, strong upper body than a thin or frail woman. On the other hand, the Maasai of Kenya prefer women with a slender, but strong, build, as they will be responsible for milking cows, and hauling water and firewood.

The characteristics in Table 11.3 come from the Bem Sex-Role Inventory, a questionnaire measuring masculinity, femininity, and androgyny, developed in 1974 by psychologist Sandra Bem. Survey participants checked the boxes corresponding to opposing gender traits, after which the participant's androgyny could be determined. More than 40 years later, the original survey is just as interesting for its stereotypes of masculine and feminine traits in the 1970s as it is for the results.

Gender Identity

Gender identity and expression may be formed through interactions with others in society. It may also be predetermined by biological factors. For instance, this is true for **transgender** people, or those who internally experience and/or express their gender identity as different from their assigned sex, also called **gender dysphoria**. One way biological factors may play a role is if minor alterations occur during fetal development in brain structure or on receptors for the hormone androgen. Those who do not experience gender dysphoria are referred to by the term **cisgender**. In other words, their gender identity matches their assigned sex at birth.

It is important to note that gender identity is independent of sexual orientation, as any person may be heterosexual, homosexual, or **bisexual**. Beyond the traditional **binary** gender division, a person may self-identify as **pansexual**, **polysexual**, or **asexual**. In other words, a person of any gender may prefer men (**androphilia**), prefer women (**gynophilia**), both, some, any, or none.

Table 11.3

"Masculine" and "Feminine" Traits of North American Men and Women

"Masculine" Traits	"Feminine" Traits
Self-reliant	Yielding
Willing to defend own beliefs	Eager to soothe hurt feelings
Independent	Soft-spoken
Leadership ability	Does not use harsh language
Willing to take risks	Childlike
Analytical	Gullible
Assertive	Loves children

Source: Bem 1974

Third Genders

Across cultures, there are many examples of societies that recognize multiple genders. In these societies, an individual could choose to take on a social identity that was outside of the two gender model. That is, a person could opt to self-identify as one of three genders: masculine man, feminine woman, or other not-man not-woman. Some societies recognize four or more genders: masculine man, feminine man, masculine woman, and feminine woman, or other variant. In many cultures gender-variant individuals are and were accepted, sought for spiritual guidance and blessings, and thought to occupy special roles in society.

One gender variant was recorded across more than 120 Native American and First Nations cultures, including the Zuni (*A:shiwi*), Crow (*Apsáalooke*), and St. Lawrence Island Yupik. Although the older anthropological literature sometimes refers to this group of individuals as *berdaches*, this is a derogatory term derived from the French word for "prostitute." The Native American community instead identifies with the term **two-spirit**.

Two-spirits are not thought of as homosexual. They are socially accepted as a **third gender**—neither man nor woman, but with elements of both. The idea that both genders could inhabit the same body was regarded as normal practice in the case of two-spirit people. Either male or female clothes could be worn on a given day.

In Native American/First Nations cultures, two-spirits are most often male-bodied people, who as young boys identified with girls and later adopted feminine gender roles. However, in some cases, they may also be female-bodied people

Figure 11.6
Hijra in Temple, Ahmadebad

Hijras are male-bodied or intersex individuals who occupy a third-gender role in India and Pakistan. Today, they are the objects of discrimination and violence.

Credit: © Serena Nanda/Images of Anthropology

who adopt a masculine gender role. Two-spirit people might have strange dreams or unexplainable illnesses that have identified them as walking between the mortal and spirit worlds. In addition, they often have special roles in society, such as healers, fortune-tellers, and matchmakers. Deceased two-spirits are recognized as such by being buried in both female dress and men's trousers.

Another example of a third gender variant is the **hijras** of India and Pakistan. They are thought to occupy a role that is between the sexes in Indian society; that is, a third gender (not-man, not-woman). Hijras are male-bodied individuals who adopt feminine behaviors such as dress, ornamentation, names, and mannerisms. Yet culturally, their rough language and aggressive behaviors distinguish them from Indian women.

The hijra is essentially a spiritual role to which a person is called. Members of the hijra community become devotees of *Buhuchara Mata*, an incarnation of the Hindu Mother Goddess. Their devotion requires a vow of sexual abstinence. For this reason, hijras are traditionally eunuchs: emasculated men who have undergone an operation to remove their penis and testicles. Because the surgery is prohibited in hospitals, the risk of infection or death can be high. Today people who self-identify as hijras are not necessarily eunuchs, but are also likely to be intersex or male-bodied homosexuals who have left home and joined a hijra community.

Hindu belief regards homosexuality as one of the permitted expressions of human sexuality and desire. The pantheon of Hindu deities includes some who are sexually ambiguous, combining aspects of maleness and femaleness, or who transform themselves from one into another. Like monks in the Buddhist tradition, hijras are expected to survive on charity and payment for services performed, such as blessing babies or dancing and singing at weddings. Unfortunately, this does not translate into acceptance for hijras in society. Today they live on the margins due to severe prejudice. It is common to see hijras begging for charity on the trains of Indian cities, extorting money from businesses, or making money as sex workers. They are the objects of discrimination and violence.

Homosexuality

Homosexuality, or the romantic or sexual attraction or sexual behavior between partners of the same sex, is common in cultures around the world and throughout time. Like gender identity, **sexual orientation** (romantic or sexual attraction to another person) may be formed socially or biologically. Although orientation is often referred to as "sexual preference," for most people, their genes determine sexual orientation.

Nevertheless, sexual orientation is expressed within a set of cultural values and expectations. Human cultures differ widely in their acceptance of orientation other than heterosexuality. Some societies see a range of sexual orientation as a natural part of human life. Other societies have low or no tolerance, even to the degree that a person may be put to death for homosexual acts, including (at the time of this writing) the nations of Iran, Saudi Arabia, and Sudan.

Within certain cultures, homosexual practices are essential to the functioning of society. For instance, among the Etoro of the Southern Highlands Province of Papua New Guinea, homosexual relations among males are linked to male development and power. In particular, the Etoro believe male oral intercourse ensures a man's physical growth and enhances his spiritual strength. Many social rules revolve around the expectations and importance of these practices.

The earliest Western evidence for same-sex relationships can be found in records of early Greece. Older males entered into sexual relationships with younger males while at the same time maintaining a marriage with a woman to pass on his genetic line. Ancient Greek men did not consider sexuality itself to be relevant to one's status in society, but whether a male was the dominant or submissive partner in the sex act.

It is hard to predict whether a society will be permissive regarding homosexuality and other gender variants. An ecological hypothesis argues that homosexuality is tolerated or accepted in societies that experience pressure from population growth or food shortages. Allowing non-binary gender variants means that not every couple will produce offspring, thus population levels will remain stable. A socio-political hypothesis makes a correlation between intolerance or punishment of homosexuality and societies in which abortion or infanticide is prohibited. This may be a result of strict religious laws.

Margaret Mead and Gender Studies

One of the first anthropologists to undertake academic studies of gender roles in the family and society was **Margaret Mead**, arguably the most famous student of Franz Boas. Mead is a hugely important figure in the field of anthropology for several reasons: she was one of the first women to undertake long-term fieldwork, and she

Figure 11.7
Tribal Warrior with Scarification
This warrior from South Sudan carries scarification designs that were given to him to represent his social role, identity, and place in the community.
Credit: © Barry D. Kass/Images of Anthropology

addressed some of the most fundamental human issues, such as family, gender roles, and childhood development, through the holistic lens of anthropology. As described in Chapter 14, Mead made her results available to a wide audience—not just other scholars—through her work as a curator in the American Museum of Natural History in New York and by writing for popular magazines.

In the 1930s, people in North America assumed that gender roles were biologically based. Mead questioned the idea that men and women were born into their roles; she felt they took them on as a result of upbringing in a particular society. To discover whether gender roles were biologically based in humans, and therefore universal, she looked at three cultures in the Sepik region of Papua New Guinea in 1935.

What she found there was surprising to those with mainstream notions of gender. Among the Arapesh, both men and women were expected to behave in ways we would call "feminine," that is, gentle, cooperative, non-aggressive, and nurturing. Among the Mundugumor, she found that both sexes were aggressive, even violent, with little interest in child care and therefore more "masculine" according to her own society's standards at the time. Finally, among the Tchambuli, she discovered the Western gender roles were reversed: women were dominant, and playing the primary economic role while men were primarily interested in aesthetics, were less responsible, and easily became emotional.

Her studies laid the foundation for our understanding that gender roles are a cultural artifact. The way we, as humans, perceive men and women to have "masculine" and "feminine" characteristics is a direct result of how cultural adaptation has shaped our understanding of what it means to be a man or woman in any particular society.

Body Modification and Gender

Body modification is one of the most common ways people express their identity and make themselves attractive. Today's make-up, piercings, and tattoos that showcase modern individuality actually have deep roots in human history. Ancient Egyptian royalty wore kohl eye pencil made of minerals to accentuate their eyes. Young Tlingit boys of the Pacific Northwest Coast wore multiple ear piercings to represent high status in the community. Many of these modifications signal that individuals have completed a **rite of passage**; that is, they have moved from one stage of life to another.

Box 11.4

Removing the Rings

Today, nearly all traditional cultures are part of the global economy. For many, this means that their cultural practices and artifacts are tourist commodities. Under the best conditions, members of an ethnic group may form a production co-op and engage in **Fair Trade** practices, which ensure that producers or craftspeople receive a living wage and safe working conditions. Under the most common conditions, however, most of the income brought in by tourism goes to non-Indigenous managers or local governments, while members of the ethnic community receive a small percentage.

The Kayan of Burma (Myanmar) is one such group in this situation. Kayan women (called *Kayan Lahwi* or *Padaung*) wear coiled brass neck rings that give the illusion of an elongated neck. In fact, the neck vertebrae do not elongate, but the weight of the rings presses down and deforms the clavicle as a young girl grows.

Because the Kayan Lahwi are unique, they are a major tourist draw for foreign visitors. After civil unrest in Burma in the 1980s and 1990s, a permanent refugee village was set up for fleeing hill tribes on the border of northern Thailand. Today, tourists visit the village to pay a few dollars to see the longneck "giraffe women."

Since the mid-2000s, some Kayan Lahwi have chosen to remove their rings in protest against the treatment of the Kayan people. Removing the rings causes discomfort for several days with residual bruising and discoloration. Eventually the muscles strengthen and discomfort subsides. Some women report feeling freer once

Figure 11.8
Kayan Lahwi
Kayan women's heavy brass coils compress the clavicle, or collar bone, as a young girl grows. After many years, it gives the impression of a very long neck. This woman lives in a tourist village in Thailand.
Credit: Daniel Chit

the rings are off, and some admit feeling sad at the loss of their cultural tradition.

Many Kayan have applied for resettlement and have been allowed to move to other countries such as New Zealand and Finland. However, Thai authorities have denied the right to leave to a group of Kayan Lahwi at the refugee village. One young woman who removed her rings in protest after being denied an offer of resettlement said she felt like a "prisoner" in the village and called the situation a "human zoo" (Harding 2008). Human rights organizations are putting pressure on the Thai government to allow the refugees to begin new lives abroad.

Young Mursi women of the Omo River Valley in Ethiopia traditionally wear a circular clay or wood plate in their lower lip in preparation for marriage. Cutting the lip for a plate during this important rite of passage symbolizes a Mursi girl's readiness for marriage, her fertility, and after marriage, her commitment to her husband. Even today, Mursi men prefer women who still meet traditional expectations of wearing lip-plates in marriage contexts. Men may insult or even de-value the bride price if the girl is not "cut" or refuses to wear her plate. The sentiments of Mursi women are divided, with some feeling a strong sense of pride and self-esteem upon wearing their plates, and others wanting to forgo the plate to become more "modern."

Māori warriors of Aotearoa, or modern New Zealand, earned the right to a full facial tattoo called a moko. The moko provided information about the wearer's tribal and family history, and acted as a marker of male identity. Female adult Māori traditionally would also wear a partial moko, with their lips and chins inked blue. These tattoos could not be bought, only earned, through life experiences. Although the images are similar, Māori designs aren't like the "tribal" tattoos that can be bought in any tattoo shop today. In fact, Māori writers and public figures have protested the imitation and commodification of their traditional designs by Western wearers who have no knowledge of the significance of these designs.

Scarification is another method of inscribing artistic symbols on the body as a marker of identity. To create scar designs, the skin will be cut or burned, with irritants such as dirt added to create a keloid (raised scar). African societies in Ethiopia and Ghana and Papuans from New Guinea are some of the peoples who have traditionally created ornamental scars on male or female bodies to mark a rite of passage, such as puberty, initiation, or readiness for marriage. Some scar designs are given to mark a particular religious or political role. As with other methods of body ornamentation, scarification is most often used to express a person's identity within a social or ethnic group.

Summary

This chapter has examined how marriage, family and gender roles structure a great deal of social life in human societies. Mirroring the Learning Objectives stated in the chapter opening, the key points are:

- Many different marriage patterns and family types can contribute to stable societies, including those built on monogamy, polygamy, and same-sex partnerships.
- Throughout most of human existence, people have lived in extended family groups for the many benefits it provides. With the increase in industrial societies, nuclear families became the norm, due to the need to move to jobs and changing family expectations.

- Because marriage is considered to be a joining of two families in most societies, rules exist to regulate marriage practices, compensation, and the responsibilities of descent.
- Although marriage among people in modern Western societies tends to be self-initiated, many societies in the world still practice arranged marriage.
- Families may trace the rights and responsibilities of their lineage through one or both parents' lines of descent.
- Gender roles are the culturally appropriate roles of a man or a woman in society, dictated by social norms. Sex refers to the biological assignment of a person's anatomy and physiology. Some people experience their gender identity as different from their biological sex, existing on a spectrum.
- Gender identity is separate from sexual orientation, which refers to romantic or sexual attraction.
- In some societies, people who experience a different gender identity are accepted in a third (or fourth) gender role.

REVIEW QUESTIONS

1. What are the different marriage and family types that exist across cultures?
2. What are the biocultural benefits of exogamy?
3. What types of compensation are given in different marriage exchanges?
4. What is the difference between sex and gender?
5. How are the identities of a homosexual, transgender, and third gender person different?

DISCUSSION QUESTIONS

1. What makes a "good family?"
2. Are marriage tendencies in North America exogamous or endogamous? Why?
3. In what ways are dating and having an arranged marriage similar?

Visit **www.lensofanthropology.com** for the following additional resources:

| SELF-STUDY QUESTIONS | WEBLINKS | FURTHER READING |

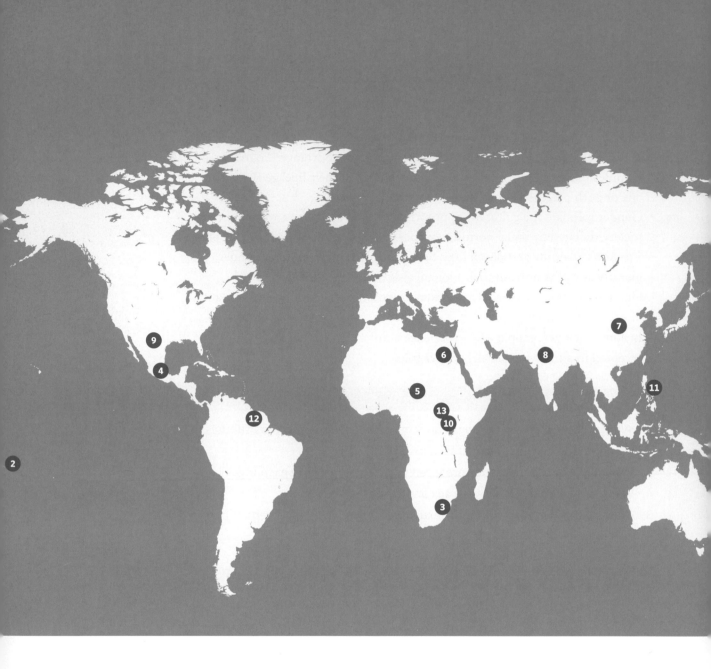

PLACES MENTIONED IN CHAPTER 12

POLITICS: KEEPING ORDER

Steal a cookie, others gossip. Invade a country, go to war. Political controls in any society depend on the level of organization. #politics

Learning Objectives

In this chapter, students will learn:
- how societies maintain order and stability within their own borders and with other societies.
- why and how societies use power and controls differently.
- the differences between societies with decentralized governments and those with centralized governments.
- the characteristics of bands, tribes, chiefdoms, and states.
- how power is used to create inequality between genders and to control access to resources.
- what kinds of conflicts ethnic groups face when they come into sustained contact.
- the fact that although state societies can pursue war to end conflicts, humans do not necessarily have violence in our genes.

Introduction

All societies, whether small or large, use a set of rules to guide their members' behavior toward one another. These rules may be official, such as a code of written laws, or unofficial, such as a set of social expectations. They may be embedded within a community's cultural or religious values ("Do not steal") or imposed on them from the outside ("No border entry"). The types of expectations, moral codes, policies, and laws will differ based on the size and complexity of the society.

This chapter examines different types of **political organization**, or the way a society maintains order internally and manages affairs externally. Through the lens of anthropology, politics refers to a wide range of actions and interactions that have to do with power. Power relations are negotiated among individuals, for instance, between a parent and child, teacher and student, chief and subject, or master and slave. On a broader scale, this interaction occurs between larger groups such as communities, organizations, governments, and nations.

Anthropology focuses on the following questions in the study of political organization: How is power distributed and used within a society? How do societies regulate the power relations between their own and other groups? Furthermore, the study of political organization examines how safety and order are maintained within a group. Is there a central authority, like a government, which imposes rules and punishes those who break them? Or does the group share the responsibility for making decisions?

Use of Power

Political relationships are managed by the use of power, authority, and prestige. A person, community of people, organization, or nation may use one, two, or all three of these strategies to control others. They may be used positively (as "carrots") or negatively (as "sticks").

Power is the ability to compel another person to do something that he or she would not do otherwise. It may be by threat of punishment or promise of reward. The use (and misuse) of power is one of the means by which people become unequal in terms of resources and social status. Social, economic, and political inequality stem from uneven access to, or distribution of, resources. Some degree of power exists in all social relationships, from the everyday interactions of neighbors to global relations between countries. Therefore, power is an important aspect of culture.

Power is used in essentially two ways: coercively or persuasively. Coercive power uses physical force or the threat of it (a "stick"). Examples of coercive violence are schoolyard bullying, hate crime violence, rape, and war. There are many examples in history of the coercion of enslaved peoples to perform manual labor under threat of physical punishment. For instance, in the second century BC, rulers of the Qin dynasty in China harnessed the labor of imprisoned slaves to construct the massive fortification of the Great Wall of China. During the construction of the different areas of the Wall, it is thought that up to a million workers died. Unfortunately, those using coercive power don't often make safety the highest priority, since laborers had to participate or suffer the consequences.

Figure 12.1
Great Wall of China
The building of the Great Wall of China took place over several hundreds of years with the work of millions of laborers. The existing sections of the Wall are mainly those fortified during the Ming Dynasty, in the fifteenth century AD.

Credit: Sashur Henninger

Persuasive power relies not on force, but on changing someone's behavior through argumentation using religious or cultural beliefs. Persuasive power offers a reward for compliance (a "carrot"), rather than a threat. This reward may be measurable, such as wealth, or it may be personal, such as increased status, power, or emotional fulfillment. In 1997, a self-proclaimed prophet named Marshall Herff Applewhite created a religious revitalization movement called "Heaven's Gate," based in Southern California. Applewhite convinced a cult of followers that they could escape the impending destruction of Earth, which only he could foresee. He taught that the promise of a better life was only attainable through suicide, at the precise time the Hale-Bopp comet passed overhead. Thirty-nine people willingly took their lives after being persuaded psychologically and emotionally.

Some individuals may have power over others, but few also have authority. **Authority** is the use of legitimate power. In large, complex societies with a centralized government, citizens grant the power of rulemaking or punishment to an individual or set of individuals, such as a ruler, congress, or police force. These entities have the authority to exercise power with the consent of their members.

Governments with democratically elected leaders bestow authority upon a prime minister or a president to lead the country. Nonetheless, the individual heading the government must also use persuasive power to convince the cabinet or congress to agree with policy decisions. This arrangement prevents all of the power and authority from remaining in the hands of one person. When a leader rules by non-democratic means, such as in a dictatorship, then power is exercised legitimately in the eyes of the law, but it may not reflect the will of the people.

Figure 12.2
Huli Big Man, Papua New Guinea
The Huli Big Man of the Southern Highlands of Papua New Guinea wears an elaborately decorated wig to demonstrate his political role.

Credit: © Lee Hunter/Images of Anthropology

Prestige is a type of social reward that can only be given to a person by others. It refers to the positive reputation or high regard of a person or other entity merited by actions, wealth, authority, or status. It may be by virtue of birth into a particular family, personal achievement, or membership in a highly regarded social group.

The "**Big Man**," found throughout Melanesia, uses his prestige as an informal leader in his community. A clever and charismatic person, he represents his tribe to outsiders and mediates conflicts when necessary. The Big Man is generally wealthy and affirms his status with great shows of generosity. The role of the Big Man confers prestige and persuasive power; however, he has no officially recognized authority to make decisions for the group. Should he fail to represent the people well, a new Big Man will be sought.

Social Controls and Conflict Resolution

Internalized Controls

Societies maintain order within their groups and in their relations with other groups using a series of controls. Some controls come from within, as part of the society's cultural values of what is right and wrong. These **internalized controls** guide a person toward the right behavior based on a moral system. They may be based on cultural standards or religious tenets, for instance, not lying because religious teachings say it is wrong. Internalized controls may also come from a mixture of sources, as seen in the incest taboo, which is likely a combination of genetic, social, and psychological avoidances (see Chapter 11).

Maintaining order through a belief system is very different from a state system that uses a set of codified laws and punishments. Internalized controls embedded in belief seem "natural." They are entrenched in the way people think about the world. For instance, people who inhabit the world's forests have deeply held beliefs that their own health and survival is intimately connected to the health of the forest. It is "normal" and "right" to them to protect the ecosystem on which they depend from deforestation.

Cultural patterns develop around a social focus on either shame or guilt, both of which function as internalized controls. **Shame cultures** are those in which conformity to social norms stems from wanting to live up to others' expectations. The criticism of others, especially those of higher social status, is to be avoided at all costs. Even suicide is considered as an alternative to "losing face" when a person is dishonored. Suicide rates among adult males can be high in shame cultures if a man feels he has brought shame to his family by losing his job or by being caught publicly in a compromising situation.

In contrast, **guilt cultures** focus on one's own sense of right and wrong and the punishment that can result from breaking the rules (especially when that punishment is meted out by supernatural entities). In general, Western cultures tend to be guilt focused, in which members suffer emotionally due to failing to meet their own expectations rather than those of others. Both guilt and shame operate to some extent in most societies as internalized controls to keep people from transgressing social norms.

Externalized Controls

Externalized controls are imposed from the outside. Rules regulate behavior by encouraging conformity to social norms. Authority figures enforce these rules within which a person, organization, community, or nation operates. External controls vary in degree from community gossip to the death sentence. Sometimes just knowing the controls exist can be enough to deter someone from breaking the rules.

Sanctions are the punishments that result from breaking rules. They may be informally meted out by community members or formally enforced by authority figures. Informal sanctions can be preventative (grounding teenagers to keep them from getting in trouble) or retributive (spanking a child). Gossip is an effective negative informal sanction, especially in smaller communities, that is both preventative and retributive. More formalized sanctions may be legally imposed and include punishments such as fines, prison, exile, or death. Countries linked by trade agreements also impose sanctions by limiting or preventing the movement of goods or funds.

The Inuit of Arctic Canada traditionally used song duels to solve problems in the community. These are externalized controls, because others determined right and wrong. The result would be informal sanctions, since they were part of what is

Figure 12.3
"Sacrifice/Poker"
by Speed Bump
Sacrifice of animals was done with the intention of appeasing the deities, spirits, or ancestors. Sacrifice of humans was more likely an external sanction, meant to punish prisoners and terrorize enemies.
Credit: © Dave Coverly

known as "customary law" (in contrast to "government law"). Song duels were held at festive community gatherings, during which the aggrieved parties would sing humorous and deprecating songs about each other. The community members present would identify the best song and presentation, declaring the "winner" of the song duel. In this way, differences would be aired openly in a community forum, and solved in a publicly accepted way.

In the state of Burma (Myanmar), pro-democracy leader Aung San Suu Kyi suffered under formal legal sanctions imposed upon her by the Burmese ruling junta in 1989. She was imprisoned in her home and kept under house arrest for 15 years. Although these sanctions were imposed on Suu Kyi to quiet the call for democracy in Burma, they did not have the result the military government desired. Impressively, during this time she attained international recognition and won several awards, including the Nobel Peace Prize in 1991. She was finally released in 2010, and has become a successful political leader in the country again.

In contrast to negative sanctions, positive rewards applaud good behavior and encourage it in the future. Informal rewards might include recognition from community members for killing an animal for the first time on a hunt, or for achievements in school. Formal rewards might include a gift of cattle upon completing a male puberty ritual (such as among the Maasai) or a military honor for bravery in battle (such as the US military's Purple Heart medal).

Types of Political Organization

There are two major types of political systems among the world's cultures: those that make decisions collectively and those that concentrate power into the hands of a few. In general, smaller societies have decentralized systems in which the group makes decisions. They use informal controls to maintain order. Larger, more complex societies require centralized governments, and thus use formal controls for stability.

Decentralized Systems
Decentralized systems have no central governing body. Therefore, community members impose sanctions on those who break the rules. This type of system is found primarily among smaller, more homogeneous societies, such as foragers or horticulturalists. In decentralized systems, social rights and responsibilities are

organized along family lines. That is, a person's place within the descent group and lineage dictates his or her role in society. Kinship relationships serve to govern people's relations with one another.

When problems arise within these groups, they will seek informal leaders to help mediate or negotiate. Informal leaders may be respected, wise, or charismatic, and are often elders with experience. However, they have no official title or real authority to enforce judgments. When people don't comply with the judgments of elders, social mechanisms serve to humiliate or coerce them back in line through gossip, loss of reputation, or social ostracism.

Centralized Systems

In **centralized** political systems, a ruling body of one or more people is given the authority to govern. This occurs in a larger, more complex, and heterogeneous society. Not all members of the population know or are related to one another, lacking the kinds of relationships governed by kinship ties or bonds of reciprocity. Therefore, the governing body creates a formal code of oral or written laws by which the population must abide, no matter whether that person is a family member or a stranger. The ruling individual or group has both the power to control others and the legal authority to do so.

Cultural anthropologist Elman Service (1962) developed a method to classify the different types of political organization in the world's societies. His ideas are based on an anthropological perspective called **cultural materialism**, in which a society's organization is directly related to whatever adaptations are necessary to survive in its environment. According to Service's classification, there are four types: band, tribe, chiefdom, and state.

Each type has a different structure of social, economic, and political organization. The more homogeneous types—band and tribe—have decentralized political organization; while the more heterogeneous types—chiefdom and state—have centralized political organization. Even though we present these four types as if they were unique and clearly distinguishable from the others, in truth, societies usually operate on multiple levels at the same time. That is, a tribal society may utilize the kinds of social controls found in band societies, while at the same time acting politically on a world stage as part of a state society. Nonetheless, knowing the different characteristics of each type of society allows us to discuss the different elements that exist.

Bands

Bands are groups of approximately 50 to 100 individuals who rely on hunting and gathering as their main means of subsistence. A band will camp together while foraging, creating temporary structures for shelter and protection, but will move frequently to seek out the next desirable location. Since bands are small, the majority makes the decisions. This includes when and where to move the group next, or what the outcome of interpersonal conflicts will be. There is no centralized government or other coercive authority.

The band's decentralized power is reinforced by the egalitarian status of the group: no one member has more access to resources or authority than any other. Any leaders are temporary, based on good decision making, charisma, or ability to communicate well. They can attempt to persuade others, but have no authority to enforce decisions. Therefore, in band societies, only informal sanctions may be used. Mediation and negotiation among antagonistic community members help to resolve differences. Gossip and ridicule can keep people in line with social expectations. Fear of reprisal from supernatural forces may also serve to guide people's behavior.

Among the Ju/'hoansi of the Kalahari Desert, an informal leader may be sought to settle a domestic dispute between husband and wife. If a solution can't be found, this same individual can also grant a divorce with the support of the community. In situations where a solution cannot be found, an individual or couple may leave their band temporarily or permanently and join another band where they have relatives.

Tribes

Tribes are groups with higher population density than bands. They are horticulturalists or pastoralists, living in separate villages spread out over a wide area. The villages are linked by clan membership to a common ancestor, which may be real (a historical person) or mythic (an animal or deity). Although villages of a single tribe are separate, they are tied to one another by clan membership, their real or fictive kinship, and a common language. Often these strong links can be useful when the tribe needs to come together to solve larger issues (see Box 12.1).

Tribal power is also decentralized, in that there is no central government to impose rules or punishments. However, leaders arise based on their skills and experience, or due to their birth into a noble or high status clan. The Melanesian "Big Man" discussed above is an example of this type of leader. Disputes can be solved through mediation or through unofficial "court-like" resolution methods in which the village comes together to hear and discuss issues.

Another way that tribes remain united over a wide area is through links between individuals that cut across village lines. **Sodalities** are groups that bring people together through common concerns, age, or interests. For instance, children of a particular age-set across multiple villages may go through a rite of passage at the same time. Boys and girls of the Dinka (*Jieng*) tribe of South Sudan may undergo

Kayapo and the Belo Monte Dam Project

Tribal peoples often unite their villages for a common cause. Sodalities, or pan-tribal associations, help bring people with similar interests and goals together across a region. Since 1988, the Kayapo (*Mebengokre*) people of the Amazonian rainforest have been uniting to protest the building of a hydroelectric dam in the Pará territory. The dam, proposed by the Brazilian government, would flood the Kayapo's native lands around the Xingú River forcing thousands of Native peoples to relocate.

When the Kayapo first protested the dam construction, high-status chiefs encouraged their fellow chiefs of Kayapo and other Amazonian peoples to show support. Thousands of Native people made the days-long trip out of the forest by boat to show strength at a meeting with Brazil's electric company. During the meeting, native men and women whose land

was under threat gave hours of speeches underscoring their claims to the land as the original inhabitants. The international media covered the highly publicized event. Even Western celebrities who advocate for environmental causes, such as the musician Sting, lent their support to the Kayapo. The show of force against the dam effectively postponed its construction.

In 2006, protests began again with the new Belo Monte Dam project proposal. Kayapo chiefs extended their political reach to bring in new allies, even meeting with representatives from the World Bank. Unfortunately, these political negotiations did not have the desired effect. As of 2014, the Belo Monte Dam project is under construction. The tribal peoples of the area will be relocated, effectively losing their land and potentially their way of life. Repercussions for the 7,000 Kayapo and other Indigenous people of Pará, whose identities and survival are intimately connected to the forest, have yet to be seen (Xing n.d.).

an initiation ceremony together. A painful facial scarification of forehead lines marks their passage from childhood to adulthood.

Chiefdoms

A **chiefdom** is found in more populous societies, in which intensive agriculture is practiced. These pre-industrial societies have a more complex structure, with villages linked together by districts. Due to the complexity and large population, a centralized government is required with formalized leadership. There is an officially recognized chief at the top of the chain of command and a bureaucracy of greater and lesser chiefs in place to manage the different levels of governance.

The chief is generally a hereditary office, not an elected one. He (a chief is most often male) comes from the wealthiest families in the chiefdom. Every society will have rules that govern inheritance of the chief's position. The seat is most commonly passed to the son of the chief (patrilineal) or the son of the chief's wife (matrilineal). In Samoa, an island nation in the South Pacific Ocean, social and political organization is governed by the *fa'amatai* system, in which each extended family holds a chiefly title. These chiefs, the *matai*, represent their families' interests in

The Samoan 'ava Ceremony

Samoans today still practice a traditional ritual drinking ceremony as part of every important occasion, called the 'ava ceremony. (In Samoa, it is pronounced with a glottal stop, sounding like a "K" before the first "a." On other islands of Oceania, it is called Kava with the hard "K" sound.) 'Ava is a drink made from the ground roots of the *Piper methisticum* plant. It may only be handled, poured, and consumed by certain persons of high status (Tuvale 2014).

On the occasion that a new *matai* (family chief) is named, an 'ava ceremony will be held in the village. The host chief and members of his 'ava party will prepare the drink and serve it to the new chief. The 'ava during the ceremony is prepared by a specially chosen individual, in a role called the 'aumaga. When the drink is ready, one of the members of the host chief's party will call the names of those present, who will approach one at a time. A few drops of

'ava are spilled on the mat as an offering before drinking the 'ava, and none should be left in the cup, as a sign of respect. Serving order is of the utmost importance to mark the status of the individuals present. In the case of a matai naming ceremony, the new matai will be served first, then the host chief, followed by orator ("talking") chiefs of both sides, and so on in order of diminishing rank.

'Ava preparation is most often performed by a daughter of the host matai. All daughters of chiefs are expected to learn the 'ava ceremony for the many occasions on which her family will host visitors or celebrate an important event. It requires training to learn each step in order, and to prepare the drink correctly. In addition, all participants in the 'ava ceremony must possess an outward mark of their worthiness to serve the community in the form of a ta-tau (tattoo): *pe'a* or full waist and leg design for men, and *malu* or leg designs for women (von Hoerschelmann 1995).

village councils (*fono*) and matters relating to the family or village on a larger scale. When a new matai takes office, it is customary to hold an *'ava* ceremony to begin the proceedings, as described in Box 12.2.

Among the Five Nations of the Iroquois Confederacy, across the area now known as upstate New York, Clan Mothers are responsible for selecting a new chief and ensuring that he performs his duties well. If he does not act in the best interests of the people, she can also remove his authority. In this matrilineal society, the hereditary title of Clan Mother is passed down among sisters and then daughters, but the title of chief is not hereditary.

Intensive agricultural societies have a surplus of goods, which allows the central governing body to demand tribute in the form of goods or food. This is one way that authority figures wield power over their subjects. The chiefly office then performs a redistributive function, hosting cultural or religious feasts to redistribute these goods to the community.

In many societies, colonial contact drastically altered the traditional political and social organization. In some cases, in order for the colonial governments to better administer the native lands that they had claimed, they created new roles for "chiefs" that did not exist before. Among Aboriginal peoples of Australia, for instance,

British governors would choose Aboriginal elders and appoint them "Kings." They would be easily identified by a metal plate hanging around their necks from a chain, stamped with their name, perhaps several images, and the word "King." Prior to contact, Aboriginal society was decentralized. As hunter-gatherers, Aboriginal groups were egalitarian and decisions were made by consensus.

States

State societies are industrial and heterogeneous, with a strong centralized government. State societies contain the largest populations seen among the different forms of political organization. A state society usually contains diverse groups within its borders. It is common to see smaller forms of political organization within a state, such as the Yanomamö tribe inhabiting an area that crosses the borders of two modern states (Brazil and Venezuela). Few true nation-states still exist in the world, in which one ethnic group inhabits one bordered region. An example of a nation-state would be Swaziland, a monarchy in Southern Africa only 200 km across, mostly inhabited by ethnic Swazi.

A state has a formalized central government with the authority to use force to control its citizens. A written code of laws formalizes right and wrong and encourages socially sanctioned behavior. When laws are broken, there is also a codified set of punishments that correspond to the severity of the offense. The government uses an official court system to determine innocence or guilt and to impose punishments.

A state society gives authority to various groups to maintain order in society. A police force is an example of a group that is given the legitimate use of authority to control citizens. The state also has the authority to use force in dealing with other states, for example, to impose sanctions, hold other states accountable for their actions, and to declare war.

Because state societies are very large, a bureaucracy is necessary to administer to all the needs of its people. There are lower-level administrators, who report to higher-level governors. All of these leaders report to a central authority. The highest authority may be an individual ruler such as an emperor, king, or queen, or it may be a collective group, such as a congress or parliament (with a ruling president or prime minister).

A central governing body may demand taxes or tribute of its citizens, which can then be used for improvements in infrastructure or operations. Due to their power of authority, they may also demand labor of their citizens. The stability of a central

Figure 12.4
"King" Mickey Johnson of Illawarra, c. 1896
Aboriginal elders were chosen as representatives of their societies by British administrators to better govern the native populations of Australia. "King" Mickey Johnson served as the titled representative for a farming district in the Illawarra district of New South Wales.
Credit: © State Library of New South Wales

Figure 12.5
Political Protest Near the Tour Eiffel
These French citizens are participating in a public political protest near the Eiffel Tower over violence in Sri Lanka. A stable democratic system allows citizens to peacefully gather to publicize issues that are important to them.

Credit: © Barry D. Kass/Images of Anthropology

government may be dependent upon how these taxes are collected and used, and whether the citizens are treated justly. If a government authority demands too much from its citizens, resentment and discontent may turn into violence.

Ancient Teotihuacan, near present-day Mexico City, has several examples of massive construction built by the labor of commoners. Around the first century AD, this vibrant political, religious, and economic center was the sixth largest city in the world. Harnessing the labor to construct giant structures like the Pyramids of the Sun and Moon was only possible due to the state's hierarchical social organization. In fact, oppression of the lower classes may also have contributed to the downfall of Teotihuacan, which collapsed in approximately AD 650. One hypothesis proposed by anthropologist Richard Adams to explain the collapse is that the disgruntled lower classes revolted in an uprising against the elite, destroying the city by fire, looting, and murder.

Social Inequality

Social stratification, or the ranking of members of a society into a hierarchy, is not a natural feature of social organization. Many societies, such as foraging band societies, follow social rules of behavior that are carefully constructed so that individual members do not have more status than others. Cooperation and sharing is built into their daily lives, and resources abound in their environment. Gossip and social ostracism result if they do not abide by these expectations.

Nevertheless, once a society settles in one location and begins to amass possessions, a stratified society results. Stratification is characterized by differential access to resources. High-ranking members of a stratified society own or have access to more possessions and opportunities than low-ranking members. Having possessions equates to wealth. Wealthy individuals gain status in the form of power and prestige. Therefore, people with the most power tend to be concentrated in a small group at the top of the social pyramid.

Stratification may also arise due to the need for specialization of roles and more complex tasks. Thus, individuals with certain occupations will have access to resources that others do not have. In addition, as societies grow, they require management of resources and people. A higher population size generally correlates to more specialization, which in turn, correlates to more social inequality.

Depending on the society and how it is structured, social hierarchies may or may not allow **social mobility**, that is, the ability to move upward or downward within the system. There are two basic types of social stratification: class and caste (see Table 12.1). **Class** stratification is based upon differences in wealth and status. Through a combination of work and opportunity, members of one class can move up into a higher class, or they can lose their status and move downward. This is referred to as **achieved status** because it is based on personal actions.

In the United States, for instance, a person may be able to move from one class to another based on hard work, resulting in income and status. This is the model of the "American Dream," which many immigrants aspire to reach. In reality, it is much harder to rise through the system, since one's cultural and physical environments play a large part in determining opportunities.

Caste, on the other hand, is a hierarchical system based on birth. The caste system doesn't allow movement from one group to another. Individuals' status in society is **ascribed**, or fixed at birth, and can't be changed. Caste may dictate a person's social standing, occupation, and who they may marry. Historically, social ranking based on ascribed status is found in societies all over the world, including Japan during the Edo period and among the Igbo of Nigeria. Of course, it is most commonly associated with Hindu India.

The Hindu caste system is an ancient ranking system that separates people into categories based on their birth into a particular set of occupations. There are four major *varnas* or divisions: Brahmin (priests), Kshatriyas (warriors and rulers), Vaisyas (merchants, farmers, craftspeople), and Shudras (laborers, servants). The

Table 12.1

Comparison of Class and Caste

Class	Caste
Determined by wealth and status (achieved status)	Determined by birth (ascribed status)
Allows social mobility	Does not allow social mobility
Influences occupation and marriage	Determines occupation (to an extent) and marriage

caste system in India was outlawed after India's independence from Britain in 1948. Nevertheless, social practices based on caste (such as marriage) and discrimination of lower castes still persist.

Gender Inequality

When looking at the question of equality between males and females in society, it may be tempting to regard male dominance as "natural." This is because in nearly all societies, men own the family's land and other resources, even when a society is matrilineal and matrilocal. This generally results in higher status and more prestigious positions for men than women. That is not to say that women don't hold positions of power, because clearly many women throughout history and today are leaders with prestige and authority. However, men tend to have more access to power, prestige, and privilege than women. The dominance of men and subordinate status of women in society is referred to as **gender stratification**.

In examining the question of male dominance, anthropologist Ernestine Friedl (1978) discovered a consistent connection between power and the distribution of food resources. She notes that in societies in which females grew and controlled access to food, women had more equal status to men than in societies in which men controlled food resources, especially meat. Across cultures, where men hunt or fish and control the distribution of that protein, gender stratification exists. Unfortunately, this can also result in poor treatment of women. Because social expectations and status vary across cultures, it is clear that gender inequality is not "natural," but connected closely to social norms.

Another example of gender stratification can be seen in the daily expectations of men's and women's behavior. If these expectations are similar, then the society regards both sexes as equal. In gender-stratified societies, however, women are faced with restrictions on their behavior from which men are largely exempt. Women's behavior may be closely monitored, with limits on where, when, and with whom a woman is seen. Her clothing may be restricted or commented upon by others, while

Figure 12.6
Egyptian Woman Wearing the Abaya
Muslim women in many countries wear varying forms of head or body coverings. This Egyptian woman wears a full-body and hair covering, called an abaya, when she goes out in public. She may choose to wear the abaya, or she may be pressured by others to wear it.

Credit: Barbara Zaragoza

men's clothing is not. Unmarried women, especially, are believed to represent the family's honor; therefore the family and community members regard her actions with suspicion. Even suspected dishonorable behavior may be punished harshly.

A woman's dress code is one way that gender inequality may be expressed externally. To outsiders, the veil that Muslim women wear throughout the Middle East, Asia, Africa, and beyond, appears to indicate extreme gender inequality. Head and body coverings are seen as a sign of restriction and oppression imposed upon them by their families or husbands. It is true that in some countries in which women veil their heads, faces, or bodies, they experience severe **gender discrimination**.

For instance, in areas of Afghanistan where the Taliban rule, women are forbidden not only from showing their faces or bodies in public, but may not laugh or sing, see a male doctor, and indeed, may not leave the house without being accompanied by a male relative. This type of severe gender discrimination affects women's mental health as well: in the 1990s, researchers from the American Medical Association found that 78 per cent of women living in a Taliban-controlled area were clinically depressed. A full 73 per cent of women reported suicidal thoughts (Rasekh, Bauer, Manos, & Iacopino 1998).

Nonetheless, wearing the veil is a complex and nuanced issue. Even though many women feel restricted and oppressed by their veils, it is also true that many educated, working women *choose* to wear the veil without experiencing pressure from their husbands or family members. For these women, wearing the veil is primarily a sign of devotion to their religious beliefs. It is also a way to take part in public life with a desired measure of modesty. Head and body coverings provide them a measure of privacy, even safety, which they would not otherwise enjoy.

Environmental Inequality: Access to Water

Social stratification reaches into all aspects of human society, even our most fundamental needs, such as food and water. Water is especially crucial since the human body is made up of 50–65 per cent water and a person can't live more than a handful of days without it. Throughout history, human communities have been built around access to water both for their own survival and for the successful growth of food crops and animals. It is not an exaggeration to say that for the living species on our planet, water equals life.

Although clean water is a fundamental human need, vast inequalities exist regarding who has access to it. Although our blue planet has plenty of water, only 2.5 per cent of it is fresh. Sixty-eight per cent of that fresh water is locked into glaciers. The remaining water is available underground in aquifers and groundwater, and above ground in rivers and streams. Because of the small percentage of water available for human use, and the unequal distribution of it throughout nations, the UN Food and Agriculture Organization (2013) predicts that two-thirds of the world's population will face water shortages by 2025. The countries—and people—suffering most from these shortages will be across the developing world.

Gender, status, and ethnic differences can impact the water rights of an individual, family, or community. For example, in sub-Saharan Africa, 60 per cent of the water collected daily is done by girls aged 15 years and under. Sometimes walking to and from the water source takes up to six hours a day. Girls with this responsibility often cannot attend school due to the time it takes to bring fresh water to their households. In some places, women are harassed or even assaulted as they carry water.

North America is no stranger to water issues. First Nations peoples across Canada struggle with water access for their **reserves**. A national study released in 2011 assessed 571 First Nations reserves (with nearly 500,000 inhabitants) to evaluate their water systems, including the supply of clean drinking water and treatment of wastewater (Aboriginal Affairs and Northern Development Canada 2011). Looking at the sources, design, operation, and monitoring of water systems in each location, the report concluded that fully 73 per cent of the reserves had medium- to high-risk water problems, either now or in the immediate future. Nearly half of all homes lack sewage pipes, and rely on outhouses, even in the winter. The lack of updated infrastructure has led to outbreaks of illness, including skin rashes, infections, and gastrointestinal problems due to high levels of bacteria and chemicals. It appears that inequality remains in terms of meeting people's basic needs.

WATER INEQUALITY IN AGRICULTURE

Rivers and their tributaries provide the water needed to irrigate fields to grow food. Some of the world's great rivers no longer reach the ocean: the Nile in Egypt, the

Yellow River in China, the Indus in Pakistan, and the Rio Grande in the western United States and Mexico. Even more disturbing is the lack of water in farmers' wells, caused by an overuse of groundwater. Every year farmers dig deeper—in certain places more than a mile—to find the water needed to irrigate their crops. Fresh water is disappearing in places where the ability to feed people depends upon it.

Feeding people is a thirsty business. Growing food uses the majority of our water supplies across the planet. It takes massive quantities of water to feed people: an average of 450 gallons to grow a pound of rice, 400 gallons for a pound of sugar, 130 gallons for a pound of wheat, and a shocking 2,650 gallons to produce a pound of coffee (Pearce 2006).

Therefore, food preferences play a role in a country's water requirements. Meat products, especially the raising of beef cattle, require more water to produce than any other foods per calorie. It takes 20 times the amount of water per calorie to raise beef than cereal grains (such as rice or wheat). Even if we compare the water cost of raising the least thirsty meat (chicken) to high plant protein sources such as pulses (dry beans, peas, or lentils), it still takes one-and-a-half times the water per calorie. Therefore, those nations with growing economies where meat consumption has exploded, such as China, have much higher water requirements than others.

Figure 12.7
Bank of the River Nile

Millions of people from Ethiopia to Sudan and Egypt depend upon the water from the Nile River for their livelihoods and survival. Every year during the dry season, the water in the Nile dries up before reaching the Mediterranean Sea.

Credit: © Barry D. Kass/Images of Anthropology

It is estimated that more than a billion people do not have regular access to clean drinking water. The situation is dire in regions all over the world, but nowhere is it more threatening than in Africa, where 19 of the 25 countries suffering from very limited access to safe drinking water are found. Among the poorest inhabitants of these nations, millions of people die annually from diarrheal infections caused by drinking water from open sources contaminated by human and animal waste. Most of these are children under five years old.

Although clean drinking water is a basic human need, it is no longer treated as a human right. **Privatization** of water makes it difficult for marginalized and rural people to access clean water. When local water supplies are privatized, governments grant the rights over the water supply to a private corporation, which then purifies the water, bottles it, and sells it back to the local people. This can be an extreme hardship when people have very little income. Often, the head of household must make the decision whether to purchase clean water or food and medical supplies.

Ethnic Politics

When ethnic groups live together, as they do in most areas of the world today, they may integrate or collide. Both usually occur simultaneously, resulting in struggles for rights, representation, or even survival. The issues arising in these areas of interface are referred to as **ethnic politics**. Sociologists divide intergroup relations into six types that can be applied to all societies. Because the application is universal, this sociological concept crosses over readily for use in anthropology.

- The first, **pluralism**, represents an ideal situation in which ethnic groups coexist in harmony. This type of multicultural society allows equal rights and representation for all groups.
- Second, **assimilation** results when the dominant society absorbs an ethnic minority culturally, socially, and finally, genetically.
- Third, legal protection of minorities occurs when a government must intervene to confer legal protections on a minority group that suffers discrimination or whose rights have been stripped.
- Fourth, population transfer has to do with forced relocation of peoples who suffer great hardships as a result of their residence location. This includes both people who have been forcibly removed by governments, such as Native/First Nations peoples relocated to reservations, and those people fleeing civil war or other persecution as refugees.

- Fifth, long-term subjugation may not ever fully assimilate people into the dominant culture, nor is the minority group forcibly removed. Instead, both groups coexist in a dominant-subjugated state.
- Finally, the most severely aggressive intergroup conflicts may lead to **genocide**, in which the dominant society attempts to wipe out the minority through **ethnic cleansing**. (Simpson & Yinger 1985)

Again, it is important to remember that even though typologies are tidy ways to define categories of relations, in practice the world is much more complex. Multiple forms of intergroup relations will exist in any society simultaneously. Unfortunately, many of these relations are characterized by violence.

Violence and War

When groups clash, the size of the group and goals of the conflict shape the confrontation. Violence in smaller horticultural or pastoral societies may take the form of a **raid**, in which members of one group aim to steal or recover items, animals, or people from another group in the same society. Tribal and pastoral societies may embark on raids to kill adversaries, or steal women, horses, or weapons from neighboring enemies. Raids are short-term incursions with a specific goal in mind.

Ongoing violent relations between two groups in the same society are called a **feud**. Feuding often begins when a member of one group kills a member of another. This begins a long-term hostile relationship in which revenge is the goal. Feuding often occurs between extended families, who continue to avenge the murders of their kin. It also can occur between groups who share fictive kinship, such as members of an urban gang. Unlike a raid, which is over in a few hours, a feud can last for generations until the two sides agree on a truce.

Warfare is different from raiding and feuding in that it is on a much larger scale. Generally the weapons and transport of armies are more technologically advanced.

Societies can divide internally into civil wars, in which different groups within the same society go to war with one another. Civil wars may begin based on religious or ethnic issues. History is full of examples. In the civil war in Rwanda, Central Africa, in the 1990s, the extremist Hutu majority committed near genocide against the Tutsis, killing 70 per cent of the Tutsi people living in Rwanda at the time.

War may also be declared by one society or nation on another. The goals of war are much larger in that one side attempts to kill as many people or destroy as much property as possible until the other side surrenders. While industrialized nations may go to war over ideological issues, they often fight over natural resources such as

Box 12.3

Talking about War

Anthropologist Carol Cohn (1987) spent a year studying the subculture of a strategic think tank for US government defense analysts who plan nuclear strategy. She wanted to find out how people can plan the business of destruction, in other words, "think about the unthinkable." Through a process of enculturation, Cohn learned the language necessary to discuss military strategy, which she calls "technostrategic." As she became fluent in this highly specialized language, she was surprised to find that she had lost the ability to think about the human costs of war.

Abstraction and **euphemisms** focus all discussion on weapons and strategy. She found that the use of several types of metaphors of domesticity allow the analysts to connect in positive ways to their work. First, the euphemisms invoke hygiene and medical healing: they talk about *clean bombs* (bombs that release power but not radiation) and *surgically clean strikes* (bombing that takes out weapons or command centers only). Second, images of country life and recreation are used: missiles are located in *silos* as if on a farm, piles of nuclear weapons loaded in a submarine are called *Christmas tree farms*, and bombs are referred to as *re-entry vehicles*, or *RVs*. Third, the weapons are talked about as if they were responsible for their own actions: for instance, the pattern in which a bomb falls is called a *footprint*, as if the bomb were dropping itself, like a foot in the sand.

This image removes human accountability for the action.

In addition, Cohn discovered male-gender attribution to the missiles. Beyond the expected phallic imagery, bomb detonations were frequently described sexually, comparing the explosion to an orgasm. Moreover, missiles are spoken about as if they were infants or little boys. The implication is that they hope the bomb will be powerful and aggressive (like a boy) and not mild or timid (like a girl). After the first successful test of the hydrogen bomb in 1952, one pleased atomic scientist wrote to another, "It's a boy" (p. 701).

Cohn began her fieldwork interested in how nuclear defense analysts discuss massive destruction and human suffering day in and day out as part of their job. Quickly, she found, they don't. Military strategy demands a language that focuses on weapons only in a quest for scientific rationality. But the costs of embracing this language privilege a distanced and aggressive (i.e., "masculine") view over any others. Human costs cannot be discussed; these are "feminine" concerns. To her surprise, Cohn discovered that once she was a speaker of this language, she could no longer express her own values, since they were outside of "rational" discourse. Not only could she not articulate her ideas using this language, but also she was written off as a "hippie" or "dumb" if she tried. Her work carries an important message: what does any language allow us to think and say?

land, water, or raw materials. Today some military budgets, such as that of the United States, allocate billions of dollars to develop weapons and technology, support the different branches of the military, equip troops, and extend their influence in countries in different parts of the world.

How does this type of war develop on such a massive scale? It has to do with population growth and surpluses of wealth that arise in a stratified, settled society. Competition among state societies for access to resources is high, especially when a massive and growing population demands them. War also arises when other methods of conflict resolution have failed, such as **diplomacy** or economic sanctions.

We may assume that war has been a part of human behavior since the beginning of our species. However, large-scale warfare can't exist without large-scale societies. In small populations like food foragers or horticulturalists, there are few resources, especially for hunter-gatherers who carry their belongings on their backs. Marriage alliances between groups make it impractical to fight other groups since relatives may live in other local groups. Avoiding conflict and confrontation is important in small-scale societies where cooperation is crucial for survival.

Large-scale warfare arises with centralized states and surpluses of food and resources. This coincides with population growth and the rise of cities. Surpluses become attractive to official leaders, who then can organize their people to fight. An army or other large-scale military force is given the authority to use force against other nations.

Not all societies value aggression as a means to solve problems. Egalitarian societies, such as foragers and horticulturalists, must cooperate for reasons of survival. Egos and arguments only divide the group, making protection and pooling of resources harder. Therefore, these groups develop cultural norms that lessen the inevitability of social tension. One way to remove the source of tension is for an individual or group to leave. Foragers such as the Ju/'hoansi, for instance, can join a neighboring band and live with relatives either temporarily or permanently.

Other groups have developed a set of social norms that limit possible sources of tension. For instance, among the Buid of Mindoro Island, Philippines, non-aggression is the most valued characteristic in a person. Social expectations reinforce this behavior to the extent that men do not face one another when speaking. Rather, they direct their comments to the larger group, which lessens the possibility of annoyance or defensiveness. Other cultural practices that minimize the risk of hostility between individuals include harvesting crops with all workers facing the same way to minimize conversation; avoiding economic debt to one another; placing little value on bravery; and rearing children without punishment. The members of the group are conditioned to avoid competition, individual leadership (ego) or authority, in an effort to keep the group stable and non-violent.

In contrast, ferocity was valued in the Carib society who lived in today's Venezuela, Guyana, and adjacent Caribbean islands at the time of the Spanish arrival to the New World. The Carib, in fighting the encroachment of the Spanish soldiers in their territory, would prepare for raids in a way that fostered violence. A Carib chief would host a feast for raiding assassins, called *kanaimà*, before a raid. While the warriors danced, the ferocious Tiger Sprit, called *Kaikusi-Yumu*, would possess their bodies, seeking vengeance for losses. The Tiger Spirit bound the assassins to

Eating One of Us—Endo-Cannibalism

Beyond wartime exo-cannibalism, several additional types of anthropophagy (person-eating) exist that have cultural and religious meaning for participants. **Endo-cannibalism** is practiced within a group, especially an extended family. This is the practice of consuming part of a deceased loved one's corpse. While eating a dead family member may not have widespread appeal, the symbolism is clear. Consuming a part of someone's body unites them together in the most intimate way possible. The Yanomamö of the Amazon forest, for example, would closely care for and then consume the ground bone ashes of a dead family member or close friend some months after funerary rites. Among the Wari, also of the Amazon, this type of mortuary cannibalism would help survivors deal with their grief over losing a loved one.

Certain groups who practiced endo-cannibalism suffered physiologically for it. The Fore of Papua New Guinea ritually consumed the brain of their deceased relatives to keep the dead person's "life-force" within the village. They also suffered from a terrible and unknown illness they called *kuru*, characterized by shaking, loss of muscle control, bouts of uncontrolled laughter, and death. This disease reached epidemic levels among Fore people in the 1950s and 1960s, especially among women and children, without anyone making the link between the behavior and symptoms. In the 1970s, a series of scientific studies finally led to an understanding of the connection between kuru and a disease that can be transmitted from person to person from infected neural tissue. This type of disease is called *transmissible spongiform encephalopathy*, also called prion protein disease.

Prion protein disease is no stranger outside of Melanesia. In the 1990s, the bovine variant of Creutzfeldt-Jacob disease commonly known as "Mad Cow" disease crossed the species barrier, killing approximately 200 people in the United Kingdom who ate tainted beef. In both human and bovine forms, prion proteins change the shape of other healthy proteins in the brain, resulting in death. There is still no treatment or cure.

murder, and was only satiated when the warrior chewed a part of the dead enemy's flesh and tasted his blood. Failure to do so would exile a warrior from his village, condemning him to wander without satisfying the spirit-demon inside. Possessing fierceness and aggression was the way to be a valued member of Carib society.

Cannibalism

Cannibalism, or **anthropophagy** (person-eating), in wartime is not unique to the Carib, even though the term "cannibal" likely originates from the Carib word for person, "caribna." In fact, **exo-cannibalism**, or eating the flesh of those outside one's society, is a common feature of war rituals. (This is different from endo-cannibalism; see Box 12.4.) Consuming the enemy is a symbolic and expressive practice that may be done to humiliate enemy prisoners. It may even be done to erase their souls from Earth so they have no chance for an afterlife.

Exo-cannibalism is also practiced to capture the enemy's strength. Ingestion of part of an enemy's body is thought to transfer power, skill, and courage to the victor. Eating the flesh of prisoners also may have had an emotional element, as an expression of rage against the enemy after battle.

While symbolic or ritual cannibalism is no longer practiced in most societies, the practice during wartime still persists. As recently as 2007, the *Washington Post* reported that modern armies in the Second Congo War and the militant fighters of the Lord's Resistance Army in Uganda, under leader Joseph Kony, ate the flesh of their captives. Reasons today for these practices are similar to traditional motives: to show disdain for captives and their armies, or as a "trophy" as part of the spoils of war (Congo's Sexual Violence Goes "Far Beyond Rape" 2007).

Are We Programmed to Be Violent?

Some researchers argue that collective violence is innate—a biological tendency of human beings. Although not all anthropologists agree with this assessment of human nature, it is an interesting question. As was explained in Chapter 4, the idea of the "Killer Ape Hypothesis" is that humans inherited violence in their genes through our shared ancestry with apes.

Chimpanzee (*Pan troglodytes*) society is aggressive and violent. The alpha males must be fierce, otherwise they will lose their position to another upcoming male. On more than a handful of occasions, adult males have been reported killing and consuming the infants of female members of the same group. Perhaps most disturbing, primatologist Jane Goodall witnessed a full-scale war in the 1970s between two factions of a large group that had divided in her study area in Gombe Stream, Tanzania.

On the other hand, if we examine the more tranquil life of the bonobo (*Pan paniscus*), who is just as related to us as the chimpanzee is, then we see that aggression and violence are not necessarily in our primate biological heritage. The bonobo uses sex rather than violence to solve conflicts. They are not known to kill other bonobos, and have only recently been recorded hunting monkeys for meat (a behavior that chimps engage in frequently). Because we are equally related to these two species, with a common ancestor that lived five to seven million years ago, we cannot say that humans carry chimp genes for violence without also admitting that we could carry peaceful bonobo genes as well.

Human societies can be violent, but they can also be peaceful. Humans allow themselves to commit acts of great violence, justifying them psychologically. When children are raised in a violent environment, in which they lack love and care, more violence is often the result. Therefore, a tendency toward violence does not seem to be an innate or biological impulse, but the result of social and cultural conditioning in one's environment.

Summary

This chapter explored political organization, which acts as a structure that holds society together and dictates the hierarchy of power. Mirroring the Learning Objectives stated in the chapter opening, the key points are:

- Political organization regulates people's behavior through a combination of the use of power, authority, and prestige with culturally sanctioned punishments and rewards.
- In decentralized political systems, such as bands and tribes, informal leaders use charisma and experience to lead. They rely on the members of the community to support the functioning of the social system through gossip, negotiation, and supernatural threats. In centralized political systems, such as chiefdoms and states, official leaders use power and authority to keep order.
- Other forms of social hierarchies exist, such as gender or environmental inequities, in which marginalized members of society do not have the same kinds of access to power and therefore lack social status or access to resources, such as the basic right to water.
- When multiple ethnic groups have sustained contact with one another, it tends to lead to oppression and the potential for violence.
- While the majority of societies experience violence, some small-scale societies value cooperation over competition and manage to avoid violence. However, when populations grow large and complex, wars begin to emerge in which large, settled societies fight for the resources of the other.
- Nonetheless, violence is not necessarily part of the human biological heritage. Even though other primates are extremely violent, humans have culture, which allows us alternate ways to achieve our goals.

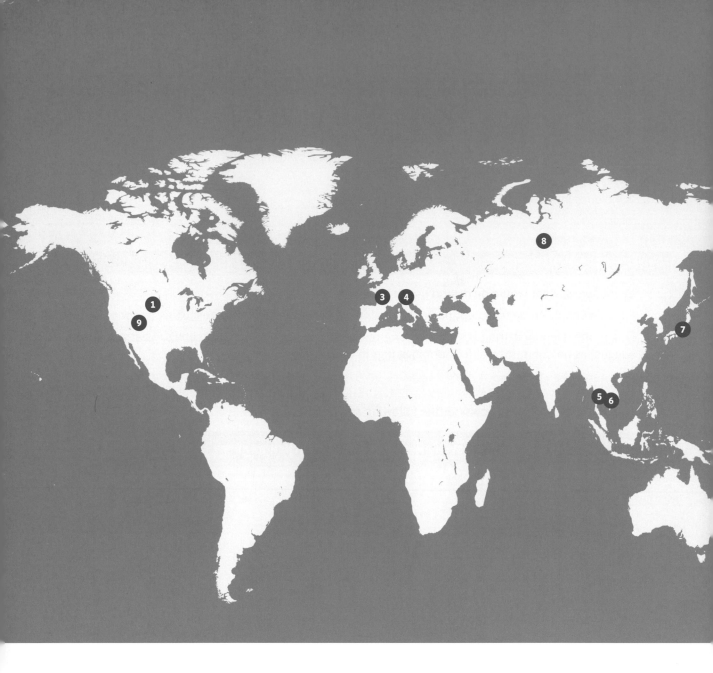

PLACES MENTIONED IN CHAPTER 13

1 Great Plains
2 Vanuatu
3 France
4 Ötztal Alps
5 Thailand

6 Cambodia
7 Japan
8 Russia
9 Four Corners, American Southwest

SUPERNATURALISM

(((Leaping into the fire as a sacrificial offering
teaches lessons about religious origins and right
and wrong behavior. #supernaturalism

Learning Objectives

In this chapter, students will learn:

- reasons for the development of supernatural belief systems.
- what the earliest evidence is for supernatural beliefs.
- what functions religious belief serves in society.
- about the roles of deities, ancestor spirits, and spirits of nature.
- about the different roles that religious practitioners play in society
- how oppressed peoples resist the imposition of a new set of beliefs.
- about the intersections of religious beliefs and other forms of cultural expression.

Introduction

Humans are unique in that they are compelled to make meaning of their lives.
People create and use symbols to connect to others in their communities, shape
their world, and define their identities. Chapter 9 explains that symbols in language
imbue people's actions and thought with significance. One area of life in which
symbols carry great meaning both personally and for society is in the realm of religious or supernatural beliefs.

Figure 13.1
Golden Buddha, Burma
The golden Buddha at the Maha Myat Muni Temple in Mandalay, Burma, has a two-inch-thick layer of gold leaf applied over many years by the hands of male pilgrims to the site.
Credit: Daniel Chit

Faith in spirits, gods, or unseen forces guides individual behavior in powerful ways, and serves important functions for the social group. The teachings of religious belief systems often underpin many aspects of social life, such as the structures of power and punishment. They also extend beyond the realm of organized religion into family life, ideas about health and healing, people's relationship to the natural world, and other areas of life. Every society also has nonbelievers among its members, and their secular, scientific, or humanist value systems serve to guide their behavior in similar ways as well.

Studying Belief Systems

Of course, beliefs vary widely throughout the world, as do the experiences and practices of religion. Because of this enormous diversity, anthropologists may not agree on a single definition of religion. It all depends on how anthropologists approach their research. In this text, we define **religion** simply as a set of beliefs and behaviors that pertain to supernatural forces or beings, which transcend the observable world.

Religious belief systems have four components: they share an interest in the supernatural (whether beings, forces, states, or places), use ritual, are guided by myths, and are symbolic. The term **supernatural** in this case doesn't imply "unnatural" or "abnormal." It simply refers to those things outside of a scientific understanding that we cannot measure or test. **Ritual** is a symbolic practice that is ordered and regularly repeated. It provides people with a way to practice their beliefs in a consistent form, connecting them to others in the same community. **Myths** are sacred stories that explain events, such as the beginning of the world or the creation of the first people. They serve to guide values and behaviors. It's important to clarify that these stories are referred to as "myth" not because we deem them untrue, but because they are outside of recorded history. Finally, religion is symbolic because it is based on the construction of meaning between a person and his or her beliefs, and among people within a community. It represents their understanding of the world.

With the guiding principle of cultural relativism, an anthropological approach does not question whether one religion is more valid than another. We examine religious beliefs both from an **emic**, or insider's, perspective, and from an **etic**, or outsider's, perspective. That is, anthropology attempts to learn how people think, act, and feel about their belief systems. Then, we analyze and interpret these aspects to produce a deeper and broader understanding. Anthropologists stay out of the kinds of arguments that claim one belief system is "truer" than another. Each is true for those who believe it.

Reasons for Supernatural Belief Systems

Attempting to trace the earliest evidence for religious beliefs poses a challenge. Like many aspects of culture, beliefs do not fossilize and lie buried in strata for us to uncover ("Look, there's a belief, right next to that hand ax!"). However, cultural practices may leave physical evidence that can be found by archaeologists, who seek to understand cultural practices through physical remains.

EARLY EVIDENCE

The earliest evidence of religion is linked to burial sites, since the idea of burial is an early marker of culture and community. Before foragers began burying their dead, they would simply leave a corpse behind and move on to a new location. Moving after a group member has died was a practical choice because it avoided exposure to the decomposition process and to scavengers who might be attracted to it. The idea of burial represents a radical change in this thinking process. Even the earliest burials may have had something to do with the possibility of preparing or assisting the body (or its essence/soul) for existence in an afterlife.

Although laying the dead in the ground is the most common mortuary practice, cultures throughout the world practice other forms of releasing a person into the spiritual realm. Therefore, there may be ancient funerary rites for which we have no physical evidence. For instance, many cultures cremate the remains of their loved ones. Hindu tradition requires a body to be cremated on a pyre of wood while family members are in attendance. Zoroastrians and Tibetan Buddhists invite scavenging vultures to remove remains by placing them in high, open places. For Zoroastrians, this practice prevents the world of the living from being contaminated by the dark forces of the dead. In contrast, Tibetan Buddhists believe this is the most generous and compassionate way to return the body to the circle of life. Although the practice is similar, the symbolism guiding it is very different.

FUNCTIONS OF RELIGION

Supernatural belief systems have both intellectual and emotional functions. One can imagine the prescientific notion that natural forces, such as weather, the sun's orbit, the changing of the seasons, or solar eclipses were caused by unseen supernatural forces. In fact, humans' big brains compel us to seek understanding and knowledge. Our ancestors wanted explanations for these kinds of natural phenomena.

Anthropologists believe that supernatural beliefs provide the crucial ability to explain those aspects of life for which we have no logical answer. Religion also helps humans cope emotionally with those anxiety-producing events that we cannot control, such as accidents, illness, or death. Prayer, offering, and sacrifice are ways for a person to seek help from supernatural beings or forces. Active participation in ritual practices allows a person who is suffering to feel involved in achieving a positive outcome. For these reasons, belief in supernatural beings and forces can provide both psychological and emotional relief.

However, the opposite can also be true. In his ethnography *The Winds of Ixtepeji*, Michael Kearney (1972) writes about the Zapotec town of Ixtepeji, Oaxaca, Mexico, in which the air is filled with malevolent forces and spirits. These *mal aigres* ("bad airs," colloquial) can enter one's home when a door is opened. They can also be manipulated by people who wish someone ill. Imagine living in a world where the very air you breathe may be ready to kill you! Not surprisingly, the townspeople have developed cultural and psychological defenses against these perceived threats. As Kearney relates, they live in a society that is characterized by sadness, distrust, and paranoia.

Nonetheless, religious belief systems generally provide support for individuals and also for the social group. Even when beliefs cause suspicion or fear, there is comfort in knowing that others in the community also experience the world in the same way. The roles that belief systems play vary widely, ranging from teaching children right and wrong to providing reasons for why things happen. The ways in which belief systems provide support include the following: creating community, instilling values, renewing faith, providing reasons for life's events, and solving problems.

Figure 13.2
Men Washing Their Feet before Entering a Mosque for Prayers
These Muslim men are washing their feet before entering a mosque for prayers in Istanbul, Turkey. In some traditions, it is important to show respect by cleansing the hands or feet, or both, before worship.

Credit: © Barry D. Kass/Images of Anthropology

1. Creating Community: Religious ceremonies and rituals bring community members together, so that individuals feel support from the group. There are many types of rituals that bring cohesiveness to a group, whether they are performed with others or alone. Services (such as those in a temple, mosque, or church) allow individual members to physically come together regularly, creating a community of worshippers. Some religious practitioners create altars in their homes, whether to gods, spirits, or their own departed ancestors. Although they may worship alone, other members of that community use the same types of altars, creating cohesion.

Some religious rituals mark life's important transitions from one social or biological role to another, such as at puberty, first menses, marriage, childbirth, or death. Anthropologists call these **rites of passage**. The three stages of a rite of passage take an individual on a journey from separation, through transition, to the final stage of reincorporation and acceptance. For example, puberty rituals, such as circumcision, may mark a boy's passage into manhood. Among the Maasai of East Africa, the Emuratta circumcision rite identifies a young man as responsible enough to protect a camp territory, to learn the skills of an adult male, to lead others, and to fight as a warrior. Months of preparation and training precede the arduous circumcision ceremony, during which no anesthesia is administered. The young man must not flinch or cry out as an elder warrior performs the surgery. Once he successfully passes the initiation, the young man is given gifts of cattle to begin his new role in Maasai society.

2. Instilling Values: Religious texts and oral tales teach ethics to guide behavior. Elements of religious education may come from written texts such as the Qur'an (Islam), Torah (Judaism), Bible (Abrahamic religions such as Christianity and Judaism), and Bhagavad Gita (Hinduism). In cultures without a written tradition, values are passed orally through poems, myths, legends, and tales. Practitioners may learn the rules of moral behavior through these texts and stories. They also learn what punishments may ensue from a failure to follow them.

For instance, ancient Hindu religious law meted out punishment (Sanskrit: *daṇḍa*) according to the transgression. This could take the form of incapacitation (mutilation or amputation), deterrence (knowing the harsh punishments that may result), and rehabilitation. Modern forms of Hindu law are based on the same basic ideas but no longer condone bodily incapacitation such as mutilation. However, in India, the death penalty still exists as a method of deterrence, as it does in many secular legal systems.

A group's oral stories provide guidelines for correct action as well. Myth is a category of story that describes the sacred origins of the world and its people. The Aztec creation myth of ancient Mexico recounts a story of the beginning of the Fifth Age of the World (el Quinto Sol). Before the current world was created, the gods gathered together. They were discussing the best way to create the sun anew to provide life for the world. They came to the conclusion that sacrifice was the means to achieve this. However, none of the gods wanted to be sacrificed. Finally, two gods offered themselves: a proud and strong god (Tecciztecatl) and the humblest and poorest god, the God with Boils (Nanahuatzin). At the last minute, the strong god lost his nerve, but the lowly god calmly offered himself up, becoming the sun. Ashamed, the strong god followed, but a more powerful god kicked a rabbit at him in protest, dimming his light. So the strong god, now weakened, became the moon, which is said to have the shape of a rabbit on its face. This origin myth teaches its followers that being strong and conceited are wrong, while acting humbly and for the benefit of others is right. It also provides a foundation for the religious practice of human sacrifice, without which the sun would cease and day and night would end.

3. Renewing Faith: Certain regular rituals elevate the mood of participants and bring on a state of happiness or transcendence. This may include such elements as song, call-and-response, hand clapping, trance states, or dance. For instance, Islamic Sufi dancers of the Mevlevi sect in Turkey perform a form of moving meditation in which they spin in circles. Practitioners, called whirling dervishes, experience closeness to the divine by abandoning the self in a trance-like dance. The Sema, or worship ceremony, is highly regulated, from the dervishes' clothing to the movements of the feet and hands.

Some revitalization activities use the threat of danger to rejuvenate faith in their belief system. An example of this is the religious snake handlers of the Pentecostal Holiness or Church of God churches across parts of North America. The handling of venomous snakes is one way members of these sects provide evidence that the Holy Spirit has saved them. The dangerous nature of this ritual generates excitement and transcendence for the community participating and witnessing the event. Unfortunately, there have been several high-profile deaths from snakebite in these rituals, causing some states to outlaw the practice.

4. Providing Reasons: Belief systems provide explanations for life's events. This speaks to the human desire to understand why we do certain things in certain ways, and why bad things happen to good people. Religious traditions also provide reasons for behaviors, such as why certain foods can or can't be eaten by people of certain religious communities. Practitioners may not know the origins of these restrictions; however, many anthropologists believe that some of the major food taboos are linked to the environmental pressures found in places where religions first developed. The Hindu taboo on eating beef and Muslim and Jewish taboos on eating pork are explored in Box 13.1.

Many belief systems teach that everything that happens in life is predetermined. Therefore, when a misfortune occurs, a believer might say, "Everything happens for a reason." A divine plan that life events fit into is less frightening and chaotic than one in which accidents happen for no reason at all.

The Wape people of Papua New Guinea believe that ghosts, demons, and witches inhabit their environment. When the main food source of the Wape was produce from horticulture, any meat brought from a forest hunt was greatly anticipated. However, the forest is a dangerous and forbidding place to the Wape. Vengeful spirits of recently dead ancestors populate it. A hunter may not find any game animals or have any luck killing the ones he sees due to the will of these spirits. Therefore, if a hunting party returns to the village with no meat, the explanation is clear: angry ancestor spirits chased the animals away.

5. Solving Problems: Since many societies attribute the causes of events to supernatural beings and forces, they also seek help from them when problems need to be

Figure 13.3
Dervish Dancer, Cairo
This Dervish dancer experiences a revitalization of faith and devotion by spinning in circles and entering a trance-like state. This worship brings the dancer into a state of divine meditation.
Credit: © Barry D. Kass/Images of Anthropology

Box 13.1

Religious Food Taboos

Religious rules and practices support a group's environment. That is, the guidelines laid down in religious stories and texts serve to maintain balance in the ecosystem. For example, spirits of the forest would never require that their human worshippers burn down trees, making the area uninhabitable. This is especially true in terms of sacred food taboos.

Why do Jews and Muslims avoid eating pork? Why do Hindus avoid beef? The etic answer calls pigs "dirty" and disease carrying. On the other hand, cows are sacred and pure, connected to the divine Mother. Elaborate symbolism supports these ideas in stories, prayers, ritual ceremonies, and texts. In seeking the emic answer, anthropologist Marvin Harris examines the environmental conditions in which these religions developed. His approach is called **cultural materialism**, in which the external pressures of the environment dictate cultural practices. This is not the only framework with which to explain cultural choices, such as diet, but it is one that focuses on the interaction of people and their environments.

Harris relates that the pig was not well adapted to the dry, hot grasslands of the Middle East where the early Abrahamic religions developed. It was used to shadier, wetter climates in which it could keep a cool body temperature (pigs have no sweat glands, making it hard for them to live in a desert-like environment). Not only must humans provide shelter and water to keep them cool, but pigs also compete for resources, eating the foods that humans live on. On the other hand, cows, sheep, and goats live happily on pasture, leaving grains for human consumption.

As farming expanded, suitable habitat for pigs decreased. It became too costly to raise pigs for meat, which is a pig's only real product. You can't milk a pig easily. And while you can make sheep's wool into clothing, can you imagine trying to wear clothing made of pig hair? Thus, pigs became unsuitable to eat and were codified as such. In this way, the ban on pork among Jews and Muslims supported the expansion of farms and the raising of pasture animals, which were "good to eat" (Harris 1985).

In Hindu cultures, cow meat was prohibited not because of the animal's lack of usefulness, but the opposite. The strong and hardy zebu cattle of India provide so many benefits alive that killing them for beef would undercut the entire system of agriculture. Their main role is to pull the plow, creating opportunities for Indian agriculture where neither other animals' nor human labor suffices. Farm cattle are fed kitchen scraps or oil patties; therefore, they do not compete with people for food resources. Even in times of drought or a failed harvest, keeping cattle on the farm ensures some long-term security.

In addition, cows provide an unlimited supply of milk and other dairy products at the center of the Indian diet, such as ghee (clarified butter), cheese, and yogurt. The giving nature of the cow is revered and protected. For all these reasons, it is easy to see why early Indian Buddhists, Hindu Brahmin priests, and, more recently, the Indian leader Mohandas Gandhi, condemned the killing of cows for their flesh.

solved. Prayer is one of the most common ways that individuals request assistance, either in a communal setting, individually, or even silently. Many ritual behaviors are done with the purpose of solving an immediate problem, such as asking for rain during a drought, consulting the astrological charts for an auspicious day for marriage, or praying for the health of a loved one. Even mundane activities merit divine cooperation, such as lighting a candle before taking an exam, or touching a statue for luck before driving a car.

The oldest evidence of Chinese script is found on what scholars call oracle bones: flat pieces of ox scapulae (shoulder blades) or the undersides of turtle shells. The writing on these pieces of bone shows that rulers during the Shang period (from the sixteenth through the eleventh centuries BC) regularly consulted fortune tellers specializing in **divination** to answer questions and solve problems. It was thought that ancestors of the Shang royal family would communicate through the heating and cracking of the bone. The diviner would read the messages left by the cracks, and then inscribe the bone with the answers. Rulers consulted oracle bones for ways to appease the ancestors before a hunt, the harvest, or wars with neighboring groups.

Figure 13.4
Oracle Bones
Ancient Chinese diviners used ox scapulae or the undersides of turtle shells to read a person's future. It was believed that the ancestors would guide the questioner toward the right decisions.
Credit: Cambridge University Library, CUL 52-R

Sacred Roles

Fundamental to supernatural beliefs is the culturally accepted existence of beings or forces that exist beyond the natural or observable world. **Supernatural beings** are personified or embodied gods, demons, spirits, or ghosts. Like humans, they may have genders (masculine, feminine, transgendered, or changeable). Beings may be known (ancestors) or unknowable (all-powerful gods beyond human comprehension). **Supernatural forces**, in contrast, are disembodied powers that exist in the world. These powers may bring good or bad luck. Forces may be manipulated or controlled for a purpose. Religious belief systems incorporate three basic types of beings and forces: deities, ancestral spirits, and spirits/forces of nature. Because culture is fluid and changing, multiple belief systems may be used simultaneously to understand the spirit world.

Deities

Deities are distant, hugely powerful beings. People ask them for aid with life's problems, assuming they are concerned with human issues and can alter the course of events. **Gods and goddesses** are found most often in societies with a hierarchical social organization, since a society's belief systems reflect its social organization. A society's gender roles are also reflected in the composition of deities, in that a male-dominated, authoritarian society will worship a masculine, authoritarian god. Societies in which women do much of the labor will worship both male and female deities. Over time, societies may change their understandings of gender roles, but codified religious tenets may not change at the same pace.

Worship of one god or goddess is called **monotheism**. Monotheistic religions posit a single, all-knowing, and all-powerful deity as the absolute ruler of the universe. Judaism, Islam, and Christianity are three modern religions that stemmed from a single religion of pastoral peoples. This pastoral society's worship of a single god evolved into these three world religions. The all-powerful deity is expressed as either the masculine Yahweh in Judaism, God as Jesus Christ in Christianity, or as the neutral/genderless Allah in Islam. Although there are important female figures in each of these traditions, the subordinate role of women in pastoral society is reflected in the few leadership roles for women in these religions, even today.

Polytheistic religions, on the other hand, worship two or more gods and goddesses in a **pantheon**. In the native Hawaiian belief system, the goddess Pele is one of the most prominent deities. She resides in the volcanoes and is associated with volcanic activity. The Hawaiian pantheon includes her brothers and sisters, such as Kā-moho-ali'i, the keeper of the water of life and shark god; Kapo, goddess of fertility; and Hi'iaka, spirit of the dance. When a pantheon exists, gods and goddesses control certain aspects of the world (sun, rain, afterlife, or children). Often, one is given more dominance than others; thus, they have power over lesser deities.

Ancestral Spirits

A belief in **ancestral spirits** comes from the idea that humans are made of two aspects, the body and the soul (essence or spirit), which separate upon death. The

Table 13.1

Excerpt from *Cantares Mexicanos #20* by Aztec Poet Nezahualcoyotl

Nahuatl	English
Tiazque yehua xon ahuiacan.	We will pass away.
Niquittoa o ni Nezahualcoyotl. Huia!	I, Nezahualcoyotl, say, enjoy!
Cuix oc nelli nemohua oa in tlalticpac?	Do we really live on earth?
Yhui. Ohuaye.	Yhui. Ohuaye. (refrain)
Anochipa tlalticpac. Zan achica ye nican . . .	Not forever on earth, only a brief time here . . .
Tel ca chalchihuitl no xamani,no teocuitlatl in tlapani, no quetzalli poztequi:	Even jades fracture, even gold ruptures, even quetzal plumes tear:
Anochipa tlalticpac. Zan achica ye nican . . .	Not forever on earth: only a brief time here . . .
Ohuaya, ohuaya.	Ohuaya, ohuaya. (refrain)

Source: Curl 2005

physical body may eventually disappear, but the soul continues to exist among the living. Spirits of one's family members may continue to live in their house or community, inhabit the physical environment, or live in another realm but visit on certain days of the year. Ancestors can be pleased or angered, which may have an impact on the health or success of the living. For instance, the Wape from Papua New Guinea, described above, believe their forest-dwelling ancestors have a direct impact on whether they bring home game from a hunt.

The Mexican holiday *Días de los Muertos* (Days of the Dead) reflects this duality of existence in body and soul. This celebration honors family members who have passed away. It merges aspects of the ancient Aztec belief system with the Gregorian or Christian calendar, imposed upon the Aztecs during the Spanish conquest of Mexico. Ancient Aztec poems recorded before AD 1550 stress that death is a natural part of the cycle of life. (See Table 13.1.)

Over the two-day holiday, deceased family members are believed to return to their homes. Fireworks may be shot off or petals strewn on the ground from the graveyard to help guide the spirits of children. Families construct altars with yellow and orange marigolds (*flores de cempoalxóchitl*, also called *cempasuchiles*), on which they place photos, food, and drinks, along with personal items (such as cigarettes or cards) for individual family members. Through the burning of copal incense, the deceased are believed to be able to enjoy these sensory pleasures. Families in rural

Figure 13.5

Días de los Muertos Altar

On the holiday of *Días de los Muertos,* or Days of the Dead, Mexicans purchase sugar skulls for friends and family in a lighthearted remembrance of mortality. Often sugar skulls are placed on altars with other items dedicated to family members who have passed away.

Credit: Anabel de Krogstad

areas may also spend the entire night in the graveyard, decorating their family graves, listening to music and singing, and sharing a feast with their neighbors.

Ancestor veneration also reinforces the social values regarding family and kinship. In traditional Chinese society, the spirits of deceased ancestors remained among the living, residing in the family shrine. Family members would regularly clean the shrine and provide offerings to please the deceased. Just as children were expected to obey and provide for their parents during their lifetimes, they were obliged to do the same after death. In fact, a woman who joined her husband's family would not be considered a full member of her husband's lineage until she died. At that time her gravestone would be placed in the family shrine, where she would be venerated along with her husband's ancestors.

Spirits of Nature

Preindustrial peoples' lives are intimately connected to the natural world in which they live. Therefore, **spirits of nature** inhabit the world around them, in the earth, sky, and water. The physical environment, whether it be forest, desert, steppe, or tundra, is filled with supernatural beings and forces that can influence the lives of people there.

Because the spirits reside in the everyday environment, believers have a more equal relationship with them. In other words, in contrast to all-powerful beings, spirits of nature may be negotiated with and potentially won over. The goal of a Ju/'hoansi healer going into trance is to convince the god who has brought the patient's sickness on to relinquish his or her hold. This is experienced as conversation rather than prayer.

There are two main belief systems under the umbrella term *spirits of nature*. The first is **animism**, or a belief that spirit beings inhabit natural objects. Any aspect of a group's natural environment may be personified by spirit beings that are involved with human lives on a day-to-day basis. The Hawaiian goddess Pele is thought to physically embody the volcano Kīlauea, on the big island of Hawaii. When Kīlauea erupts, it is because Pele is angry. Small things can annoy her as well, such as when visitors remove rocks of her lava from the island. A curse is said to follow those thefts, until the stones are returned and she can be appeased.

The second type of spirit belief is **animatism**, or the belief that supernatural forces reside in everyday things. The forces are impersonal—not spirit beings, but powers—that have control over people's lives. Supernatural forces can reside anywhere in

Figure 13.6
Llama Fetus as Talisman
This dried llama fetus is used as a talisman for luck and prosperity. Shamans across Peru and Bolivia advise families to keep a llama fetus nearby when building or moving to a new home.
Credit: © Mike Kass/Images of Anthropology

the natural world, such as in the air, earth, or water. These forces may be helpful or harmful. Religious specialists may be able to harness this power for human purposes. For instance, an object such as an arrow may be imbued with power to ensure a successful hunt.

Special items that have concentrated power, such as charms to ward off evil, may be carried or worn for luck. The Turkish *nazar* is a talisman that depicts an eye of blue-and-white glass. It is carried to protect the bearer from the "evil eye," a supernatural force caused by envious stares that can result in sickness, whether intentionally or not. In many cultures, it is thought that the evil eye is cast when a barren woman feels envy of another's child. An infant wearing the nazar will be protected, as it captures and neutralizes the force.

Another animatistic force is the power of *n/um*, the Ju/'hoansi healing force. The Ju/'hoansi believe that all people possess n/um, but some cultivate the power to harness it in trance. As mentioned above, the goal of the healer is to reach the god responsible for the patient's illness and negotiate with him or her to give the person back. To achieve this, the healer will enter into a trance through the percussive claps and song of the group gathered to witness. Once the healer is deeply into trance, his or her n/um is thought to boil up and down the spine. At this point, the healer will lay hands on the sick person, and attempt to communicate with the god controlling the illness. If the healer is successful, the n/um will seize the illness and suck it up into the healer's spine, sending it flying out of the healer's mouth with a cry. Since trance sends the healer into an altered physiological state with a lowered heart rate, family members and other healers must aid the trancing healer until he or she regains full consciousness.

Religious Practitioners

Priests/Priestesses

Priests and **priestesses** are full-time religious practitioners. They are often found in societies that are based on hierarchical status, in which there is a major gap between those with power and those without it. Although they may be called to this profession, priests do not usually have direct access to the gods. The priest specializes in carrying out the required rituals of the religion. This may include conducting services, interpreting sacred texts, or carrying out particular duties for members of the religious community.

Figure 13.7
Body-Piercing Ritual among Tamil Hindu
This young Tamil Hindu man is participating in the Panguni Uthiram festival, in Tamil Nadu, India, in which he pierces his cheeks with a stake to show his devotion. On this ceremonial day, devotees pierce body parts and also carry offerings and images of the gods in chariots.
Credit: © Avena Matondang/ Images of Anthropology

Shamans

Shamans are part-time religious practitioners who specialize in communicating with spirits, ancestors, or deities. They are more likely to be found in societies in which social and political life is more egalitarian than hierarchical. People who are called to the practice of shamanism may experience visions or dreams, after which they are given the gift of healing. They may also survive long illnesses or near-death experiences. Because shamans are people who communicate with supernatural beings and forces, often any inexplicable personality traits signal that a person has one foot in this world and another in the world of the spirits. After a person with these gifts is identified, he or she will be trained by more experienced practitioners to become a full shaman.

Shamans make contact with the spirit world in several different ways. Some may use trance, like the Ju/'hoansi, to contact the gods who have planted illness in a person's body. Others use artistic means, such as the Navajo (*Diné*), who create sandpaintings that call the gods to aid in healing. Some may use hallucinogenic substances; the Yanomamö, for instance, snort *ebene* (crushed *Virola* tree bark) to provoke visions. Yanomamö shamans have the ability to communicate with spirits called *xapiripë* who manifest themselves as tiny lights. The xapiripë can heal sickness, help hunters find game animals, and protect community members. Their protection, as manipulated by shamans, is especially important now, given the encroachment of non-Yanomamö settlers and the destruction of the forest, as discussed in Box 13.2.

Because shamans have an influence on the outcome of events, we say that they are practitioners of magic. As such, shamans have a strong voice in determining the outcome of community issues. Even a member of the community who might be otherwise marginalized for odd behavior ends up with the power to speak for the spirits. With this power, a shaman can pass judgments on community members who have transgressed norms.

Religious Resistance

Belief systems, like all other aspects of culture, are subject to change and modification over time, whether by internal or external pressures. Conquest and colonialism generally impose a dominant society's religious belief system on the subordinate society. Communities often resist these imposed and enforced changes to the core values and symbols of their society. They may attempt to merge the two systems or resist by inventing a new tradition.

When the Spanish explorers led by Hernán Cortés conquered the Aztec forces of Cuauhtémoc and Motecuhzoma in Mexico City in 1521, they imposed the Catholic

Box 13.2

Disappearing Forest of the Yanomamö

Public awareness of the deforestation of the Amazonian rainforest began in North America in the 1980s, when the extent to which logging, mining, and development had changed the forest environment came to light. Decades later, rainforests all over the world are still losing the battle to both legal and illegal activity.

What effects come from deforestation? Loss of the forest removes animal and plant habitats, leading to extinction. The loss of biodiversity creates challenges for the organisms that remain, because it upsets the food cycle. Since medicine comes from plants, the loss of unknown plant life is detrimental to the development of medical advances. In addition, erosion kills the microorganisms that keep soil alive, leading to vast areas of infertile land. The loss of trees and resulting decomposition of leftover tree trunks emit approximately 1.5 tons of carbon into the air, contributing to 20 per cent of human-caused carbon emissions. All the emissions, plus the loss of the forest as a carbon sink, contribute directly to the buildup of greenhouse gases, the warming of the oceans, and the alarming effects of climate change (CSIRO Australia 2007).

As one might imagine, the loss of forest has been tragic for the Yanomamö and other Native peoples of Brazil and Venezuela. In 1973, the Brazilian government built a Trans-Amazonian Highway, opening up interior land to commercial exploitation and settlers. The influx of workers and settlers had a devastating impact on the health and lives of the Yanomamö. Nearly 20 per cent of the population died from new diseases, such as smallpox and malaria, to which they had no immunity. Hundreds of native people, including women and children, have been beaten and killed by *garimpeiros* (non-Yanomamö prospectors). By 1990, 70 per cent of Yanomamö land had been taken from native control for use in commercial activities, leaving them with only 30 per cent of their original land (Bier 2005).

According to Davi Kopenawa (2013), a Yanomamö shaman and spokesperson, shamans of the Amazonian rainforest recognize the terrible destruction of their ancestral lands. Nonetheless, they work harder than ever to extend their influence and protection to the entire rainforest and generously, to non-Yanomamö people. "The shamans do not only repel the dangerous things to protect the inhabitants of the forest. They also work to protect the white people who live under the same sky. This is why if [the shamans] die, the white people will remain alone and helpless on their ravaged land.... If they persist in devastating the forest, all the unknown and dangerous beings that inhabit and defend it will take revenge" (p. 404).

religion with one God on the Aztec people, who worshipped a pantheon of gods. One way for the Aztec people to hold on to some of their beliefs while outwardly assimilating to the new religious system was to merge them, in a synthesis anthropologists refer to as **syncretism**. Syncretic beliefs bring the old and new belief systems together in ways that make sense to people who are forced to undergo a complete revision of their worldview. Tonantzin, the Aztec mother goddess, was reimagined as the Catholic Virgin Mother. Huitzilopochtli, the god of war and sacrifice and the most revered Aztec god in the pantheon, merged into the idea of the Catholic God. When oppressed Aztecs went to worship, they could still retain their old symbols in a new form.

Whole societies forced to undergo major religious conversions as part of the colonization process might seek active ways to resist and change their fate. One of these ways is to create a **religious revitalization movement**, through which people can appeal to their old gods for help and deliverance. Revitalization movements generally begin with a charismatic leader who reports having visions or other communication with deities or spirits.

Anthropologist Anthony F.C. Wallace (1956) first described the five-step process through which a culture would attempt to actively revitalize its religious beliefs to save it from religious oppression. Prior to contact, a small society would be adapted to its traditional beliefs and practices. Then, the meeting of two cultural systems creates conflict, with sudden and oppressive changes resulting in people not being able to satisfy their needs. This may stem from a colonial situation. Then, major changes in the group's cultural and religious environment make it nearly impossible for their emotional or social needs to be met. This extreme situation leads to the birth of a revitalization process, in which a new cultural pattern is developed and communicated to help deal with these changes. Once the new cultural pattern becomes accepted, people become generally more satisfied with their lives. Even if their situation doesn't change completely, the new practices rekindle hope for the future.

One well-known revitalization movement is the **Ghost Dance**, which began with the Northern Paiute (Numa) and spread to Native American nations across the West and into the Great Plains. Many Native communities used circle dances for ritual and prayer. After American settlers encroaching on their lands interrupted their traditional lifeways, Native peoples sought answers and an end to their suffering. When a Paiute prophet named Wovoka preached that a type of five-day circle dance could lead them back to happiness and to reuniting with their ancestors in Heaven, the idea caught on and spread. Wovoka claimed that God had said all evil would be gone from the world, leaving them with peace and happiness, if all Natives would perform the dance.

Cargo cults are another form of revitalization movement in which acts are performed to hasten the return of happiness and material wealth. Beginning after European contact with islands in the Pacific in the 1800s, groups of Natives began to believe that the wealth ("cargo") enjoyed by the European invaders actually was destined for them. If they practiced the right supernatural rituals, then ships would come in, bringing all of the cargo they desired.

On Vanuatu, a Melanesian island, a specific cargo cult developed centering on a mythical American serviceman named John Frum (John "from" America) in the

1940s, after the American military had occupied the island. Practitioners believed that if they returned to their traditional customs and rejected Western ones, John Frum would bring their "cargo" and all non-Native people would leave the island. Rituals celebrating John Frum include flag raising, marching, and caring for a painted landing strip on which the cargo will fly in. John Frum Day is celebrated annually on February 15th and has become the ideological focal point of a modern-day political party.

Supernatural Beliefs and Cultural Expression

Although the practice of religion is a very personal experience, it is also embedded in wider cultural practices. Religious beliefs are expressed in symbols such as images and iconography, and in music, dance, rituals, and patterns of behavior. For this reason, religious beliefs and the arts are closely connected as expressive systems. That is, the inner experience of an individual may be expressed in external ways and shared in communal ones. Because values and beliefs are thoroughly embedded in cultural practices, religious expression appears in many areas of life, including the craft of healing.

Religion and Early Cave Art

There may be some very basic connections between religion and art in the evolution of modern human beings. First, they may have developed around the same time in human history, around 40,000 years ago. Second, both are understood to be signs of behavioral modernity; in other words, along with cooking and language, the existence of religion and art are signs that *Homo sapiens* had reached a modern stage of social and cultural development. Third, after 40,000 years ago, early humans appear to have made art for spiritual reasons, to attempt to manipulate or communicate with forces beyond their control. Visual representation may be the most fundamental way to try to connect with the supernatural realm.

Some of the earliest art can be seen in sites with cave paintings (**pictographs**) and engravings (**petroglyphs**) discussed in Chapter 5. There are many reasons why early humans might have painted and carved the walls of caves, including for rituals or ceremonies, to recreate the lives of the people who lived in the region, to document game animals, or for aesthetic reasons. Multiple sites have abstract paintings such as geometric designs, the meanings of which are difficult to decipher. The most common interpretation of cave art is that it has religious significance.

Some of this art on the walls of caves seems to provide evidence for the use of **magic**, or the use of powers to contact and control supernatural forces or beings.

Magic seeks to manipulate the outcome of events. For instance, in South Africa, a series of ancient caves show pictographs of geometric grids, zigzag lines, dots, and spirals. Based on ethnographic research among the San people who have inhabited that area for thousands of years, these shapes are similar to the patterns seen by a person who is deep in trance or who has ingested hallucinogenic drugs. Interestingly, the same shapes are also similar to the visions seen by sufferers of migraine headaches. These links connect this cave art to the universal physiological alterations of the human brain under those conditions (Lewis-Williams, 1998).

In the Northern Hemisphere, cave pictographs at Lascaux, in France, depict hundreds of large game animals, many superimposed upon each another. One interpretation of this layered painting was that the animals were painted on a sacred spot in the cave to practice magic. The location of the paintings might have been a particularly powerful spot, and so many paintings were placed there to harness the same power.

Interpretations of some representational animal art see the animals as painted before a hunt to ensure success. If true, this would be evidence of **imitative magic**, or creating something to represent real life, then manipulating it in a way that imitates the desired effect. In other words, "like produces like": painting an animal may signify the wish to encounter and kill it on the hunt. Another example of imitative magic would be a shaman creating an effigy that resembles an actual person, and then sticking it with a pin to cause pain in the person's body.

Religion and Body Art

People have manipulated their bodies for religious reasons for thousands of years. Physical devotion may involve painting one's body, shaving one's head, not cutting one's hair, pulling heavy items with hooks inserted in the skin of the back, fasting, or making pilgrimages entirely on one's knees. Humans have also been permanently marking the skin with tattoos to harness healing forces or protective powers for thousands of years. These sacred tattoos both refer to the symbols of a religious belief system and produce a magical outcome. In this way, they are similar to religious language and writing, which both speak of a belief system while invoking the power of the belief system (see Box 13.3).

In 1991, an ancient mummy was found thawing out of the ice in the Ötztal Alps, on the Austrian-Italian border. Called Ötzi the Ice Man due to the site of his death, he may have been attacked and murdered there 5,300 years ago. Subsequent analysis of his body has provided a wealth of information about his life, including the fact that he suffered from a host of ailments. At the points on his body where he would have experienced physical pain, Ötzi has over 50 tattoo marks at 12 different sites. The placement of the tattoos, mostly along his back, shows that they would have

Talking about Religious Speech

Religious traditions offer a linguistic origin of life itself as well as a divine origin of human language. For instance, the biblical story of Genesis relates the creation myth of both Judaism and Christianity: "God said, 'Let there be light,' and there was light" (Genesis 1:3). It is language that brings life to the heavens and earth. Then, on the sixth day of creation, God made Adam and Eve, and bestowed upon them the power of speech. In a later passage, the Tower of Babel incident causes God to split the single human language into many different languages. According to this tradition, divine events caused the origin and development of all human languages.

Religious speech comes in many forms and is used under many different circumstances. Of course, religious speech is connected with the five functions of faith-based belief systems that were explored at the beginning of this chapter. Much religious speech is ritualistic, such as the weekly prayer at an Islamic mosque. Some is spontaneous, such as a blessing or curse uttered in the course of everyday conversation. What seem to be most important are the context of the utterance and the intent of the speaker. As long as these two conditions are right, the actual content of religious speech often is not as important.

For individuals, communication with supernatural beings and forces takes a wide variety of forms. It may be done aloud, as in chanting or spell casting, or silently, as in meditation or prayer. Spirits may speak through an individual when called upon, in a practice called channeling, giving the medium the power to speak sacred words.

Individuals may also use words or sounds, known as mantras, to reach a state of unity with the divine. One of the most widely practiced is the Sanskrit mantra "Om mani padme hum." This mantra is chanted in the Mahayana Buddhist tradition in Tibet, as well as anywhere else this tradition has taken root. While the individual sounds have meaning, an important part of the chanting of a mantra is the resonance of the sacred sounds themselves.

had to be applied by another person, likely a healing specialist, attempting to ease the pain. This type of tattooing marks him as a person who may have had wealth or status, since he had access to the art of a healer.

Sacred tattoo designs are also placed on the body for magical protection and power. The Thai, Shan of Burma, and Khmer of Cambodia share the tradition of *sak yant*, or *yantra* tattooing. Buddhist monks or yantra specialists apply the designs on young men, who wear them for protection. These tattoos have a long history, beginning in the first century BCE with Khmer warriors, who tattooed their entire bodies so they could be invisible to harm. Today, members of street gangs and soldiers in the military also wear yantra tattoos as a type of charm to ward off misfortune.

Several cultures practiced facial tattooing for spiritual reasons that were also linked to social practices. Ainu women of northern Japan and Russia wore lip tattoos that were applied before marriage. In addition to the social function, lip tattoos also had religious meaning. They were thought to repel evil spirits that could enter the

Figure 13.8
Medicinal Leeches for Sale, Istanbul
Although one may find them "gross," leeches have successfully been used in medicine across the world and throughout time to improve blood flow to a part of the body as it heals, their saliva acting as a natural anesthetic. Leeches have again grown in popularity in the Western medical world as a natural cure, and some hospitals, such as Johns Hopkins and the University of Maryland, keep them on site.

Credit: © Barry D. Kass/Images of Anthropology

woman's body through the mouth. Bearing the lip tattoo also signified that a woman would have a place among her ancestors in the afterlife.

Religion and Healing

The area of health is a realm in which there are intimate connections between religion and art. A subset of anthropology, called **medical anthropology**, examines people's ideas about illness, healing, and the body, using a holistic view. Supernatural explanations may arise when unexplained circumstances, such as sickness or death, befall a group. Therefore, healing practices also often invoke supernatural beings or forces as part of the healing process. Specialists in **ethnomedicine** focus on socio-cultural understandings of these aspects. Because medical practitioners in non-Western societies will often use expressive methods as part of the healing process (such as song, dance, or visual displays), artistic practices are intimately tied to human communication with the supernatural realm.

Traditional understandings of medicine are woven into the cultural worldviews of societies, who use religious practices to diagnose and cure illness. For instance, Diné healers of the Four Corners area of the American Southwest create sandpaintings to heal ill members of their community. As they perform healing ceremonies, healers are seeking to restore harmony between the human and spirit worlds. In a Diné sandpainting ritual, the patient will sit on a painting created by healing specialists as songs and chants are sung. The patient's family is present and plays an important role providing support. Through the ritual process, the illness moves out of the patient's body and becomes absorbed into the painting. Now toxic, the painting must be destroyed within a day. This is art made for a particular purpose. Once it has done its duty, it is swept away, taking the illness with it.

Once an illness is diagnosed, there are many ways to address the cure. Modern Western medicine uses chemicals in the form of medications that have been identified as effective through scientific testing. Non-Western forms of medicine focus more on restoring the balance of the whole person than on treating symptoms individually. Today, many healers will call upon both types of medicine, knowing that certain cases call for particular remedies.

Ethnomedicine is the practice of medicine using local knowledge of plants and other foodstuffs. Nonspecialists practice it; that is, anyone can access the materials to heal. However, specialists may train to learn deeper knowledge and may

Table 13.2
Plants Used in Modern Pharmaceuticals

Common Name of Plant	Scientific Name of Plant	Pharmaceutical Using Plant Derivative	Healing Properties
Chili	Capsicum frutescens	Capsaicin	Pain relief
Foxglove	Digitalis lanata	Digoxin	Heart disease/Arrhythmia
Garlic	Allium sativum	Raw garlic/Garlic oil/ Aged garlic extract	Heart disease
Tea Tree	Melaleuca alternifolia	Tea tree oil	Antibacterial/Antifungal
Thyme	Thymus vulgaris	Thymol	Antibacterial/Anti-inflammatory
White Willow	Salix alba	Salicylic acid/Aspirin	Headache/Pain/Anti-inflammatory

be sought out by patients. In fact, over 2,500 plants were used as medicine by the Indigenous peoples of North America. Knowing that most modern medicines come from constituents found in plants, it makes sense that plants themselves would also be used to heal in traditional societies. Table 13.2 contains a brief list of plants that are used in traditional healing and that have also been incorporated into modern Western medicine.

Some of the medical practices still used to treat people all over the world today are thousands of years old. They may be based on ancient texts and ages of received wisdom and experience. Traditional medicine often goes beyond prescribing a treatment of symptoms, attempting to also understand and diagnose the entire person.

Traditional Chinese Medicine (TCM) uses natural materials such as herbs, plants, and animal parts to strengthen the body's natural defenses and to restore harmony when it is ill. Rather than focusing on individual organs, a practitioner will attempt to understand the body's systems (digestion, respiration, etc.) by looking at the patient in a holistic way. Once a blockage or disruption in the patient's **qi** (pronounced "chee"), or life force, has been determined, the practitioner will prescribe natural remedies to be taken in tea or medicinal decoctions.

Some of the systems that may be out of balance include the Four Natures, or the temperature balance of the body. Herbs classified as hot or warm may be taken to restore balance to a person who has become too "cold," and cold or cool herbs are used to correct problems of "heat" in the body. These descriptions don't pertain to actual temperature differences, but to the classification system only. Other treatments, such as breathing exercises, acupuncture, acupressure, **moxibustion**, or **cupping**, may be used to restore the flow of qi.

In addition, the Five Tastes are employed in different ways to modify certain functions in the body. A practitioner may use salty, sweet, sour, bitter, or acrid (pungent) flavors to address certain organs or specific functions. By correcting imbalances in these areas, TCM seeks to improve overall health.

The practice of Indian **Ayurveda** is similar to Traditional Chinese Medicine in that it is also based on restoring balance to the body systems. Ayurveda is based on a three-part balance of air/space ("wind"), fire/water ("bile"), and water/earth ("phlegm"). Practitioners will assess a patient with all of their senses to identify any imbalances.

As in TCM, substances have qualities that may be harnessed to provide more of something a patient lacks. For instance, natural materials such as herbs may be classified as hot/cold. However, they also may be soft/hard, dull/sharp, slimy/non-slimy, or many other qualities in opposition. Herbal, animal, and mineral medicinals are prescribed to restore a patient's balance, as are yoga postures, breathing, and even psychological work.

Summary

This chapter examined how belief systems guide people's behavior in society by providing a symbolic framework for aspects of cultural life. Mirroring the Learning Objectives stated in the chapter opening, the key points are:

- Evidence for early religious practices focuses on burials, especially those with grave goods.
- Supernatural beliefs help individuals and entire religious communities explain events and cope emotionally with things they can't control. In addition, beliefs function in various ways to guide people's behavior, create cohesion within the group, and maintain ecological practices that support their own success in a given environment.
- Different types of sacred beings and forces inhabit the worlds of different types of societies. For instance, hierarchical societies will often worship deities, societies with a strong moral code for the respect of elders will revere ancestors, and small-scale groups who rely on the natural world for resources will populate the natural environment with beings and forces.
- Priests, priestesses, and shamans intervene on behalf of the spirit world and relay messages to those inhabiting the world beyond.
- Throughout history, many traditional societies have been forced to adopt the religion of a society that has come to dominate their region. Rather than

surrender their deeply held beliefs, people develop revitalization movements, bringing hope that supernatural beings will help things return to the way they were.

- Because supernatural beliefs are central to social structure, they are found in many other forms of cultural expression, including art, body modification, and ethnomedicine.

REVIEW QUESTIONS

1. What does it mean to say that human culture is founded on symbolic systems?
2. How and why do anthropologists think the earliest religions developed?
3. What kinds of political systems tend to correlate with the veneration of deities, ancestors, and spirits in nature?
4. What are the functions of religious belief in society, both on an individual and social level?
5. What are some differences between the roles of priests and shamans?
6. How do religion and art overlap?

DISCUSSION QUESTIONS

1. Use the five functions of religion stated here to describe the functions of your own belief system. If you do not subscribe to a formal religion, then describe your system of morals and values.
2. What are some differences between scientific and spiritual systems of healing? What are some similarities?
3. Have you personally undergone a medical treatment that relied on traditional knowledge of ethnomedicine? How was the experience different from Western scientific medical treatments?

Visit **www.lensofanthropology.com** for the following additional resources:

| SELF-STUDY QUESTIONS | WEBLINKS | FURTHER READING |

PLACES MENTIONED IN CHAPTER 14

1 Neah Bay (Pacific Northwest Coast)
2 Paraguay
3 Isla Grande de Tierra del Fuego
4 Ivory Coast (Cote d'Ivoire)

5 Chiapas, México
6 South America
7 New Guinea
8 South Pacific Ocean

ANTHROPOLOGY AND SUSTAINABILITY

(((A stable and healthy environment is fundamental to meeting people's needs. Anthropologists can help. #anthropologyandsustainability

Learning Objectives

In this chapter, students will learn
- the connections between anthropology and sustainability.
- useful definitions of sustainability that resonate with the anthropological perspective.
- how anthropologists have approached the study of people and ecosystems throughout the history of the discipline of anthropology.
- some of the current frameworks in environmental anthropology, including the study of Traditional Ecological Knowledge (TEK) and ethnoecology.
- the importance for anthropologists of some of the major issues in sustainability studies.
- ways that anthropologists can help inform the discussion about a sustainable future.

Introduction

One of the key concerns of anthropology across the subfields is the way humans adapt to their environments. Biological anthropologists may examine foraging strategies among primates or the ways people have adapted to climate change. Archaeologists study the remains of people's lives situated within a particular ecological and regional context. Cultural anthropologists may focus on how people create and modify their beliefs and behaviors to adapt to particular environmental pressures. In sum, anthropology has been concerned with issues of **human ecology** since the discipline's inception, and can provide a long-term view of human adaptations. This chapter examines the intersections between the fields of **sustainability** and anthropology, and looks at how anthropologists can be instrumental in finding sustainability solutions.

Both anthropologists and sustainability researchers put people at the center of their research. That is, both fields focus on how people live: what works for them in terms of adaptive strategies and what doesn't work (both today and in the past). Both fields also recognize that for any issue, there are multiple ways to understand and engage with it. That is, both emic and etic perspectives are valid. With so many examples of human societies throughout time faced with similar challenges, anthropology provides a wealth of detailed knowledge from the inside of how these societies have solved their problems—or not.

In addition to human-environment interactions, anthropologists are interested in the connections between local and global processes. Cultural anthropology provides a close-up view of local processes through fieldwork, and then a larger analysis allows them to be situated in the global context. Archaeology discovers how global changes in climate led to the dispersal or demise of peoples. Biological anthropology highlights physiologic or demographic changes in human populations resulting from long-term environmental change. Therefore, the anthropological lens is uniquely suited to inform global projects that seek sustainability solutions.

It's important to clarify that anthropologists do not believe that traditional peoples lived in some sort of primitive state of organic balance with their environments. Sometimes this myth is invoked to provide an ideal model of a sustainable society. The argument goes that if modern people could return to the "simpler" and more "natural" ways of our ancestors, then the problem of sustainability would be solved. While we can certainly identify practices in traditional societies that conserve the environment, each cultural practice is bound up in a complex web of beliefs and behaviors that may be fundamentally different from our own. There is no "going back" to some simple ideal. We can only move forward.

History of Human-Environmental Issues

Anthropological research underscores the interconnectedness of life. Today, a web of complex relationships around the globe connects people and products. Corporate decisions made in an office in Paris or Beijing can set off a stream of events that involve people, environmental resources, and politics in Sri Lanka or Bolivia. The chain is largely invisible to the consumer, who knows little to nothing about where a product was made, by whom, and under what conditions. Modern marketing stresses every decision as a personal one, based only on identity and personal choice. For most consumers, owning an item that expresses something about who we are—or who we want to be—becomes the most important consideration, over cost or the process of production. If we, as consumers, knew about some of the less ethical links in the chain, we might make different decisions.

The way early humans perceived their place in nature was markedly different than it is today. As discussed in Chapters 6 and 10, before the development of agriculture, bands of people hunted and gathered, planted small horticultural plots, or practiced a pastoral lifestyle. These adaptations required intimate knowledge of the ecosystem within which they lived. Economies were, for the most part, local. To survive, it was crucial to know where to gather or hunt, when to plant and harvest, or when to take the animals to pasture. People's foodways placed them within the natural world, as part of it, albeit a part that learned to manipulate it for human needs. People may not have had "natural" instincts when it came to sustainability, but for most of human history they certainly perceived themselves in the world through a different lens.

With the rise of intensive cultivation approximately 9,000 years ago, human societies began to change their relationship to the land. Intensive agricultural techniques require more labor, technology, and inputs into the soil than small-scale horticulture. Although productivity increased, allowing societies to feed growing populations, large-scale cultivation changed the ecological balance. Large plots of land needed to be cleared for planting. Farmers domesticated animals for food and labor, requiring close contact with animal waste. The use of draft animals allowed deeper plowing, but also released into the air new pathogens that impacted human health.

Industry began to grow exponentially several hundred years ago. Nations' resources and wealth developed at a faster rate than ever before. For the first time, goods flowed around the globe from industrialized countries, especially from those in the Northern Hemisphere. These goods were often produced outside of these countries, in nonindustrialized nations. These developing nations provided natural resources and raw materials but saw little of the profit. The problems of social, economic, and political inequities stemming from this period lie at the root of many of the sustainability issues of our time. The exploitation of underdeveloped areas for the profit of corporations in developed nations creates great inequities.

After 1950, in a period economists call The Great Acceleration, demands for fuel, food, timber, water, and other natural resources exploded. This was primarily due to the growth of populations and human consumption. With this era began the highest level of deforestation and destruction of the world's ecosystems ever seen on the planet. Global resources seemed limitless, and little attention was paid to conservation.

Figure 14.1
Fishing on the Tonlé Sap, Cambodia
People who rely on the availability of natural resources, such as this Cambodian family who fish from a river of the Tonlé Sap, often suffer when those resources are diverted, polluted, or privatized.
Credit: © Lee Hunter/Images of Anthropology

Anthropologist David Maybury-Lewis (2006) argues that the real change around this time occurred within human societies and personal values. Society's priorities shifted from collective needs to individual needs. Maybury-Lewis argues that Western society especially glorifies the individual's rights and desires. It releases the individual from the complex bonds of family and kinship that rooted people in their communities for nearly all of human history. He sees evidence for this refocusing of social values in the changes that took place in child rearing (a move to independence training), social status (now conferred by power and money, not tolerance or compassion), and the structure of the modern nuclear family (free from the obligations of extended families).

All of these changes in society and culture have led to incredible advancements. Limitless creativity has released ambition, competition, and achievement as never before. Unfortunately, it has isolated individuals from not only other people but also the natural world. Modern industrial societies have developed a sense of ownership and entitlement over the land, air, and water. The shift in social and cultural values has led to our modern environmental crisis.

As an anthropologist who is also an advocate for the rights of traditional societies, Maybury-Lewis (2006) is deeply invested in these issues. He poses several questions: "What would it take for us to try to live in harmony with nature or to rehumanize our economic systems? How can we mediate between the individual and

Table 14.1
Human Impacts on the Biosphere

1. Evidence for global warming due to human production of CO_2 and other greenhouse gases is now unequivocal.

2. Between 5 and 20 per cent of the approximately 14 million plant and animals species on earth are threatened with extinction.

3. The Living Planet Report compiled by the World Wide Fund for Nature (WWF) reports that from 1970 to 2010, the average number of vertebrate species on earth has been reduced by 52 per cent. [In 40 years, the planet has lost more than half of its species of mammals, amphibians, reptiles, birds, and fish. Specifically, there has been a reduction in land and freshwater species by an average of 39 per cent, and marine species by an average of 76 per cent (WWF 2014).]

4. Overharvesting has devastated both ocean and inshore fisheries. The population of large predatory fish has been reduced by more than 90 per cent of preindustrial levels.

5. More than two million people globally die prematurely every year due to outdoor and indoor air pollution and respiratory disease.

6. Per capita availability of fresh water is declining globally, and contaminated water remains the single greatest environmental cause of human sickness and death.

7. We currently use up the resources of 1.5 earths. (This is possible because we use resources faster than they can regenerate. For example, trees are cut down faster than they can grow and carbon is released into the atmosphere and oceans faster than it can be absorbed.)

Source: Adams and Jenreneaud 2008; WWF 2014.

the family, between genders and generations? Should we strive for a less fragmented view of physical reality or of our place in the scheme of things?" (pp. 398–399). He makes the case that reconnecting in these ways will catalyze the shift in culture needed to embrace sustainable solutions.

The International Union for Conservation of Nature (IUCN) compiled a list of human impacts on the **biosphere**. This document examines the state of the world's natural resources today. Table 14.1 lists some of the most severe impacts humans have made on the planet.

Defining Sustainability

A general definition of *sustainability* is the ability to keep something in existence, to support or continue a practice indefinitely. Clearly, this is problematic when applied to the earth, as it doesn't have limitless resources. Our planet is an example of a **closed-loop system**, or a system that has finite resources and cannot sustain indefinite growth. Therefore, the most general definition of the term *sustainability* cannot be applied accurately to life on earth.

To address this dilemma, sustainability scholarship focuses on the well-being of people, now and in the future. The most commonly used definition is the one originally developed by the 1987 Brundtland Commission of the United Nations. The commission described sustainability as "meeting the needs of the present without compromising the ability of future generations to meet their own needs" (United Nations 1999).

There are echoes in this definition of a much-quoted passage on considering the impacts of our actions today on the next seven generations. Perhaps falsely attributed to Chief Seattle of the Duwamish and Suquamish Nations, the original context of this quote may reside in the Great Binding Law of the Iroquois Nation (Haudenosaunee):

In all of your deliberations in the Confederate Council, in your efforts at law making, in all your official acts, self-interest shall be cast into oblivion. Cast not over your shoulder behind you the warnings of the nephews and nieces should they chide you for any error or wrong you may do, but return to the way of the Great Law which is just and right. Look and listen for the welfare of the whole people and have always in view not only the present but also the coming generations, even those whose faces are yet beneath the surface of the ground—the unborn of the future Nation. (Murphy 2001, par. 28)

Modern Iroquois leaders continue to invoke this idea. Oren Lyons is a Faithkeeper of the Turtle Clan of the Seneca Nations, one of the five original nations of the Iroquois Confederacy. He is an activist, author, and leader who has won awards for his work on Indigenous rights and development. Lyons also talks of protecting resources for the next seven generations. He says, "We are looking ahead, as it is one of the first mandates given us as chiefs, to make sure every decision that we make relates to the welfare and well-being of the seventh generation to come." He asks today's world leaders, "What about the seventh generation? Where are you taking them? What will they have?" (Vecsey & Venables 1980:173–174). The idea of the "seventh generation" is a powerful reminder that people today are stewards of the future resources of the planet.

The United States Environmental Protection Agency (EPA) uses an environmentally focused description of sustainability, in that it takes into account all of the features of human society that depend on the environment. The EPA (n.d.) writes, "Sustainability is based on a simple principle: Everything that we need for our survival and well-being depends, either directly or indirectly, on our natural environment. Sustainability creates and maintains the conditions under which humans and nature can exist in productive harmony, that permit fulfilling the social, economic, and other requirements of present and future generations. Sustainability is important to making sure that we have and will continue to have, the water, materials, and resources to protect human health and our environment" (par. 1–2).

The approaches of both the Brundtland Commission and the EPA resonate with the anthropological perspective. Anthropology is a holistic science, which seeks to interpret the connections among all aspects of human life. We focus on whether and how people get their needs met—just as these definitions do.

Environmental resources are linked to food getting and work patterns, which affect social life, economic stability, family structures, and child rearing. People make meaning of these aspects of life through culture: symbolism, belief systems, myth, and artistic expression. Therefore, a stable and healthy environment is fundamental to meeting people's needs. Furthermore, it supports human "well-being" and "productive harmony," points that the EPA's definition highlights.

Components of Sustainable Development

Sustainable development is often described as having three components. These different components were named the **three pillars of sustainability** at the Rio Earth Summit in Brazil in 1992. As shown in Figure 14.2, the pillars are social, environmental, and economic. Ideally, each of these aspects of human life must be supported and in balance if we are to reach the goal of a sustainable world.

Environmental sustainability is the ability of the environment to renew resources and accommodate waste at the same rate at which resources are used and waste is generated. It implies that human practices should protect and preserve those aspects of the physical environment that sustain life. This includes not only our major life-giving ecosystems—such as the land and soil, atmosphere, freshwater resources and oceans—but also all natural resources, from the smallest biomes to the most complex living systems.

Social sustainability is the ability of social systems (such as families, communities, regions, or nations) to provide for the needs of their people so that they can attain a stable and healthy standard of living. Aspects of social sustainability include equity, justice, fair governance systems, human rights, quality of life, and diversity. A socially sustainable society would be one in which people can rely on a dependable infrastructure for health, order, education, and employment, while also feeling interconnected to others in social and cultural life.

Economic sustainability is the ability of the economy to support indefinite growth while ensuring a minimum quality

Figure 14.2
The Three Pillars of Sustainability
The three pillars of sustainability (social, environmental, and economic) are shown in this diagram as equal components of a healthy and stable system.

of life for all members of society. However, there is an inverse relationship between economic growth and environmental conservation. That is, economic development generally causes environmental degradation (but not always in the same region). Therefore, sustainable economic development would address overconsumption in the developed world and find ways to manage resource use and the environmental impacts of growing economies.

Where the three pillars overlap, certain goals need to be met in order to increase the likelihood of a sustainable outcome. For instance, as seen in Figure 14.2, where the environment interfaces with society, life should be "bearable." Where society interfaces with the economy, life should be "equitable." Finally, where economic and environmental issues overlap, life should be "viable."

While the three-pillar model provides a good place to begin a sustainability discussion, alternate models have also been proposed. One of these models shows the fundamental importance of the environment to provide for sustained life on earth, as discussed above. If the environment is depleted, social structures will collapse and there will be no economic output. Therefore, our first priority should be to protect the environment, as it is the foundation of social and economic life. Figure 14.3 represents an environment-centered approach.

How might the models of sustainability translate into practice on the ground for those interested in pursuing sustainability projects? Rather than sustainability science remaining in the universities, corporate accounting offices, and governmental policy offices, steps toward sustainability in the local context should be taken with the full participation of the people the work is aimed to help. This engaged approach to sustainability research is similar to that already used by applied and public anthropologists involved in participatory action research (PAR). In PAR projects, the community's needs and goals are identified through a process of participant observation and consultation. Then, external factors that impact the needs of the local community can be analyzed. Finally, the collaborative team identifies solutions. Since projects trying to solve local problems (clean water, effective farming techniques, higher harvest yields) often require funding from outside agencies, the reports emerging from such studies also need to meet the requirements of those organizations supporting development.

Tragedy of the Commons

In the mid-twentieth century, ecologist Garrett Hardin (1968) illustrated the nature of the sustainability problem with a scenario. He called it the **tragedy of the commons**. *The commons* may refer to any publicly shared resource, such as water, land, or air. In Hardin's

Figure 14.3
Concentric Model of Sustainability
The concentric model of sustainability uses the three-pillar approach in a way that responds more accurately to the realities of life on earth. This model emphasizes the importance of the environment, for without a productive and healthy environment, the social and economic realms of life would not be able to function.

Through the Lens of Anthropology: An Introduction to Human Evolution and Culture

original analogy, it refers to an open pasture shared by herdsmen and their cattle. The inevitability of the tragedy comes from overpopulation.

At first, there is enough space in the commons for all the cattle, and enough pasture for all to graze freely. However, each herdsman wishes to grow his herd by adding another head of cattle. The benefits to him personally are obvious, since he will have a larger herd. The cost, on the other hand, is that there will be less pasture for all animals to share. He chooses the former, because the benefits of adding cattle are his alone. On the other hand, the costs of losing a little pasture due to the addition of one more animal are distributed among herders. Clearly, to this individual herdsman, the benefits outweigh the costs. Unfortunately, each herdsman has the same private goal: to maximize his herd and his profit. Eventually, with this mindset, the tragedy occurs: the pasture becomes overgrazed, and there are no resources left for anyone.

The analogy can be applied to human use of natural resources. If each person acts in his or her own best interest, then the depletion of resources follows. Hardin argues that people will naturally act selfishly when they weigh the pros and cons of the situation.

How do policy makers try to avoid what they see as an imminent tragedy? Hardin argues that a degree of financial coercion is necessary, especially through charging more money to individuals for the resources used and pleasures enjoyed. Governmental agencies take this approach, seeing "tragedy" as the inevitable result of collective resource use. Therefore, resource **privatization** by corporations and government regulation are seen as the only ways to prevent total ecological destruction. Unfortunately, conservation does not always result from these policies.

Under certain circumstances, the problem of the commons may actually be self-regulating. Anthropologists cite many examples of groups of people that regulate their own joint use. Individual users of an area may voluntarily cooperate to constrain or conserve the use of resources.

For instance, among rural South Indian farming villages, anthropologist Robert Wade (1988) found that farmers cooperated when they had the power to affect outcomes. With an understanding of how their actions affected overall success, farmers cooperated to share irrigation to the benefit of all. Part of their success was a strict set of social guidelines governing behavior that prevented any individual farmer from "free riding" to the detriment of another.

In another example, the Makah people of the Pacific Northwest Coast made the decision to protect the gray whale, their most cherished resource, even when it meant they would suffer in other ways. Traditionally, Makah people hunted whale—as part of their varied seafood diet—by canoe and harpoon. In addition, the whale is an essential part of their religious mythology and cultural traditions. Whaling was so

The Guaraní and Commercial Agroforestry

The Guaraní are an Indigenous group who live in the subtropical rainforests of Paraguay and Brazil. They hunt, fish, gather, and garden, relying on mixed methods of food strategies. The Guaraní support the long-term health of the forest by using **agroforestry** techniques that mimic the diversity of the natural environment. For instance, trees are used to provide cover for shade crops below, which may be planted among the wild plants that already exist. As opposed to clear-cutting and the planting of single crops, this technique preserves the **biodiversity** of the area and retains micronutrients in the soil.

The Guaraní are not new to external influences. In the sixteenth century, the arrival of Europeans marked the beginning of their long-term relationship with outsiders. At the time, the European settlers wanted forest goods and provided items such as soap and machetes in exchange. Unlike other Native groups, however, the Guaraní were able to continue mixed-use strategies in the forest and maintain their cultural identity, while engaging with non-Native peoples.

Today, outsiders to the forest demand more resources and more land than ever before. This has made it difficult for the Guaraní to retain their traditional strategies, especially because they have been relocated onto much smaller protected reserves of land. Rather than work for developers or move from the forest into the city, Guaraní people have kept their lifestyle culturally and economically viable through commercial practices that support the long-term health of the forest.

Anthropologist Richard Reed (2009) found the Guaraní are able to harvest a variety of goods throughout the forest ecosystem and sell them in the larger marketplace without overexploiting any one area. In particular, when harvesting yerba leaves for the international *mate* (tea) market, harvesters are careful to cut only young leaves annually, and more mature stems every three years. This helps ensure the survival of the plant. When the yerba harvest is over for the season, the Guaraní may shift to hunting animals for their skins or producing citrus essential oils. Relying on multiple goods, methods, seasons, and microzones of the forest ensures that the effects of participating in the market economy are distributed. It also ensures that the forest is well managed and remains viable into the future.

International purchasing partners, such as retail body care companies, may then market these products as authentically supporting rainforest conservation. This creates a positive solution for producers, distributors, and consumers. Reed argues that this type of commercial agroforestry model can and should be adapted for others who inhabit or wish to develop the forest.

important that in 1855, the tribe gave up 90 per cent of their ancestral land for the ability to continue hunting whale. However, gray whale numbers got dangerously low in the first half of the twentieth century, earning the gray whale a place on the Endangered Species List in 1970 (United States Endangered Species Act). Rather than continuing to reap the benefits of their treaty, the Makah decided voluntarily to stop whaling. In this case, the group acted to protect the natural resource instead of in their own self-interest. The numbers of gray whales grew while they were protected, and in 1994 the species was removed from the Endangered Species List. The treaty had reserved the Makah's right to hunt whale in Neah Bay. Therefore, the entire Makah community planned, trained, and were successful in harvesting one whale by canoe in 1999, revitalizing their cultural and spiritual connections to whaling for the first time in 70 years.

Hardin's (1968) original model does not take into account the potential for an internalized code of conduct that prevents individuals from acting selfishly. Clearly, cultural norms and values influence the outcome. Therefore, to assume that the tragedy of the commons is inevitable may itself be a tragedy if one summarily imposes the model upon an area without taking into account the particular cultural context.

Anthropological Approaches to Sustainability Studies

Since the early twentieth century, anthropologists have sought to understand the relationship between people and their environments. This relationship is referred to as ecological because it stresses this fundamental connection. Several different frameworks or models have been used, each building on—and reacting to—the ideas that came before. The following section introduces some of the major theories and how they seek to understand the human-environment relationship.

Cultural Ecology

Julian Steward (1955/2006) is largely considered the first anthropologist to develop a **paradigm** based on the interactions of people in their particular environments. His ideas came out of a major debate in anthropology on how much of a people's culture developed in direct response to environmental pressures. This idea was known as determinism, and asserted that the limitations of the environment determined people's behavior.

Steward was the primary proponent of the theory of **cultural ecology**, which began in the 1940s. During periods of fieldwork among the Shoshone (*Newe*) of the Nevada Great Basin area, he saw how the specific environmental pressures of the Great Basin ecosystem limited the possibilities of food procurement. In particular, the Shoshones' traditional plant-based foraging diet had been drastically reduced by settlers' introduction of herds of sheep and cattle.

Steward believed that food-getting practices directly affected social and economic life, creating a central set of behaviors that he called the **culture core**. To identify features of the culture core, an ethnographer would need to examine the technology used in food procurement, the patterns of social life directly linked to those practices, and then, finally, how other aspects of life were influenced by social patterns.

For instance, the Shoshone hunted and gathered as their foraging strategy. Both hunting and foraging takes place in groups, divided into men's and women's work.

The sexual division of labor would influence political life, in that control of the protein resources gives certain individuals more power than others. Simply put, Steward argued that the production of food was central to the organization of Shoshone society.

This model also argues that societies using similar technologies would form similar social patterns. He cites the Bushmen (foragers of the Kalahari Desert in Southern Africa) and Fuegians (Native peoples of Tierra del Fuego, at the tip of South America) as examples of two societies organized into similar patrilocal bands. Their environments are different, but in this case, the behavior of the game they hunt is similar (nonmigratory, nonherding), and the tools they use, such as spears, are also similar. This causes the groups to organize themselves patrilocally because it is most efficient for this type of hunting.

At the time, the cultural ecology model established itself as a model of multilinear cultural evolution in opposition to the predominant model of universal (linear) evolution. As noted in Chapter 1, the theory of universal evolution argued that all cultures went through the same steps as they modernized. This implied a hierarchy of development from simple to complex. Steward rejected that notion. He focused instead on the particulars of each culture: their environmental limitations and resources, their patterns of behavior pertaining to subsistence, and any area of social life influenced by these patterns.

Ecological Anthropology

Steward's cultural ecology model eventually transformed into a field called **ecological anthropology**. This framework is similar to a cultural ecology model, in that culture and social organization are the outcomes of a group's adaptation to the particular challenges of their environment. While cultural ecology focuses on culture as the unit of analysis, ecological anthropologists define the population as the unit of study. Within ecological anthropology, a framework called systems theory is used to measure the inputs and outputs of the system.

SYSTEMS THEORY

The **systems theory** model examines a particular geographic area inhabited by people as a closed-loop system. It understands the population to be in a state of equilibrium within its environment of finite resources. Research focuses on the flow of energy and matter, as well as information, in an attempt to quantify how the system functions. This framework borrows ideas from biological studies of natural ecosystems.

Anthropologist Roy Rappaport (1968), who studied the Tsembaga Maring of Papua New Guinea in the mid-twentieth century, used a systems theory approach.

He studied how the Maring functioned within their ecosystem, in which everything was connected: plants, animals, and humans. Rappaport saw how the products of human culture created measurable effects in the flow of material goods through the ecosystem. For example, the ceremonial sacrifice of pigs created the sudden availability of tons of pork to be consumed. He noted that the timing of pig-slaughtering rituals was linked to a regular cycle of war, when injured warriors would require extra animal protein for strength.

Political Ecology

For researchers looking to understand the relationship between ecology and power, a related framework called **political ecology** developed. Using this model, anthropologists and other scholars focus on the complex relationships between the environment, economics, and politics. These studies focus especially on the developing world, where people who are marginalized tend to lack access to or control of resources.

Issues studied by political ecologists include ecological justice, such as deforestation of an inhabited area of the rainforest; human rights, such as the right to clean drinking water; and cultural identity, such as the right to pursue traditional modes of hunting. There are also many forms of resistance that Indigenous or minority groups mount in the face of decisions that may be detrimental to their health and well-being. Therefore, political ecologists also focus on environmental activism in the many forms it takes around the world.

Environmental Anthropology

Today, hundreds of practicing and teaching anthropologists interested in these issues belong to the Anthropology and Environment Society, a section of the American Anthropological Association. Within this section, one might find members who identify themselves as ecological anthropologists, political ecologists, or human geographers. Many, however, use the term **environmental anthropologist**, to represent their broad interests. There are several frameworks that environmental anthropologists may use to inform their research, including Traditional Ecological Knowledge and ethnoecology.

TRADITIONAL ECOLOGICAL KNOWLEDGE (TEK)

While it is important to avoid stereotyping the "simple" lives of Indigenous peoples, there is much to be learned from the knowledge and practices that a group has developed and handed down over generations. The study of **Traditional Ecological Knowledge (TEK)** seeks to understand the collective and cumulative knowledge that a group of people has gained through living in their particular ecosystem. (TEK may also be called Indigenous knowledge or local knowledge, especially outside of Canada.) In **natural resource management** studies, TEK is used much as the scientific principles of ecology and biology are, with the understanding that there are multiple sources of knowledge regarding a given issue.

Studies that use local knowledge to inform their research seek to understand the broad and deep knowledge local groups have of the interrelationships among people, plants, animals, and nature. In particular, projects might focus on traditional methods of food procurement, such as hunting, gathering, trapping, fishing, and farming. It might also examine ways in which people manage their local ecosystem, such as through forestry, water use, and soil management. When applied to policymaking, these understandings may be used as tools in not only short-term resource management but also plans for the long-term sustainability of a given area.

However, TEK has the potential to be misused by external agencies. For instance, there have been many examples since the 1990s of governmental agencies using TEK data as simply another piece of externally calculated scientific data. This removes the local knowledge from its deeply complex cultural context. Attempting to apply a cultural "fact" as a discrete piece of data is similar to removing an artifact from an archaeological site and trying to make some sense of it in the absence of contextual clues. Furthermore, if First Nations peoples do not have control over how this information is embedded into new contexts, such as in external reports used to develop policy, then it ceases to be of use to them. It may even be detrimental to their voice being included in future land management debates.

The fundamental conflict between Indigenous and scientific understandings of the natural world is exemplified by Inuit understandings of glaciers in the Mount Saint Elias ranges, as described in Julie Cruikshank's book *Do Glaciers Listen?* (2005). She describes the scientific concepts of nature as something separate from the social world of people and culture; in other words, glaciers are areas of pristine wilderness that can be studied and measured. For the local Inuit residents, on the other hand, the glacier is a social being, enmeshed in their community histories. In the Inuit view, glaciers can be pleased or angered, with results for the local community. Therefore, when scientific researchers include TEK in their studies, they have no way to represent the full and complex relationships and knowledge that local residents have of their environment.

This data may be taken further out of context and used as a marketing tool. Many popular "miracle foods" today are publicized as providing health or other specific benefits to Indigenous peoples, with the assumption that urban consumers can also derive these same benefits by incorporating these foods into their diets. Some examples include açai berry (a "superfood" from the Americas), noni fruit (a "wonder drug" from Polynesia), and quinoa (the "ancient Inkan Grain"). There is

much more to know about how these foods are produced and consumed, and the cultural context that surrounds them. Benefits may be exaggerated to the unaware consumer. In fact, the high demand for these trendy foods may impact Native ecosystems in negative ways. Thus, while urban consumers are attempting to derive benefits from Native foods, they may at the same time be disrupting Native environments and economies.

ETHNOECOLOGY

Researchers who identify themselves as **ethnoecologists** tend to emphasize traditional peoples' knowledge of flora and fauna. Like other environmental anthropologists, they look at the interactions a group of people has with its natural environment. In particular, ethnoecology tends to focus on Native concepts of plants and their uses for food, medicine, or ritual.

Understanding the unique ways in which a group classifies its environment can provide anthropologists with a key to understanding their **worldview**. For instance, in early ethnoecological studies, anthropologist Harry Conklin (1986) discovered that the Hanunóo people of Mindoro Island, Philippines, use a fundamentally different color classification scheme than ours, based on their forest environment. In the forest, light/dark and fresh/dry characteristics play an important part in perception. Therefore, the Hanunóo use four major categories of color: "darkness" (dark colors including black, deep blues, greens, and purples); "lightness" (light colors including white and other pale hues); "redness" (colors of dry plant life such as reds, oranges, and yellows); and "greenness" (colors of fresh plant life such as light greens and browns).

Of course, Hanunóo people can see all of the variations in the color spectrum that any other person sees, and express them as well, using modifications to the basic color scheme. The four-category division simply reflects how they interpret the colors in a way that is relevant to their lives. Ethnoecologists use this kind of data to understand the way that people understand their role in the world around them.

Figure 14.4
Glacier Bay
To the Inuit, glaciers are sentient and social beings that play a role in community life. Researchers who use discrete bits of data and represent them as traditional knowledge lack the full cultural context. Some of the cultural context may be crucial to conservation.
Credit: Luis A. Gonzalez

Issues in Sustainability Studies

Population Growth

Underscoring the urgency of the sustainability discussion is the rate at which the world's population is growing. For most of human history, the world's population remained more or less steady, with slow growth resulting from the beginnings of agriculture. With the effects of the Industrial Revolution in the eighteenth and nineteenth centuries, the world's population began to leap forward in exponential growth. There were many factors at work here, and the results were lower mortality rates and higher life expectancies. After that time, the world's population began to explode from 1.6 billion in 1900 to 7 billion in 2012. The US Census Bureau (2013) projects we will reach 9 billion by about 2050.

As you look at Table 14.2, note the years between milestones of one billion more people on earth. Each increment of one billion more people on earth has come at a faster rate. The population growth rate is currently holding steady at about one billion more people on earth every 12 to 16 years.

The direct relevance of population growth for sustainability is that it results in environmental depletion. This is especially true when increased population leads to higher consumption and economic growth. In other words, the more populations expand and economic growth increases, the more natural and nonrenewable resources need to be exploited. This effect, on a global scale, has the worst impacts on people in societies producing the goods to support growth.

In particular, the growth of economies in the developed world has the most severe effect on environmental resources in the developing world. This is because most natural resources for energy and products are sought outside developed countries. For example, to produce smartphones and other digital products, minerals must be extracted from mines. In the Democratic Republic of the Congo (DRC), armed terror groups largely control the extraction. The groups, run by local warlords, are known for the stripping of land and control of natural resources. Because much of

Table 14.2
World Population Growth

Population (billions)	1	2	3	4	5	6	7	8	9
Year	1804	1927	1959	1974	1987	1999	2012	2026	2042
Years between milestones	–	123	32	15	13	12	13	14	16

Source: http://www.census.gov/popclock/

Through the Lens of Anthropology: An Introduction to Human Evolution and Culture

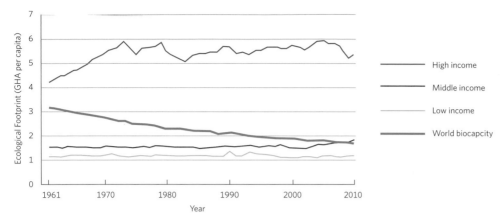

Figure 14.5
The Inverse Relationship between Economic Growth and Environmental Degradation
This figure shows the ecological footprint (in global hectares) per capita from 1961 to 2010 comparing high-, middle-, and low-income nations. The green line shows the declining world's resources, called world biocapacity.
Source: WWF Living Planet Report Summary 2014 (wwf_lpr2014_sum.pdf)

their enterprise is illegal, the environmental destruction is accompanied by other social, political, and economic problems, such as arms trafficking and sexual violence against women.

Figure 14.5 shows the vast difference between the **ecological footprint** of high-income and low-income countries. While the economy has grown over the past 50 years in high-income countries, such as the United States and Canada, the economy has remained relatively steady in the countries with the lowest income. Notice the decreasing ability of the earth's resources to support life (identified as **world biocapacity**), represented by the green line. It is clear that high-income countries have a greater impact on the decreasing ability of the earth to provide the resources to support life.

Globalization of Food

Industrial food production, distribution, and consumption are enmeshed in global processes. These interconnected systems and processes are referred to as **globalization**. In the modern global economy, people in places all over the world are linked in a complex, yet largely invisible, chain of producers and consumers.

Globalization is the integration of economic, social, political, and geographic boundaries and processes. Global studies scholar Manfred Steger (2003) defines it as "a multidimensional set of social processes that create, multiply, stretch and intensify worldwide social interdependencies and exchanges while at the same time fostering in people a growing awareness of deepening connections between the local and the distant" (p. 34) Because inequalities exist structurally, generally the poorest people suffer the most inequity as a result of globalization. This is seen clearly in our food system.

There are three major transformations that have affected food access since the industrialization and globalization of the food system (Pelto & Pelto 2013).

1. Food production and distribution are embedded in an increasingly intertwined and rapidly growing network of global interdependency.

Figure 14.6

Street Scene: Alexandria, Egypt, with Marlboro Billboard

The processes of globalization result in the marketing and sales of products from the Western world to countries all over the globe, including those who may not share our cultural values. This process is also called Westernization.

Credit: © Barry D. Kass/Images of Anthropology

2. In developed nations, this leads to better nutrition due to a wider availability of diverse foods.

3. In underdeveloped nations, the elite benefit while the majority of people who were dependent on local production and methods suffer economically and nutritionally.

Due to interdependent food networks, urban dwellers in modern industrial society have access to a smorgasbord of world cuisines and international foodstuffs. People who love new tastes and textures and have the resources to afford them can enjoy exotic meals and unique products. Consumers can purchase foods when they're not in season from a global buffet of nearly unlimited choice. Nutritious and ripe produce is available even in the middle of winter, something our ancestors couldn't have imagined. Eating a wide range of healthy products supports the health of those who can access those foods.

On the other hand, the globalization of the market creates a set of issues for food production and distribution that should be examined critically. Developing nations engaged in the production of raw materials for food often lack the same protections as the countries in which demand originates. With fewer environmental protections, the soil and waterways of producing nations may be polluted by pesticide runoff or other waste products. With fewer labor protections, laborers may work under conditions that are maladaptive: unhealthy, illegal, or potentially dangerous. The farming of cacao beans for the chocolate industry as described in Box 14.2 provides an example.

Box 14.2
Chocolate Production

Serious costs are borne by laborers in industries with little regulation or oversight, such as the chocolate industry. Seventy-five per cent of all chocolate the world eats begins as raw cacao in West Africa. The West African cacao industry relies on half a million underage workers to produce the cacao bean. In Ivory Coast alone, 200,000 children, many of them trafficked from other countries, work under conditions that UNICEF refers to as "slave labor" (UNICEF 2007). According to a study done by Tulane University in 2009, up to 70 per cent of the workforce in Ivory Coast consists of children under 14 years old. Only 2 to 6 per cent of those children report being paid for their labor. Many of them are forced to work up to 100 hours a week, suffer physical abuse, and never return home to their parents. Ironically, most cacao farmers have never seen or tasted chocolate in the finished product.

Anthropologist Amanda Berlan (2008) did her fieldwork among Ghanaian cacao famers. In contrast to the Tulane study groups above, her informants are participants in the **Fair Trade** system. Farming for companies committed to the Fair Trade model ensures a fair price for the product, supports ethical business and environmental practices, and provides financial support to farmers. In her field setting, she did not uncover child labor and a collapsing social structure. Berlan found that these cacao farmers were active participants in decision making regarding their farming practices and compensation.

This is in stark contrast to the Fair Trade marketing narratives that use images of starving African children to sell chocolate products. Such moral marketing uses guilt to attract customers, and then frees them through the purchase of the product. Berlan argues that the images of helpless African farmers don't reflect the reality of the Ghanaian farmers among whom she did her fieldwork. These two contrasting examples underscore the importance of examining each issue in its local context, something that is fundamental to the process of doing anthropology.

Companies seeking to provide an ethically sound product may seek out anthropologists to help them develop it. An example of this is Askinoisie Chocolate, an artisan chocolate company, seeking the assistance of anthropologist Jeanine Gasco. Gasco has run an ethnoecology field school through CSU Dominguez Hills since 2000 in the Soconusco region of Chiapas, a center of cacao farming (Harmon 2010). Working as a collaborative team, Gasco, Soconusco cacao farmers, and the founders of Askinoisie Chocolate developed strategies to produce higher-quality cacao. The result of the collaboration was Askinoisie's purchase of six tons of cacao in 2007 to produce single-origin Soconusco chocolate bars. This example illustrates the benefits for companies of having an anthropologist on the team when seeking to work directly with food producers.

FOOD PRODUCTION IN DEVELOPED NATIONS

Even within industrial nations, food production isn't transparent. With all the information available today in the Age of Information, not all developed countries require that information about the origins of food be provided. For instance, in North America, meat, grains, and produce, along with hundreds of processed foods, appear in the grocery store. The everyday consumer has little or no idea where the food items on the shelves of the local grocery store originate, how ingredients were grown, raised, or synthesized in a lab, or what chemical additives do in the product.

Demand for certain food items in modernized nations creates pressure on industries to produce more and faster. In the United States, conventionally raised chickens are fed arsenic to speed up the growth process. Because arsenic is a human poison, independent studies raise health concerns for consumers. Since the process of raising **conventional** chicken (and other meat) for consumption is not public knowledge, a consumer would not be aware of these potential health risks unless he or she was specifically looking for them. In fact, in some American states, it is illegal to photograph or record meat-processing operations; consumers are officially cut off.

However, consumers in industrial societies today do have access to information about environmental damage and health risks resulting from the industrial food system, especially through the Internet. Those with the means can seek information and opt to make more deliberate choices about food sources. This has led to an interest in buying **organic** foods from farms that promote ecological balance and biodiversity. Certified organic foods in the US and Canada must be free of chemical pesticides or fertilizers and not **genetically modified**.

In addition to purchasing organic foods, a growing percentage of consumers are choosing to buy their food from local sources. These consumers are seeking to narrow the gap between "farm" and "fork." They wish to reconnect to the regional food system by purchasing directly from local farmers operating small-scale, sustainable farms. Direct marketing of food has grown in popularity in recent years with the proliferation of farmer's markets and **Community Supported Agriculture (CSA)** programs.

Members of a CSA purchase a share of the farm in advance for which they receive a box of freshly picked produce weekly. Some transparency returns to the food production process when consumers know their farmers, and they find satisfaction in knowing they are supporting the local economy and that their food is grown without the costs of long-distance distribution. They enjoy being able to ask questions about the production process and visiting the farms where their food is grown.

CSA programs also exist for sustainably raised beef, pork, and other meats, as well as eggs and fish. Applied anthropologist Susan Andreatta worked with a team of community specialists, fishermen, and local businesses in Carteret County, North Carolina, to develop a CSF (Community Supported Fishery). In a model similar to the CSA one, customers pay in advance for a regular supply of fresh, locally caught fish. Andreatta found that a demand existed for local seafood, and when North Carolina seafood was marketed as the "Carteret Catch," consumers were much more likely to purchase it than imported fish. In addition, her research in the community showed more than 80 per cent of restaurant-goers were willing to pay a premium for local seafood. The identification, branding, and direct marketing of local seafood resulted in consumer satisfaction as well as a boost to the local economy (Nash & Andreatta 2011).

FOOD INEQUALITY IN DEVELOPED NATIONS

Not everyone is able to purchase organic and local foods. It's true that eating season-ally, when a surplus of produce is harvested, brings down the cost of food items. But certainly organic meat, eggs, processed foods, and out-of-season produce are more expensive in stores than similar conventional products. This creates a divide between rich and poor, with only the wealthy having access to the healthier choices. Some scholars, pointing to the structural inequalities of the system, refer to this as food oppression.

In addition to cost, geographic accessibility further marginalizes people in low-income neighborhoods. Many inner-city areas do not have a farmer's market, or even a local grocery store. These areas are called **food deserts** because they lack food options to which other communities have access. Inner-city communities rely instead on more conveniently located fast-food restaurants and small retail stores that stock processed foods. Unfortunately, this also limits residents' access to healthier foods such as fresh produce. To help close the **grocery gap**, cities across the United States (such as Berkeley, California; Elmsford, New York; and Concord, Massachusetts) have created zoning restrictions to curb further development of fast-food and "drive-thru" eateries, and convenience stores.

Community garden membership is another way to increase access to healthy food for people in low-income areas. Community gardens in urban areas allow local people to utilize plots of land (often garden beds) in areas where residents may live in apartments or condos without space to start a garden. Community gardens are one way that immigrant families can plant crops from their home countries that they might not find in local supermarkets. Research shows that working in commu-nal gardens—be it in prisons, residence homes for the elderly, domestic violence shelters, or schools—helps people connect to the land and to their food in ways that decreases stress and behavioral issues. It also raises their awareness about how food is grown and leads them to choose healthier options.

How Can Anthropologists Help?

More than any other academic discipline, anthropology uses a long-range, holis-tic perspective that connects the dots between local and global systems. Therefore, anthropologists are uniquely suited to engage with sustainability issues on multiple levels. In particular, these include using the methods and theories of anthropol-ogy, disseminating information, and, for those who teach, engaging students and campuses.

Box 14.3

Talking about the Connection between Language Diversity and Biodiversity

This century, we will likely see plant and animal extinctions at a greater rate than ever before. Compared to extinction levels before humans inhabited the planet, the rates of species extinction from a range of environments are 100 to 1,000 times faster. As noted in Chapter 9, human languages are also going extinct at a faster rate than ever. Of the approximately 6,900 languages spoken in the world today, linguists estimate up to 90 per cent will have died out with no remaining speakers by the end of the century.

The high extinction rates are not the only point that can be compared, however. When researchers measure language diversity and species diversity, they find that these tend to correspond to the same geographic areas. In other words, in the areas of the world that have been identified as biodiversity **hotspots** and high biodiversity wilderness areas, there is a high correlation to the diversity of languages. In fact, 70 per cent of all languages spoken on earth are found within these high biodiversity zones, including Melanesia, Central and South America, West Africa, and New Guinea. Over 2,000 of these languages are native to these regions (Gorenflo, Romaine, Mittermeier, & Walker-Painemilla 2012).

Why should there be a correlation between biological and linguistic diversity? Reasons appear to vary based on the area. However, several arguments appear to have some validity. The first possible reason is ecological: that greatly diverse and plentiful areas contain a large number of cultural and linguistic groups within them who do not need to compete for the same resources, and thus have a high degree of social distance. Another reason is based on the historical context: when Europeans expanded to all corners of the globe, they tended to settle in temperate climates. Therefore, the tropical areas remained less affected. Certain ecosystems have their own stories. For instance, the island of Madagascar hosts a great number of native species in a highly diverse environment due to millions of years of evolution separate from the mainland of the African continent. On the other hand, humans settled there only roughly 2,000 years ago, bringing with them a single language. In terms of linguistic evolution, there has not been much time to diversify.

Identifying these zones of high linguistic and biodiversity can be important in developing plans to preserve them. The study above concludes that an important link is the Indigenous management practices of their ecosystem, which acts to preserve these areas and species. That is, areas, such as in the Brazilian rainforest, that have many Indigenous populations have the highest rates of diverse native species. Unfortunately, there are few speakers left of most of these languages, which is why it is so important to employ anthropologists in the conservation process.

First, the basis of anthropological practice and theory is to learn about people. Anthropologists spend years among people in developing nations—people who are largely invisible to consumers in the developed world. Experience in the field, alongside people who suffer the inequities of global systems, provides an intimate understanding of their struggles. With both local and global knowledge, anthropologists can help provide the kinds of solutions that researchers in other fields may not be able to offer.

Anthropologist John Bodley (2008) makes the case that anthropologists should be an essential part of the discussion on sustainable development. The advantages of our evolutionary and cross-cultural approaches provide a deep and broad perspective on societal change. He argues that it is the scale and scope of our societies that have created the major problems of today: environmental problems, hunger, poverty, and conflict. A reduction in **culture scale** would help to mitigate some of these problems in our globally linked, commercial societies. Bodley concludes that the long-term success of small-scale tribal societies should serve as a guiding model. As the experts on 100,000 years of tribal societies, anthropologists have much to say about successfully living in regional ecosystems supported by local economic markets, and small-scale social communities.

Second, armed with the knowledge of human history and societies, anthropologists can bring it to the larger public, helping people understand the effects of their actions. The discipline of anthropology has a great responsibility to publish and present information in ways that will reach the general public. Statistics and charts give facts, but the actual stories of a people's struggles tie us emotionally to their plight. Consumer behavior can change rapidly when knowledge leads to compassion.

Pioneering anthropologist Margaret Mead did just that: she brought knowledge of human societies to the public. Mead worked among islanders of the South Pacific and Indonesia, exploring major questions of the early twentieth century, such as race, gender, child rearing, and the **nature versus nurture** controversy. She was able to translate her conclusions into formats that nonanthropologists could readily understand.

Although later researchers have questioned the validity of all her data, Mead's lasting legacy is the way in which she was able to reach a wider public. As a curator in the American Museum of Natural History in New York for 50 years, she designed exhibits shown to visitors. She appeared on radio and television programs, and taught at several colleges. Importantly, she published regularly in *Redbook*, a women's magazine. In this way, Mead reached the general public with critical information about human beings and culture, breaking down stereotypes and paving the way for the women's rights movement in the 1960s.

Finally, the majority of anthropologists teach at colleges and universities. In this setting, anthropologists have the potential to effect major change, especially among students and the campus community. Sustainability Studies is now a major at many institutions, training students in an interdisciplinary way to work with development solutions. Even urban college campuses are building organic farms to offer degrees in urban agriculture and supply their cafeterias with fresh, organic produce. Many campuses have created offices of sustainability and lead the way in green building for new campus structures, water conservation on campus, and recycling or composting programs. Anthropologists appear in these roles as leaders, alongside biologists, environmental scientists, and ecologists.

At Emory University in Atlanta, Georgia, anthropologist Peggy Barlett (2005) helped develop a series of sustainability workshops to engage faculty on her campus. Based on the successful Ponderosa Project at Northern Arizona University, the Piedmont Project seeks to connect the campus community with the local geography and ecosystem of the Piedmont region. Workshop participants hear speakers on local sustainability issues, spend time outdoors in the Piedmont forest, and draw on their own expertise as inspiration for including sustainability topics in their classes. Barlett concludes that the success of this model results from not only learning new information but also reconnecting physically with nature—with the resulting emotional shift that participants experience. This type of intellectual and experiential workshop now serves as a model for campuses everywhere.

Summary

This chapter explored the relationship between the field of anthropology and the challenges and scope of sustainability. Mirroring the Learning Objectives stated in the chapter opening, the key points are:

- Anthropology is interested in the human-environment relationship: what has worked and what has failed, over a long span of time and in every corner of the globe. Therefore, anthropology can inform discussions about sustainability.
- Sustainable development has at least three aspects: social, economic, and environmental. The environmental piece is the most basic foundation, for without healthy air, soil, or water, human society would collapse.
- Earlier in history, humans had a very different interaction with their local ecosystems in small bands of foragers. As populations grew, we drew more resources from the environment. Things increased exponentially in the middle of the twentieth century, and the environment has suffered proportionally.
- There have been multiple theoretical approaches to these questions within anthropology, all looking at the relationships between people and their ecosystems.
- Some of the most pressing questions include the issues of population growth and food security.

- Anthropologists can provide much of this data from their ethnographic and archaeological fieldwork, their biological research, and applied anthropology projects in which they seek to solve problems for people.

REVIEW QUESTIONS

1. What are some of the unique contributions that the study of the fields of anthropology can make to the discussion of sustainability solutions?
2. How have the ways that anthropologists have approached ecological studies changed over the years?
3. How is the loss of biodiversity encouraging current studies of ethnoecology and Traditional Ecological Knowledge?
4. Why is population growth a fundamental problem for sustainability?
5. How are anthropologists engaging with sustainability studies currently?

DISCUSSION QUESTIONS

1. The health of our planet's oceans is suffering due to human practices. How has global use of the ocean resulted in a "tragedy of the commons?"
2. Can you think of ways that alternative food movements are aligned with Bodley's idea of "culture scale?"
3. Have you had a personal experience that caused you to think differently about nature or our place in it?
4. What are some responses of modern consumers to the industrial food system?

Visit **www.lensofanthropology.com** for the following additional resources:

| SELF-STUDY QUESTIONS | WEBLINKS | FURTHER READING |

Glossary

Note: The numbers that follow the definitions indicate the chapters where the term is discussed.

Acheulean a cultural tradition, based primarily on specific kinds of stone tools, associated primarily with *Homo erectus* and *Homo ergaster* 5

achieved status a social role a person achieves due to work and opportunity 12

adaptive radiation a process by which one species occupies a new ecological niche, quickly increasing its population and diversifying into new species 2, 3

affiliative friendly 2

affinal related by marriage 11

agriculture a farming technique that can support a large population, using advanced tools and irrigation, and requiring more preparation and maintenance of the soil; also known as intensive cultivation 1, 6, 10

agroforestry an approach to food procurement in which mixed-use food-getting techniques that mimic the natural environment are used 14

allele an alternate form of a gene 3, 11

allele frequency the relative proportion of a particular allele occurring, compared to other alleles that could be selected 3

ancestor veneration worship of one's ancestors 13

ancestral spirits the essence of one's family ancestors who have remained in contact with the mortal world 13

androphilia the romantic or sexual attraction to males 11

animal husbandry the use and breeding of animals for purposes that benefit humans 10

animatism the belief that spiritual forces inhabit natural objects 13

animism the belief that spiritual beings inhabit natural objects 13

Anthropocene a proposed geological period to describe the years in which humans have had a significant impact on the environment, observable in the geological record; there is no consensus on the validity of the term to describe the geological period or when such a period began 2

anthropological perspective evolutionary, holistic, and comparative methods applied to the study of humans 1

anthropology the study of human biology and culture, past and present, through evolutionary, holistic, and comparative perspectives 1

anthropophagy cannibalism, literally "people eating" 12

applied anthropology a field of anthropology in which the researcher uses knowledge of anthropological methods, theory, and perspectives to solve human problems 1, 8

archaeological record the material remains of the human past and, in some cases, the description of the human past based on the material remains 5

archaeological site any location where there is physical evidence of past human activity 1, 5

archaeology the study of humans through the remains of their physical activities 1

arranged marriage the practice in which parents find a suitable husband or wife for their child 11

artifact any portable object showing evidence of being made or used by people 1, 5

ascribed status a social role of a person that is fixed at birth 12

asexual without sexual desires 11

assimilation the result when a dominant society absorbs an ethnic minority culturally, socially, and finally, genetically 12

Atlantis fictional land and civilization described by Plato, in which both the land and civilization are destroyed 7

atlatl spear thrower 5

authority having legitimate power by law 12

Ayurveda a system of healing used in India that focuses on the restoration of balance to the body's systems 13

balanced reciprocity a form of exchange in which the value of goods is specified as well as the time frame of repayment 10

band a small egalitarian society of food foragers who live and travel together 6, 10

base camps discrete areas with physical evidence that people were temporarily occupying a place for resource processing or habitation 5

Beringia a large, unglaciated land mass connecting North America and Asia during the last ice age 6

Big Man an informal leader who possesses authority based on prestige and persuasive power, found in Melanesian societies 6, 12

bilateral descent the act of tracing one's genealogy through both the mother and father's line 11

binary having two parts; in gender studies, it refers to a two-gender system of masculine males and feminine females 11

biodiversity the variety of life on earth, including plants, animals, and microorganisms; the diversity of living organisms in a given ecosystem, area, or the world 14

biological adaptation a physical adaptation that allows an organism to survive better in its environment 8

biological anthropology the branch of anthropology focusing on human biology, including evolution and contemporary variability 1

biosphere the earth's ecosystems and living organisms 14

bipedalism moving mostly by using two legs 1

bisexual attracted romantically or sexually to both males and females 11

Body Mass Index (BMI) a measure of body fat calculated using a person's height and weight 10

body modification the practice of altering the body for reasons of identity, attractiveness or social status 11

brachiation a form of locomotion primarily by arm-over-arm swinging 2

bride price a form of marriage compensation in which the family of the groom is required to present valuable gifts to the bride's family 11

bride service a form of marriage compensation in which the family of the groom is required to work for the bride's family 11

bushmeat meat from wild animals, usually referring to animals from forested regions of Africa 2

Cahokia a World Heritage Site near St. Louis, Missouri 1

cargo cult a religious revitalization movement in Melanesia that uses ritual to seek help and material wealth 13

cargo system a political and religious system among the Maya in which members must serve the community in a volunteer position for at least one year; a leveling mechanism 10

carrying capacity the number of people that can be sustained with the existing resources of a given area 6, 10

caste a hierarchical system based on birth; most commonly associated with Hindu India 12

caste system a system of social stratification in India in which a person is born into a hereditary group traditionally linked to certain occupations 11

Catarrhini primate infraorder, including Old World monkeys, apes, and humans 2

cave art art painted or incised on cave walls, including petroglyphs and pictographs 5

centralized system a political system with a centralized governing body that has the power and authority to govern 12

ceramics baked clay 6

Cercopithecoidea a primate superfamily, including the Old World monkeys 1

chemical inputs synthetic additives, such as pesticides and fertilizers, that raise the yield of crops in industrial agriculture 10

chiefdom a type of political organization found in settlements of typically from a few thousand to tens of thousands of people, characterized by social inequality and hereditary leadership, and based on horticulture **6, 12**

child marriage the practice in which parents marry young girls to older men who offer to provide for them **11**

cisgender a term to describe people who internally experience and/or express their gender identity as aligned with their assigned sex **11**

city a settlement supporting a dense population with a centralized government, specialization, and socio-economic hierarchy **6, 7, 10**

civilization a type of society characterized by a state-level of political organization, a system of writing, at least one city, and monumental architecture **6, 7**

clan a social division that separates members of a society into two groups; also called a moiety **11**

class a form of social stratification based on differences in wealth and status **12**

closed-loop system a system that has finite resources and cannot sustain indefinite growth **14**

coastal migration route probably the route of first migrants to the Americas, along the coast of Alaska and British Columbia **6**

code switching the practice of moving easily between speech styles or languages in a conversation or single utterance **9**

colonialism the domination and subjugation of Indigenous peoples by Europeans and their descendants **1**

commercial archaeology *see* cultural resource management.

community people who share a physical location; people who live, work, and play together **8**

Community Supported Agriculture (CSA) a direct-marketing program in which consumers pay up front for boxes of fresh produce that are delivered on a regular basis from the farms where it is grown **14**

Confined Animal Feeding Operations (CAFOs) industrial farming enterprises in which large numbers of animals are prepared for human consumption; the basis of conventional meat production **10**

consanguineal related by blood **11**

conventional describes food-growing processes in industrial societies in which pesticides and other chemicals are used **14**

cooperative society a pattern of social life in which resources are shared among the group **10**

coprolite preserved feces, usually referring to human feces **5**

creole a pidgin language that remains relevant and, in the next generation, becomes the dominant language of a group **9**

cultural adaptation a belief or behavior that allows an organism with culture (especially humans) to better thrive in their environment 8

cultural anthropology the branch of anthropology focusing on contemporary cultures 1

cultural appropriation the use of an element of a minority or oppressed culture by a dominant culture, in an inappropriate context, such as the way in which Euro-Americans use elements of Native American culture for fashion, logos, and mascots 1

cultural ecology a framework of understanding culture by examining the limitations of the environment and food-getting practices 14

cultural identity a term used to describe the aspects of our social lives that are not linked to one particular ethnicity, such as socio-economic level, gender, or interests 8

cultural landscape a distinctive geographic area with cultural significance 5

cultural materialism a framework for understanding society that is directly related to whatever adaptations are necessary to survive in its environment 12, 13

cultural model a widely shared understanding about the world that helps us organize our experience in it; determines the metaphors used in communication 9

cultural relativism the idea that all cultures are equally valid, and that every culture can be understood only in its own context 1, 8

cultural resource management doing archaeology in advance of development projects; often abbreviated as CRM and also known as commercial archaeology 1

culture core a set of features of culture that are similar in societies practicing the same food-getting strategies; an aspect of the cultural ecology model 14

culture scale the scope or reach of culture; implied is the idea that smaller-scale societies are more sustainable than larger-scale societies 14

culture-bound disorder a mental disorder specific to particular ethnic groups 8

cupping a healing practice used in Traditional Chinese Medicine in which cups of heated air are placed on painful areas of the body 13

decentralized system a political system with no centralized governing body in which decisions are made by the community 12

deities gods and goddesses 13

dental arcade the shape of tooth rows, such as parabolic (wider at back than front) or u-shaped 4

dental formula the kind and number of teeth, usually described for one quarter of the mouth 2

dependence training a set of child-rearing practices that supports compliance to the family unit over individual needs 8

descent group a social group of people who trace their descent from a particular ancestor 11

diasporic spread to different parts of the world, especially used in reference to ethnic or cultural groups 8

diastema a space between teeth 4

diplomacy the relations and negotiations between nations 12

divination the art of reading the future 13

DNA deoxyribonucleic acid; a molecule that contains the genetic instructions for living organisms 3

domestication shaping the evolution of a species for human use 6, 10

dowry a form of marriage compensation in which the family of the bride is required to present valuable gifts to the groom's family or to the couple 11

dowry death deaths of women in the homes of their in-laws due to unmet dowry demands 11

ecofacts botanical remains, animal remains, and sediments in archaeological sites that have cultural relevance 5

ecological anthropology a framework of understanding culture that uses systems theory to understand a population as a closed-loop system 14

ecological footprint humanity's demand on the earth's natural ecosystems 14

economic sustainability the ability of the economy to support indefinite growth while ensuring a minimum quality of life for all members of society 14

economics how goods and services are produced, distributed, and consumed in a society 10

egalitarian describes a society in which every member has the same access to resources and status; non-hierarchical 2, 10

emic an insider's view; the perspective of the subject 8, 13

empire a kind of political system with one state being territorially expansive and exerting control over others, such as the Roman or Inka empires 7

enculturation the process by which culture is passed from generation to generation 8

endo-cannibalism eating the flesh of people within one's society, especially within one's family 12

endogamy the practice of marrying within one's social or ancestral group 11

entomophagy the practice of eating insects for food 8

environmental anthropologist an anthropologist interested in the relationships between people and the environment 14

environmental sustainability the ability of the environment to renew resources and accommodate waste at the same rate at which resources are used and waste is generated 14

epigenetics the study of how parts of the genome may become activated or deactivated as an organism develops 3

ergonomics the science of designing things so they create little or no physical stress on the human body 1

ethnic cleansing violent and aggressive intergroup conflicts in which one group attempts to commit genocide of the other 12

ethnic politics the struggles for rights, representation, or survival that result when multiple ethnicities live in the same geographic region 12

ethnicity a term used to describe the heritage, geographic origin, language, and other features of a person 8

ethnocentrism the idea that our own customs are normal while the customs of others are strange, wrong, or even disgusting 8

ethnoecologist a person who studies the interactions a group of people has with their natural environment, focusing especially on the use of flora and fauna 14

ethnographer a cultural anthropologist who studies a group of people in a field setting 8

ethnographic research the process of studying culture, undertaken in a field setting 1, 8

ethnography the written or visual product of ethnographic (field) research 1, 8

ethnolinguistics the study of the relationship between language and culture; a subset of linguistic anthropology 9

ethnomedicine traditional, non-Western medicine 13

etic an outsider's view; an objective explanation 8, 13

eugenics a pseudoscience of "race improvement" 8

euphemisms polite or socially acceptable words or phrases that are used in place of ones that are unpleasant or offensive 12

exo-cannibalism eating the flesh of people outside one's society 12

exogamy the practice of marrying outside one's social or ancestral group 11

extended family a family unit consisting of blood-related members and their spouses; a mix of consanguineal and affinal kin 11

externalized controls rules that regulate behavior by encouraging conformity to social norms; may be negative (punishments) or positive (rewards) 12

extinctions that which occurs when a taxonomic group, usually a species, ceases to exist, either because it could not adapt to changing circumstances or because it evolved into a new species 3

Fair Trade a social and economic model aimed to support food and craft producers in developing countries by promoting equity and fair pricing 11, 14

family of orientation blood-related family members, including parents, siblings, grandparents, and other relatives 11

family of procreation the family unit created by marriage or partnership, including spouses/partners and children 11

faunal remains animal remains in palaeoanthropological and archaeological sites, usually restricted to bones and hair but also possibly including fur, nails, claws, horn, antler, skin, and soft tissue 5

feature a non-portable object or patterning created by people and recognized archaeologically, such as a fire hearth 5

feud ongoing violent relations between two groups in the same society 12

fictive kinship including non-blood relations in the family with all the expectations of blood-related family members 11

folivory a diet focusing on leaves and other rough plant foliage 2

food deserts neighborhoods in which the majority of available food is processed or fast food 14

food foragers people who utilize the food resources available in the environment; also called hunter-gatherers 10

food producers people who transform the environment with the goal of food production, using farming and/or animal husbandry 6, 10

food production transforming the environment with the goal of producing food using farming and/or animal husbandry 6, 10

food security the availability of and access to safe and nutritious food 1

foodways the methods, knowledge, and practices regarding food in a particular society 10

foraging utilization of food resources available in the environment; also known as food foraging or hunting and gathering 1, 6, 10

foramen magnum the hole at the base of the skull, through which the spinal column enters the brain 4

forced marriage the practice in which parents demand their child marry someone the parents have chosen 11

fossil in anthropology, a term used to describe any preserved early human bones or teeth 4

fossil record in anthropology, the assemblage of early human remains, or the interpretation of human evolution based on human remains 4

fraternal polyandry the practice of women marrying brothers 11

frugivory a diet focusing on fruit 2

garbology the study of contemporary garbage using the methods of archaeology 7

gender a person's internal experience of their identity as male, female, both, or neither, as well as the expression of that identity in social behavior 11

gender discrimination the apparent or real dominance of men and subordinate status of women in society 12

gender dysphoria the experience that one's gender identity does not match their assigned sex at birth 11

gender identity a person's internal experience of their identity as male, female, both, or neither, as well as the expression of that identity in social behavior 11

gender roles the culturally appropriate or expected roles of individuals in society 11

gender spectrum the varieties of gender identity that exist on a continuum 11

gender stratification the hierarchical division of males and females in society 12

gendered speech different speech patterns based on the cultural expectations of each sex 9

gene a unit of heredity 3

gene flow the movement of genes between populations 3

generalized reciprocity a form of specialized sharing in which the value of a gift is not specified at the time of exchange, nor is the time of repayment 10

genetic drift the random factor in evolution, including changes in allele frequencies by chance rather than selection 3

genetically modified (GM) altered at the level of the gene; refers particularly to food crops that have been modified by introducing genes from another organism to enhance or create desired traits in the species 10, 14

genetics the study of a particular gene or groups of genes, especially as it relates to inheritance 3

genocide the death of an entire ethnic group 12

genome the complete genetic make-up of an organism 3

genomics the study of genomes 3

genotype the genetic make-up of an organism 3

genus a taxonomic category, above the level of species 2, 3

Ghost Dance a religious revitalization movement, started among the Northern Paiute, that used a five-day circle dance to seek help from the supernatural realm 13

globalization the integration of economic, social, political, and geographic boundaries in complex chains of interconnected systems and processes 14

glycemic index a measure of the rise in blood glucose (sugar) after eating 10

gods and goddesses distant and powerful supernatural beings 13

gradualism the idea that evolutionary change is a long, slow process 3

Great Rift Valley an area in East Africa where many important palaeoanthropological sites are located 4

grocery gap the absence in a community of grocery stores or ways to purchase fresh produce 14

group people who share culture; they may or may not live in the same physical location, but often in the same region 8

group marriage the marriage practice of having multiple spouses from both sexes 11

guilt culture a culture that focuses on one's own sense of right and wrong and the punishment that can result from breaking the rules 12

gynophilia the romantic or sexual attraction to females 11

habitation sites areas with physical evidence indicating that people were living there, at least temporarily 5

Haplorhini a suborder of Primates, including monkeys, apes, and humans 2

hearth a discrete area where people controlled a fire 5

heterogeneous sharing few identity markers 8

hijra a third-gender role found in India and Pakistan in which male-bodied or intersexed individuals adopt female mannerisms and dress 11

historical particularism the notion that each culture is a product of its own unique history, and that there are several ways of successfully adapting 1

holistic describes the viewpoint that all aspects of biology and/or culture are interrelated 1

Homininae the biological family to which humans belong; some also consider Homininae to include gorillas, chimpanzees, and bonobos 1

Hominoidea a superfamily of the infraorder Catarrhini; Hominoidea includes apes and humans 2

Homo sapiens the genus and species to which humans today belong 1

homogeneous sharing similar identity markers 8

homosexuality the romantic or sexual attraction or sexual behavior between partners of the same sex 11

horticulturalists food producers who cultivate the land in small-scale farms or gardens 6, 10

horticulture land cultivation in small-scale farms or gardens 1, 6, 10

hotspot region in which there is a high concentration of native plant and animal species and a high rate of biodiversity loss 14

household a domestic unit of residence in which members contribute to child rearing, inheritance, and the production and consumption of goods 11

human at a minimum, *Homo sapiens*, although most anthropologists define it as any member of the genus *Homo* or biological family Homininae 1

human ecology the study of the complex relationships between humans and their environments 14

Human Terrain System US Army program involving anthropologists deployed with military units in active conflict zones 1, 8

hunter-gatherers people who utilize the food resources available in the environment; also called food foragers 10

Hylobatidae one of the three families of the superfamily Hominoidea; Hylobatidae includes gibbons and siamangs, otherwise known as Lesser Apes 2

hypothesis a possible explanation that may be tested using scientific methods 3

ice-free corridor space between two ice sheets covering most of Canada during the last ice age, providing a possible route from Beringia to areas south 6

ideal behavior how people believe they behave or would like to behave; the norms of a society 8

identity markers cultural characteristics of a person, such as ethnicity, socio-economic class, religious beliefs, age, gender, and interests 8

ideology refers to beliefs and values, including religion 1

imitative magic a form of magic in which a practitioner creates something to represent real life, then manipulates it in a way that imitates the desired effect; the magical idea that like produces like 13

incest taboo prohibition against sexual relations with immediate family members 11

independence training the set of child-rearing practices that foster a child's self-reliance 8

index sign an emotional expression that carries meaning directly related to the response 9

Indigenous describes people who can trace their ancestry in an area into the distant past; Indigenous peoples in North America include Native Americans, First Nations, Indians, Eskimos, and Inuit 1

industrialism methods of producing food and goods using highly mechanized machinery and digital information 10

informants study subjects of an anthropologist; also referred to variously as collaborators, field subjects, or associates 8

Inheritance of Acquired Characteristics the (incorrect) idea that characteristics acquired during one's lifetime could be passed on to offspring 3

Inka ancient culture of the Peruvian Andes; the spelling preferred over "Inca" by modern scholars 7, 11

insectivory diet focusing on insects 2

intensive agriculture a farming technique that can support a large population using advanced tools and irrigation, and requiring more preparation and maintenance of the soil 10

internalized controls impulses that guide a person toward right behavior based on a moral system 12

intersex having a combination of physiologic or morphological elements of both sexes 11

Inuit Indigenous peoples inhabiting Arctic Canada, Alaska, and Greenland; in Alaska, the term *Eskimo* remains commonly used while in Canada and Greenland, it is a racial slur 7, 10

judgment sample a method of choosing informants based on their knowledge or skills 8

key informant a person with whom the ethnographer spends a great amount of time because of the person's knowledge, skills, or insight 8

kinesics the cultural use of body movements, including gestures 9

kinship family relations; involves a complex set of expectations and responsibilities 11

Kula Ring a system of balanced reciprocity in which gifts circulate among trading partners in the Trobriand Islands 10

language a symbolic system expressing meaning through sounds or gestures 9

language registers different styles of speaking within a single language 9

lens of anthropology a particular way to view the world, through the perspectives, ideas, methods, theories, ethics, and research results of anthropology 1

leveling mechanism a social and economic obligation to distribute wealth so that no one member of a group accumulates more than anyone else 10

lingua franca a language used for business transactions where speakers of multiple languages must communicate 9

linguistic anthropology the branch of anthropology focusing on human languages 1

linguistic relativity principle the idea, studied by Benjamin Whorf, that the language one speaks shapes the way one sees the world 9

lithic scatter an accumulation of lithic (stone) flakes left behind from making stone tools 5

Lomekwian a proposed new tool tradition or industry based on what appears to be 3.3-million-year-old tools at the Lomekwi locality in Kenya, Africa 5

Lower Palaeolithic cultural time period from about 2.6 million to about 500,000 years ago 5

magic the use of powers to contact and control supernatural forces or beings 13

maladaptive leading to harm or death; not productive for a culture's survival in the long run 8

Margaret Mead pioneering figure in early cultural anthropology; one of the first female anthropologists to undertake long-term fieldwork 11

market economy an economic system in which prices for goods and services are set by supply and demand 10

marriage the practice of creating socially and legally recognized partnerships in society 11

marriage compensation gifts or service exchanged between the families of a bride and groom 11

mass extinctions widespread and rapid extinctions, usually restricted to situations in which at least half of all living species become extinct 3

matrilineal descent tracing one's genealogy through the mother's line 11

matrilocal a residence pattern in which a husband moves to his wife's household of orientation 11

medical anthropology a subfield of cultural anthropology which examines ideas about health and healing 13

Mesoamerica the term used in anthropology to describe the area now encompassing Mexico and Central America 7

Mesolithic from about 15,000 to 10,000 years ago; also known as the Middle Stone Age 5

Mesopotamia when referring to ancient times, the area around modern-day Iraq 7

midden a discrete accumulation of refuse 5

Middle Palaeolithic cultural time period from about 500,000 to 40,000 years ago 5

moiety a social division that separates members of a society into two groups; also called a clan 11

money anything that is used to measure and pay for the value of goods and services 10

monoculture a technique used in industrial farming in which a single crop is planted on a large number of acres 10

monogamy the marriage practice of having a single spouse 11

monotheism a religious belief system worshipping a single god or goddess 13

morpheme the smallest part of a word that conveys meaning 9

moxibustion a healing practice used in Traditional Chinese Medicine in which a burning stick of herbs is placed near acupuncture points on the body 13

multipurpose money commodities that can be used for other practical purposes besides simply as money 10

mutation an error in the replication of DNA 3

myth a sacred story that explains the origins of the world or people in it 13

natural resource management practices aimed to conserve natural resources such as air, water, and land and to maintain the quality of life for those who inhabit these areas 14

nature versus nurture the debate over which aspects of human life are fixed in one's genetic makeup, and which are learned through culture 14

negative reciprocity a deceptive practice in which the exchange is unequal; an exchange in which the seller asks more than the value of the item 10

Neolithic from about 10,000 to 5,000 years ago; also known as the New Stone Age 5

neolocal a residence pattern in which a husband and wife move to their own household after marriage 11

nobles high-status members of a society, with rank often inherited 10

nomadic moving within a large area frequently to access food resources 10

nuclear family a family unit consisting of two generations, most often parents and their children 11

nurture kinship non-blood relationships based on mutual caring and attachment 11

Nutrition Transition a shift in diet and activity level that accompanies modernization and results in obesity and related health problems 10

Occam's razor the notion that the simplest explanation is usually the best; also known as Occam's Rule 7

Oldowan a cultural tradition, based primarily on specific kinds of stone tools, associated primarily with *Homo habilis* and *Homo rudolfensis* 5

olfaction sense of smell 2

omnivorous diet including a wide variety of plants and animals 2

ontogeny the development of an individual from conception to maturity 2

optimal foraging theory the concept that individuals are driven to maximize the benefits and minimize the costs of food procurement 10

organic describes food-growing processes in which the use of chemical pesticides, herbicides, or fertilizers; irradiation; and genetic modification are prohibited 14

palaeoanthropology the study of early humans, using both archaeology and biological anthropology 1

palaeoenvironment ancient environment 5

Palaeolithic from 2.6 million to about 15,000 years ago; also known as the Old Stone Age 5

Paleo Diet a fad diet, based on the notion that people should be eating "like our ancestors" before the domestication of plants and animals 6

Pan genus to which chimpanzees and bonobos belong 2

pansexual not limited in romantic or sexual attraction by sex or gender; polysexual 11

pantheon a set of gods and goddesses in a religious belief system 13

paradigm set of concepts; a model 14

paralanguage the ways we express meaning through sounds beyond words alone; a subset of semantics 9

participant observation a research method used in anthropology in which an ethnographer lives with a group of people and observes their regular activities 1, 8

participatory action research an applied anthropological method of field research and implementation of solutions; relies on close collaboration with the target community 8, 14

pastoralism a way of life that revolves around domesticating animals and herding them to pasture 1, 6, 10

patrilineal descent tracing one's genealogy through the father's line 11

patrilocal a residence pattern in which a wife moves to her husband's household of orientation 11

peasants low-status members of a society who farm for a living 10

personality the unique way an individual thinks, feels and acts 8

petroglyph inscription on stone 5, 13

phenotype the physical expression of a genotype; what an organism looks like 3

phonemics the study of how sounds convey meaning 9

phonetics the study of the sounds in human speech 9

physical anthropology also known as biological anthropology 1

phytoliths plants turned to stone 5

pictograph painting on stone 5, 13

pidgin a language that is a mixture of features of two or more languages; develops during periods of extended contact where no lingua franca exists 9

Platyrrhini Primate infraorder, commonly known as New World monkeys 2

pluralism an ideal concept of a multicultural society in which ethnic groups coexist in harmony 12

political ecology a framework of understanding culture that focuses on the complex relationships between the environment, economics, and politics 14

political organization the way a society maintains order internally and manages affairs externally 12

polyandry the marriage practice of having two or more husbands at the same time 11

polygamy the marriage practice of having two or more spouses 11

polygyny the marriage practice of having two or more wives at the same time 11

polysexual not limited in romantic or sexual attraction by sex or gender; pansexual 11

polytheistic describes a religious belief system in which multiple gods and goddesses are worshipped 13

Pongidae one of the three families of the superfamily Hominoidea; some use Pongidae to refer to the three genera of Pongo, Gorilla, and Pan while others use it only for Pongo 2

Pongo genus to which orangutans belong 2

popular culture mainstream culture in a society, including mass media, television, music, art, movies, and books 1

potassium argon dating dating technique based on measuring the ratio of potassium and argon in volcanic sediments 4

pottery baked clay container 6

power the ability to compel another person to do something that he or she would not do otherwise 12

pragmatics the context within which language occurs 9

prehensile the ability to grasp 2

prehistory the time before written records were kept in an area 1

prestige the positive reputation or high regard of a person or other entity merited by actions, wealth, authority, or status 12

priest (priestess) a full-time religious practitioner 13

primate one of the taxonomic orders of the class Mammalia 1

primatology the study of primates, usually in the wild, using the framework of anthropology 1

privatization selling ownership of public resources to private companies 12, 14

prognathism having a protruding face 4

proxemics the cultural use of space, including how close people stand to one another 9

pseudoarchaeology the study of the human past, but not within the framework of science or scholarly archaeology 7

punctuated equilibrium the idea that evolutionary change may alternate between periods of slow, gradual change and short periods of significant change 3

qi the body's life force in Traditional Chinese Medicine; pronounced "chee" 13

qualitative a term used to describe the research strategy or perspective of anthropologists focusing on observations, actions, symbols, interviews, and words to gather data 1

quantitative a term used to describe the research strategy or perspective focusing on methods designed to produce data in the form of numbers 1

race a term used to describe varieties or subspecies of a species; inaccurately used to refer to human differences 1, 8

radiocarbon dating dating technique based on measuring how much carbon 14 is in preserved organic remains 4

raid violence in which members of one group aim to steal or recover items, animals, or people from another group in the same society 12

random sample a method of choosing informants randomly 8

real behavior how people actually behave as observed by an ethnographer in the field 8

reciprocity a set of social rules that govern the specialized sharing of food and other items 10

redistribution an economic system in which goods and money flow into a central entity, such as a governmental authority or a religious institution 10

religion a set of beliefs and behaviors pertaining to supernatural forces or beings that transcend the observable world 13

religious revitalization movement a process by which an oppressed group seeks supernatural aid through the creation of new ritual behaviors 13

reserves land set aside for Canada's First Nations peoples; in the United States, these areas are called reservations 12

resource processing sites areas where physical remains indicate that people were harvesting and/or processing resources 5

rhinarium the fleshy part at the end of the nose of Strepsirrhini, and many other animals 2

rites of passage rituals marking life's important transitions from one social or biological role to another 11, 13

ritual a symbolic practice that is ordered and regularly repeated 13

rock art paintings on rock (pictographs) and inscriptions on rock (petroglyphs) 5

Rosetta Stone a slab of basalt with three different kinds of writing; provided key for deciphering Egyptian hieroglyphics 7

salvage ethnography ethnography done with a sense of urgency to record cultures, based on the assumption that the cultures are rapidly disappearing 1

sanction punishment that results from breaking rules 12

savannah an environment common in tropical and subtropical Africa, consisting of wild grasses and sparse tree growth 4

scarification inscribing scars on the body as a marker of identity 11

science a framework for investigating and understanding things, including a specific set of principles and methods 1, 3

semantics the study of how words and phrases are put together in meaningful ways 9

serial monogamy the marriage practice of taking a series of partners, one after the other 11

sex the biological and physiological differences of human beings based on sex chromosomes, hormones, reproductive structures, and external genitalia 11

sexual division of labor the division of tasks in a community based on sex 10

sexual orientation the romantic or sexual attraction to another person 11

sexual selection when mates are chosen based on characteristics unrelated to survival 3

shaman a part-time religious practitioner 13

shame culture a culture in which conformity to social expectations stems from wanting to live up to others' expectations 12

sign in communication, something that stands for something else 9

silent language the very specific set of non-verbal cues such as gestures, body movements, and facial expressions that is acquired by speakers of a language 9

snowball sample a method of finding informants through association with previous informants 8

social density the frequency and intensity of interactions among group members in a society 10

social distance the degree of separation or exclusion between members of different social groups 10

social mobility the ability of members of society to rise in social class 12

social stratification the ranking of members of society into a hierarchy 12

social sustainability the ability of social systems (such as families, communities, regions, or nations) to provide for the needs of their people so that they can attain a stable and healthy standard of living 14

society people who share a large number of social or cultural connections; in the animal world, a group of animals born with instincts that cause them to occupy a particular place in the group hierarchy 8

sodality group that brings people together through common concerns, age, or interests 12

special-purpose money items used only to measure the value of things and lacking a practical purpose 10

specialization the development of certain skills that others in the group do not share; characteristic of complex societies 10

speciation the evolution of new species or the process of creating species 3

species a population that can mate and produce fertile offspring in natural conditions 2

speech verbal communication using sounds 9

speech community a group that shares language patterns 9

spirits of nature unobservable beings and forces that inhabit the natural world 13

state a type of political organization in a highly populated, industrial society with strong centralized government 6, 12

Strepsirhini a suborder of Primates, including lemurs and lorises 2

subculture a group of people within a culture who are connected by similar identity markers, may include ethnic heritage or interests 8

subsistence food procurement; basic food needs for survival 1, 10

superfamily a taxonomic category; a subdivision of infraorder 2

supernatural describes those aspects of life that are outside of a scientific understanding and that we cannot measure or test; religious 13

supernatural beings personified or embodied beings, such as deities or spirits, that exist beyond the observable world 13

supernatural forces disembodied powers, such as luck, that exist beyond the observable world 13

sustainability the ability to keep something in existence, to support a practice indefinitely 14

swidden (shifting) cultivation a farming technique in which plant material is burned and crops are planted in the ashes 10

symbol something that stands for something else with little or no natural relationship to its referent; a type of sign 9

syncretism a synthesis of religious belief systems 13

syntax the study of how units of speech are put together to create sentences 9

systems theory a model of understanding an ecosystem that assumes the ecosystem is a closed-loop system with finite resources 14

taphonomy the study of what happens to organic remains after death 4

taxa a category in the system of biological classification of organisms 2

taxonomic order subdivision of a taxonomic class in the biological classification system; primates are an order of the class Mammalia 2

technology the tools, skills, and knowledge used by people to survive 10

terra cotta army approximately 8,000 life-size warriors made of terra cotta in China, presumably guarding the tomb of an emperor 7

terraced describes a farming technique that uses graduated steps on hilly terrain 10

theory in science, an extremely well-supported idea; an idea that has not been disproven 3

third gender a gender role accepted in some societies as combining elements of male and female genders 11

three pillars of sustainability a model of sustainable development with three components: sustainability of the environment, society, and the economy 14

totem a mythological ancestor linking people together in kinship ties 11

Traditional Chinese Medicine (TCM) a system of healing used in China that focuses on strengthening the body's systems and improving the flow of qi 13

Traditional Ecological Knowledge (TEK) the collective and cumulative knowledge that a group of people has gained over many generations living in their particular ecosystem 1, 10, 14

Traditional Use Studies (TUS) anthropological studies focusing on the ways in which Indigenous people have used their lands and resources and continue to do so 1

tragedy of the commons the idea that individual actors sharing a natural resource will inevitably act in their own best interest, eventually depleting the resource 14

transgender a term used to describe people who internally experience and/or express their gender identity as different from their assigned sex at birth 11

transhumance a pattern of seasonal migration in which pastoralists move back and forth over long distances, to productive pastures 10

tribe a type of political organization with a decentralized power structure, often seen among horticulturalists or pastoralists 6, 12

two-spirit a Native American person who identifies as a third-gender occupying a role between males and females with characteristics of each 11

uniformitarianism the idea that the processes that created landscapes of the past are the same processes in operation today 3

unilineal descent tracing one's genealogy through either the mother or father's line 11

unilinear theory an evolutionary model that proposed societies progressed from savagery through barbarism and then to civilization; now entirely discredited 1

Upper Palaeolithic cultural time period from about 40,000 to 12,000 years ago 5

utterance an uninterrupted sequence of spoken or written language 9

vocalizations intentional sounds humans make to express themselves, but not actually words 9

voice qualities the background characteristics of a person's voice, including pitch, rhythm, and articulation 9

warfare an extended violent conflict in which one side attempts to kill as many people or destroy as much property as possible until the other side surrenders 12

world biocapacity the ability of the earth's resources to support life 14

World Heritage Site a site of outstanding heritage value, designated by the United Nations Educational, Scientific, and Cultural Organization (UNESCO) 1, 7

worldview the way a group understands and interprets the world; includes all aspects of their culture 14

References

Abel, A. (1997). Paleohooters: Men as brute hunters, women as shapely sucklers: Who turned prehistory into "Baywatch"? *Saturday Night, 112*(6), 15–16.

Aboriginal Affairs and Northern Development Canada (2011, July 4). *Fact sheet—The results of the national assessment of First Nations water and wastewater systems.* Retrieved from Aboriginal Affairs and Northern Development Canada: http://www.aadnc-aandc.gc.ca/eng/1313762701121/1313762778061

Adams, W.M., & Jeanreneaud, S. J. (2008). *Transition to sustainability: Towards a diverse and humane world.* Retrieved from CMS Data: http://cmsdata.iucn.org/downloads/transition_to_sustainability__en__pdf_1.pdf

American Anthropological Association Executive Board (2004, February 26). Statement on marriage and the family. Retrieved from American Anthropological Association: http://www.aaanet.org/issues/policy-advocacy/Statement-on-Marriage-and-the-Family.cfm

American Anthropological Association (2014). American Anthropological Association (AAA) code of ethics. Retrieved from American Anthropological Association: http://www.aaanet.org

American Cancer Society (2014, September 5). What are the key statistics about melanoma skin cancer? Retrieved from American Cancer Society: http://www.cancer.org/cancer/skincancer-melanoma/detailedguide/melanoma-skin-cancer-key-statistics

Arnold, K., & Zuberbühler, K. (2013). Female putty-nosed monkeys use experimentally altered contextual information to disambiguate the cause of male alarm calls. *PLoS ONE, 8*(6), e65660. doi:10.1371/journal.pone.0065660

Asch, T., & Chagnon, N. (Directors). (1974). *A man called Bee: A study of the Yanomamo* [Motion Picture]. DER.

Atkins, B. T., & Rundell, M. (2008). *The Oxford guide to practical lexicography.* New York: Oxford University Press.

Balee, W. (1994). *Footprints of the forest: Ka'apor ethnobotany—the historical ecology of plant utilization by an Amazonian people.* New York: Columbia Press.

Barlett, P.F. (2005). Reconnecting with place: Faculty and the Piedmont Project at Emory University. In P.F. Barlett (Ed.), *Urban place: Reconnecting with the natural world* (pp. 39–60). Cambridge, MA: MIT Press.

Bem, S. (1974). The measurement of psychological androgyny. *Journal of Counseling & Clinical Psychology, 42*(2), 155–62. http://dx.doi.org/10.1037/h0036215

Ben & Jerry's (n.d.). Rainforest Crunch—Ben and Jerry's. Retrieved from Vermont's Finest Ben & Jerry: http://www.benjerry.com/flavors/flavor-graveyard/rainforest-crunch

Berlan, A. (2008). Making or marketing a difference: An anthropological examination of the marketing of Fair Trade cocoa from Ghana. In G. de Neve et al. (Eds.), *Hidden hands in the market: Ethnographies of Fair Trade, ethical consumption, and corporate responsibility: Vol. 28. Research in economic anthropology* (pp. 171–94). Bingley, England: Emerald Group Publishing. http://dx.doi.org/10.1016/S0190-1281(08)28008-X

Berman, J.C. (1999). Bad hair days in the palaeolithic: Modern (re)constructions of the cave man. *American Anthropologist, 101*(2), 288–304. http://dx.doi.org/10.1525/aa.1999.101.2.288

Bier, S. (2005, August). *Conflict and human rights in the Amazon: The Yanomamö*. Retrieved from ICE Case Studies: http://www1.american.edu/ted/ice/yanomami.htm

Bisulca, P. (1996). Penobscot: A people and their river. *Conservation Matters* (Summer). Retrieved from Penobscot Nation: http://www.penobscotnation.org

Bodley, J. (2008). *Anthropology and contemporary human problems*. Lanham, MD: AltaMira Press.

Bryson, B. (2003). *A short history of nearly everything*. Toronto, ON: Doubleday Canada.

Burress, C. (2004, February 27). Scientists counter Bush view/Families varied, say anthropologists. Retrieved from sfgate.com: http://www.sfgate.com/news/article/Scientists-counter-Bush-view-Families-varied-2817424.php

Bush, G.W. (2004, February 24). Transcript of Bush statement. Retrieved from CNN.com: http://www.cnn.com/2004/ALLPOLITICS/02/24/elec04.prez.bush.transcript/

Canadian Cancer Society (2014). Melanoma statistics—Canadian Cancer Society. Retrieved from Canadian Cancer Society: https://www.cancer.ca/en/cancer-information/cancer-type/skin-melanoma/statistics/?region=on

Carroll, J.B. (Ed). (2003). *On the origin of species by means of natural selection/Charles Darwin*. Peterborough, ON: Broadview Press.

CDC Office on Smoking and Health. (2014, February 14). CDC—Fact sheet—Youth and tobacco use—Smoking & tobacco use. Retrieved from Centers for Disease Control and Prevention: http://www.cdc.gov/tobacco/data_statistics/fact_sheets/youth_data/tobacco_use/index.htm#estimates

Chance, N.A. (1990). *The Inupiat and arctic Alaska*. San Diego, CA: Harcourt Brace.

Chapman, C.A., & Chapman, L.J. (1990). Dietary variability in primate populations. *Primates, 31*(1), 121–28. http://dx.doi.org/10.1007/BF02381035

Clack, T., & M. Brittain (Eds.). (2007). *Archaeology and the media*. Walnut Creek, CA: Left Coast Press.

Coe, M.D. (2013). *Mexico: From the Olmecs to the Aztecs* (7th edition). New York: Thames & Hudson.

Cohn, C. (1987). Sex and death in the rational world of defense intellectuals. *Signs, 12*(4), 687–718. http://dx.doi.org/10.1086/494362

Conklin, H.C. (1986). Hanunóo color categories. *Journal of Anthropological Research, 42*(3), 441–46.

Cordain, L. (2011). *The Paleo diet: Lose weight and get healthy by eating the foods you were designed to eat* (Revised edition). Hoboken, NJ: John Wiley.

Counihan, C. (1999). *The anthropology of food and body: Gender, meaning, and power*. London: Routledge.

Counihan, C. (2009). *A tortilla is like life: Food and culture in the San Luis valley of Colorado*. Austin, TX: University of Texas Press.

Crandall, B.D., & Stahl, P.W. (1995). Human digestive effects on a micromammalian skeleton. *Journal of Archaeological Science, 22*(6), 789–797. http://dx.doi.org/10.1016/0305-4403(95)90008-X

Cruikshank, J. (2005). *Do glaciers listen? Local knowledge, colonial encounters, and social imagination*. Vancouver, BC: UBC Press.

CSIRO Australia. (2007, May 11). Confirmed: Deforestation plays critical climate change role. *ScienceDaily*. Retrieved from Science Daily: http://www.sciencedaily.com/releases/2007/05/070511100918.htm

Cultural Survival. (2014). Cultural survival—Advancing Indigenous peoples rights and cultures worldwide. Retrieved from Cultural Survival: https://www.culturalsurvival.org

Curl, J. (2005). *Ancient American poets*. Tempe, AZ: Bilingual Review Press.

Darwin, C. (1859). *On the origin of species by means of natural selection or the preservation of favoured races in the struggle for life*. London: John Murray.

Darwin, C. (1871). *The descent of man and selection in relation to sex*. London: John Murray.

Darwin, C. (1977). *The origin of species by means of natural selection or the preservation of favored races in the struggle for life and The descent of man and selection in relations to sex*. New York: Modern Library.

de Queiroz, A. (2014). *The monkey's voyage: How improbable journeys shaped the history of life*. New York: Basic Books.

de Waal, F.B. (1992). Intentional deception in primates. Evolutionary anthropology: Issues. *News Review (Melbourne), 1*(3), 86–92.

Deloria, V. J. (1988). *Custer died for your sins: An Indian manifesto*. Norman, OK: University of Oklahoma Press.

EPA (United States Environmental Protection Agency) (n.d.). Sustainability basic information. Retrieved from United States Environmental Protection Agency: http://www.epa.gov/sustainability/basicinfo.htm

Evans-Pritchard, E.E. (1940). *The Nuer: A description of the modes of livelihood and political institutions of a Nilotic people*. London: Oxford University Press.

Fedorak, S.A. (2009). *Pop culture: The culture of everyday life*. Toronto, ON: University of Toronto Press.

Fiske, S. (2007, May). Improving the effectiveness of corporate culture. Retrieved from Anthropology News: http://www.aaanet.org/cmtes/copapia/upload/Briody.pdf http://dx.doi.org/10.1525/an.2007.48.5.44

Friedl, E. (1978, April). Society and sex roles. *Human Nature, 1*, 68–75.

Gardner, R.A., Gardner, B.T., & Van Cantfort, T.E. (1989). *Teaching sign language to chimpanzees*. Albany, NY: SUNY Press.

Geertz, C. (1973). *The interpretation of cultures*. New York: Basic Books.

Gonzalez, L.T. (2013). Modern arranged marriage in Mumbai. *Teaching Anthropology: SACC Notes, 19*(1 & 2), 34–43.

Gorenflo, L., Romaine, S., Mittermeier, R., & Walker-Painemilla, K. (2012). Co-occurrence of linguistic and biological diversity in biodiversity hotspots and high biodiversity wilderness areas. *Proceedings of the National Academy of Sciences of the United States of America, 109*(21), 8032–37. http://dx.doi.org/10.1073/pnas.1117511109

Gottlieb, P. (2012, May 23). U.S. halts Makah whaling study after seven years over "new scientific information." Retrieved from Peninsula Daily News: http://www.peninsuladailynews.com/article/20120523/NEWS/305239987/us-halts-makah-whaling-study-after-seven-years-over-new-scientific-information

Gould, S. J. (1997, March). Nonoverlapping magisteria. *Natural History, 106*, 16–22.

Hall, E.T. (1990). *The hidden dimension*. New York: Anchor Books.

Hardin, G. (1968). The tragedy of the commons. *Science, 162*(3859), 1243–48. http://dx.doi. org/10.1126/science.162.3859.1243

Harding, A. (2008, January 30). BBC News Asia Pacific Burmese women in Thai "human zoo." Retrieved from BBC News: http://news.bbc.co.uk/2/hi/asia-pacific/7215182.stm

Harmon, J. (2010, July 29). Anthropology students get a taste of cacao farming in Chiapas. Retrieved from California State University Dominguez Hills—Dateline Dominguez: http://www.csudhnews.com/2010/07/anthropology-students-get-a-taste-of-cacao -farming-in-chiapas/

Harris, M. (1985). *Good to eat: Riddles of food and culture*. Long Grove, IL: Waveland Press.

Hayden, B. (2003). Were luxury foods the first domesticates? Ethnoarchaeological perspectives from Southeast Asia. *World Archaeology, 34*(3), 458–469. http://dx.doi.org/ 10.1080/0043824021000026459a

Heslin, R. (1974). Steps toward a taxomony of touching. Annual meeting of the Midwestern Psychological Association. Chicago, IL: MPA.

Holtorf, C. (2005). *From Stonehenge to Las Vegas: Archaeology as popular culture*. Walnut Creek, CA: Altamira.

Humes, E. (2012). *Our dirty love affair with trash*. New York: Avery.

Intergovernmental Panel on Climate Change (IPCC). (2014). *Climate change 2014: Synthesis report*. Contribution of Working Groups I, II and III to the Fifth Assessment Report of the Intergovernmental Panel on Climate Change [Core Writing Team, R.K. Pachauri and L.A. Meyer (eds.)].Geneva: IPCC.

Kaliff, A. (2011). Fire. In T. Insoll (Ed.), *The Oxford handbook of the archaeology of ritual and religion* (pp. 51–62). Oxford: Oxford University Press.

Kearney, M. (1972). *The winds of Ixtepeji: World view and society in a Zapotec town*. Long Grove, IL: Waveland Press.

Kopenawa, D. (2013). *The falling sky: Words of a Yanomami shaman*. Cambridge, MA: The Belknap Press of Harvard University Press. http://dx.doi.org/10.4159/ harvard.9780674726116

Lakoff, G., & Kovecses, Z. (1987). The cognitive model of anger inherent in American English. In D. Holland, D. Holland, & N. Quinn (Eds.), *Cultural models in language and thought* (pp. 195–221). New York: Cambridge University Press. http://dx.doi.org/10.1017/ CBO9780511607660.009

Lakoff, R. (1973). Language and woman's place. *Language in Society, 2*(1), 45–80. http:// dx.doi.org/10.1017/S0047404500000051

Lee, R.B. (2013). *The Dobe Ju/'hoansi* (4th edition). Stamford, CT: Cengage Learning.

Lewis-Williams, J. (1998). The signs of all times: Entoptic phenomena in Upper Paleolithic art. *Current Anthropology, 29*(2), 209–45.

Lewis, M.P. (2013). *Ethnologue: Languages of the world* (17th edition). Online version: http://www.ethnologue.com. Dallas, TX: SIL International.

Linnaeus, C. (1758). Linnaeus—1758 systema naturae (Biodiversity Heritage Library OAI Repository). Retrieved from Internet Archive CiteBank.org: https://archive.org/details/ cbarchive_53979_linnaeus1758systemanaturae1758

Malinowski, B. (1929). *The sexual life of savages in north-western Melanesia*. New York: Eugenics Publishing Company.

Marlowe, F. (2010). *The Hadza: Hunter-gatherers of Tanzania*. Berkeley, CA: University of California Press.

Mathiasson, J.S., & Mathiasson, S. (1992). *Living on the land: Change among the Inuit of Baffin Island*. Toronto, ON: University of Toronto Press.

Maybury-Lewis, D. (2006). On the importance of being tribal: Tribal wisdom. In N. Haenn & R.R. Wilk (Eds.), *The environment in anthropology: A reader in ecology, culture, and sustainable living* (pp. 390–99). New York: New York University.

McCann, A., & Brandom, R. (2012, August 23). How to say LOL in 14 different languages. Retrieved from BuzzFeed: http://www.buzzfeed.com/atmccann/how-to-say-lol-in-14-different-languages

McGovern, P.E. (2009). *Uncorking the past: The quest for wine, beer, and other alcoholic beverages*. Los Angeles, CA: University of California Press.

McIlwraith, T. (2012). *"We are still Didene": Stories of hunting and history from northern British Columbia*. Toronto, ON: University of Toronto Press.

McWhorter, J. (2013, February). Txtng is killing language. JK!!! Retrieved from TED: Ideas Worth Spreading: http://www.ted.com/talks/john_mcwhorter_txtng_is_killing_language_jk.html

Mead, M. (1935). *Sex and temperament in three primitive societies* (2001 edition). New York: Harper Collins.

Muckle, R. (2012). *Indigenous peoples of North America: A concise anthropological overview*. Toronto, ON: University of Toronto Press.

Muckle, R. (2014). *Introducing archaeology* (2nd edition). Toronto, ON: University of Toronto Press.

Murphy, G. (2001, October 1). Great Law of Peace of the Haudenosaunee. Retrieved from Iroquois Confederacy and the U.S. Constitution: http://www.iroquoisdemocracy.pdx.edu/html/greatlaw.html

Nabhan, G.P. (2002). *Coming home to eat: The sensual pleasures and global politics of local foods*. New York: W.W. Norton and Company.

Nagle, R. (2013). *Picking up: On the streets and behind the trucks with the sanitation workers in New York City*. New York: Farrar, Straus and Giroux.

Nanda, S. (1990). *Neither man nor woman: The hijras of India*. Belmont, CA: Wadsworth.

Nanda, S. (2000). Arranging a marriage in India. In P.R. Devita (Ed.), *Stumbling toward truth: Anthropologists at work* (pp. 196–204). Long Grove, IL: Waveland Press.

Nash, B., & Andreatta, S. (2011, November 10). New business models for small-scale fishermen and seafood processors. Retrieved from NOAA Central Library—National Oceanographic Data Center: http://www.lib.noaa.gov/about/news/2011_NOAA_NCSG_Webinar_Final.pdf

Nowell, A., & Chang, M.L. (2014). Science, the media, and interpretations of Upper Palaeolithic figurines. *American Anthropologist 116*(3), 562–77.

Pearce, F. (2006). *When the rivers run dry: Water—The defining crisis of the twenty-first century*. Boston, MA: Beacon Press.

Pelto, G.H., & Pelto, P. J. (2013). Diet and delocalization: Dietary changes since 1750. In D.L. Dufour, A. H. Goodman, & G.H. Pelto (Eds.), *Nutritional anthropology: Biocultural perspectives on food and nutrition* (pp. 353–61). New York: Oxford University Press.

Peters-Golden, H. (2012). *Culture sketches: Case studies in anthropology* (6th edition). New York: McGraw-Hill.

Pirog, R., Van Pelt, T., Enshayan, K., & Cook, E. (2001, June). Food, fuel, and freeways: An Iowa perspective on how far food travels, fuel usage, and greenhouse gas emissions. Retrieved from the Leopold Center for Sustainable Agriculture: http://www.leopold. iastate.edu/pubs-and-papers/2001-06-food-fuel-freeways

Popkin, B. (2001). The nutrition transition and obesity in the developing world. *Journal of Nutrition, 131*(3), 871S–35.

Rappaport, R.A. (1968). *Pigs for the ancestors*. New Haven, CT: Yale University Press.

Rasekh, Z., Bauer, H., Manos, M., & Iacopino, V. (1998). Women's health and human rights in Afghanistan. *Journal of the American Medical Association, 280*(5), 449–55. http://dx.doi. org/10.1001/jama.280.5.449

Rathje, W.L. (2002). Garbology: The archaeology of fresh garbage. In B.J. Little (Ed.), *Public benefits of archaeology* (pp. 85–100). Gainesville, FL: University of Florida Press.

Reed, R. (2009). *Forest dwellers, forest protectors: Indigenous models for international development*. Upper Saddle River, NJ: Pearson/Prentice Hall.

Rindels, M. (2013, April 17). To save endangered languages, tribes turn to tech: American Indian tribes turn to technology in race to save endangered languages. Retrieved from Yahoo News: http://news.yahoo.com/save-endangered-languages-tribes-turn-070726855.html

Russel, M. (Ed). (2002). *Digging holes in popular culture: Archaeology and science fiction*. Oxford: Oxbow.

Sagan, C. (1979). *Transcript for "The case of the ancient astronauts."* Boston, MA: WGBH Educational Foundation.

Schablitsky, J. (Ed.). (2007). *Box office archaeology: Refining Hollywood's portrayals of the past*. Walnut Creek, CA: Left Coast Press.

Service, E. (1962). *Primitive social organization*. New York: Random House.

Seymour, S. (1999). *Women, family, and child care in India: A world in transition*. New York: Cambridge University Press.

Shostak, M. (1981). *Nisa: The life and words of a !Kung woman*. Cambridge, MA: Harvard University Press.

Simpson, G.E., & Yinger, J.M. (1985). *Racial and cultural minorities: An analysis of prejudice and discrimination (Environment, development and public policy: Public policy and social services)*. New York: Springer.

Soukup, K. (2006). Travelling through layers: Inuit artists appropriate new technologies. *Canadian Journal of Communication, 31*(1). http://www.cjc-online.ca/index.php/journal/article/view/1769/1889

Steger, M. (2003). *Globalization: A very short introduction*. Oxford: Oxford University Press.

Stephenson, W. (2013, January 22). Indian farmers and suicide: How big is the problem? Retrieved from BBC News Magazine: http://www.bbc.com/news/magazine-21077458

Steward, J. (2006). The concept and method of cultural ecology. In N. Haenn & R.R. Wilk (Eds.), *The environment in anthropology: A reader in ecology, culture, and sustainable living* (pp. 5–9). New York: New York University Press. (Original work published 1955)

Stiles, D., Redmond, I., Cress, D., Nellemann, C., & Formo, R.K. (Eds.). (2013). *Stolen apes—The illicit trade in chimpanzees, gorillas, bonobos, and orangutans. United Nations Environment Program and UNESCO.* Oslo, Norway: Birkeland Trykkeri.

Tannen, D. (2007). *You just don't understand: Women and men in conversation.* New York: William Morrow Paperbacks.

Townsend, P. (2009). *Environmental anthropology: From pigs to policies.* Long Grove, IL: Waveland Press.

Tsunoda, T. (2006). *Language endangerment and language revitalization: An introduction.* Berlin, Germany: Walter de Gruyter. http://dx.doi.org/10.1515/9783110896589

Tulane University. (2009, June 23). Oversight of public and private initiatives to eliminate the worst forms of child labor in the cocoa sector in Cote d'Ivoire and Ghana. Retrieved from Tulane University: http://www.childlabor-payson.org/Child%20 Labor%20in%20the%20Cocoa%20Supply%20Chain_June2009.pdf

Turner, V.W. (1967). *The forest of symbols: Aspects of Ndembu ritual.* Ithaca, NY: Cornell University Press.

Tuttle, R.H. (2014). *Apes and human evolution.* Cambridge, MA: Harvard University Press. http://dx.doi.org/10.4159/harvard.9780674726536

Tuvale, T. (2014). An account of Samoan history up to 1918, Kava: Its ceremonial use. Retrieved from Victoria University of Wellington Library: http://nzetc.victoria.ac.nz/ tm/scholarly/tei-TuvAcco-t1-body1-d16.html

UN Food and Agriculture Organization. (2013). *FAO Water Unit—Water news: Water scarcity.* Retrieved from FAO Water: http://www.fao.org/nr/water/issues/scarcity.html

UNICEF. (2007, February). UNICEF Cote D'Ivoire: Fighting child trafficking. Retrieved from UNICEF: http://www.unicef.org/wcaro/english/WCARO_CI_Prog_En_ ChildTrafficking.pdf

UNICEF. (2014). UNICEF statistics. Retrieved from UNICEF Data: Monitoring the Situation of Women and Children: www.unicef.org/statistics

United Nations. (1999, December 16). A/RES/42/187 Report of the World Commission on Environment and Development. Retrieved from United Nations: http://www.un.org/ documents/ga/res/42/ares42-187.htm

United States v. Windsor (2013) 570 U.S. 12, 12–307.

United States Army. (2014, July 28). The Human Terrain System. Retrieved from http:// humanterrainsystem.army.mil

United States Census Bureau. (2013, December). *International programs information gateway.* Retrieved from US Census Bureau: http://www.census.gov/population/international/ data/idb/informationGateway.php

Vecsey, C., & Venables, R.W. (1980). *American Indian environments: Ecological issues in Native American history.* Syracuse, NY: Syracuse University Press.

Verhaar, J.W. (1990). Melanesian pidgin and Tok Pisin. Proceedings of the First International Conference on Pidgins and Creoles in Melanesia (p. 204). Philadelphia, PA: John Benjamins Publishing.

von Hoerschelmann, D. (1995). The religious meaning of the Samoan kava ceremony. *Anthropos, 90*, 193–95.

Wade, R. (1988). *Village republics: Economic conditions for collective action in South India.* New York: Cambridge University Press.

Wallace, A.F.C. (1956). Revitalization movements. *American Anthropologist, 58*(2), 264–81.

Wansink, B., & Sangerman, C. (2000, July). Engineering comfort foods. *American Demographics*, 66–67.

Washington Post. (2007, July 31). Congo's sexual violence goes "far beyond rape." Retrieved from Washington Post: http://www.washingtonpost.com/wp-dyn/content/article/2007/07/30/AR2007073001849.html

West, C., & Zimmerman, D.H. (1987). Doing gender. *Gender & Society, 1*(2), 125–51. http://dx.doi.org/10.1177/0891243287001002002

WHO. (2014, February). WHO—Female genital mutilation. Retrieved from World Health Organization: http://www.who.int/mediacentre/factsheets/fs241/en/

Wiessner, P. (2002). Hunting, healing, and *Hxaro* exchange: A long-term perspective on !Kung (Ju/'oansi) large-game hunting. *Evolution and Human Behavior, 23*(6), 407–36. http://dx.doi.org/10.1016/S1090-5138(02)00096-X

Wilk, R.R. (1985). The ancient Maya and the political present. *Journal of Anthropological Research, 41*, 307–26.

Wrangham, R. (2009). *Catching fire: How cooking made us human.* New York: Basic Books.

WWF. (2014, September). Living planet report 2014: Summary. Retrieved from World Wide Fund for Nature (WWF): wwf_lpr2014_sum.pdf

Xing, B. (n.d.). Case study: Kayapó and the Belo Monte. Retrieved from Indigenous Culture in the Amazon, Duke University: http://sites.duke.edu/amazonindigenousculture/kayapo-and-the-belo-monte/

Zuk, M. (2013). *Paleofantasy: What evolution really tells us about sex, diet and how we live.* New York: W.W. Norton and Company.

Index

Page numbers for figures, tables, and maps are indicated by italics.